P9-DVR-903

CONTENTS

Manual organization
Service hints
Safety first
Expendable supplies
Shop tools
Emergency tool kit
Troubleshooting and tune-up equipment

Starting system
Charging system
Engine performance
Engine oil pressure light
Fuel system (carburetted)
Fuel system (fuel injected)
Fuel pump test (mechanical, electric)
Emission control systems
Engine noises
Electrical accessories
Cooling system
Clutch
Manual transmission/transaxle
Automatic transmission
Brakes
Steering and suspension
Tire wear analysis
Wheel balancing

Routine checks
Periodic checks
Periodic maintenance
Engine tune-up

PORSCHE 911

1965-1982
SHOP MANUAL

SYDNIE A. WAUSON
Editor

JEFF ROBINSON
Publisher

CLYMER PUBLICATIONS

*World's largest publisher of books
devoted exclusively to automobiles and motorcycles*

12860 MUSCATINE STREET · P.O. BOX 20 · ARLETA, CALIFORNIA 91331

Copyright © 1972, 1976, 1978, 1981, 1983 Clymer Publications

All rights reserved. No part of this publication may be reproduced, stored in a retrieval system or transmitted, in any form or by any means, electronic, mechanical, photocopying, recording or otherwise, without the written permission of Clymer Publications.

FIRST EDITION
Published December, 1972

SECOND EDITION
Revised by Jim Combs to include 1973-1976 models
Published June, 1976

THIRD EDITION
Revised by Jim Combs to include 1977-1978 models
First Printing November, 1978
Second Printing November, 1979

FOURTH EDITION
Revised by Ron Wright to include 1979-1981 models
First Printing October, 1981

FIFTH EDITION
Revised by Kalton C. Lahue to include 1982 models
First Printing June, 1983

Printed in U.S.A.

ISBN: 0-89287-060-5

Production Coordinator, Marina M. Lerique

.

COVER:
Photographed by Michael Brown Photographic Productions, Los Angeles, California.
Assisted by Tom Lunde.
Automobile courtesy of Volkswagen of America Inc.
Porsche Audi Division

PORSCHE 911
1965-1982
SHOP MANUAL

QUICK REFERENCE DATA

SPARK PLUG CROSS REFERENCE

Bosch	BERU	Champion
W145 T30	145/14/3	—
W175 M30	175/14/3L	—
W200 T35	—	UL-828
W215 P21	215/14/3P	—
W225 T30	225/14/3	—
W230 T30	240/14/3	—
W235 P21	235/14/3P	—
W265 P21	265/14/3P	—

SPARK PLUG SPECIFICATIONS

Model/Year	Type	Gap
911		
1966-1969	Bosch W200 T35	0.024-0.028 in. (0.6-0.7 mm)
1976	Bosch W175 M30	0.028 in. (0.7 mm)
911T carburetted		
1965-1968	Bosch W250 P21	0.014 in. (0.35 mm)
1968-1971	Bosch W230 T30	0.024 in. (0.55 mm)
911 fuel injected		
1972	Bosch W235 P21	0.024 in. (0.55 mm)
1973-1974	Bosch W215 P21	0.024 in. (0.55 mm)
911E		
1968	Bosch W265 P21	0.014 in. (0.35 mm)
1969-1973	Bosch W265 P21	0.024 in. (0.55 mm)
911S		
1968	Bosch W265 P21	0.014 in. (0.35 mm)
1969-1973	Bosch W265 P21	0.024 in. (0.55 mm)
1974-1976	Bosch W235 P21	0.024 in. (0.55 mm)
1977	Bosch W225 T30	0.028 in. (0.7 mm)
911SC		
1978-1979	Bosch W145 T30	0.032 in. (0.8 mm)
1980-on	Bosch W225 T30	0.032 in. (0.8 mm)

BREAKER POINT AND VALVE SPECIFICATIONS

Point gap	
1974, 1977	0.014 in. (0.35 mm)
All others	0.016 in. (0.4 mm)
Dwell angle	
Marelli distributor	
1965-1971	40 ±3°
1972-1977	37 ±3°
Bosch distributor	38 ±3°
Valve clearance (intake and exhaust)	0.004 in. (0.1 mm)
Valve timing	
1977	0.40-0.54 mm
1978-1979	0.90-1.10 mm
1980-on	1.4-1.7 mm

BREAKER POINT ADJUSTMENT

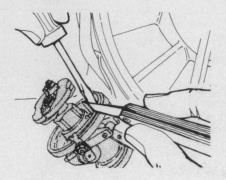

MARELLI DISTRIBUTOR

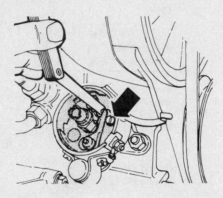

EARLY BOSCH DISTRIBUTOR

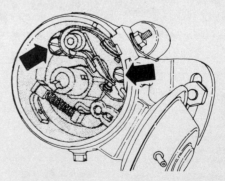

LATE BOSCH DISTRIBUTOR

CYLINDER NUMBERING

FRONT

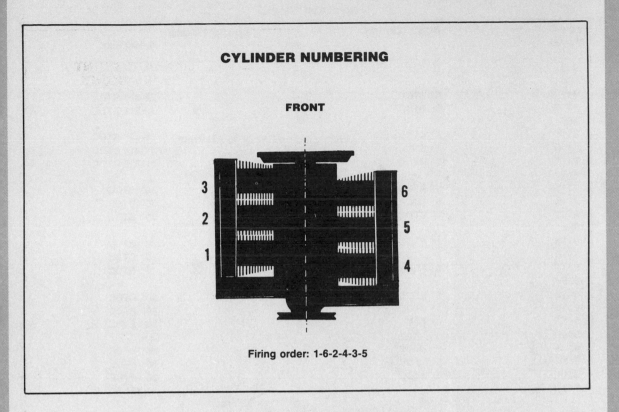

Firing order: 1-6-2-4-3-5

APPROXIMATE REFILL CAPACITIES

Engine oil	
1965-1972	9.5 qts. (9 liters)
1973-on	10.6 qts. (10 liters)
Transaxle	3-4 qts. (2.8-3.8 liters)
Fuel tank	
1965-1973	16.4 gal. (62 liters)
1974-on	21.2 gal. (80 liters)

RECOMMENDED LUBRICANTS

	Temperature Range	Recommended Type
Engine Oil (1)		
	Below 5° F (15° C)	SAE 10W
	Between 5° F & 32° F	
	(-15° C to° C)	SAE 20-20W
	Above 32° F (0° C)	SAE 30
Transaxle hypoid gear oil (2,3)	All temperatures	SAE 90
Brake fluid	All temperatures	DOT 3 or DOT 4

(1) API service SE or SF oil rating.
(2) Without limited-slip differential.
(3) With limited-slip differential, must be marked "For limited-slip differentials."

XIII

IGNITION TIMING[1]

Year/ Model	Static Timing	Strobe Timing	
		Idle	6,000 rpm[2]
1965	0° TDC	-	-
1966			
911	5° BTDC[3]	-	32-33° BTDC
911S	5° BTDC[3]	-	30-31° BTDC
1967			
911	5° BTDC[4]	3° ATDC @ 850-950 rpm[5,6]	18-32° BTDC
911S	5° BTDC[4]	-	30-31° BTDC
911T	5° BTDC[4]	-	28-32° BTDC
1968			
911S	5° BTDC[4]	-	30° BTDC
911E	0° TDC	-	30° BTDC
911T	5° BTDC[4]	-	30° BTDC
1969			
911S	5° BTDC[4]	-	30° BTDC
911E	5° BTDC[4]	-	30° BTDC
911T	0° TDC	-	35° BTDC
1970			
911S	5° BTDC[4]	-	30° BTDC
911E	5° BTDC[4]	-	30° BTDC
911T	0° TDC	-	30° BTDC
1971			
911S	5° BTDC[4]	-	30° BTDC
911E	5° BTDC[4]	-	30° BTDC
911T	5° BTDC[4]	-	30° BTDC
1972-1976	-	5° ATDC @ 900 rpm[7]	32-38° BTDC[6]
1977			
California	-	15°ATDC @ 1,000 rpm[8]	Not specified
49-State	-	0° TDC @ 950-1,000 rpm[8]	Not specified
1978-1979	-	5° BTDC @ 950 rpm[8]	26° BTDC[6,8]
1980-on	-	5° BTDC @ 950 rpm[6,8]	19-25° BTDC

1. Use the specifications in this table only if the emission control decal in your engine compartment is missing or illegible. If the decal specifications differ from those in this table, always use the ones on the decal.
2. Unloaded engine.
3. 0.218 in. (5.5 mm) right.
4. 0.198 in. (5 mm) right.
5. 0.119 in. (3 mm) left.
6. Vacuum line disconnected.
7. Vacuum line connected.
8. ±2°.

INTRODUCTION

This detailed, comprehensive manual covers the 1965-1982 Porsche 911. The expert text gives complete information on maintenance, repair and overhaul. Hundreds of photos and drawings guide you through every step. The book includes all you need to know to keep your car running right.

Where repairs are practical for the owner/mechanic, complete procedures are given. Equally important, difficult jobs are pointed out. Such operations are usually more economically performed by a dealer or independent garage.

A shop manual is a reference. You want to be able to find information fast. As in all Clymer books, this one is designed with this in mind. All chapters are thumb tabbed. Important items are indexed at the rear of the book. Finally, all the most frequently used specifications and capacities are summarized on the *Quick Reference* pages at the front of the book.

Keep the book handy. Carry it in your glove box. It will help you to better understand your car, lower repair and maintenance costs, and generally improve your satisfaction with your vehicle.

CHAPTER ONE

GENERAL INFORMATION

The troubleshooting, tune-up, maintenance, and step-by-step repair procedures in this book are written for the owner and home mechanic. The text is accompanied by useful photos and diagrams to make the job as clear and correct as possible.

Troubleshooting, tune-up, maintenance, and repair are not difficult if you know what tools and equipment to use and what to do. Anyone not afraid to get their hands dirty, of average intelligence, and with some mechanical ability can perform most of the procedures in this book.

In some cases, a repair job may require tools or skills not reasonably expected of the home mechanic. These procedures are noted in each chapter and it is recommended that you take the job to your dealer, a competent mechanic, or machine shop.

MANUAL ORGANIZATION

This chapter provides general information and safety and service hints. Also included are lists of recommended shop and emergency tools as well as a brief description of troubleshooting and tune-up equipment.

Chapter Two provides methods and suggestions for quick and accurate diagnosis and repair of problems. Troubleshooting procedures discuss typical symptoms and logical methods to pinpoint the trouble.

Chapter Three explains all periodic lubrication and routine maintenance necessary to keep your vehicle running well. Chapter Three also includes recommended tune-up procedures, eliminating the need to constantly consult chapters on the various subassemblies.

Subsequent chapters cover specific systems such as the engine, transmission, and electrical systems. Each of these chapters provides disassembly, repair, and assembly procedures in a simple step-by-step format. If a repair requires special skills or tools, or is otherwise impractical for the home mechanic, it is so indicated. In these cases it is usually faster and less expensive to have the repairs made by a dealer or competent repair shop. Necessary specifications concerning a particular system are included at the end of the appropriate chapter.

When special tools are required to perform a procedure included in this manual, the tool is illustrated either in actual use or alone. It may be possible to rent or borrow these tools. The inventive mechanic may also be able to find a suitable substitute in his tool box, or to fabricate one.

The terms NOTE, CAUTION, and WARNING have specific meanings in this manual. A NOTE provides additional or explanatory information. A CAUTION is used to emphasize areas where equipment damage could result if proper precautions are not taken. A WARNING is used to stress those areas where personal injury or death could result from negligence, in addition to possible mechanical damage.

SERVICE HINTS

Observing the following practices will save time, effort, and frustration, as well as prevent possible injury.

Throughout this manual keep in mind two conventions. "Front" refers to the front of the vehicle. The front of any component, such as the transaxle, is that end which faces toward the front of the vehicle. The "left" and "right" sides of the vehicle refer to the orientation of a person sitting in the vehicle facing forward. For example, the steering wheel is on the left side. These rules are simple, but even experienced mechanics occasionally become disoriented.

Most of the service procedures covered are straightforward and can be performed by anyone reasonably handy with tools. It is suggested, however, that you consider your own capabilities carefully before attempting any operation involving major disassembly of the engine.

Some operations, for example, require the use of a press. It would be wiser to have these performed by a shop equipped for such work, rather than to try to do the job yourself with makeshift equipment. Other procedures require precision measurements. Unless you have the skills and equipment required, it would be better to have a qualified repair shop make the measurements for you.

Repairs go much faster and easier if the parts that will be worked on are clean before you begin. There are special cleaners for washing the engine and related parts. Brush or spray on the cleaning solution, let it stand, then rinse it away with a garden hose. Clean all oily or greasy parts with cleaning solvent as you remove them.

WARNING
Never use gasoline as a cleaning agent. It presents an extreme fire hazard. Be sure to work in a well-ventilated area when using cleaning solvent. Keep a fire extinguisher, rated for gasoline fires, handy in any case.

Much of the labor charge for repairs made by dealers is for the removal and disassembly of other parts to reach the defective unit. It is frequently possible to perform the preliminary operations yourself and then take the defective unit in to the dealer for repair, at considerable savings.

Once you have decided to tackle the job yourself, make sure you locate the appropriate section in this manual, and read it entirely. Study the illustrations and text until you have a good idea of what is involved in completing the job satisfactorily. If special tools are required, make arrangements to get them before you start. Also, purchase any known defective parts prior to starting on the procedure. It is frustrating and time-consuming to get partially into a job and then be unable to complete it.

Simple wiring checks can be easily made at home, but knowledge of electronics is almost a necessity for performing tests with complicated electronic testing gear.

During disassembly of parts keep a few general cautions in mind. Force is rarely needed to get things apart. If parts are a tight fit, like a bearing in a case, there is usually a tool designed to separate them. Never use a screwdriver to pry apart parts with machined surfaces such as cylinder head and valve cover. You will mar the surfaces and end up with leaks.

Make diagrams wherever similar-appearing parts are found. You may think you can remember where everything came from — but mistakes are costly. There is also the possibility you may get sidetracked and not return to work for days or even weeks — in which interval, carefully laid out parts may have become disturbed.

Tag all similar internal parts for location, and mark all mating parts for position. Record number and thickness of any shims as they are removed. Small parts such as bolts can be identified by placing them in plastic sandwich bags that are sealed and labeled with masking tape.

Wiring should be tagged with masking tape and marked as each wire is removed. Again, do not rely on memory alone.

When working under the vehicle, do not trust a hydraulic or mechanical jack to hold the vehicle up by itself. Always use jackstands. See **Figure 1**.

Disconnect battery ground cable before working near electrical connections and before disconnecting wires. Never run the engine with the battery disconnected; the alternator could be seriously damaged.

Protect finished surfaces from physical damage or corrosion. Keep gasoline and brake fluid off painted surfaces.

Frozen or very tight bolts and screws can often be loosened by soaking with penetrating oil like Liquid Wrench or WD-40, then sharply striking the bolt head a few times with a hammer and punch (or screwdriver for screws). Avoid heat unless absolutely necessary, since it may melt, warp, or remove the temper from many parts.

Avoid flames or sparks when working near a charging battery or flammable liquids, such as brake fluid or gasoline.

No parts, except those assembled with a press fit, require unusual force during assembly. If a part is hard to remove or install, find out why before proceeding.

Cover all openings after removing parts to keep dirt, small tools, etc., from falling in.

When assembling two parts, start all fasteners, then tighten evenly.

The clutch plate, wiring connections, brake shoes, drums, pads, and discs should be kept clean and free of grease and oil.

When assembling parts, be sure all shims and washers are replaced exactly as they came out.

Whenever a rotating part butts against a stationary part, look for a shim or washer. Use new gaskets if there is any doubt about the condition of old ones. Generally, you should apply gasket cement to one mating surface only, so the parts may be easily disassembled in the future. A thin coat of oil on gaskets helps them seal effectively.

Heavy grease can be used to hold small parts in place if they tend to fall out during assembly. However, keep grease and oil away from electrical, clutch, and brake components.

High spots may be sanded off a piston with sandpaper, but emery cloth and oil do a much more professional job.

Carburetors are best cleaned by disassembling them and soaking the parts in a commercial carburetor cleaner. Never soak gaskets and rubber parts in these cleaners. Never use wire to clean out jets and air passages; they are easily damaged. Use compressed air to blow out the carburetor, but only if the float has been removed first.

Take your time and do the job right. Do not forget that a newly rebuilt engine must be broken in the same as a new one. Refer to your owner's manual for the proper break-in procedures.

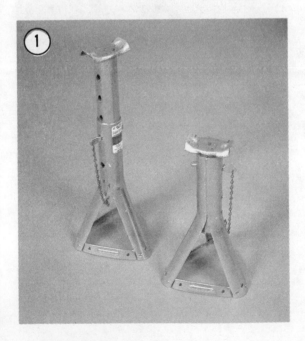

SAFETY FIRST

Professional mechanics can work for years and never sustain a serious injury. If you observe a few rules of common sense and safety, you can enjoy many safe hours servicing your vehicle. You could hurt yourself or damage the vehicle if you ignore these rules.

1. Never use gasoline as a cleaning solvent.

2. Never smoke or use a torch in the vicinity of

flammable liquids such as cleaning solvent in open containers.

3. Never smoke or use a torch in an area where batteries are being charged. Highly explosive hydrogen gas is formed during the charging process.

4. Use the proper sized wrenches to avoid damage to nuts and injury to yourself.

5. When loosening a tight or stuck nut, be guided by what would happen if the wrench should slip. Protect yourself accordingly.

6. Keep your work area clean and uncluttered.

7. Wear safety goggles during all operations involving drilling, grinding, or use of a cold chisel.

8. Never use worn tools.

9. Keep a fire extinguisher handy and be sure it is rated for gasoline (Class B) and electrical (Class C) fires.

EXPENDABLE SUPPLIES

Certain expendable supplies are necessary. These include grease, oil, gasket cement, wiping rags, cleaning solvent, and distilled water. Also, special locking compounds, silicone lubricants, and engine cleaners may be useful. Cleaning solvent is available at most service stations and distilled water for the battery is available at most supermarkets.

SHOP TOOLS

For proper servicing, you will need an assortment of ordinary hand tools (**Figure 2**).

As a minimum, these include:

a. Combination wrenches
b. Sockets
c. Plastic mallet
d. Small hammer
e. Snap ring pliers
f. Gas pliers
g. Phillips screwdrivers
h. Slot (common) screwdrivers
i. Feeler gauges
j. Spark plug gauge
k. Spark plug wrench
l. Torque wrench

Special tools necessary are shown in the chapters covering the particular repair in which they are used.

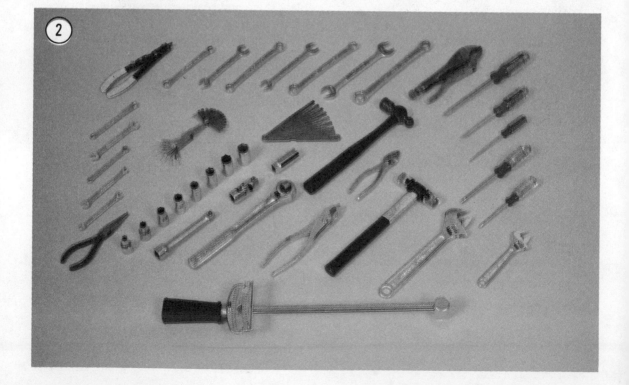

Engine tune-up and troubleshooting procedures require other special tools and equipment. These are described in detail in the following sections.

EMERGENCY TOOL KIT

A small emergency tool kit kept in the trunk is handy for road emergencies which otherwise could leave you stranded. The tools listed below and shown in **Figure 3** will let you handle most roadside repairs.

a. Combination wrenches

b. Crescent (adjustable) wrench

c. Screwdrivers — common and Phillips

d. Pliers — conventional (gas) and needle nose

e. Vise Grips

f. Hammer — plastic and metal

g. Small container of waterless hand cleaner

h. Rags for cleanup

i. Silver waterproof sealing tape (duct tape)

j. Flashlight

k. Emergency road flares — at least four

l. Spare drive belts (cooling fan, alternator, etc.)

TROUBLESHOOTING AND TUNE-UP EQUIPMENT

Voltmeter, Ohmmeter, and Ammeter

For testing the ignition or electrical system, a good voltmeter is required. For automotive use, an instrument covering 0-20 volts is satisfac-

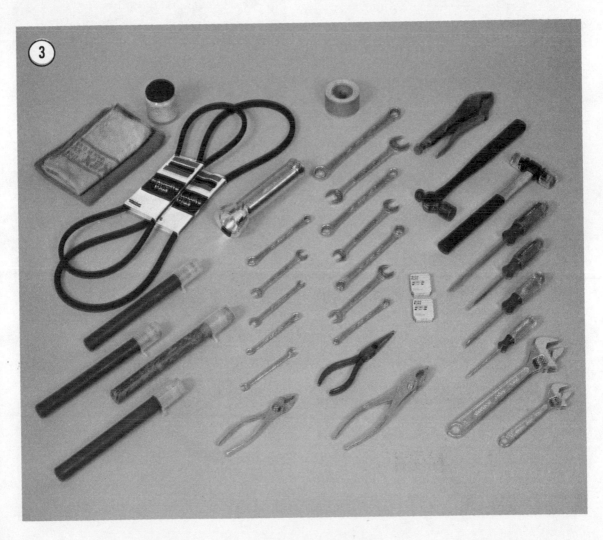

tory. One which also has a 0-2 volt scale is necessary for testing relays, points, or individual contacts where voltage drops are much smaller. Accuracy should be ± ½ volt.

An ohmmeter measures electrical resistance. This instrument is useful for checking continuity (open and short circuits), and testing fuses and lights.

The ammeter measures electrical current. Ammeters for automotive use should cover 0-50 amperes and 0-250 amperes. These are useful for checking battery charging and starting current.

Several inexpensive VOM's (volt-ohm-milliammeter) combine all three instruments into one which fits easily in any tool box. See **Figure 4**. However, the ammeter ranges are usually too small for automotive work.

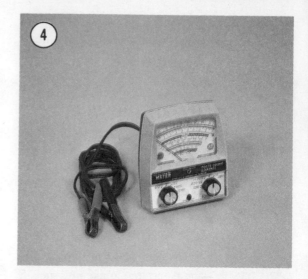

Hydrometer

The hydrometer gives a useful indication of battery condition and charge by measuring the specific gravity of the electrolyte in each cell. See **Figure 5**. Complete details on use and interpretation of readings are provided in the electrical chapter.

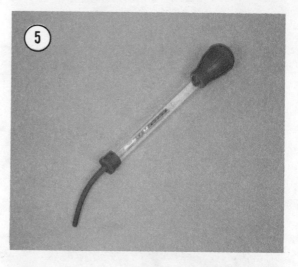

Compression Tester

The compression tester measures the compression pressure built up in each cylinder. The results, when properly interpreted, can indicate general cylinder and valve condition. See **Figure 6**.

Most compression testers have long flexible extensions built-in or as accessories. Such an extension is necessary since the spark plug holes are deep inside the metal air cooling covers.

Vacuum Gauge

The vacuum gauge (**Figure 7**) is one of the easiest instruments to use, but one of the most difficult for the inexperienced mechanic to interpret. The results, when interpreted with other findings, can provide valuable clues to possible trouble.

To use the vacuum gauge, connect it to a vacuum hose that goes to the intake manifold. Attach it either directly to the hose or to a T-fitting installed into the hose.

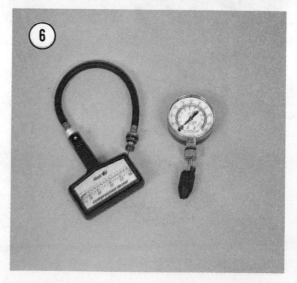

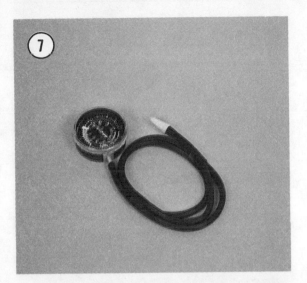

NOTE: *Subtract one inch from the reading for every 1,000 ft. elevation.*

Fuel Pressure Gauge

This instrument is invaluable for evaluating fuel pump performance. Fuel system trouble-shooting procedures in this manual use a fuel pressure gauge. Usually a vacuum gauge and fuel pressure gauge are combined.

Dwell Meter (Contact Breaker Point Ignition Only)

A dwell meter measures the distance in degrees of cam rotation that the breaker points remain closed while the engine is running. Since this angle is determined by breaker point gap, dwell angle is an accurate indication of breaker point gap.

Many tachometers intended for tuning and testing incorporate a dwell meter as well. See **Figure 8**. Follow the manufacturer's instructions to measure dwell.

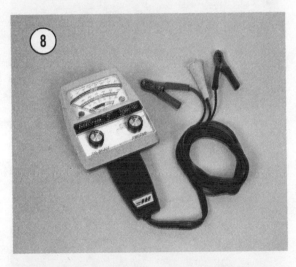

Tachometer

A tachometer is necessary for tuning. See **Figure 8**. Ignition timing and carburetor adjustments must be performed at the specified idle speed. The best instrument for this purpose is one with a low range of 0-1,000 or 0-2,000 rpm for setting idle, and a high range of 0-4,000 or more for setting ignition timing at 3,000 rpm. Extended range (0-6,000 or 0-8,000 rpm) instruments lack accuracy at lower speeds. The instrument should be capable of detecting changes of 25 rpm on the low range.

Strobe Timing Light

This instrument is necessary for tuning, as it permits very accurate ignition timing. The light flashes at precisely the same instant that No. 1 cylinder fires, at which time the timing marks on the engine should align. Refer to Chapter Three for exact location of the timing marks for your engine.

Suitable lights range from inexpensive neon bulb types ($2-3) to powerful xenon strobe lights ($20-40). See **Figure 9**. Neon timing lights are difficult to see and must be used in dimly lit areas. Xenon strobe timing lights can be used

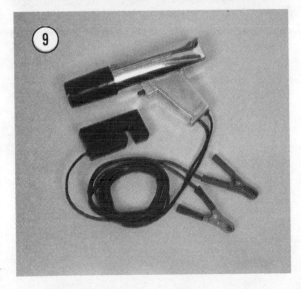

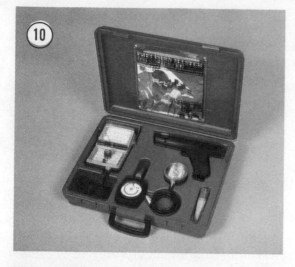

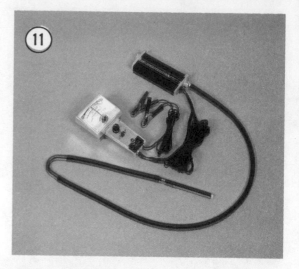

outside in bright sunlight. Both types work on this vehicle; use according to the manufacturer's instructions.

Tune-up Kits

Many manufacturers offer kits that combine several useful instruments. Some come in a convenient carry case and are usually less expensive than purchasing one instrument at a time. **Figure 10** shows one of the kits that is available. The prices vary with the number of instruments included in the kit.

Exhaust Gas Analyzer

Of all instruments described here, this is the least likely to be owned by a home mechanic. This instrument samples the exhaust gases from the tailpipe and measures the thermal conductivity of the exhaust gas. Since different gases conduct heat at varying rates, thermal conductivity of the exhaust is a good indication of gases present.

An exhaust gas analyzer is vital for accurately checking the effectiveness of exhaust emission control adjustments. They are relatively expensive to buy ($70 and up), but must be considered essential for the owner/mechanic

to comply with today's emission laws. See **Figure 11**.

Fire Extinguisher

A fire extinguisher is a necessity when working on a vehicle. It should be rated for both *Class B* (flammable liquids — gasoline, oil, paint, etc.) and *Class C* (electrical — wiring, etc.) type fires. It should always be kept within reach. See **Figure 12**.

CHAPTER TWO

TROUBLESHOOTING

Troubleshooting can be a relatively simple matter if it is done logically. The first step in any troubleshooting procedure must be defining the symptoms as closely as possible. Subsequent steps involve testing and analyzing areas which could cause the symptoms. A haphazard approach may eventually find the trouble, but in terms of wasted time and unnecessary parts replacement, it can be very costly.

The troubleshooting procedures in this chapter analyze typical symptoms and show logical methods of isolation. These are not the only methods. There may be several approaches to a problem, but all methods must have one thing in common — a logical, systematic approach.

STARTING SYSTEM

The starting system consists of the starter motor and the starter solenoid. The ignition key controls the starter solenoid, which mechanically engages the starter with the engine flywheel, and supplies electrical current to turn the starter motor.

Starting system troubles are relatively easy to find. In most cases, the trouble is a loose or dirty electrical connection. **Figures 1 and 2** provide routines for finding the trouble.

CHARGING SYSTEM

The charging system consists of the alternator (or generator on older vehicles), voltage regulator, and battery. A drive belt driven by the engine crankshaft turns the alternator which produces electrical energy to charge the battery. As engine speed varies, the voltage from the alternator varies. A voltage regulator controls the charging current to the battery and maintains the voltage to the vehicle's electrical system at safe levels. A warning light or gauge on the instrument panel signals the driver when charging is not taking place. Refer to **Figure 3** for a typical charging system.

Complete troubleshooting of the charging system requires test equipment and skills which the average home mechanic does not possess. However, there are a few tests which can be done to pinpoint most troubles.

Charging system trouble may stem from a defective alternator (or generator), voltage regulator, battery, or drive belt. It may also be caused by something as simple as incorrect drive belt tension. The following are symptoms of typical problems you may encounter.

1. *Battery dies frequently, even though the warning lamp indicates no discharge* — This can be caused by a drive belt that is slightly too

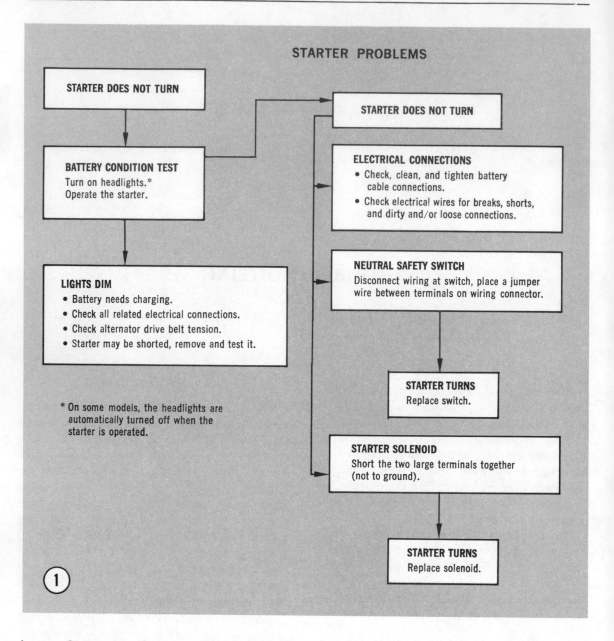

STARTER PROBLEMS

STARTER DOES NOT TURN

STARTER DOES NOT TURN

BATTERY CONDITION TEST
Turn on headlights.*
Operate the starter.

ELECTRICAL CONNECTIONS
• Check, clean, and tighten battery cable connections.
• Check electrical wires for breaks, shorts, and dirty and/or loose connections.

NEUTRAL SAFETY SWITCH
Disconnect wiring at switch, place a jumper wire between terminals on wiring connector.

LIGHTS DIM
• Battery needs charging.
• Check all related electrical connections.
• Check alternator drive belt tension.
• Starter may be shorted, remove and test it.

* On some models, the headlights are automatically turned off when the starter is operated.

STARTER TURNS
Replace switch.

STARTER SOLENOID
Short the two large terminals together (not to ground).

STARTER TURNS
Replace solenoid.

①

loose. Grasp the alternator (or generator) pulley and try to turn it. If the pulley can be turned without moving the belt, the drive belt is too loose. As a rule, keep the belt tight enough that it can be deflected about ½ in. under moderate thumb pressure between the pulleys (**Figure 4**). The battery may also be at fault; test the battery condition.

2. *Charging system warning lamp does not come on when ignition switch is turned on* — This may indicate a defective ignition switch, battery, voltage regulator, or lamp. First try to

start the vehicle. If it doesn't start, check the ignition switch and battery. If the car starts, remove the warning lamp; test it for continuity with an ohmmeter or substitute a new lamp. If the lamp is good, locate the voltage regulator and make sure it is properly grounded (try tightening the mounting screws). Also, the alternator (or generator) brushes may not be making contact. Test the alternator (or generator) and voltage regulator.

3. *Alternator (or generator) warning lamp comes on and stays on* — This usually indicates

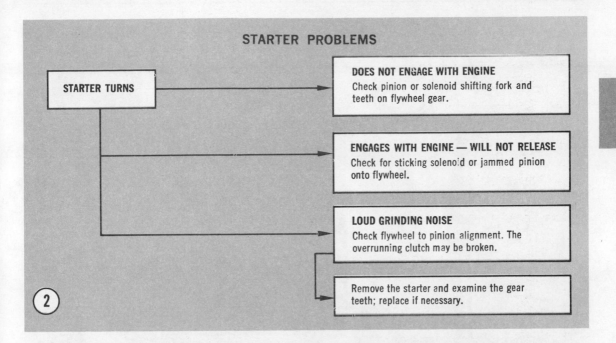

STARTER PROBLEMS

STARTER TURNS

DOES NOT ENGAGE WITH ENGINE
Check pinion or solenoid shifting fork and teeth on flywheel gear.

ENGAGES WITH ENGINE — WILL NOT RELEASE
Check for sticking solenoid or jammed pinion onto flywheel.

LOUD GRINDING NOISE
Check flywheel to pinion alignment. The overrunning clutch may be broken.

Remove the starter and examine the gear teeth; replace if necessary.

②

③
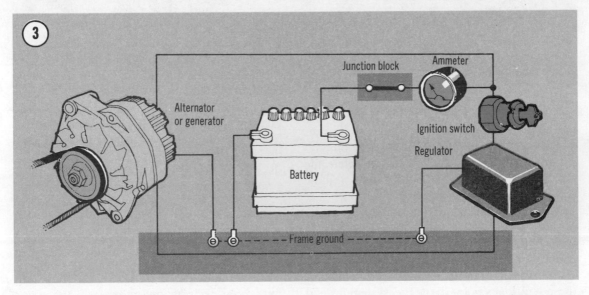

Junction block — Ammeter

Alternator or generator

Ignition switch

Regulator

Battery

Frame ground

that no charging is taking place. First check drive belt tension (**Figure 4**). Then check battery condition, and check all wiring connections in the charging system. If this does not locate the trouble, check the alternator (or generator) and voltage regulator.

4. *Charging system warning lamp flashes on and off intermittently* — This usually indicates the charging system is working intermittently. Check the drive belt tension (**Figure 4**), and check all electrical connections in the charging

system. Check the alternator (or generator). *On generators only*, check the condition of the commutator.

5. *Battery requires frequent additions of water, or lamps require frequent replacement* — The alternator (or generator) is probably overcharging the battery. The voltage regulator is probably at fault.

6. *Excessive noise from the alternator (or generator)* — Check for loose mounting brackets and bolts. The problem may also be

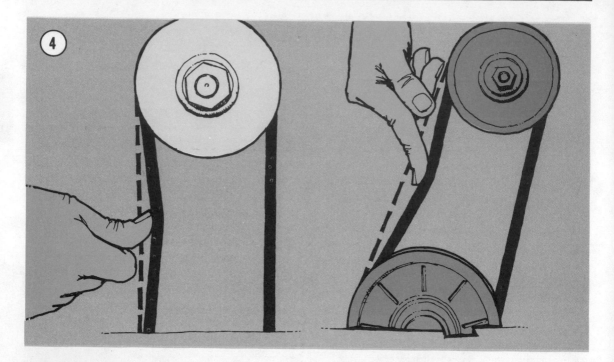

worn bearings or the need of lubrication in some cases. If an alternator whines, a shorted diode may be indicated.

IGNITION SYSTEM

The ignition system may be either a conventional contact breaker type or an electronic ignition. See electrical chapter to determine which type you have. **Figures 5 and 6** show simplified diagrams of each type.

Most problems involving failure to start, poor performance, or rough running stem from trouble in the ignition system, particularly in contact breaker systems. Many novice troubleshooters get into trouble when they assume that these symptoms point to the fuel system instead of the ignition system.

Ignition system troubles may be roughly divided between those affecting only one cylinder and those affecting all cylinders. If the trouble affects only one cylinder, it can only be in the spark plug, spark plug wire, or portion of the distributor associated with that cylinder. If the trouble affects all cylinders (weak spark or no spark), then the trouble is in the ignition coil, rotor, distributor, or associated wiring.

In order to get maximum spark, the ignition coil must be wired correctly. Make sure that the double wire from the battery is attached to terminal No. 15 on the ignition coil and that the single wire from the distributor is attached to terminal No. 1 on the ignition coil.

The troubleshooting procedures outlined in **Figure 7** (breaker point ignition) or **Figure 8** (electronic ignition) will help you isolate ignition problems fast. Of course, they assume that the battery is in good enough condition to crank the engine over at its normal rate.

ENGINE PERFORMANCE

A number of factors can make the engine difficult or impossible to start, or cause rough running, poor performance and so on. The majority of novice troubleshooters immediately suspect the carburetor or fuel injection system. In the majority of cases, though, the trouble exists in the ignition system.

The troubleshooting procedures outlined in **Figures 9 through 14** will help you solve the majority of engine starting troubles in a systematic manner.

Some tests of the ignition system require running the engine with a spark plug or ignition coil wire disconnected. The safest way to do this is to disconnect the wire with the engine

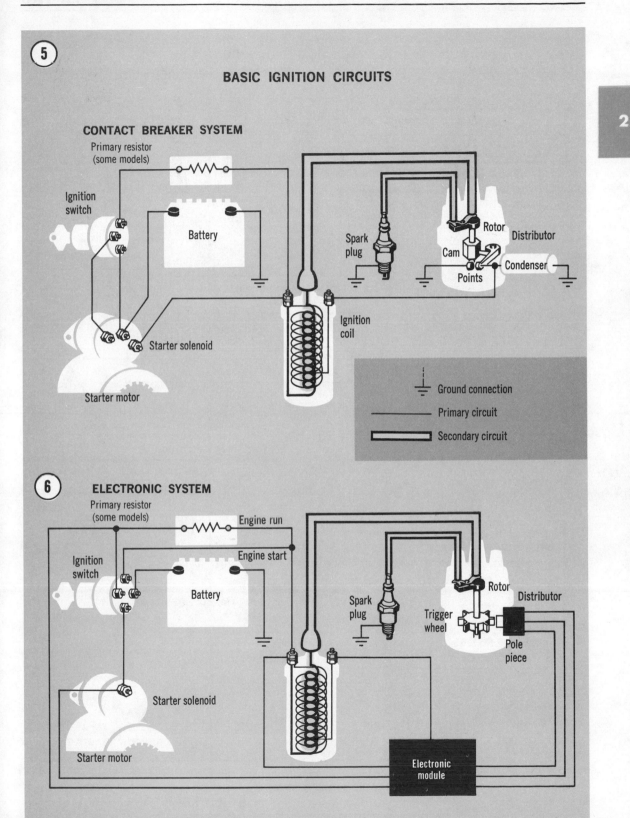

⑤

BASIC IGNITION CIRCUITS

CONTACT BREAKER SYSTEM

Primary resistor
(some models)

Ignition
switch

Battery

Spark
plug

Rotor

Distributor

Cam

Condenser

Points

Ignition
coil

Starter solenoid

Starter motor

Ground connection

Primary circuit

Secondary circuit

⑥

ELECTRONIC SYSTEM

Primary resistor
(some models)

Engine run

Ignition
switch

Engine start

Battery

Spark
plug

Rotor

Distributor

Trigger
wheel

Pole
piece

Starter solenoid

Starter motor

Electronic
module

2

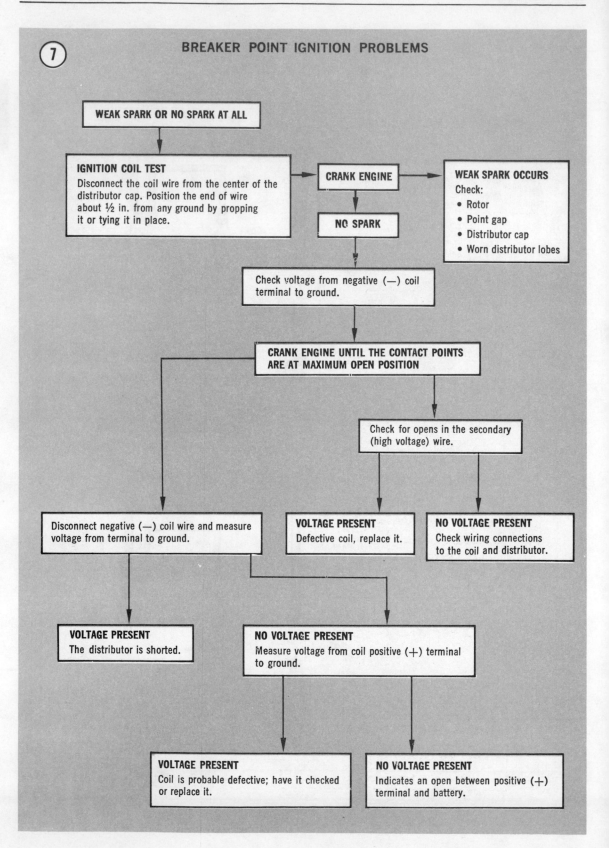

⑦ BREAKER POINT IGNITION PROBLEMS

WEAK SPARK OR NO SPARK AT ALL

IGNITION COIL TEST
Disconnect the coil wire from the center of the distributor cap. Position the end of wire about ½ in. from any ground by propping it or tying it in place.

CRANK ENGINE

NO SPARK

WEAK SPARK OCCURS
Check:
• Rotor
• Point gap
• Distributor cap
• Worn distributor lobes

Check voltage from negative (—) coil terminal to ground.

CRANK ENGINE UNTIL THE CONTACT POINTS ARE AT MAXIMUM OPEN POSITION

Check for opens in the secondary (high voltage) wire.

Disconnect negative (—) coil wire and measure voltage from terminal to ground.

VOLTAGE PRESENT
Defective coil, replace it.

NO VOLTAGE PRESENT
Check wiring connections to the coil and distributor.

VOLTAGE PRESENT
The distributor is shorted.

NO VOLTAGE PRESENT
Measure voltage from coil positive (+) terminal to ground.

VOLTAGE PRESENT
Coil is probable defective; have it checked or replace it.

NO VOLTAGE PRESENT
Indicates an open between positive (+) terminal and battery.

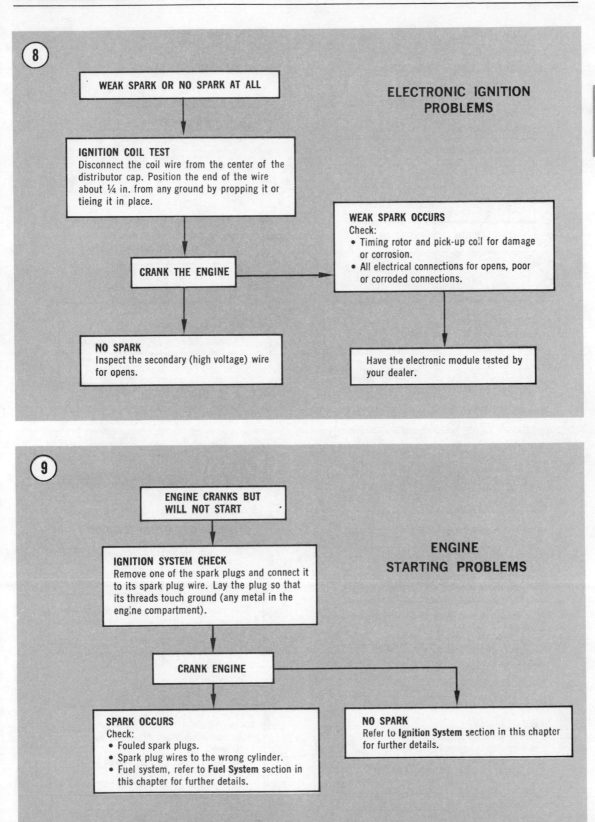

8

WEAK SPARK OR NO SPARK AT ALL

ELECTRONIC IGNITION
PROBLEMS

IGNITION COIL TEST
Disconnect the coil wire from the center of the
distributor cap. Position the end of the wire
about ¼ in. from any ground by propping it or
tieing it in place.

WEAK SPARK OCCURS
Check:
• Timing rotor and pick-up coil for damage
  or corrosion.
• All electrical connections for opens, poor
  or corroded connections.

CRANK THE ENGINE

NO SPARK
Inspect the secondary (high voltage) wire
for opens.

Have the electronic module tested by
your dealer.

9

ENGINE CRANKS BUT
WILL NOT START

ENGINE
STARTING PROBLEMS

IGNITION SYSTEM CHECK
Remove one of the spark plugs and connect it
to its spark plug wire. Lay the plug so that
its threads touch ground (any metal in the
engine compartment).

CRANK ENGINE

SPARK OCCURS
Check:
• Fouled spark plugs.
• Spark plug wires to the wrong cylinder.
• Fuel system, refer to **Fuel System** section in
  this chapter for further details.

NO SPARK
Refer to **Ignition System** section in this chapter
for further details.

2

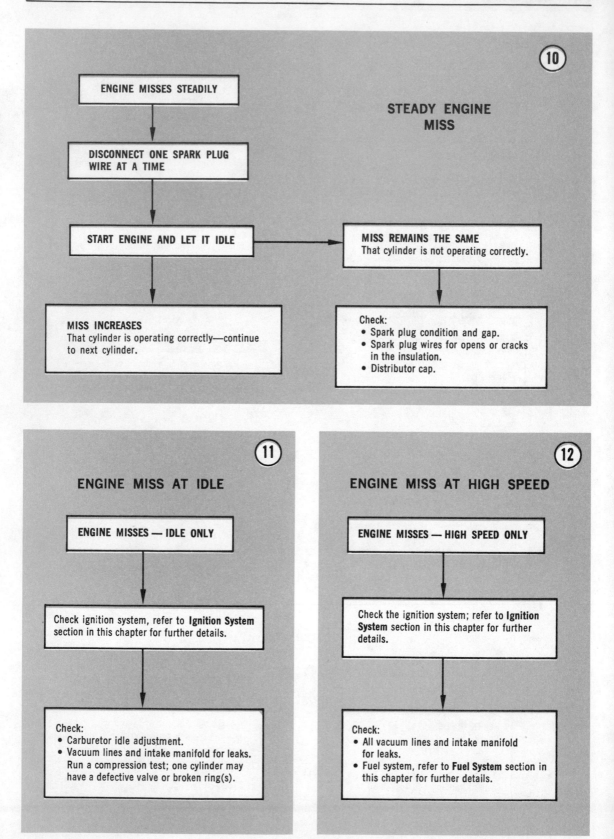

STEADY ENGINE MISS

ENGINE MISSES STEADILY

↓

DISCONNECT ONE SPARK PLUG WIRE AT A TIME

↓

START ENGINE AND LET IT IDLE →

MISS REMAINS THE SAME
That cylinder is not operating correctly.

↓

MISS INCREASES
That cylinder is operating correctly—continue to next cylinder.

Check:
• Spark plug condition and gap.
• Spark plug wires for opens or cracks in the insulation.
• Distributor cap.

ENGINE MISS AT IDLE

ENGINE MISSES — IDLE ONLY

↓

Check ignition system, refer to **Ignition System** section in this chapter for further details.

↓

Check:
• Carburetor idle adjustment.
• Vacuum lines and intake manifold for leaks. Run a compression test; one cylinder may have a defective valve or broken ring(s).

ENGINE MISS AT HIGH SPEED

ENGINE MISSES — HIGH SPEED ONLY

↓

Check the ignition system; refer to **Ignition System** section in this chapter for further details.

↓

Check:
• All vacuum lines and intake manifold for leaks.
• Fuel system, refer to **Fuel System** section in this chapter for further details.

2

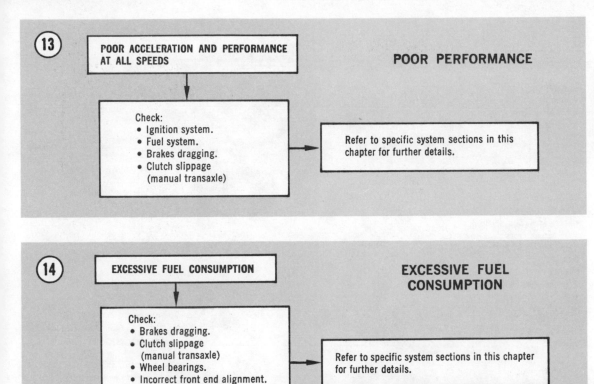

⑬

POOR ACCELERATION AND PERFORMANCE AT ALL SPEEDS

POOR PERFORMANCE

Check:
- Ignition system.
- Fuel system.
- Brakes dragging.
- Clutch slippage (manual transaxle)

Refer to specific system sections in this chapter for further details.

⑭

EXCESSIVE FUEL CONSUMPTION

EXCESSIVE FUEL CONSUMPTION

Check:
- Brakes dragging.
- Clutch slippage (manual transaxle)
- Wheel bearings.
- Incorrect front end alignment.
- Ignition system.
- Fuel system.

Refer to specific system sections in this chapter for further details.

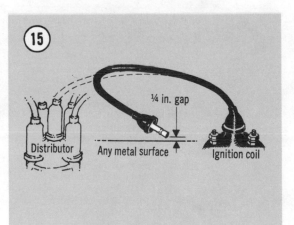

stopped, then prop the end of the wire next to a metal surface as shown in **Figures 15 and 16**.

WARNING
Never disconnect a spark plug or ignition coil wire while the engine is running. The high voltage in an ignition system, particularly the newer high-energy electronic ignition systems could cause serious injury or even death.

Spark plug condition is an important indication of engine performance. Spark plugs in a properly operating engine will have slightly pitted electrodes, and a light tan insulator tip. **Figure 17** shows a normal plug, and a number of others which indicate trouble in their respective cylinders.

NORMAL
- Appearance—Firing tip has deposits of light gray to light tan.
- Can be cleaned, regapped and reused.

CARBON FOULED
- Appearance—Dull, dry black with fluffy carbon deposits on the insulator tip, electrode and exposed shell.
- Caused by—Fuel/air mixture too rich, plug heat range too cold, weak ignition system, dirty air cleaner, faulty automatic choke or excessive idling.
- Can be cleaned, regapped and reused.

OIL FOULED
- Appearance—Wet black deposits on insulator and exposed shell.
- Caused by—Excessive oil entering the combustion chamber through worn rings, pistons, valve guides or bearings.
- Replace with new plugs (use a hotter plug if engine is not repaired).

LEAD FOULED
- Appearance — Yellow insulator deposits (may sometimes be dark gray, black or tan in color) on the insulator tip.
- Caused by—Highly leaded gasoline.
- Replace with new plugs.

LEAD FOULED
- Appearance—Yellow glazed deposits indicating melted lead deposits due to hard acceleration.
- Caused by—Highly leaded gasoline.
- Replace with new plugs.

OIL AND LEAD FOULED
- Appearance—Glazed yellow deposits with a slight brownish tint on the insulator tip and ground electrode.
- Replace with new plugs.

FUEL ADDITIVE RESIDUE
- Appearance — Brown-colored, hardened ash deposits on the insulator tip and ground electrode.
- Caused by—Fuel and/or oil additives.
- Replace with new plugs.

WORN
- Appearance — Severely worn or eroded electrodes.
- Caused by—Normal wear or unusual oil and/or fuel additives.
- Replace with new plugs.

PREIGNITION
- Appearance — Melted ground electrode.
- Caused by—Overadvanced ignition timing, inoperative ignition advance mechanism, too low of a fuel octane rating, lean fuel/air mixture or carbon deposits in combustion chamber.

PREIGNITION
- Appearance—Melted center electrode.
- Caused by—Abnormal combustion due to overadvanced ignition timing or incorrect advance, too low of a fuel octane rating, lean fuel/air mixture, or carbon deposits in combustion chamber.
- Correct engine problem and replace with new plugs.

INCORRECT HEAT RANGE
- Appearance—Melted center electrode and white blistered insulator tip.
- Caused by—Incorrect plug heat range selection.
- Replace with new plugs.

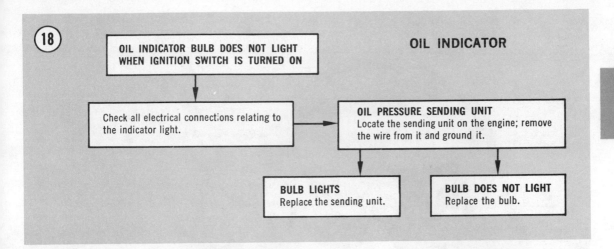

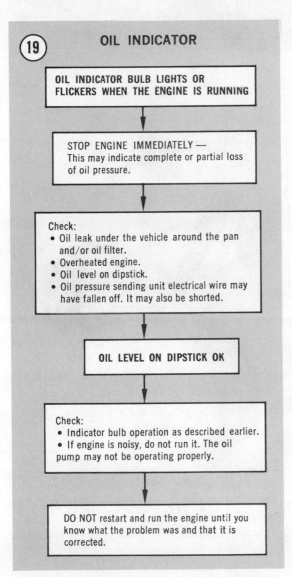

ENGINE OIL PRESSURE LIGHT

Proper oil pressure to the engine is vital. If oil pressure is insufficient, the engine can destroy itself in a comparatively short time.

The oil pressure warning circuit monitors oil pressure constantly. If pressure drops below a predetermined level, the light comes on.

Obviously, it is vital for the warning circuit to be working to signal low oil pressure. Each time you turn on the ignition, but before you start the vehicle, the warning light should come on. If it doesn't, there is trouble in the warning circuit, not the oil pressure system. See **Figure 18** to troubleshoot the warning circuit.

Once the engine is running, the warning light should stay off. If the warning light comes on or acts erratically while the engine is running there is trouble with the engine oil pressure system. *Stop the engine immediately*. Refer to **Figure 19** for possible causes of the problem.

FUEL SYSTEM (CARBURETTED)

Fuel system problems must be isolated to the fuel pump (mechanical or electric), fuel lines, fuel filter, or carburetor(s). These procedures assume the ignition system is working properly and is correctly adjusted.

1. *Engine will not start* — First make sure that fuel is being delivered to the carburetor. Remove the air cleaner, look into the carburetor throat, and operate the accelerator

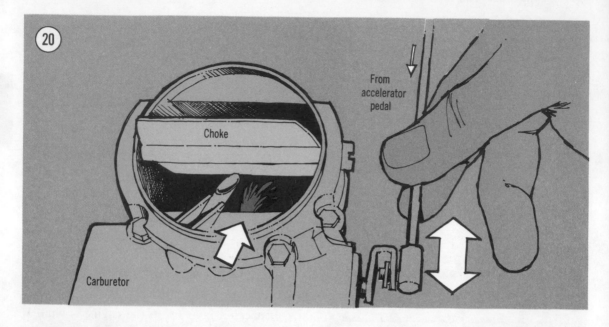

From accelerator pedal

Choke

Carburetor

linkage several times. There should be a stream of fuel from the accelerator pump discharge tube each time the accelerator linkage is depressed (**Figure 20**). If not, check fuel pump delivery (described later), float valve, and float adjustment. If the engine will not start, check the automatic choke parts for sticking or damage. If necessary, rebuild or replace the carburetor.

2. *Engine runs at fast idle* — Usually this is caused by a defective automatic choke heater element. Ensure that the heater wire is connected and making good contact. Check the idle speed, idle mixture, and decel valve (if equipped) adjustment.

3. *Rough idle or engine miss with frequent stalling* — Check idle mixture and idle speed adjustments.

Poor idle may also be caused by a defective or dirty electromagnetic cutoff valve. Check that the electromagnetic cutoff valve wire is connected to the valve (on the carburetor) and making good contact. If it is, turn the ignition switch on, disconnect the wire and touch it to the valve terminal. If the valve is working, there should be a slight click heard each time the wire touches. If the valve is defective, turn the small setscrew on the end of the valve fully counter-clockwise. This permanently opens the valve,

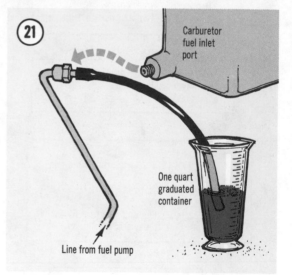

Carburetor fuel inlet port

One quart graduated container

Line from fuel pump

permitting the car to idle properly until the valve can be cleaned or replaced.

NOTE: *The engine may "diesel" in this condition. Replace the valve as soon as possible.*

4. *Engine "diesels" (continues to run) when ignition is switched off* — Check idle mixture (probably too rich), ignition timing, and idle speed (probably too fast). Check the throttle solenoid (if equipped) and electromagnetic cutoff valve for proper operation. Check for overheated engine.

5. *Stumbling when accelerating from idle* —
Check the idle speed and mixture adjustments.
Check the accelerator pump.

6. *Engine misses at high speed or lacks power*
— This indicates possible fuel starvation.
Check fuel pump pressure and capacity as
described in this chapter. Check float needle
valves. Check for a clogged fuel filter or air
cleaner.

7. *Black exhaust smoke* — This indicates a
badly overrich mixture. Check idle mixture and
idle speed adjustment. Check choke setting.
Check for excessive fuel pump pressure, leaky
floats, or worn needle valves.

8. *Excessive fuel consumption* — Check for
overrich mixture. Make sure choke mechanism
works properly. Check idle mixture and idle
speed. Check for excessive fuel pump pressure,
leaky floats, or worn float needle valves.

FUEL SYSTEM
(FUEL INJECTED)

Troubleshooting a fuel injection system requires more thought, experience, and know-
how than any other part of the vehicle. A
logical approach and proper test equipment are
essential in order to successfully find and fix
these troubles.

It is best to leave fuel injection troubles to
your dealer. In order to isolate a problem to the
injection system make sure that the fuel pump
is operating properly. Check its performance as
described later in this section. Also make sure
that fuel filter and air cleaner are not clogged.

FUEL PUMP TEST
(MECHANICAL AND ELECTRIC)

1. Disconnect the fuel inlet line where it enters
the carburetor or fuel injection system.

2. Fit a rubber hose over the fuel line so fuel
can be directed into a graduated container with
about one quart capacity. See **Figure 21**.

3. To avoid accidental starting of the engine,
disconnect the secondary coil wire from the
coil.

4. Crank the engine for about 30 seconds.

5. If the fuel pump supplies the specified
amount (refer to the fuel chapter later in this

book), the trouble may be in the carburetor or
fuel injection system. The fuel injection system
should be tested by your dealer.

6. If there is no fuel present or the pump cannot supply the specified amount, either the fuel
pump is defective or there is an obstruction in
the fuel line. Replace the fuel pump and/or inspect the fuel lines for air leaks or obstructions.

7. Also pressure test the fuel pump by installing a T-fitting in the fuel line between the fuel
pump and the carburetor. Connect a fuel pressure gauge to the fitting with a short tube
(**Figure 22**).

8. Reconnect the primary coil wire, start the
engine, and record the pressure. Refer to the
fuel chapter later in this book for the correct
pressure. If the pressure varies from that
specified, the pump should be replaced.

9. Stop the engine. The pressure should drop
off very slowly. If it drops off rapidly, the
outlet valve in the pump is leaking and the
pump should be replaced.

EMISSION CONTROL SYSTEMS

Major emission control systems used on
nearly all U.S. models include the following:

    a. Positive crankcase ventilation (PCV)

    b. Thermostatic air cleaner

    c. Air injection reaction (AIR)

    d. Fuel evaporation control

    e. Exhaust gas recirculation (EGR)

Emission control systems vary considerably
from model to model. Individual models con-
tain variations of the five systems described
here. In addition, they may include other
special systems. Use the index to find specific
emission control components in other chapters.

Many of the systems and components are
factory set and sealed. Without special expensive test equipment, it is impossible to adjust
the systems to meet state and federal requirements.

Troubleshooting can also be difficult without
special equipment. The procedures described
below will help you find emission control parts
which have failed, but repairs may have to be
entrusted to a dealer or other properly equipped
repair shop.

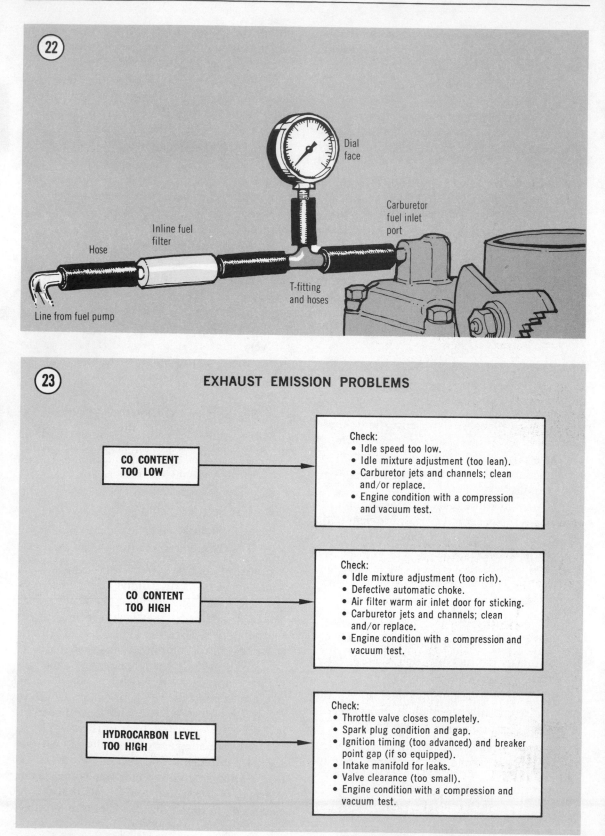

㉒

Dial
face

Inline fuel
filter

Hose

Carburetor
fuel inlet
port

Line from fuel pump

T-fitting
and hoses

㉓   EXHAUST EMISSION PROBLEMS

CO CONTENT TOO LOW

Check:
- Idle speed too low.
- Idle mixture adjustment (too lean).
- Carburetor jets and channels; clean and/or replace.
- Engine condition with a compression and vacuum test.

CO CONTENT TOO HIGH

Check:
- Idle mixture adjustment (too rich).
- Defective automatic choke.
- Air filter warm air inlet door for sticking.
- Carburetor jets and channels; clean and/or replace.
- Engine condition with a compression and vacuum test.

HYDROCARBON LEVEL TOO HIGH

Check:
- Throttle valve closes completely.
- Spark plug condition and gap.
- Ignition timing (too advanced) and breaker point gap (if so equipped).
- Intake manifold for leaks.
- Valve clearance (too small).
- Engine condition with a compression and vacuum test.

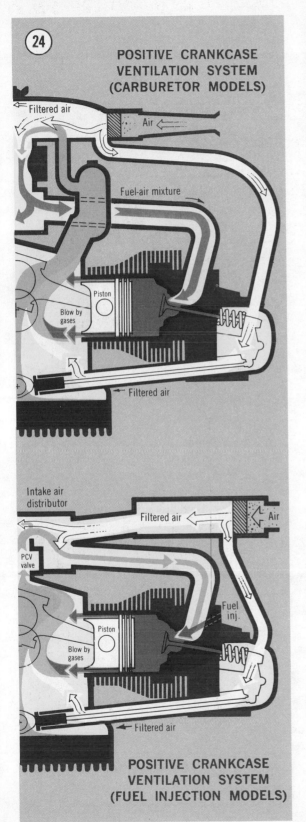

POSITIVE CRANKCASE
VENTILATION SYSTEM
(CARBURETOR MODELS)

POSITIVE CRANKCASE
VENTILATION SYSTEM
(FUEL INJECTION MODELS)

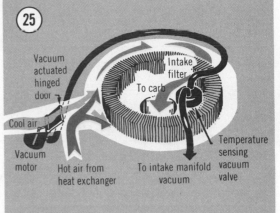

With the proper equipment, you can test the carbon monoxide and hydrocarbon levels. **Figure 23** provides some sources of trouble if the readings are not correct.

Positive Crankcase Ventilation

Fresh air drawn from the air cleaner housing scavenges emissions (e.g., piston blow-by) from the crankcase, then the intake manifold vacuum draws emissions into the intake manifold. They can then be reburned in the normal combustion process. **Figure 24** shows a typical system.

Thermostatic Air Cleaner

The thermostatically controlled air cleaner maintains incoming air to the engine at a predetermined level, usually about 100°F or higher. It mixes cold air with heated air from the exhaust manifold region. The air cleaner includes a temperature sensor, vacuum motor, and a hinged door. See **Figure 25**.

The system is comparatively easy to test. See **Figure 26** for the procedure.

Air Injection Reaction System

The air injection reaction system reduces air pollution by oxidizing hydrocarbons and carbon monoxide as they leave the combustion chamber. See **Figure 27**.

The air injection pump, driven by the engine, compresses filtered air and injects it at the exhaust port of each cylinder. The fresh air mixes with the unburned gases in the exhaust and pro-

(26)

THERMOSTATIC AIR CLEANER

THERMOSTATIC AIR CLEANER

Normal operation — Closed for cold engine.
— Open for warm engine.

OPENS AND CLOSES
Is operating correctly.

DOES NOT OPEN OR CLOSE
Check for binding linkage or a leak in the vacuum line.

(27)

A.I.R. SYSTEM

Filtered air

Air pump

Back-up valve

To other cylinders

To muffler

Air injection valve

(28)

AIR INJECTION REACTOR

AIR INJECTION REACTOR

PUMP NOT PRODUCING AIR PRESSURE
(Approximately 1 psi)

PUMP NOT RUNNING
AT PROPER SPEED

REMOVE THE AIR FILTER
(if so equipped)

Check:
• Drive belt tension.
• Oil the bearings (if there are provisions to do so).
• Air filter (some models have their own small air filter).

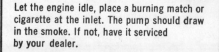

Let the engine idle, place a burning match or cigarette at the inlet. The pump should draw in the smoke. If not, have it serviced by your dealer.

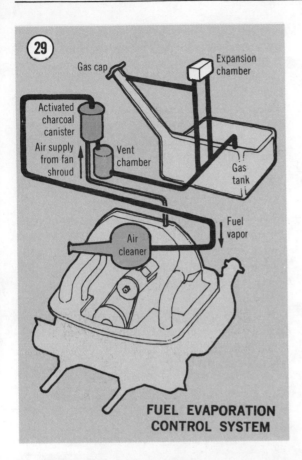

**FUEL EVAPORATION
CONTROL SYSTEM**

motes further burning. A check valve prevents exhaust gases from entering and damaging the air pump if the pump becomes inoperative, e.g., from a drive belt failure.

Figure 28 explains the testing procedure for this system.

Fuel Evaporation Control

Fuel vapor from the fuel tank passes through the liquid/vapor separator to the carbon canister. See **Figure 29**. The carbon absorbs and stores the vapor when the engine is stopped. When the engine runs, manifold vacuum draws the vapor from the canister. Instead of being released into the atmosphere, the fuel vapor takes part in the normal combustion process.

Exhaust Gas Recirculation

The exhaust gas recirculation (EGR) system is used to reduce the emission of nitrogen oxides (NO_x). Relatively inert exhaust gases are introduced into the combustion process to slightly reduce peak temperatures. This reduction in temperature reduces the formation of NO_x.

Figure 30 provides a simple test of this system.

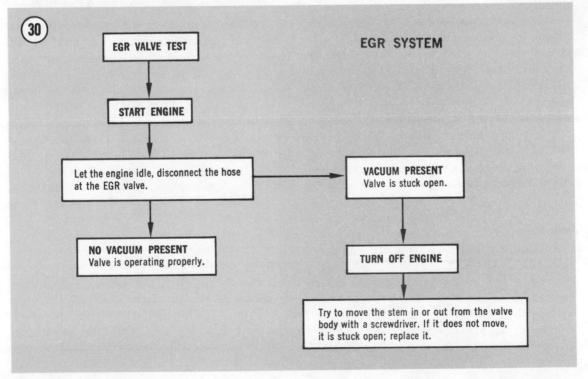

ENGINE NOISES

Often the first evidence of an internal engine trouble is a strange noise. That knocking, clicking, or tapping which you never heard before may be warning you of impending trouble.

While engine noises can indicate problems, they are sometimes difficult to interpret correctly; inexperienced mechanics can be seriously misled by them.

Professional mechanics often use a special stethoscope which looks similar to a doctor's stethoscope for isolating engine noises. You can do nearly as well with a "sounding stick" which can be an ordinary piece of doweling or a section of small hose. By placing one end in contact with the area to which you want to listen and the other end near your ear, you can hear sounds emanating from that area. The first time you do this, you may be horrified at the strange noises coming from even a normal engine. If you can, have an experienced friend or mechanic help you sort the noises out.

Clicking or Tapping Noises

Clicking or tapping noises usually come from the valve train, and indicate excessive valve clearance.

If your vehicle has adjustable valves, the procedure for adjusting the valve clearance is explained in Chapter Three. If your vehicle has hydraulic lifters, the clearance may not be adjustable. The noise may be coming from a collapsed lifter. These may be cleaned or replaced as described in the engine chapter.

A sticking valve may also sound like a valve with excessive clearance. In addition, excessive wear in valve train components can cause similar engine noises.

Knocking Noises

A heavy, dull knocking is usually caused by a worn main bearing. The noise is loudest when the engine is working hard, i.e., accelerating hard at low speed. You may be able to isolate the trouble to a single bearing by disconnecting the spark plugs one at a time. When you reach the spark plug nearest the bearing, the knock will be reduced or disappear.

Worn connecting rod bearings may also produce a knock, but the sound is usually more "metallic." As with a main bearing, the noise is worse when accelerating. It may even increase further just as you go from accelerating to coasting. Disconnecting spark plugs will help isolate this knock as well.

A double knock or clicking usually indicates a worn piston pin. Disconnecting spark plugs will isolate this to a particular piston, however, the noise will *increase* when you reach the affected piston.

A loose flywheel and excessive crankshaft end play also produce knocking noises. While similar to main bearing noises, these are usually intermittent, not constant, and they do not change when spark plugs are disconnected.

Some mechanics confuse piston pin noise with piston slap. The double knock will distinguish the piston pin noise. Piston slap is identified by the fact that it is always louder when the engine is cold.

ELECTRICAL ACCESSORIES

Lights and Switches (Interior and Exterior)

1. *Bulb does not light* — Remove the bulb and check for a broken element. Also check the inside of the socket; make sure the contacts are clean and free of corrosion. If the bulb and socket are OK, check to see if a fuse has blown. The fuse panel (**Figure 31**) is usually located under the instrument panel. Replace the blown fuse. If the fuse blows again, there is a short in that circuit. Check that circuit all the way to the battery. Look for worn wire insulation or burned wires.

If all the above are all right, check the switch controlling the bulb for continuity with an ohmmeter at the switch terminals. Check the switch contact terminals for loose or dirty electrical connections.

2. *Headlights work but will not switch from either high or low beam* — Check the beam selector switch for continuity with an ohmmeter at the switch terminals. Check the switch contact terminals for loose or dirty electrical connections.

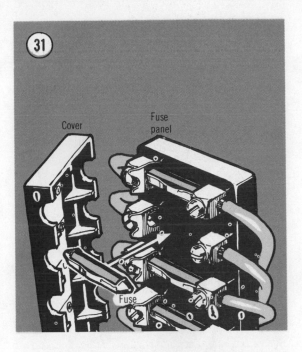

Cover   Fuse panel

Fuse

3. *Brake light switch inoperative* — On mechanically operated switches, usually mounted near the brake pedal arm, adjust the switch to achieve correct mechanical operation. Check the switch for continuity with an ohmmeter at the switch terminals. Check the switch contact terminals for loose or dirty electrical connections.

4. *Back-up lights do not operate* — Check light bulb as described earlier. Locate the switch, normally located near the shift lever. Adjust switch to achieve correct mechanical operation. Check the switch for continuity with an ohmmeter at the switch terminals. Bypass the switch with a jumper wire; if the lights work, replace the switch.

Directional Signals

1. *Directional signals do not operate* — If the indicator light on the instrument panel burns steadily instead of flashing, this usually indicates that one of the exterior lights is burned out. Check all lamps that normally flash. If all are all right, the flasher unit may be defective. Replace it with a good one.

2. *Directional signal indicator light on instrument panel does not light up* — Check the light bulbs as described earlier. Check all electrical connections and check the flasher unit.

3. *Directional signals will not self-cancel* — Check the self-cancelling mechanism located inside the steering column.

4. *Directional signals flash slowly* — Check the condition of the battery and the alternator (or generator) drive belt tension (**Figure 4**). Check the flasher unit and all related electrical connections.

Windshield Wipers

1. *Wipers do not operate* — Check for a blown fuse and replace it. Check all related terminals for loose or dirty electrical connections. Check continuity of the control switch with an ohmmeter at the switch terminals. Check the linkage and arms for loose, broken, or binding parts. Straighten out or replace where necessary.

2. *Wiper motor hums but will not operate* — The motor may be shorted out internally; check and/or replace the motor. Also check for broken or binding linkage and arms.

3. *Wiper arms will not return to the stowed position when turned off* — The motor has a special internal switch for this purpose. Have it inspected by your dealer. Do not attempt this yourself.

Interior Heater

1. *Heater fan does not operate* — Check for a blown fuse. Check the switch for continuity with an ohmmeter at the switch terminals. Check the switch contact terminals for loose or dirty electrical connections.

2. *Heat output is insufficient* — Check that the heater door(s) and cable(s) are operating correctly and are in the open position. Inspect the heat ducts; make sure that they are not crimped or blocked.

3. *Exhaust fumes in passenger compartment* — Open all windows and inspect heat exchangers and heating system immediately.

WARNING
Do not continue to operate the vehicle with deadly carbon monoxide fumes present in the passenger compartment.

COOLING SYSTEM

Engine cooling is provided by an engine driven fan which draws in outside air for the cylinders and cylinder heads. Thermostatically controlled air flaps limit the amount of cold air when engine is cold to provide rapid warm up.

If the engine is running abnormally hot, check fan drive condition and tension, air control ring adjustment and/or air control thermostat.

If overheating is extreme, the engine will have to be removed and the cooling duct system removed and inspected.

CLUTCH

All clutch troubles except adjustments require removal of the engine/transaxle assembly to identify and cure the problem.

1. *Slippage* — This is most noticeable when accelerating in a high gear at relatively low speed. To check slippage, park the vehicle on a level surface with the handbrake set. Shift to 2nd gear and release the clutch as if driving off. If the clutch is good, the engine will slow and stall. If the clutch slips, continued engine speed will give it away.

Slippage results from insufficient clutch pedal free play, oil or grease on the clutch disc, worn pressure plate, or weak springs. Also check for binding in the clutch cable and lever arm which may prevent full engagement.

CAUTION
This is a severe test. Perform this test only when slippage is suspected, not periodically.

2. *Drag or failure to release* — This trouble usually causes difficult shifting and gear clash, especially when downshifting. The cause may be excessive clutch pedal free play, warped or bent pressure plate or clutch disc, excessive clutch cable guide sag, broken or loose linings, lack of lubrication in gland nut bearing or felt ring. Also check condition of main shaft splines.

3. *Chatter or grabbing* — A number of things can cause this trouble. Check tightness of

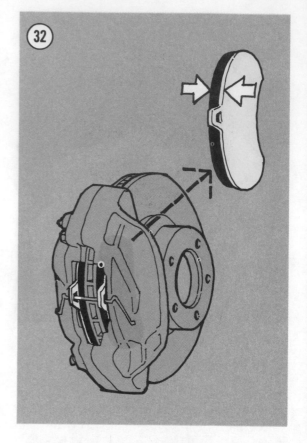

engine mounts and engine-to-transmission mounting bolts. Check for worn or misaligned pressure plate and misaligned release plate, or excessive cable guide sag.

4. *Other noises* — Noise usually indicates a dry or defective release or pilot bearing. Check the bearings and replace if necessary. Also check all parts for misalignment and uneven wear.

MANUAL TRANSAXLE

Transaxle troubles are evident when one or more of the following symptoms appear:

a. Difficulty changing gears

b. Gears clash when downshifting

c. Slipping out of gear

d. Excessive noise in NEUTRAL

e. Excessive noise in gear

f. Oil leaks

Transaxle repairs, except for one oil seal, are not possible without expensive special tools.

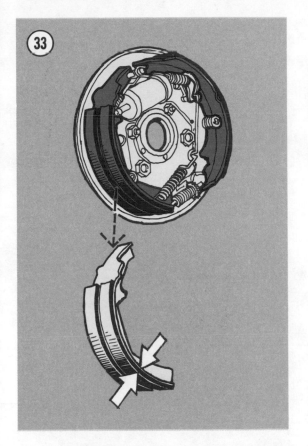

The main shaft oil seal, however, is easily replaced after removing the engine.

Transaxle troubles are sometimes difficult to distinguish from clutch troubles. Eliminate the clutch as a source of trouble before installing a new or rebuilt transaxle.

AUTOMATIC AND SEMI-AUTOMATIC TRANSAXLE

Most automatic and semi-automatic trans-axle repairs require considerable specialized knowledge and tools. It is impractical for the home mechanic to invest in the tools, since they cost more than a properly rebuilt transmission.

Check fluid level and condition frequently to help prevent future problems. If the fluid is orange or black in color or smells like varnish, it is an indication of some type of damage or failure within the transmission. Have the transmission serviced by your dealer or competent automatic transmission service facility.

Refer to transaxle chapter for specific trouble-shooting procedures.

BRAKES

Good brakes are vital to the safe operation of the vehicle. Performing the maintenance specified in Chapter Three will minimize problems with the brakes. Most importantly, check and maintain the level of fluid in the master cylinder, and check the thickness of the linings on the disc brake pads (**Figure 32**) or drum brake shoes (**Figure 33**).

If trouble develops, **Figures 34 through 36** will help you locate the problem. Refer to the brake chapter for actual repair procedures.

STEERING AND SUSPENSION

Trouble in the suspension or steering is evident when the following occur:

a. Steering is hard

b. Vehicle pulls to one side

c. Vehicle wanders or front wheels wobble

d. Steering has excessive play

e. Tire wear is abnormal

Unusual steering, pulling, or wandering is usually caused by bent or otherwise misaligned suspension parts. This is difficult to check without proper alignment equipment. Refer to the suspension chapter in this book for repairs that you can perform and those that must be left to a dealer or suspension specialist.

If your trouble seems to be excessive play, check wheel bearing adjustment first. This is the most frequent cause. Then check ball-joints as described below. Finally, check tie rod end ball-joints by shaking each tie rod. Also check steering gear, or rack-and-pinion assembly to see that it is securely bolted down.

TIRE WEAR ANALYSIS

Abnormal tire wear should be analyzed to determine its causes. The most common causes are the following:

a. Incorrect tire pressure

b. Improper driving

c. Overloading

d. Bad road surfaces

e. Incorrect wheel alignment

2

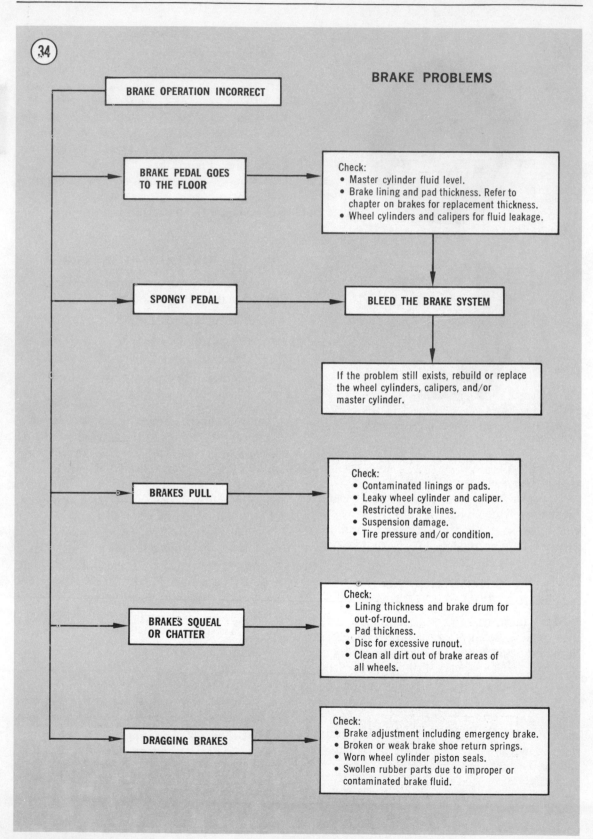

(34)

BRAKE PROBLEMS

BRAKE OPERATION INCORRECT

BRAKE PEDAL GOES
TO THE FLOOR

Check:
• Master cylinder fluid level.
• Brake lining and pad thickness. Refer to
  chapter on brakes for replacement thickness.
• Wheel cylinders and calipers for fluid leakage.

SPONGY PEDAL

BLEED THE BRAKE SYSTEM

If the problem still exists, rebuild or replace
the wheel cylinders, calipers, and/or
master cylinder.

BRAKES PULL

Check:
• Contaminated linings or pads.
• Leaky wheel cylinder and caliper.
• Restricted brake lines.
• Suspension damage.
• Tire pressure and/or condition.

BRAKES SQUEAL
OR CHATTER

Check:
• Lining thickness and brake drum for
  out-of-round.
• Pad thickness.
• Disc for excessive runout.
• Clean all dirt out of brake areas of
  all wheels.

DRAGGING BRAKES

Check:
• Brake adjustment including emergency brake.
• Broken or weak brake shoe return springs.
• Worn wheel cylinder piston seals.
• Swollen rubber parts due to improper or
  contaminated brake fluid.

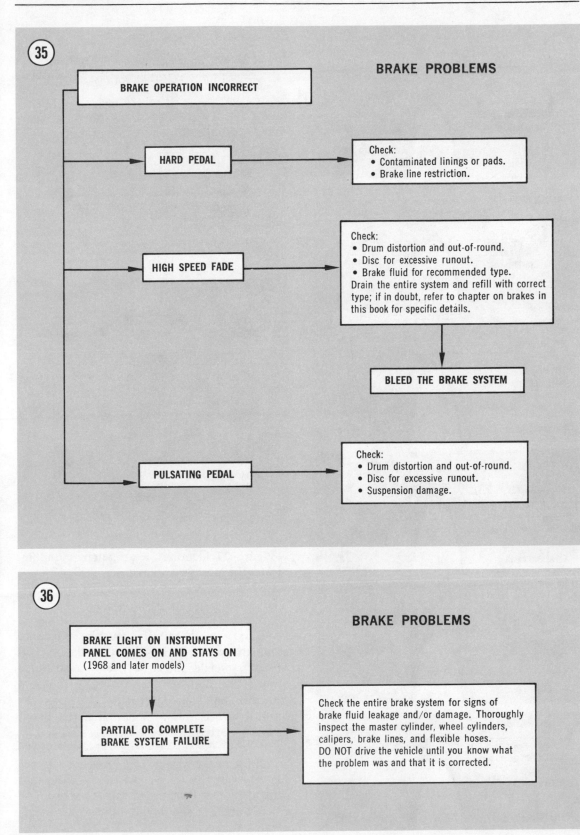

35 BRAKE PROBLEMS

BRAKE OPERATION INCORRECT

HARD PEDAL

Check:
- Contaminated linings or pads.
- Brake line restriction.

HIGH SPEED FADE

Check:
- Drum distortion and out-of-round.
- Disc for excessive runout.
- Brake fluid for recommended type.
Drain the entire system and refill with correct type; if in doubt, refer to chapter on brakes in this book for specific details.

BLEED THE BRAKE SYSTEM

PULSATING PEDAL

Check:
- Drum distortion and out-of-round.
- Disc for excessive runout.
- Suspension damage.

36 BRAKE PROBLEMS

BRAKE LIGHT ON INSTRUMENT PANEL COMES ON AND STAYS ON
(1968 and later models)

PARTIAL OR COMPLETE BRAKE SYSTEM FAILURE

Check the entire brake system for signs of brake fluid leakage and/or damage. Thoroughly inspect the master cylinder, wheel cylinders, calipers, brake lines, and flexible hoses.
DO NOT drive the vehicle until you know what the problem was and that it is corrected.

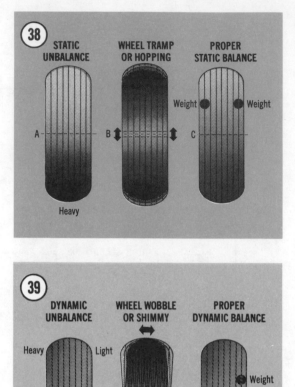

Figure 37 identifies wear patterns and indicates the most probable causes.

WHEEL BALANCING

All four wheels and tires must be in balance along two axes. To be in static balance (**Figure 38**), weight must be evenly distributed around the axis of rotation. (A) shows a statically unbalanced wheel; (B) shows the result — wheel tramp or hopping; (C) shows proper static balance.

To be in dynamic balance (**Figure 39**), the centerline of the weight must coincide with the centerline of the wheel. (A) shows a dynamically unbalanced wheel; (B) shows the result — wheel wobble or shimmy; (C) shows proper dynamic balance.

LUBRICATION, MAINTENANCE AND TUNE-UP

To ensure good performance, dependability and safety, regular preventive maintenance is necessary. This chapter outlines periodic lubrication and maintenance for a car driven by an average owner. A car driven more than average may require more frequent attention, but even without use, rust, dirt and corrosion cause unnecessary damage. Whether performed by a Porsche dealer or by the owner, regular routine attention helps avoid expensive repairs.

The recommended schedule in this chapter includes routine checks which are easily performed at each oil change and periodic

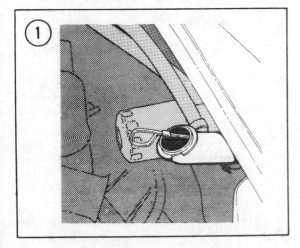

maintenance to prevent future trouble. The last part of this chapter suggests a simplified engine tune-up procedure which expedites this important task. **Table 1** lists routine fuel stop checks. **Tables 2-4** summarize all periodic maintenance. Recommended lubricants and fuels are found in **Table 5**. **Tables 1-8** are at the end of the chapter.

NOTE
*Porsche's warranty requirement states that the vehicle must be maintained and serviced in accordance with Porsche specifications. See **Tables 2-4** and your Porsche Warranty and Maintenance booklet. When performing maintenance procedures, make sure to keep accurate records, as well as dated bills of parts (and service performed by independent garages) to serve as proof that the services were performed when required.*

ROUTINE CHECKS

The following simple checks should be performed at each fuel stop. See **Table 1**.
1. Check engine oil. Oil should be checked with engine warm, *idling* and on level ground. See **Figure 1**. Level should be between the 2 marks on the dipstick; never below and never above. Top up if necessary.

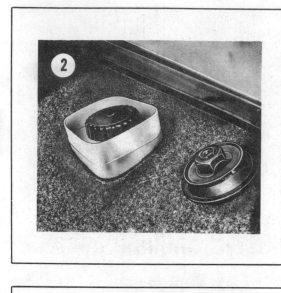

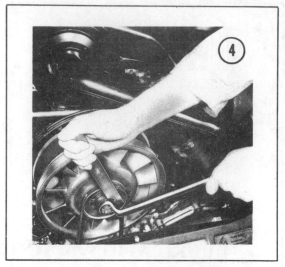

2. Check battery electrolyte level. It should be even with the top of the vertical separators. Top up with *distilled* water.

3. Check that the brake fluid level is at the top mark. See **Figure 2**. Use brake fluid clearly marked DOT 3 or DOT 4 only.

4. Check fan belt tension and condition. Tension is correct when belt can be depressed 1/2-3/4 in. (10-15 mm) under slight thumb pressure. See **Figure 3**.

5. Check tire pressure when tires are cold. Front tire pressure should be 26 psi; rear tire pressure, 29 psi. For speeds over 125 mph (200 kph), increase pressures by 5 psi.

6. Check windshield washer container level. The container holds about 2 quarts.

PERIODIC CHECKS

Cooling Fan Belt

Since cooling fan belt tension and condition affect engine cooling, check frequently. When correct, the belt should deflect about 1/2-3/4 in. (10-15 mm) under light thumb pressure. See **Figure 3**. Check condition of belt; replace it if worn or cracked.

To replace and/or adjust the fan belt, hold the alternator pulley with the tool provided in the tool kit. See **Figure 4**. Remove the pulley nut. Remove the defective belt and install a new one.

Adjust belt tension by varying the number of shims between pulley halves. Decreasing

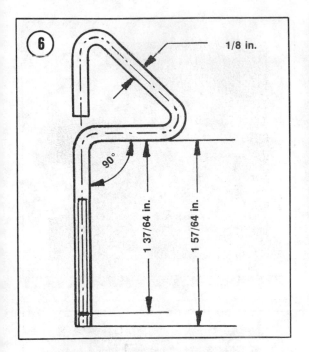

the number tightens the belt; increasing the number loosens the belt. Store extra shims on the outside of the pulley under the concave washer. See **Figure 5**. Adjust belt tension carefully. If it is too loose, the engine can overheat and the battery may not charge. If too tight, belt life will be low and the alternator bearings will wear prematurely.

Engine Compression

At specified intervals and before every engine tune-up, check cylinder compression as described in this chapter under *Compression Check*.

Engine Compartment Check

At specified intervals, check entire engine compartment for leaking or deteriorated oil and fuel lines. Check electrical wiring for breaks in insulation caused by deterioration or chafing. Check for loose or missing nuts, bolts and screws.

Exhaust Emission Control Check

After every engine tune-up, check carbon monoxide (CO) content of exhaust gas. Use a good quality exhaust gas analyzer, following the manufacturer's instructions. With the engine idling, CO content should be:

- a. Through 1976–2.5-3.0%.
- b. 1977–1.5-3.0%.
- c. 1978-1979 (measured ahead of converter)–1.5-3.5%.
- d. 1980-on–0.4-0.8%.

Air Pump Oil Level

At specified intervals, check the oil level in the exhaust emission control air pump. To do this, make a dipstick with the dimensions shown in **Figure 6**. Insert dipstick into filler hole until horizontal portion contacts plug seat (**Figure 7**). Oil level should be between the upper mark and the tip of the dipstick. If necessary, top up with Type A automatic transmission fluid.

> *CAUTION*
> *Do not overfill. If level is above upper mark, siphon some oil out.*

Air Pump Belt Tension

At specified intervals, check air pump belt tension on exhaust emission controlled vehicles. The belt should deflect about 1/2 in. (10 mm) when depressed by light finger

pressure halfway between pulleys. See **Figure 8**. Loosen the retaining bolt on the right side of the pulley (**Figure 9**). Move the pump to achieve the correct belt tension (**Figure 8**), then tighten the retaining bolt.

Steering and Suspension

At specified intervals, check entire steering and suspension systems. Check ball-joint and tie rod end dust seals. Check tie rods for tightness and damage. Check tire wear which may indicate damaged or worn suspension parts. Check shock absorbers for oil streaks indicating leaks; replace if necessary.

Jack the front wheels up. Move front wheels by hand. Steering wheel should turn as soon as wheel turns; there should be no free play. If free play is present, adjust rack-and-pinion steering. See Chapter Twelve.

Wheel Bearings

At specified intervals, check wheel bearing adjustment. See Chapter Twelve.

Brakes

At specified intervals, check brake pad thickness. The thickness shown in **Figure 10**

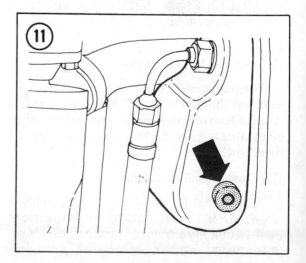

should be at least 0.08 in. (2 mm). If less, replace all 4 front or rear pads to keep brakes balanced. Never replace pads on one wheel only. Check handbrake and adjust if necessary; see Chapter Thirteen.

Windshield Wiper Blades

Long exposure to weather and road film hardens the rubber wiper blades and destroys their effectiveness. Replace the blades when they smear or otherwise fail to clean the windshield.

Tire and Wheel Inspection

At specified intervals, check the condition of all tires. Check local traffic regulations concerning minimum tread depths. Most recommend replacing tires with tread less than 1/32 in. deep. Check lug nuts for tightness.

PERIODIC MAINTENANCE

Engine Oil Change

The oil change interval varies depending upon the type of driving you do. For normal driving, including some in city traffic, change oil at specified intervals (**Tables 2-4**). If driving is primarily short distance with considerable stop-and-go city traffic, change oil more often, possibly even twice as often. Change oil at least twice a year if the car is driven only a few hundred miles a month.

Any oil used must be rated "FOR API SERVICE SD OR SE." Non-detergent oils are *not recommended*. See **Table 5** for recommended oil grades.

To drain engine oil:
1. Warm engine to operating temperature.
2. Remove drain plug from oil tank (**Figure 11**) and center of oil strainer (**Figure 12**).
3. Let oil drain for at least 10 minutes.
4. Remove and clean oil strainer. See Chapter Four. Install clean oil strainer with new gaskets.
5. Install oil drain plugs.
6. Change oil filter as described in this chapter.
7. Remove oil filler cap (**Figure 13**). Refill with quantity of oil specified in **Table 5** for your engine. See **Figure 14** or **Figure 15**.
8. Check level on dipstick.

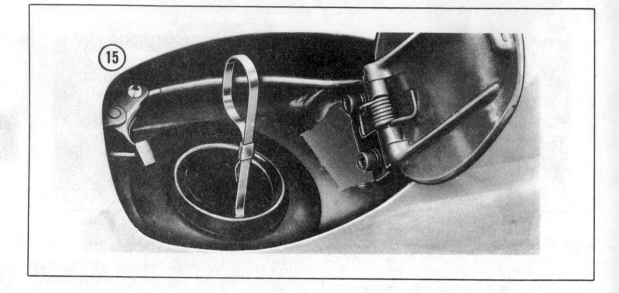

NOTE
The engine must be idling to check oil level.

Engine Oil Filter

At specified intervals, replace the oil filter. This should be done after the oil is drained and before new oil is poured in. All models have a full flow spin-off filter located on the right side of the engine compartment. Unscrew and discard the old filter and screw on a new one. Tighten the filter about 1/2 turn *by hand* after the filter gasket contacts the metal base. Start the engine and check for leaks.

Air Cleaner

All 911 models use disposable "dry-type" paper element air cleaners. Service the air cleaner at specified intervals.

To replace the paper element, remove the wing nuts or unsnap the clips around the cover (**Figure 16**). Remove cover and discard the element. Wipe inside of air cleaner housing with a lightly oiled lintless cloth. Insert new element and install cover.

Distributor Lubrication (Breaker Point Models)

At specified intervals, apply a thin coat of high-temperature grease to the contact surfaces of the breaker cam.

CAUTION
Do not get any grease on the breaker points. Dirty points pit and burn rapidly.

Transaxle Oil Change

Change transaxle oil at specified intervals. Oil must be at normal operating temperature before draining. Remove drain plug from bottom of transaxle and let oil drain for at least 10-15 minutes. Clean and install drain plug. Wipe dirt away from filler plug area and remove plug. Fill transaxle slowly with approximately 2 1/2 U.S. quarts of a lubricant specified in **Table 5**. It is good practice to fill with 2 or 3 pints, wait several minutes, then add the rest. Oil level should reach the bottom of the oil filler hole.

CAUTION
Do not overfill. Before installing plug, let any excess oil drain out. Excess oil can damage seals.

The Sportomatic torque converter shares engine oil and need not be serviced separately.

Clutch

At specified intervals, check clutch pedal free play on manual transmission cars. Depress pedal by hand. Clutch free play should be 13/16-1 in. (20-25 mm).

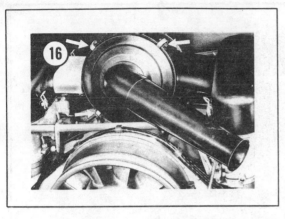

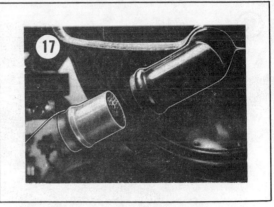

On Sportomatics, check clutch adjustment and gearshift switch adjustment as described in Chapter Ten.

Exhaust System

At specified intervals, examine the muffler, tailpipe(s) and heat exchangers for rust, holes and other damage. Replace any damaged or deteriorated parts.

Oxygen Sensor

At specified intervals, replace the oxygen sensor, if so equipped. See Chapter Five.

Carburetors

At specified intervals, lubricate the carburetor controls and linkages. Use 1-2 drops of engine oil at all pivot points. Do not use too much oil; excessive oil attracts dirt which can cause dangerous throttle sticking. Disconnect and lubricate each ball-joint. Porsche recommends high-temperature grease, but many mechanics prefer graphite powder to prevent the possibility of throttle sticking.

Fuel Filter

At the intervals specified in **Tables 2-4**, inspect and clean the fuel pump filters.

Crankcase Ventilation System

Every 12,000 miles, clean the flame arrester in the air cleaner. To do this, disconnect the oil breather line and then pull the flame arrester out. See **Figure 17**.

Auxiliary Gasoline Heater

Every year, prior to the cold season, clean the glow plug and fuel line connectors in the heater. In addition, clean the metering jet in the fuel pump.

Remove glow plug and test it as described in Chapter Five. Make sure the glow plug gap is 0.10 in. (2-2.5 mm). Disconnect the fuel line between the heater and fuel pump; clean both connectors and reinstall the line. Unscrew the jet (**Figure 18**), clean it in solvent and reinstall it. Check all electrical connections. Test heater; if there is any trouble, take it to your dealer for service.

ENGINE TUNE-UP

In order to maintain a car in proper running condition, the engine must receive periodic tune-ups. Procedures outlined here are performed at the intervals specified in **Tables 2-4**. Ignition timing specifications are found in **Table 6**, breaker point and valve specifications in **Table 7** and spark plug specifications in **Table 8**.

Since different systems in an engine interact to affect overall performance, tune-ups must be accomplished in the following order:
  a. Compression check.
  b. Valve clearance adjustment.
  c. Ignition adjustment and timing.
  d. Fuel system adjustment.

Compression Check

A compression test measures the ability of the cylinders to hold compression. If one or

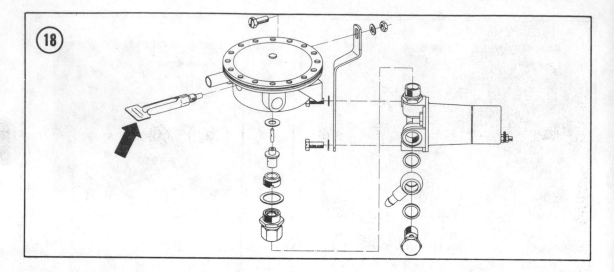

more cylinders have low compression and are allowed to remain uncorrected, completing the following engine tune-up procedures will not improve engine performance. A compression tester with a long flexible extension is required since the spark plug holes are deep inside the air cooling covers.

A "dry" and a "wet" compression test are usually performed together and their results interpreted to isolate cylinder and/or valve trouble. However, the wet compression test is unreliable when performed on the Porsche 911 engine. To perform the wet test, about one tablespoon of oil is normally poured into the spark plug hole before checking compression. Since Porsche cylinders are horizontal, oil does not spread evenly over the piston crown–a necessity for this test.

Only the dry compression test should be performed on the 911 engine:

1. Warm the engine to normal operating temperature. Make sure that the choke valve and throttle valve are completely open.

2. Remove the spark plugs.

3. Connect the compression tester to one cylinder according to manufacturer's instructions.

4. Have an assistant crank the engine over until there is no further rise in pressure.

5. Remove the tester and record the reading on paper.

6. Repeat Steps 3-5 for each cylinder.

When interpreting the results, actual readings are not as important as the difference between readings. All readings should be approximately 132-162 psi (9-11 kg/cm^2). Readings below 114 psi (8 kg/cm^2) indicate that an engine overhaul is due. A maximum difference of 28 psi (2 kg/cm^2) between any 2 cylinders is acceptable. Greater differences indicate worn or broken rings, sticking or leaking valves or a combination of both. Compare with vacuum gauge readings to isolate the trouble more closely.

Vacuum gauges are discussed in Chapter One. Follow the manufacturer's procedures to interpret results.

Valve Clearance

This is a series of simple mechanical adjustments which are performed while the engine is cold. Valve clearances for your engine must be carefully set. If the clearance is too small, the valves may be burned or distorted. Large clearances result in excessive noise. In either case, engine power is reduced.

Before adjusting valves, remove both rocker arm covers and all spark plugs. This makes the engine easier to turn by hand and plugs require cleaning or replacement at this time anyway. See *Spark Plug Replacement* in this chapter.

NOTE
Valve arrangement for 911 engines is intake on top, exhaust on bottom.

Adjust all valves to 0.004 in. (0.10 mm) in the following cylinder number order:

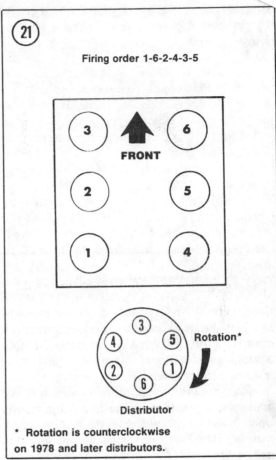

Firing order 1-6-2-4-3-5

FRONT

Distributor

* Rotation is counterclockwise
on 1978 and later distributors.

3

1-6-2-4-3-5. To begin, turn engine over until rotor points to notch on distributor housing and "Z1" mark on crankshaft pulley aligns with the blower housing notch. See **Figure 19**. This indicates that the No. 1 cylinder is at TDC on its compression stroke.

Adjust valve clearance for No. 1 cylinder valves; this is the left rear cylinder. Loosen the adjusting screw locknut, insert a feeler gauge and adjust until a slight drag is felt on the gauge. See **Figure 20**. Tighten locknut and recheck clearance to be sure it has not changed.

Rotate the crankshaft pulley 120° clockwise until the next pulley mark aligns with the housing mark. Adjust No. 6 cylinder valves. Rotate pulley to next notch (120°) and adjust No. 2 cylinder valves. Repeat this procedure for Nos. 4, 3 and 5 cylinders in that order, turning the pulley 120° each time. When

finished, install the rocker arm covers with new gaskets.

Spark Plug Replacement

1. Blow out any foreign matter from around the spark plugs with compressed air.

CAUTION
When plugs are removed, dirt from around them can fall into the spark plug holes. This could cause expensive engine damage.

2. Mark the spark plug wires with the cylinder number so they can be reconnected properly. See **Figure 21** for cylinder and spark plug wire positioning.

NOTE
Use a small strip of masking tape around each wire.

3. Disconnect the spark plug wires. Pull off by grasping the connector, *not* the spark plug wire.

4. Remove the spark plugs, using a plug socket with a rubber insert designed to grip the plug. Place the plugs in order so that you know which cylinder they came from.

5. Examine each spark plug and compare its condition to the color illustrations in Chapter Two. Spark plug condition is an indicator of engine condition and warns of developing trouble.

6. Replace the spark plugs at the intervals specified in **Tables 2-4**. If the plugs are to be reused, clean the electrodes thoroughly with sandpaper. If the plugs are difficult to clean, discard them.

Gapping and Installing the Plugs

Spark plugs should be carefully gapped to ensure a reliable, consistent spark. Use a special gapping tool with a wire gauge. See **Figure 22** or **Figure 23**.

1. Remove each spark plug from the box and measure its gap. See **Figure 23**. Compare with specifications in **Table 8**. If the gap is correct, you will feel a slight drag as the gauge is pulled through.

2. If the gap is incorrect, adjust it by bending the side electrode *with the gapping tool*. See **Figure 24**. Do not bend the center electrode. Do not tap on the side electrode.

3. Put aluminum anti-seize compound on the threads of each spark plug.

4. Screw each spark plug in by hand until it seats. Very little effort is required. If force is necessary, the plug is cross-threaded; unscrew it and try again.

5. Tighten the spark plugs. If you have a torque wrench, tighten to 22 ft.-lb. (3 mkg). If a torque wrench is unavailable, tighten an additional 1/4 turn after the plug seats.

> *CAUTION*
> *Do not overtighten. This will damage the plug gaskets and prevent a tight seal.*

6. Install the spark plug wires. Make sure each is connected to the proper spark plug. See **Figure 21**.

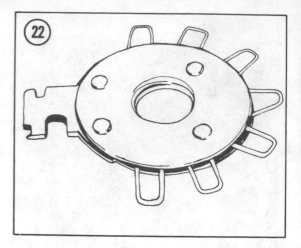

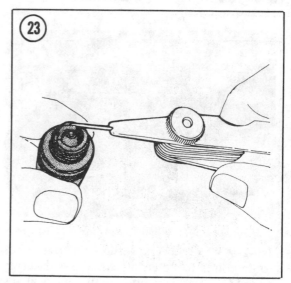

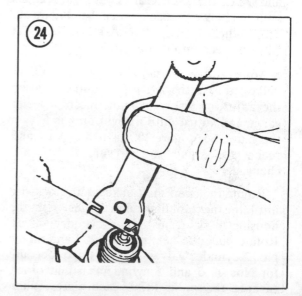

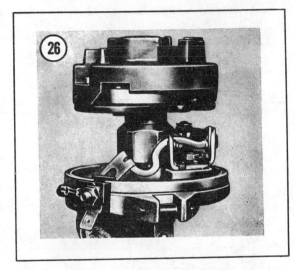

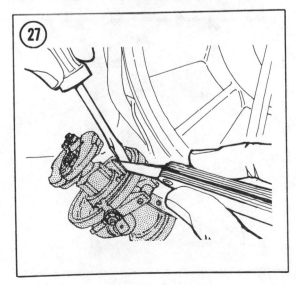

CAUTION
Make sure that the rubber seals on the spark plug wires are in good condition and seal properly. Replace them if necessary. These seals prevent loss of cooling air.

Breaker Point Replacement (1965-1977)

Check breaker points for signs of pitting, discoloration and misalignment. If this is a 12,000 mile (1965-1974) or 15,000 mile (1975-1977) tune-up, replace the points and condenser.

Several different distributors are used in the 911. Point replacement differs slightly on each one.

Marelli distributor

The Marelli distributor used on some models is characterized by a very tall distributor cap. To replace the points:

1. Remove the distributor cap and mark the position of the rotor.
2. Disconnect the primary lead to the distributor. Remove the retaining nut at the distributor base (**Figure 25**) and pull the distributor out.

NOTE
Do not turn engine over with distributor removed. If you must turn it, refer to **Distributor Installation** *procedure in Chapter Eight.*

3. Remove both breaker point retaining screws. Loosen screw on wire lead terminal. See **Figure 26**.
4. Install new points exactly like the old ones. Turn rotor until cam lobe opens the points fully. Set point gap to specifications by inserting a feeler gauge between the contacts and moving the fixed contact base. Tighten retaining screw to hold points in this position. See **Figure 27**.
5. Position rotor according to mark made earlier. Install distributor and tighten retaining nut. Reconnect primary wire to distributor and reinstall distributor cap.

Bosch distributors

Bosch distributors have a short distributor cap and are plainly marked. It is not necessary to remove the distributor to change breaker points.

First remove the distributor cap and rotor, then disconnect the primary lead. On early Bosch distributors (part No. 901.602.021.04):

1. Loosen the nut holding the leaf spring. Remove the C-ring on the breaker arm pivot, disconnect the wire lead and lift the arm off.

2. Remove the screw holding the fixed contact base and lift the base out. Install new points in exactly the same way as the old points.

3. To adjust gap, turn engine over until a distributor cam lobe opens the contacts fully. Loosen the retaining screw (**Figure 28**), insert a feeler gauge and set the point gap. Tighten the screw.

4. Install the distributor rotor and cap.

On later Bosch distributors:

1. Remove the distributor cap and rotor. The rotor on some models is held by a screw as shown in **Figure 29**.

2. Remove 2 screws holding the breaker points (**Figure 30**). Disconnect the wire lead and lift the old points from the distributor. Install new points.

3. Turn engine over until a distributor cam lobe opens the contacts fully. Loosen the retaining screw, insert a feeler gauge and set the point gap. Tighten the screw.

4. Install the rotor and distributor cap.

Dwell Angle Adjustment
(Breaker Point Models)

More accurate measurement of breaker point gap is possible by measuring dwell angle. Proper dwell angle depends upon distributor type as follows:

a. Marelli (1965-1971)-- $40 \pm 3°$.

b. Marelli (1972-on)-- $37 \pm 3°$.

c. Bosch-- $38 \pm 3°$.

Ignition Timing Adjustment
(Breaker Point Models)

After adjusting breaker point gap, set the ignition timing. Timing is set in 3 stages:

a. Static timing with test lamp.

b. Dynamic timing at idle with strobe.

c. Dynamic timing at 6,000 rpm with strobe.

To adjust timing, proceed as follows:

1. Crank the engine over until the TDC mark is visible.

2. Make a pencil or white paint mark on the crankshaft pulley to correspond with the static timing point shown in **Table 6**. For example, the mark should be at 5° BTDC on a 1966 911S. This is equivalent to a mark 0.217 in. (5.5 mm) to the right of TDC ("Z1"). If the static timing point is 0° TDC, use "Z1"; no additional mark is needed.

NOTE
Once you have found the proper mark for your engine, file a small notch permanently in the pulley. This will save time next tune-up.

3. Follow the *Static Timing* procedure in this chapter.
4. Determine from **Table 6** if dynamic timing at idle is necessary for your engine. If so, make another mark (or file a notch) at 3° or 5° ATDC, i.e., 3 mm or 5 mm to the *left* of TDC ("Z1"). Perform *Dynamic Timing Adjustment (at Idle)* using the mark.
5. Determine from **Table 6** if check of total advance is necessary. If it is, perform *Dynamic Timing Check (at 6,000 rpm)*.

Static timing

1. Remove the distributor cap.
2. Crank engine over by hand until timing mark indicated in **Table 6** aligns with the blower housing notch or timing pointer.
3. Loosen the distributor housing clamp nut.
4. Connect a 12-volt test lamp from the primary lead on the distributor to ground.
5. Switch the ignition ON.
6. Rotate the distributor body until the test lamp goes off (points closed). Slowly rotate

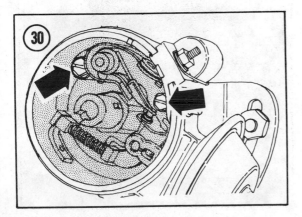

distributor in the opposite direction just until the light goes on (points opened). Tighten the distributor in this position.
7. Reinstall the distributor cap and disconnect the test lamp.

Dynamic timing adjustment (at idle)

1. Mark the crankshaft pulley with the appropriate timing mark shown in **Table 6**.
2. Connect the timing light to the No. 1 spark plug following the manufacturer's instructions.
3. Run the engine at the specified speed.

NOTE
*Determine from **Table 6** if the vacuum advance hose must be connected or disconnected.*

4. If necessary, loosen the distributor housing and turn it until the timing mark made in Step 1 of this procedure aligns with the blower housing mark or timing pointer when illuminated by the timing light. Tighten the distributor in this position.

Dynamic timing check (at 6,000 rpm)

1. Connect the timing light to the No. 1 spark plug according to manufacturer's instructions.
2. Check **Table 6** and determine if vacuum advance should remain connected or be disconnected.
3. Run the engine at 6,000 rpm.
4. The 30 or 35 degree mark (**Table 6**) on the pulley should align with the blower housing notch or timing pointer when illuminated by the strobe. Alignment may be off 2° (equivalent to 2 mm on pulley rim) in either direction. If alignment is more than 2° off, go back to *Dynamic Timing Adjustment (at Idle)* procedure and reset timing by 2-5° to get total advance specifications (**Table 6**).

Breakerless Distributor

A breakerless distributor is used on 1978 and later engines. The firing order for 1978 and later engines is identical to that for previous 911 engines (1-6-2-4-3-5); however, the distributor shaft and rotor now turn counterclockwise. In all previous engines (1965-1977), they turned clockwise. Distributor rotation is indicated by an arrow on the distributor housing. See **Figure 31**.

NOTE
All 1980-on distributors use a double vacuum unit for vacuum retard and advance. The retard hose is blue; the advance hose is red.

Correct valve timing is extremely important on 1978 and later engines. The timing overlap should be checked and adjusted, if necessary, during every tune-up. See Chapter Four for procedure.

Ignition Timing (1978-1979)

To set ignition timing on 1978-1979 engines, perform the *Dynamic Timing Adjustment (at Idle)* and *Dynamic Timing Check (at 6,000 rpm)* described for breaker point systems.

Ignition Timing (1980-on)

1. Connect a tachometer and timing light to the engine according to manufacturer's instructions.
2. Start the engine and warm to normal operating temperature.
3. Remove the advance and retard vacuum hoses at the distributor. See **Figure 32**. Check emission control decal to see if hoses are to be plugged during procedure. If so, plug the hoses as required.
4. Check and adjust the idle speed, if necessary, to 950 ±50 rpm as described in this chapter.
5. Shut the engine off.
6. Locate the timing mark on the flywheel (**Figure 33**). Refer to **Table 6** for timing specifications.
7. Mark the timing mark and pointer mark with white paint. This will make them easier to see.
8. Have an assistant hold the engine speed at 900-1,000 rpm.

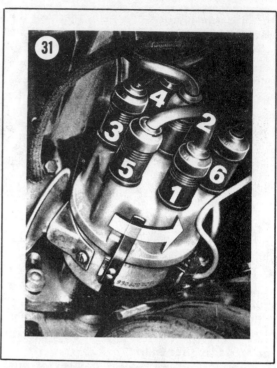

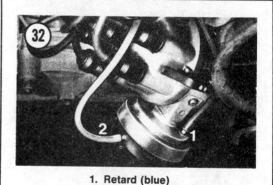

1. Retard (blue)
2. Advance (red)

A. Idle speed adjusting screw
B. Idle mixture control screw
C. Air bypass control screw

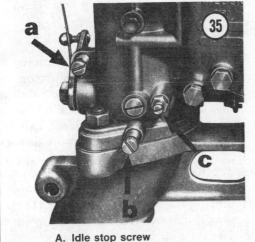

A. Idle stop screw
B. Idle mixture adjusting screw
C. Idle air adjusting screw

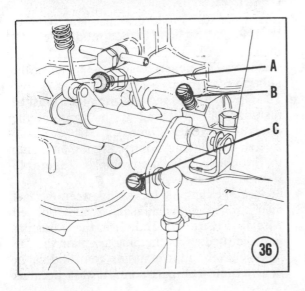

9. Aim the timing light at the marks. If the timing mark aligns with the pointer, the timing is correct. If not, loosen the distributor hold-down clamp, turn the distributor to change timing, then tighten the clamp.

10. When timing is correctly set, reconnect the vacuum advance and retard hoses to the distributor and reset the idle speed as described in this chapter.

Carburetor Adjustment (1965-1971)

1. Bring the engine to operating temperature (oil temperature should be about 60° C).

2. Remove the air cleaner assembly. See Chapter Six.

3. Disconnect the throttle rod on each side shown in **Figure 34**.

4. Turn 2 idle speed stop screws (one on each side) equally until the engine idles between 1,000-1,200 rpm. See A, **Figure 35** (Weber); C, **Figure 36** (Solex); or A, **Figure 37** (Zenith).

5. Place a Unisyn or other carburetor synchronization tool over the left rear throat. Adjust the Unisyn so that the ball is about halfway up the tube.

6. Place the Unisyn on each remaining throat. If the Unisyn ball does not return to the same point, the throat must be adjusted.
   a. On Solex carburetors, disconnect the throttle rod for that throat, readjust its length (A, **Figure 36**) and reconnect.
   b. On Weber or Zenith carburetors, adjust the air adjusting screw for that throat. See C, **Figure 35** (Weber) or C, **Figure 37** (Zenith).

7. Reduce idle speed to 800-900 rpm with the idle speed stop screws. See **Figure 35** (Weber), **Figure 36** (Solex) or **Figure 37** (Zenith).

8. Adjust the idle mixture screw at each throat (6 in all) until the engine runs smoothly.

9. Recheck synchronization.

10. Recheck idle mixture settings.

11. Reconnect throttle linkage.

12. Reinstall air cleaner assembly.

13. Recheck idle mixture settings.

Throttle Valve Compensator Adjustment

After carefully adjusting the carburetors, adjust the throttle valve compensator on cars equipped with exhaust emission controls.

The compensator is correctly adjusted if the engine speed drops from 3,000 rpm to about 1,000 rpm 4-6 seconds after quickly releasing the throttle. If adjustment is incorrect:

1. Loosen the adjusting screw setscrew. See **Figure 38**.

2. Turn the adjusting screw fully in (clockwise).

3. Accelerate the engine quickly, then release the throttle. The engine should be idling at about 2,000-2,200 rpm.

4. If the engine speed is not 2,000-2,200 rpm, shorten the connecting rod to the compensator to raise the speed or lengthen the rod to decrease speed. See **Figure 39**.

5. Readjust the compensator screw until idle speed is 900-950 rpm.

6. Increase engine speed to 3,000 rpm, quickly release throttle and measure time it takes to return to 900-950 rpm. Readjust screw clockwise to shorten time required and counterclockwise to lengthen time required.

7. Tighten adjusting screw setscrew.

8. Recheck rpm drop time.

Idle Speed Adjustment (1977-1979)

Adjust idle speed to specifications by turning the adjusting screw located on the throttle housing (**Figure 40**). Make sure that the oil tank cap is tightly installed before making the adjustment, as a loose cap will result in a lower idling speed (approximately 200 rpm lower). The reason is that the oil tank ventilating hose runs from the tank to the rubber boot connecting the air sensor to the throttle housing (6, **Figure 41**) and loosening or removing the oil tank cap allows additional air to be pulled into the intake system.

Idle Mixture Adjustment (1977-1979)

Air/fuel idle mixture adjustment requires the use of an accurate carbon monoxide (CO) meter.

1A. On 1977 models, install the meter in the tailpipe.

1B. On 1978-1979 models, the probe must be installed in the fitting at the front of the catalytic converter (**Figure 42**).

2. Remove the line connecting the air pump to the check valve and plug it. **Figure 43** shows the line plugged.

3. Remove the plug located between the fuel distributor and the air sensor boot (looped wire in **Figure 41**) and turn the adjusting screw located under the plug to obtain the CO reading given in the emission control decal in your engine compartment. If this decal is

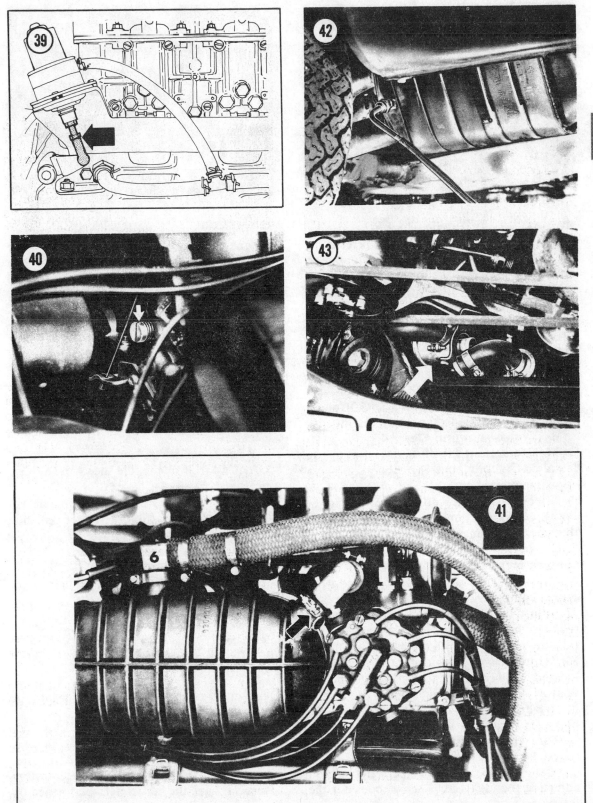

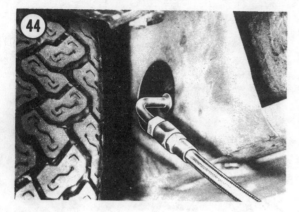

missing, set 1977 models to 1.5-3.0 percent and 1978-1979 models to 1.5-3.5 percent.

4. After the correct CO reading is obtained, install the plug and the air hose, remove the meter and plug the catalytic converter fitting plug (1978-1979 models).

Idle Speed/
Idle Mixture Adjustment
(1980)

1. Connect a tachometer to the engine according to manufacturer's instructions.

2. Connect a carbon monoxide (CO) meter exhaust pickup line to the catalytic converter connection as shown in **Figure 44**.

3. Make sure that the oil tank cap is tightly installed before making the following adjustments.

4. Check the valve adjustment (Chapter Four). Check ignition timing as described in this chapter. Adjust timing as required.

5. Warm the engine to normal operating temperature.

6. Disconnect the oxygen sensor plug in the engine compartment (left side). See **Figure 45**.

7. Adjust the idle speed to specification by turning the adjusting screw located on the throttle housing. See **Figure 40**.

8. Remove the mixture control unit plug located between the fuel distributor and venturi (looped wire in **Figure 41**). Then insert adjusting tool part No. P 377 into the plug. See **Figure 46**.

9. Turn the adjusting tool, as required, to adjust for idle speed CO concentration. The CO should be 0.4-0.8 percent. When adjusting the idle control screw, consider the following:

a. Minimal screw adjustment will change the CO level considerably.

b. Turn the screw clockwise for a richer mixture.

c. Turn the screw counterclockwise for a leaner mixture.

d. Always adjust CO level from lean to rich setting.

10. After making the CO adjustment, remove the adjusting tool.

11. Accelerate the engine slightly, then read the CO concentration at idle. Repeat Step 9 as required to obtain the correct idle speed CO concentration.

12. When the correct CO mixture adjustment is obtained, recheck the idle speed and adjust, if necessary.

13. Remove the CO meter pickup line at the catalytic converter (**Figure 44**). Coat the catalytic converter tester connecting cap with Bosch assembly paste VS 140 16 Ft or Optimoly HT before installing.

14. Install and attach all previously removed parts.

Idle Speed/
Idle Mixture Adjustment
(1981-on)

To adjust idle speed, use the procedure for 1980 models.

Mixture controls are fitted with an anti-tamper lock screw to prevent unauthorized tampering with the fuel mixture setting. If the idle mixture CO concentration is suspect, have the adjustment performed by an authorized Porsche service department.

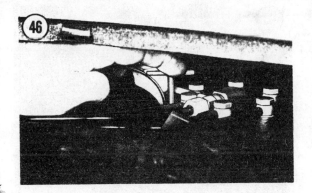

Fuel Injection Adjustments

The fuel injection system is a very precise, complex and expensive system. No adjustments or repairs, other than those described in Chapter Six, should be attempted by anyone not thoroughly trained and experienced with the system. If you suspect trouble with the fuel injection system, have your Porsche dealer or a qualified specialist troubleshoot and service the system.

3

Table 1 FUEL STOP CHECKS

Item	Procedure
Engine oil	Check level
Battery electrolyte	Check level
Brake fluid	Check level
Fan belt	Check tension
Tire pressures	Check
Windshield washers	Check container level

Table 2 SCHEDULED MAINTENANCE (1965-1974)

Every 3,000 miles
- Change engine oil and filter.
- Replace air cleaner element.
- Lubricate door hinges and locks.

Every 6,000 miles
- Check transaxle fluid level.
- Check front and rear wheel bearing adjustment and adjust as required.
- Inspect ball-joint seals and check ball-joint end play. Lubricate front suspension.
- Change engine oil and filter.
- Lubricate distributor.
- Lubricate carburetor.
- Check engine compression.
- Inspect and/or clean breaker points.
- Check and adjust ignition timing as required.
- Inspect and/or clean spark plugs.
- Check valve clearance and adjust as required.
- Inspect brake linings and clean and/or replace as required.
- Inspect and/or clean fuel filter.
- Check air pump oil fluid level.
- Check and/or adjust air pump drive belt.
- Inspect exhaust system components. Tighten and/or replace components as required.
- Inspect tire and wheel condition. See Chapter Two.
- Check front end alignment and adjust as required.

Every 12,000 miles
- Replace spark plugs.
- Replace breaker points and rotor.
- Adjust ignition timing.
- Inspect and/or clean crankcase ventilation system.

Every 30,000 miles
- Change transaxle oil.

Table 3 SCHEDULED MAINTENANCE (1975-1979)

Required Maintenance for the Emission Control System

First 1000 miles
- Change engine oil.
- Replace oil filter.
- Adjust drive belts.
- Check valve clearance and adjust if necessary.
- Check rocker arm shafts for tightness.   (continued)

Table 3 SCHEDULED MAINTENANCE (1975-1979) (continued)

First 1,000 miles (continued)

- Retighten manifold mounting bolts.
- Check evaporative control system connections.
- Check engine idle and exhaust emission and adjust if required.

Every 15,000 miles

- Change engine oil and filter.
- Adjust drive belts.
- Check valve clearance and adjust if necessary.
- Check rocker arm shafts for tightness.
- Check engine compression.
- Replace spark plugs.
- Check ignition timing and adjust if required.
- Check ignition wiring, distributor cap and rotor and replace parts as required.
- Replace the fuel filter.
- Check evaporative control system connections.
- Clean the crankcase ventilation filter.
- Check entire exhaust system for leakage or damaged parts. Replace or repair as required.
- Check engine idle and exhaust emission and adjust if required.
- Replace the air cleaner element.
- Check the air pump, control valves, air injection hoses, and connections. Tighten or replace parts as required.
- Replace the air pump filter.
- Check the anti-backfire valve.

Every 30,000 miles

- Check the EGR system.
- Replace the EGR filter.
- Check condition of the crankcase ventilation hoses. Replace as required.

Required Maintenance and Lubrication Service

First 1,000 miles

- Change the transaxle oil.
- Check the front wheel bearing play and adjust as required.
- Check the clutch pedal free play and adjust as required.
- Check operation of lights, horns, wipers and washer systems.

First 1,000 miles (continued)
- Check the headlight adjustment and adjust as required.
- Check tire pressure and adjust as required.

Every 15,000 miles
- Lubricate door hinges and locks.
- Lubricate accelerator linkage.
- Change transaxle oil.
- Check windshield washer operation and fluid level.
- Check front axle, steering gear, tie-rod connections and rubber boots for tightness and leaks and adjust or repair as required.
- Adjust clutch pedal free play.
- Check entire brake system. Adjust or replace parts as required.
- Check operation of lights, horns, wipers and washer systems.
- Check the headlight adjustment and adjust as required.
- Check tire pressure and adjust as required.
- Check ignition/steering lock and buzzer alarm system.

Table 4 SCHEDULED MAINTENANCE (1980-ON)

Required Maintenance for the Emission Control System

First 1000 miles
- Change engine oil.
- Replace oil filter.
- Adjust drive belts.
- Check valve clearance and adjust if necessary.
- Check engine idle and exhaust emission and adjust if required.

Every 15,000 miles
- Change engine oil and filter.
- Adjust drive belts.
- Check valve clearance and adjust if necessary.

Every 30,000 miles
- Change engine oil and filter.
- Adjust drive belts.
- Replace spark plugs (or every 2 years, whichever occurs first).
- Replace air cleaner.
- Replace fuel filter.
- Replace oxygen sensor.
- Reset oxygen sensor counter.

Required Maintenance and Lubrication Service

First 1,000 miles
- Check the front wheel bearing play and adjust as required.
- Check the clutch pedal free play and adjust as required.
- Check operation of lights, horns, wipers and washer systems.
- Check the headlight adjustment and adjust as required.
- Check tire pressure and adjust as required.

Every 15,000 miles
- Lubricate door hinges and locks.
- Lubricate accelerator linkage.
- Change transaxle oil.
- Check windshield washer operation and fluid level.
- Check front axle, steering gear, tie-rod connections and rubber boots for tightness and leaks and adjust or repair as required.
- Adjust clutch pedal free play.
- Check entire brake system. Adjust or replace parts as required.
- Check operation of lights, horns, wipers and washer systems.
- Check the headlight adjustment and adjust as required.
- Check tire pressure and adjust as required.
- Check ignition/steering lock and buzzer alarm system.
- Check battery electrolyte level.

Table 5 RECOMMENDED LUBRICANTS AND FUEL

	Temperature Range	Recommended Type
Engine oil	Below 5° F (minus 15° C)	SAE 10W
	Between 5° F & 32° F (minus 15° C to 0° C)	SAE 20-20W
	Above 32° F (0° C)	SAE 30
Transaxle	All temperatures	SAE 90[1]
Fuel[2]	-	98 octane, premium, (1965-1971)
		91 octane, regular, (1972)

1. With limited slip differential, must be marked for "limited slip differentials."
2. On 1980 and later models with an oxygen sensor, use unleaded fuel only.

Table 6 IGNITION TIMING [1]

Year/ Model	Static Timing	Strobe Timing Idle	6,000 rpm[2]
1965	0° TDC	-	-
1966			
911	5° BTDC[3]	-	32-33° BTDC
911S	5° BTDC[3]	-	30-31° BTDC
1967			
911	5° BTDC[4]	3° ATDC @ 850-950 rpm[5, 6]	18-32° BTDC
911S	5° BTDC[4]		30-31° BTDC
911T	5° BTDC[4]	-	28-32° BTDC
1968			
911S	5° BTDC[4]	-	30° BTDC
911E	0° TDC	-	30° BTDC
911T	5° BTDC[4]	-	30° BTDC
1969			
911S	5° BTDC[4]	-	30° BTDC
911E	5° BTDC[4]	-	30° BTDC
911T	0° TDC	-	35° BTDC
1970			
911S	5° BTDC[4]	-	30° BTDC
911E	5° BTDC[4]	-	30° BTDC
911T	0° TDC	-	30° BTDC
1971			
911S	5° BTDC[4]	-	30° BTDC
911E	5° BTDC[4]	-	30° BTDC
911T	5° BTDC[4]	-	30° BTDC
1972-1976	-	5° ATDC @ 900 rpm[7]	32-38° BTDC[6]
1977			
California	-	15° ATDC @ 1,000 rpm[8]	Not specified
49-state	-	0° TDC @ 950-1,000 rpm[8]	Not specified
1978-1979	-	5° BTDC @ 950 rpm[8]	26° BTDC[6, 8]
1980-on	-	5° BTDC @ 950 rpm[6, 8]	19-25° BTDC

1. Use the specifications in this table only if the emission control decal in your engine compartment is missing or illegible. If the decal specifications differ from those in this table, always use the ones on the decal.
2. Unloaded engine.
3. 0.218 in. (5.5 mm) right.
4. 0.198 in. (5 mm) right.
5. 0.119 in. (3 mm) left.
6. Vacuum line disconnected.
7. Vacuum line connected.
8. ±2°.

3

Table 7 BREAKER POINT AND VALVE SPECIFICATIONS

Point gap	
1974, 1977	0.014 in. (0.35 mm)
All others	0.016 in. (0.4 mm)
Dwell angle	
Marelli distributor	
1965-1971	40 ±3°
1972-1977	37 ±3°
Bosch distributor	38 ±3°
Valve clearance (intake and exhaust)	0.004 in. (0.1 mm)
Valve timing	
1977	0.40-0.54 mm
1978-1979	0.90-1.10 mm
1980-on	1.4-1.7 mm

Table 8 SPARK PLUG SPECIFICATIONS

Model/Year	Type	Gap
911		
1966-1969	Bosch W200 T35	0.024-0.028 in. (0.6-0.7 mm)
1976	Bosch W175 M30	0.028 in. (0.7 mm)
911T carburetted		
1965-1968	Bosch W250 P21	0.014 in. (0.35 mm)
1968-1971	Bosch W230 T30	0.024 in. (0.55 mm)
911 fuel injected		
1972	Bosch W235 P21	0.024 in. (0.55 mm)
1973-1974	Bosch W215 P21	0.024 in. (0.55 mm)
911E		
1968	Bosch W265 P21	0.014 in. (0.35 mm)
1969-1973	Bosch W265 P21	0.024 in. (0.55 mm)
911S		
1968	Bosch W265 P21	0.014 in. (0.35 mm)
1969-1973	Bosch W265 P21	0.024 in. (0.55 mm)
1974-1976	Bosch W235 P21	0.024 in. (0.55 mm)
1977	Bosch W225 T30	0.028 in. (0.7 mm)
911SC		
1978-1979	Bosch W145 T30	0.032 in. (0.8 mm)
1980-on	Bosch W225 T30	0.032 in. (0.8 mm)

4

ENGINE

Several engines have been offered in the 911 series. They are all very similar and differ mainly in specifications and carburetion.

The 911 is a 6-cylinder, horizontally opposed air-cooled engine. See **Figure 1** and **Figure 2**. Each cylinder has its own finned barrel and aluminum head. Three heads in a bank bolt to a housing that contains an overhead camshaft and rocker arms to operate the valves.

The cylinders mount on an aluminum crankcase manufactured in 2 halves. Eight main bearings support the crankshaft. The crankshaft contains a twin oil pump driven by the crankshaft through gears and an intermediate shaft. The intermediate shaft also drives 2 camshafts through chains. A system of tensioners and guides keeps the chains under proper tension and control.

Table 1 provides general engine specifications.

Tables 1-9 are at the end of the chapter.

ENGINE

Removal/Installation

The engine/transaxle must be removed as a single unit.

1. Prop the engine compartment lid open or remove it.
2. Drain engine oil. See Chapter Three.
3. Drain transaxle oil. See Chapter Three.
4. Put the transmission in neutral and block the front tires.
5. Disconnect all battery cables.
6. Disconnect hot air duct (**Figure 3**) and oil tank vent from air cleaner.
7. Loosen clamps and remove air cleaner cover.

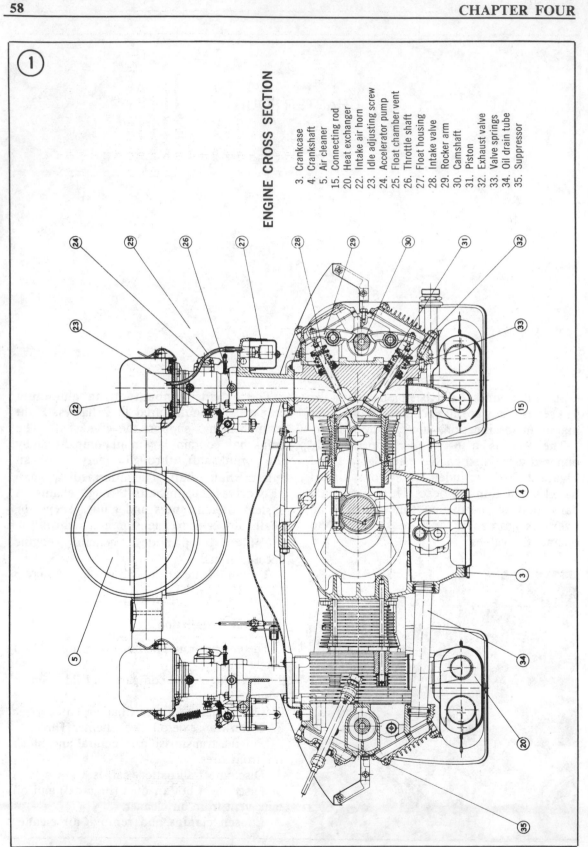

ENGINE CROSS SECTION

3. Crankcase
4. Crankshaft
5. Air cleaner
15. Connecting rod
20. Heat exchanger
22. Intake air horn
23. Idle adjusting screw
24. Accelerator pump
25. Float chamber vent
26. Throttle shaft
27. Float housing
28. Intake valve
29. Rocker arm
30. Camshaft
31. Piston
32. Exhaust valve
33. Valve springs
34. Oil drain tube
35. Suppressor

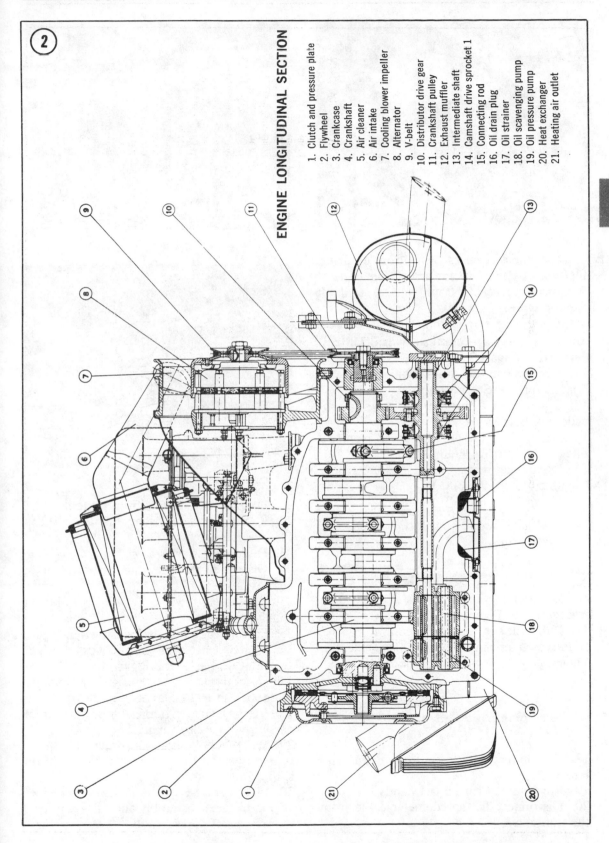

ENGINE LONGITUDINAL SECTION

1. Clutch and pressure plate
2. Flywheel
3. Crankcase
4. Crankshaft
5. Air cleaner
6. Air intake
7. Cooling blower impeller
8. Alternator
9. V-belt
10. Distributor drive gear
11. Crankshaft pulley
12. Exhaust muffler
13. Intermediate shaft
14. Camshaft drive sprocket 1
15. Connecting rod
16. Oil drain plug
17. Oil strainer
18. Oil scavenging pump
19. Oil pressure pump
20. Heat exchanger
21. Heating air outlet

8. Disconnect electrical wires from electrical fuel pump. See right-side arrow, **Figure 4**.

9. Disconnect cable from voltage regulator (center arrow, **Figure 4**).

10. Disconnect wires from terminals 1 and center high voltage terminal of ignition coil (left arrow, **Figure 4**).

11. Disconnect fuel lines from carburetor float chambers. See **Figure 5**.

12. Disconnect throttle linkage from bellcrank (left arrow, **Figure 6**).

13. Disconnect oil breather hose from oil filter (center arrow, **Figure 6**).

14. Disconnect wire from oil pressure sender (right arrow, **Figure 6**).

NOTE
The following 3 steps apply only to the Sportomatic.

15. Disconnect oil lines from torque converter oil pump. See **Figure 7**.

16. Disconnect vacuum hoses from vacuum reservoir. See **Figure 8**.

17. Pull rubber cap off control valve. Remove cotter pin and disconnect cable. See **Figure 9**.

NOTE
The remaining steps apply to all models unless otherwise specified.

18. Disconnect oil hoses from engine oil tank.

19. Raise rear of car on jackstands.

20. Disconnect the speedometer cable from the transaxle.

21. Disconnect oil hoses from oil tank.

22. Remove axle half shafts as described in Chapter Eleven.

23. Disconnect starter cables.

24. Disconnect hot air ducts from front of heat exchangers.

25. Loosen and withdraw clutch cable at clutch release lever. See Chapter Nine.

26. Disconnect ground strap shown in **Figure 10**. Disconnect wire from back-up light switch at transaxle. See **Figure 10**.

27. Disconnect throttle linkage from forward cross shaft at transaxle. See **Figure 10**.

28. Remove center-tunnel cover at rear of passenger area. See **Figure 11**.

29. Remove bolt shown in **Figure 12**. Move gearshift lever to withdraw coupling from shift rod.

30. Place garage-type floor jack at center of engine/transaxle assembly and raise it to take the weight off the assembly.

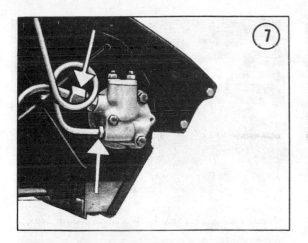

1. Ground strap
2. Cross shaft
3. Back-up switch

4

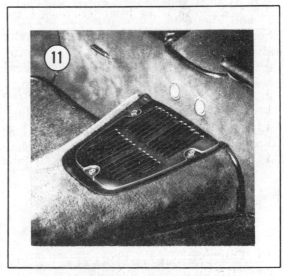

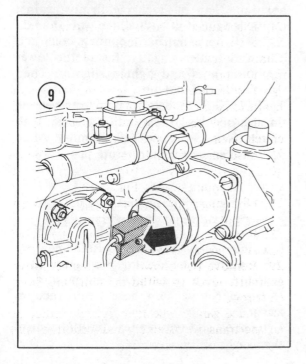

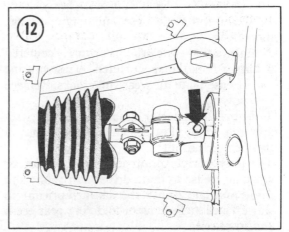

31. Remove bolts securing rear engine support to body. See **Figure 13**.
32. Remove bolts securing transaxle support. See **Figure 14**.
33. Lower engine/transaxle carefully while balancing it on jack. On Sportomatic models, disconnect electrical cables to temperature switch and sensor as soon as they are accessible. See **Figure 15**.
34. Pull jack to rear. See **Figure 16**.
35. Installation is the reverse of these steps.

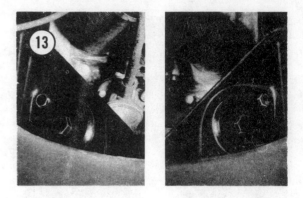

ENGINE/TRANSAXLE SEPARATION (MANUAL)

1. Disconnect rear throttle rod.
2. On 1970-on models, remove starter. Install a spacer and Allen head screw in each of the 3 holes in the pressure plate. See **Figure 17** and **Figure 18**. These parts are available from your Porsche dealer. Tighten the screws alternately and evenly to relieve spring tension on release bearing. Turn release bearing 90° through access hole as shown in **Figure 19**.
3. Remove 2 lower engine mounting nuts. Remove 2 upper engine mounting nuts. Pull engine straight back until clutch release plate clears the main drive shaft.

CAUTION
Do not let engine tilt or let engine weight put any load on drive shaft or clutch parts.

ENGINE/TRANSAXLE JOINING (MANUAL)

1. Clean transaxle case and engine flange thoroughly.
2. Ensure that clutch disc is properly centered (Chapter Nine). Inspect clutch release bearing and release plate for wear and cracks. Replace if necessary.
3. Lubricate starter shaft bushing with graphite grease. Put 2-3 cc graphite grease in flywheel gland nut.
4. Apply molybdenum disulfide powder or graphite grease to main drive shaft spline and pilot journal. Apply the same lubricant to starter pinion gear teeth and ring gear teeth (on flywheel).

5. Put transmission in gear to steady main drive shaft.
6. Rotate engine with the fan belt so that the clutch plate hub lines up with the main drive shaft splines. Take care that gland nut needle bearing, clutch release bearing and drive shaft are not damaged when pushing engine forward.

CAUTION
Do not let engine tilt or let engine weight put any load on drive shaft or clutch parts.

7. Guide lower engine mounting studs into position, then push engine firmly against transaxle until it is flush all the way around.
8. Install upper engine mounting bolts and nuts and tighten slightly. Install the lower mounting nuts and tighten slightly. Then tighten all bolts and nuts.
9. On 1970-on models, rotate release bearing through opening in case until it engages with release fork. See **Figure 19**. Remove Allen bolts and spacers from pressure plate.

ENGINE/TRANSAXLE SEPARATION (SPORTOMATIC)

1. Disconnect oil hose and pressure line from temperature sensor housing. See **Figure 20**.
2. Loosen oil hose clamp at transmission.
3. Disonnect vacuum hose from vacuum servo.
4. Unhook and remove rear throttle control rod.

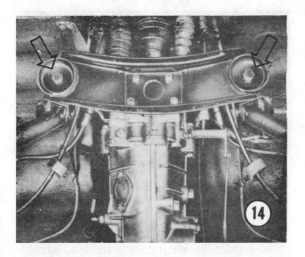

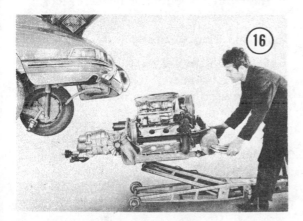

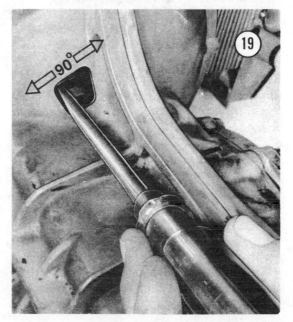

4

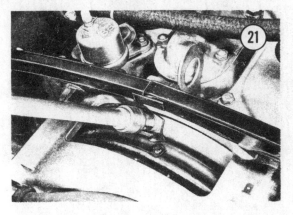

5. Remove 12-point bolts which hold the torque converter to the drive plate. See **Figure 21**.

6. Remove 2 lower mounting nuts.

7. Remove 2 upper engine mounting nuts.

8. Separate engine and transaxle. Leave torque converter in transaxle and secure with a strap. See **Figure 22**.

ENGINE/TRANSAXLE JOINING (SPORTOMATIC)

1. Clean transaxle case and engine flanges thoroughly.

2. Lubricate starter shaft bushing with graphite grease.

3. Remove strap from torque converter.

4. Join engine and transaxle and bolt them together. Tighten to 34 ft.-lb. (4.7 mkg).

5. Rotate engine crankshaft so that drive plate-to-torque converter bolts can be installed. Tighten them to 17-19 ft.-lb. (2.4-2.6 mkg).

6. Connect rear throttle control rod.

7. Connect vacuum hose to vacuum servo.

8. Connect oil hose and pressure line to temperature sensor housing.

9. Adjust clutch free play as described in Chapter Nine.

ENGINE DISASSEMBLY/ASSEMBLY

The following sequences are designed so that the engine need not be disassembled any further than necessary. Unless otherwise indicated, procedures for major assemblies in these sequences are included in this chapter. The procedures are arranged in the approximate order in which they are performed.

To perform a step, turn to the procedure for the major assembly indicated, e.g., cylinder head and perform the removal and inspection procedures. Move to the next step, perform the removal and inspection procedures, etc., until the engine is disassembled. To reassemble, reverse the disassembly sequence and perform the installation procedure for the major assembly involved.

Decarbonizing or Valve Service

1. Remove cover plates and fan.

2. Remove valve rocker assemblies.

3. Remove camshaft housing.

4. Remove cylinder heads.

5. Remove and inspect valves, guides and seats.

6. Assembly is the reverse of these steps.

Valve and Ring Service

1. Perform Steps 1-4 for valve service.

2. Remove cylinders.

3. Remove rings. It is not necessary to remove the pistons unless they are damaged.

4. Assembly is the reverse of these steps.

General Overhaul Sequence

1. Remove carburetors or injectors (Chapter Six).

1965-1975

1976-ON

12. Remove cylinders and pistons.
13. Remove breather stack.
14. Remove thermostat and oil pressure sender.
15. Remove flywheel.
16. Disassemble crankcase.
17. Remove crankshaft and connecting rods.
18. Remove oil pump and intermediate shaft.
19. Assembly is the reverse of these steps.

OIL PRESSURE RELIEF AND BYPASS VALVES

The oil pressure relief valve is located on the bottom front edge of the crankcase. The bypass valve is slightly above the oil pressure relief valve on the left side. See **Figure 23**. Both are serviced in the same manner.

Removal

1. Remove slotted plug and sealing ring. See **Figure 23**.
2. Withdraw spring and valve piston. See **Figure 24** (1975 and earlier on left, 1976-on on right).

Inspection

1. Check the crankcase bore and piston for signs of scoring or seizure. Dress the bore

2. Remove distributor.
3. Remove cooling air ducts and cover plates.
4. Remove rear engine mount.
5. Remove fuel pump (except 1976-on models).
6. Remove muffler.
7. Remove crankshaft pulley and blower housing (Chapter Five).
8. Remove heat exchangers (Chapter Five).
9. Remove camshafts.
10. Remove oil cooler.
11. Remove cylinder heads.

with crocus cloth and replace the piston if necessary.

2. Measure spring length. Unloaded length should be 2.75 in. (70 mm). Ensure that spring ends cannot scratch the bore when installed.

Installation

1. Insert piston and spring in bore.
2. Install slotted cap with metal sealing ring. See **Figure 24**.

> *CAUTION*
> *On engines through No. 901282, the oil pressure relief valve sealing ring is thicker than the bypass valve sealing ring and is made of aluminum. Do not interchange the two. The crankcase bore on later engines is modified so that both valves use the same sealing ring.*

OIL STRAINER

The oil strainer can be removed for cleaning with the engine installed. Refer to **Figure 25** for the following procedure.

Removal

1. Remove nuts securing cover plate to crankcase and remove cover plate.
2. Remove oil strainer and gaskets.

Inspection

1. Check that the oil suction pipe is tight and not bent to one side of the large opening. If not, the engine must be dismantled and the crankcase peened around the pipe. See *Crankcase Inspection* procedure.
2. Clean all parts in solvent and remove all traces of old gasket.
3. Ensure that the cover plate is not bent. Straighten or replace if necessary.

Installation

1. Install all parts in the order shown in **Figure 25**. Use 2 new gaskets and be sure that the oil suction pipe fits the opening in the oil strainer exactly.
2. Secure cover plate. Do not overtighten nuts or the plate will bend and cause leaks.

REAR OIL SEAL

The rear oil seal is a simple O-ring. It may be replaced with the engine installed.

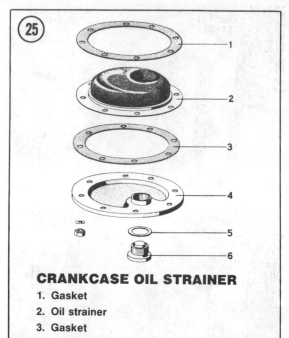

CRANKCASE OIL STRAINER
1. Gasket
2. Oil strainer
3. Gasket
4. Oil strainer cover plate
5. Sealing ring
6. Magnetic threaded plug

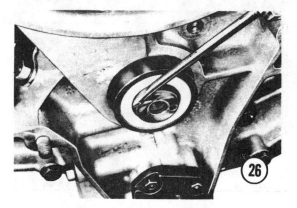

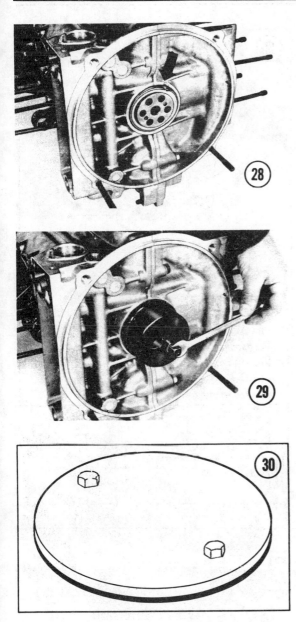

FRONT OIL SEAL

The engine must be removed to replace the front oil seal.

Removal

1. Remove flywheel or drive plate (Sportomatic) as described in this chapter.
2. Deform old seal by striking it with a punch and hammer through the slot in the crankcase. See **Figure 28**.
3. Pry seal out with a screwdriver or similar tool.

Installation

1. Clean recess between crankcase and crankshaft thoroughly. Remove any burrs from oil seal seat. If necessary, chamfer edges of crankcase opening slightly so that oil seal seats without damage. Clean out metal flakes carefully.
2. Install oil seal with closed side out. One method is to put the seal in place and gently tap it with a hammer and block of wood. Work slowly and evenly around the seal until it is flush with the bottom of the crankcase recess. Another method requires a special tool (Porsche P215 shown in **Figure 29**) which presses the seal in evenly. This is easily improvised with a metal plate and 2 bolts to fit flywheel mounting holes. See **Figure 30**. Tighten bolts alternately and evenly a few turns at a time.
3. Oil inner lips of seal at crankshaft.
4. Reinstall flywheel.

VALVE ROCKER ASSEMBLY

A new valve cover design is used on 1980 and later models. It is identified by the addition of ribs running lengthwise across the cover surface. New exhaust valve cover gaskets coated on both sides with silicon beads are also used. These gaskets can be used on all 911 models; however, the gasket can only be used once and must be replaced each time the cover is removed.

Removal

1. Clean away road dirt around valve covers.
2. Disconnect spark plug wires.

Replacement

1. Remove crankshaft pulley as described elsewhere in this chapter.
2. Pry out the O-ring with a screwdriver as shown in **Figure 26**.

> *CAUTION*
> *Do not damage the crankshaft with the screwdriver.*

3. Lightly coat a new O-ring with oil.
4. Install the O-ring as shown in **Figure 27**.
5. Install crankshaft pulley.

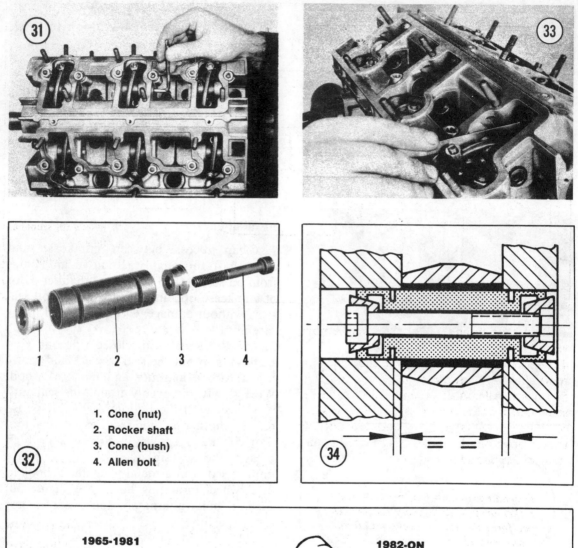

1. Cone (nut)
2. Rocker shaft
3. Cone (bush)
4. Allen bolt

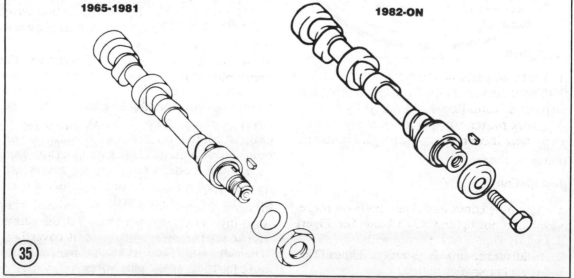

1965-1981

1982-ON

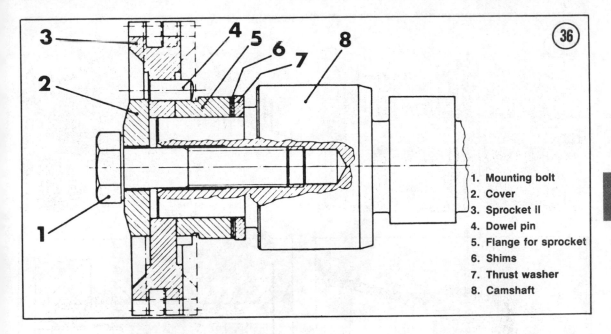

1. Mounting bolt
2. Cover
3. Sprocket II
4. Dowel pin
5. Flange for sprocket
6. Shims
7. Thrust washer
8. Camshaft

3. Remove nuts and lockwashers and remove valve covers.

4. Mark rocker arms so that they may be reinstalled in the same place.

5. Loosen Allen bolt in center of each rocker shaft that is to be removed. See **Figure 31**.

6. Push rocker shaft out and lift out the rocker arm. Mark rocker shafts as they are removed to aid reassembly.

NOTE
*Depending on camshaft position, some rocker arms will be under tension. **Do not force the rocker shaft out**. Rotate crankshaft to relieve the tension, then remove the shaft.*

Inspection

1. Clean all parts in solvent.

2. Check rocker shafts for wear, scoring and signs of seizure. Replace if necessary.

3. Check rocker arms inside bore and at each end where it bears on the valve and camshaft.

Installation

1. Assemble cones and Allen bolts on rocker shafts. Do not tighten Allen bolts. See **Figure 32**.

2. Hold rocker arm in position in head and insert rocker shaft.

CAUTION
Insert rocker shaft for cylinders 1, 3, 4 and 6 so that the Allen bolt head faces toward the center rocker arms.

3. The rocker shaft must be centered in its bore. To do this, insert a feeler gauge between the rocker arm and the camshaft housing. Push the rocker shaft into its bore until the feeler gauge slips into the rocker shaft groove. See **Figure 33**. Push the shaft additionally until the feeler gauge is held firmly.

4. Withdraw the feeler gauge.

5. Push the shaft in approximately 0.060 in. (1.5 mm) more in the same direction as in Step 3. This will center the shaft as shown in **Figure 34**.

6. Install the valve covers and reconnect the spark plug wires.

CAMSHAFT

A new camshaft sprocket (Sprocket II) design is used on 1982 and later engines. The large nut and washer formerly used has been replaced by a hex head bolt and an 8 mm thick cover. **Figure 35** shows the 2 cam designs. **Figure 36** is a cross-sectional view showing the correct placement of the shims, thrust washer, new sprocket and cover/bolt. The new sprocket retains the punch marks used for basic camshaft timing. A new wrench

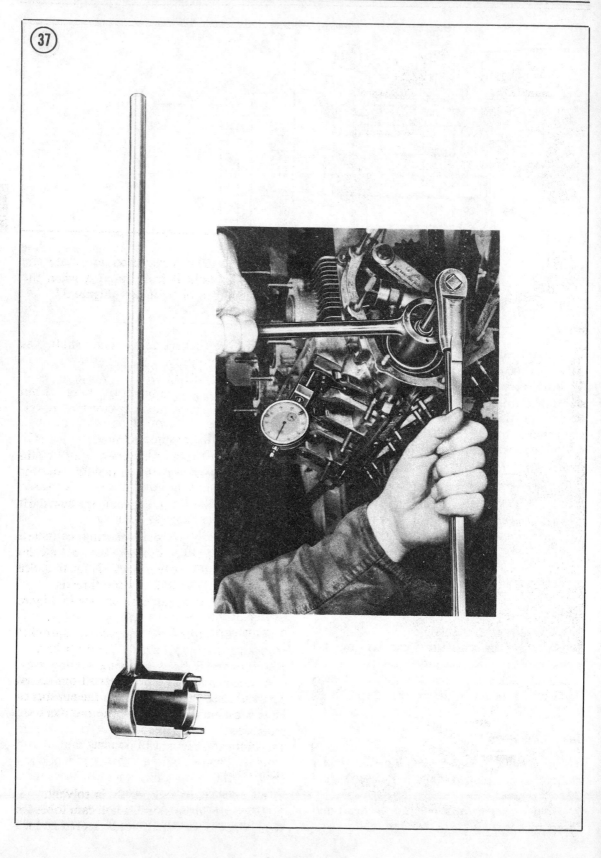

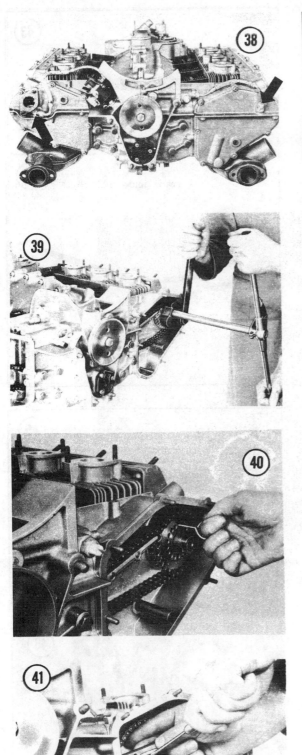

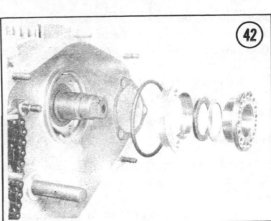

(part No. 9191) is required to rotate the camshaft or hold it from moving when the bolt is loosened or tightened (**Figure 37**).

Removal

1. Remove rocker arms and shafts as described previously.
2. Remove muffler.
3. Remove oil connecting hose from crankcase to chain housing cover at cover. See **Figure 38**.
4. Remove chain housing cover.
5. Remove chain tensioner and chain tensioning sprocket. See procedure in this chapter.
6. Remove large nut securing camshaft sprocket. See **Figure 39**.
7. Pull out dowel pin securing camshaft sprocket. Porsche dealers use a special threaded rod (Porsche tool P212) for this. See **Figure 40**. The tool has metric threads.
8. Remove chain guide as shown in **Figure 41**.
9. Pull off camshaft sprocket, sprocket mounting flange and small Woodruff key.
10. Remove 3 bolts securing sealing ring, O-ring, and gasket. Remove parts from end of camshaft. See **Figure 42**. Count the number of shim washers so that the same numbers are reinstalled.
11. Pull camshaft out of housing.

Inspection

1. Clean all parts thoroughly in solvent.
2. Inspect bearing journals and cam lobes for wear. Cam lobes should not be scored and the

edges should be square. Slight damage may be removed with a silicon carbide oilstone. Use 100-120 grit initially, then polish with a 280-320 grit.

3. Clean oilways with compressed air.

4. Check camshaft run-out at the center bearing journal. See **Figure 43**.

Installation

When installing timing chain guides on 1978 and later engines, note that 5 of the 6 guides have been modified to provide quieter operation. These new guides are made of brown plastic, while the older ones are black. The location of the 5 new guides (the darker ones) is shown in **Figure 44**. Make sure they are placed correctly.

1. Slide camshaft into housing. Ensure that it rotates smoothly and freely.

2. Install new gasket over camshaft.

3. Fit new O-ring over aluminum sealing ring. Hold in place with grease.

4. Install sealing ring and secure with 3 bolts.

5. Attach dial indicator to end of camshaft and move the camshaft back and forth. End play with all new parts is 0.006-0.0078 in. (0.15-0.20 mm). Replace sealing ring if end play exceeds 0.0157 in. (0.4 mm).

6. Install thrust washer and shim washers (**Figure 42**). Install the same number of shim washers removed in Step 10, *Removal*.

7. Install sprocket flange with Woodruff key.

8. Fit sprocket on camshaft large nut. Do not install dowel pin or large nut yet.

> *NOTE*
> *Sprockets used on left and right banks are identical. However, when installed on the left bank (cylinders 1-3), the deep recess shown in **Figure 45** faces out toward the rear of the engine. When the sprocket is mounted on the right bank (cylinders 4-6), the deep recess faces inward toward the front of the engine.*

9. Push the intermediate shaft and right bank camshaft toward the front of the engine as far as they will go.

10. With a straightedge and depth gauge, measure distance (A) from the rear face of the drive sprocket to the crankcase edge. See

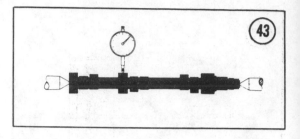

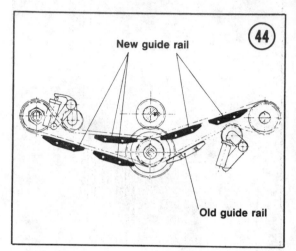

New guide rail

Old guide rail

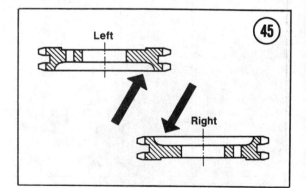

Left

Right

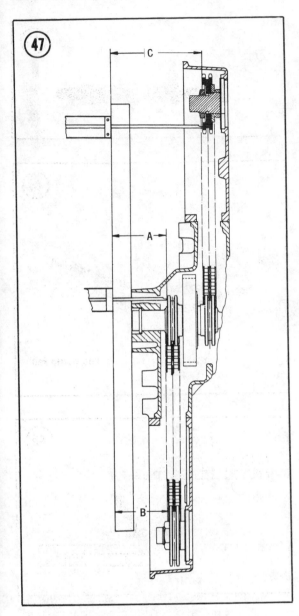

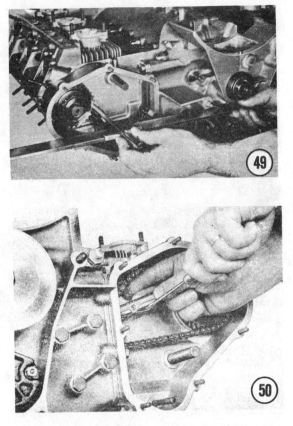

4

Figure 46 and **Figure 47**. Note the hole below the intermediate shaft which permits access to the drive sprocket face.

11. Measure distance (B), the depth of the right camshaft sprocket face, in the same way. See **Figure 47** and **Figure 48**.

12. Compare measurements (A) and (B). If the difference in the 2 measurements exceeds 0.01 in. (0.25 mm), remove the camshaft sprocket and flange and adjust the number of shim washers to correct the difference. Reinstall flange and sprocket.

13. Measure distance (C) as shown in **Figure 47** and **Figure 49**.

14. Add 2.157 in. (54.8 mm) to measurement (A), Step 10. Compare this new figure to measurement (C). If the difference exceeds 0.01 in. (0.25 mm), remove left sprocket and flange and adjust number of shims to correct difference. Reinstall flange and sprocket.

15. Install heat exchangers if removed.

16. Lift retaining spring away from chain guide and slide chain guide onto crankcase studs. See **Figure 50**.

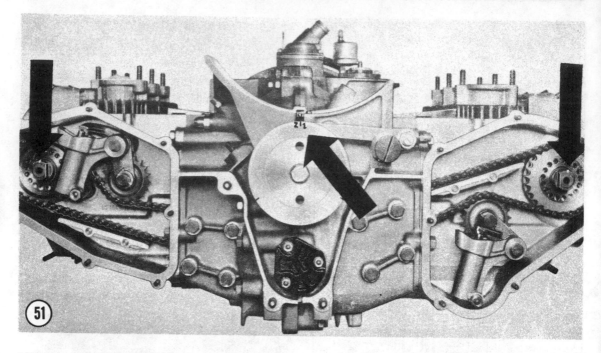

51

17. Install chain tensioner as described later.

18. Rotate crankshaft until the "Z1" marked on the crankshaft pulley aligns with the crankcase seam. See **Figure 51**.

19. Rotate camshafts until punch marks point straight up. See **Figure 51**.

20. Fit the dowel pin through whichever sprocket hole lines up with a flange hole.

21. Install large sprocket nut and tighten to 72 ft.-lb. (10 mkg).

22. Install rocker arms and shafts.

CAUTION
Valve timing is not correct at this point. Rotating either the crankshaft or camshaft could cause valves and pistons to collide and damage each other. To prevent damage, rotate the crankshaft very slowly and carefully. When the slightest resistance is felt, stop, back off a little, then rotate either or both camshafts to move the valve out of the way.

23. Adjust valve timing as described later in this chapter.

CYLINDER HEADS

Each cylinder has its own cylinder head. The 3 cylinder heads for one bank are joined by a camshaft housing containing the camshaft and rocker arms for that bank.

The cylinder heads may be removed individually or all 3 cylinders on one bank may be removed simultaneously. Both procedures are described below.

Cylinder Head Bank Removal

Only parts associated with the desired bank need to be removed.

1. Remove rear engine support shown in **Figure 52**.

2. Remove muffler and heat exchanger as described in Chapter Five.

3. Perform Steps 3-10 of *Camshaft Removal*.

4. Remove nuts securing chain housing to crankcase and remove housing.

5. Loosen cylinder head nuts with Allen wrench. See **Figure 53**.

6. Remove cylinder head nuts and lift off complete assembly shown in **Figure 54**.

Cylinder Head Inspection

1. Without removing the valves, remove all carbon deposits from the combustion chambers with a wire brush. A blunt screwdriver or chisel may be used if care is taken not to damage the head or valves.

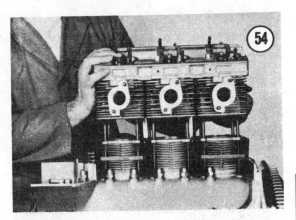

4

2. After all carbon is removed from the combustion chamber, both valves and intake and exhaust ports, clean the entire head with solvent.

3. Clean away all carbon on the piston crown. Do not remove the carbon ridge at the top of the cylinder bore.

4. Check for cracks in the combustion chamber and exhaust ports. Cracked heads must be replaced.

5. Check all studs for tightness. If a stud cannot be tightened, have a machinist drill the hole out and install Heli-coil threaded insert.

6. Push the valve stem ends sideways with your thumb. If there is any play, the valve guides are probably worn. Replace them as described later if there is any doubt.

Cylinder Head Bank Installation

Before installing cylinder heads, see *Inspection*, above.

NOTE
On engines up to No. 900727, see
Cylinder Head Replacement.

1. Remove rocker arms and shafts as described earlier to prevent camshaft bearing damage during installation.

2. Ensure that sealing surfaces on cylinder head and cylinders are clean and in good condition.

3. Install new gaskets on cylinders. Perforations face toward the cylinders.

4. Install new rubber O-rings on oil return pipes and install the pipes in the crankcase.

5. Lower cylinder head/camshaft housing assembly into position. Make sure that oil return pipes seat properly in the camshaft housing and crankcase.

6. Install washers and cylinder head nuts; tighten finger-tight.

7. Install chain housing on crankcase. Tighten nuts shown in **Figure 55** and loop chain over camshaft as shown.

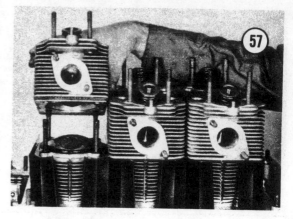

8. Tighten diagonally opposite cylinder head nuts evenly and progressively until all are tightened to 22-24 ft.-lb. (3.0-3.3 mkg).

9. Perform Steps 2-23 of *Camshaft Installation*.

10. Install heat exchangers, muffler and rear engine support.

Individual Cylinder Head Removal

Only parts associated with the desired cylinder head need to be removed.

1. Remove rear engine support shown in **Figure 52**.

2. Remove muffler and heat exhanger.

3. Perform Steps 3-11 of *Camshaft Removal*.

4. Remove nuts securing chain housing to crankcase and remove housing.

5. Remove rocker arms and shafts as described in this chapter.

6. Remove 12 nuts securing camshaft housing to cylinder heads. The three shown in **Figure 56** require an 8 mm Allen wrench.

7. Remove nuts securing desired cylinder head(s) and lift head(s) off. See **Figure 57**.

Individual Cylinder Head Installation

Before installing a cylinder head, see *Inspection*, above.

NOTE
On engines up to No. 900727, see
Cylinder Head Replacement.

1. Ensure that sealing surfaces on cylinder head and cylinders are clean and in good condiiton.

2. Install new gasket on cylinder. Perforations face toward the cylinder. See **Figure 58**.

3. Install cylinder head.

4. Install washers and cylinder head nuts; tighten finger-tight.

5. Install new rubber O-rings on oil return pipes and install the pipes in the crankcase.

6. Ensure that camshaft housing and cylinder head surfaces are clean and in good condition. Coat these surfaces with sealing compound (Permatex Aviation Form-a-Gasket No. 3 or equivalent).

7. Install camshaft housing in place. Make sure that oil return pipes seat in camshaft housing and crankcase properly. Install washers and housing nuts finger-tight.

8. Tighten diagonally opposite cylinder head nuts evenly and progressively until all are tightened to 22-24 ft.-lb. (3.0-3.3 mkg).

9. Tighten diagonally opposite camshaft housing nuts evenly and progressively until all are tightened to 16-18 ft.-lb. (2.2-2.5 mkg).

CAUTION
Periodically, while tightening these nuts, insert camshaft and make certain that it turns freely. If there is any binding, remove the camshaft housing and find out the reason.

10. Install chain housing on crankcase. Tighten nuts shown in **Figure 55** and loop chain over camshaft.

11. Install camshaft as described in this chapter.

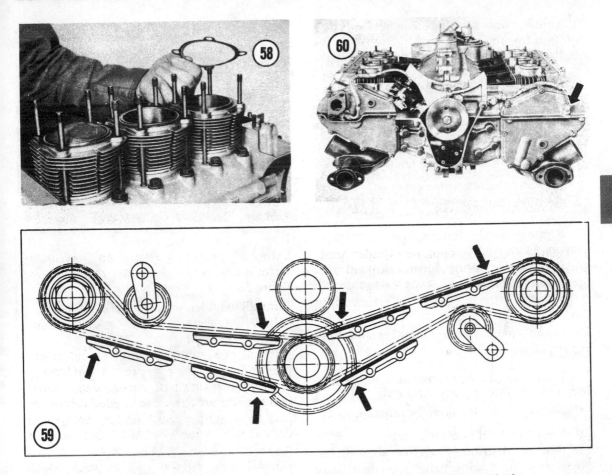

12. Install heat exchanger, muffler and rear engine support.

Cylinder Head Replacement
Up to Engine No. 900727

On engines up to No. 900727, the depth of the valve cut-outs on the pistons is less than in later engines. When cylinder head is replaced on these engines, clearance between piston and valve must not be less than 0.0314 in. (0.8 mm). Measure as described below. If clearance is insufficient, grind the valve seat so the valve sets in the head deeper.

To Measure Clearance

1. Place several small balls of a special measuring compound (Plastilin) in the valve cut-offs.
2. Install cylinder head, camshaft and rocker arms.
3. Adjust valve timing as described in another section.

4. Rotate engine several revolutions.
5. Remove cylinder head and measure thickness of measuring compound. This is the minimum clearance between valve and piston.

**CHAIN AND CHAIN
TENSION SYSTEM**

Several chain guides and 2 oil-operated tensioners keep the chains running smoothly. These parts are shown in **Figure 59**. **Figure 44** shows the modified guide system used on 1978 and later engines. While it is possible to perform some of these operations with the engine installed, it is actually easier to remove the engine/transaxle first.

Chain Housing Cover Removal

1. Disconnect oil lines to chain housing cover. See **Figure 60**.

2. Remove nuts securing chain housing cover and remove the cover.

3. Installation is the reverse of these steps.

Chain Guide Replacement

Each chain housing contains one guide. The crankcase contains 4 additional guides held in place by studs.

To Replace Chain Housing Guides

1. Remove chain housing cover.

2. Remove camshafts as described in this chapter.

3. Remove chain housing nuts shown in **Figure 55** and lift housing off.

4. Pry retainer spring down and unscrew 2 stud bolts holding chain guide. Lift guide out.

NOTE
Do not drop chain guide into crankcase or you may have to disassemble the crankcase to retrieve it.

5. Installation is the reverse of these steps.

Chain Tensioner Removal/Installation

1. Remove chain housing covers.

2. Remove distributor cap. Turn crankshaft over until rotor points to notch on distributor housing and "Z1" on crankshaft pulley aligns with the crankcase seam. This indicates position No. 1 is at TDC on compression stroke.

3. Wedge the chain tension wheels so that they maintain tension after chain tensioner has been removed. It is also possible to tie them to a cover stud with strong wire to maintain tension.

4. Remove nut securing chain tensioner and remove it. See **Figure 61**.

5. Installation is the reverse of these steps. Porsche mechanics use a special tool (Porsche P214) to compress the tensioner piston during installation. See **Figure 62**.

Chain Tensioner Disassembly/Assembly (1965 to Mid-1970)

Refer to **Figure 63** for following procedure.

1. Depress piston, then pry C-ring out of tensioner.

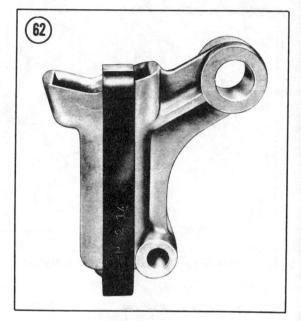

WARNING
The piston is under considerable spring tension. Do not allow it to fly out.

2. Carefully remove piston, ball, ball valves, spring and spring guide.

3. Clean all parts in solvent.

4. Examine piston and cylinder bore in tensioner body for signs of wear or scoring. Replace questionable parts.

5. Insert all parts in the order shown in **Figure 63**. Secure piston with C-ring.

6. Hold tensioner body in a vise with soft jaws.

7. Fill oil cup with engine oil.

8. Insert a 0.039 in. (1 mm) diameter steel wire through the hole in the piston. See **Figure 64** and **Figure 65**.

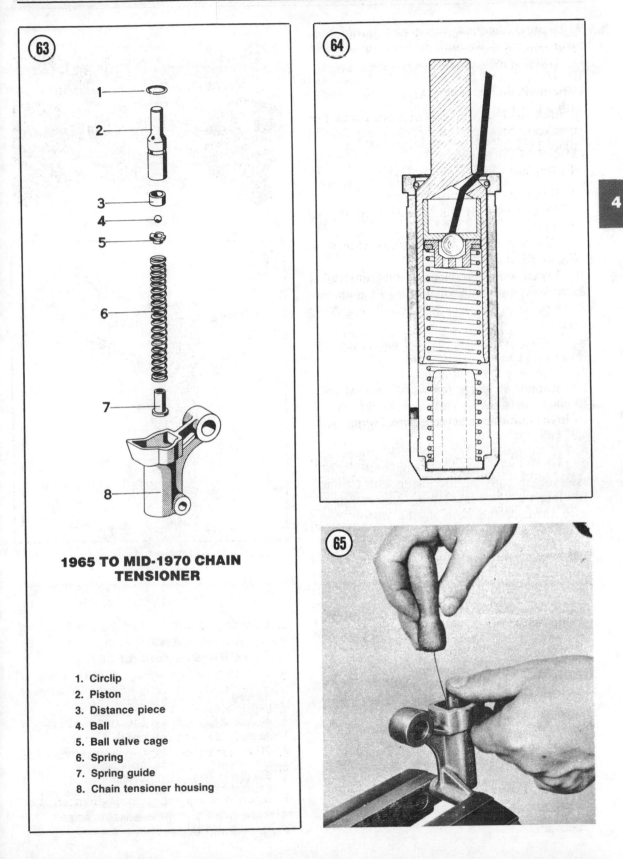

1965 TO MID-1970 CHAIN TENSIONER

1. Circlip
2. Piston
3. Distance piece
4. Ball
5. Ball valve cage
6. Spring
7. Spring guide
8. Chain tensioner housing

4

9. Depress the ball valve and pump the piston up and down until no more air bubbles are visible. Remove wire.

10. Hold piston down with a tool such as Porsche P214. A substitute is easily made with a piece of spring steel.

Chain Tensioner Disassembly/Assembly (Mid-1970 and Later)

Refer to **Figure 66** for following procedure.

> *WARNING*
> *Internal parts are under considerable spring tension. Do not allow them to fly out.*

1. Depress spring retainer and pry out C-ring.
2. Remove oil retainer with long nose pliers.
3. Depress piston and pry out C-ring. See **Figure 67**.
4. Remove remaining internal parts. Do not lose small ball.
5. Clean all parts in solvent.
6. Examine all parts for wear and scoring. Replace questionable parts.
7. Install intermediate piece with O-ring, ball and ball retainer in piston.
8. Fill tensioner body with SAE 30 engine oil.
9. Install spring guide, spring and piston assembly in body. Secure piston with C-ring.
10. Insert a 0.039 in. (1 mm) diameter steel wire through the hole in the piston. See **Figure 64** and **Figure 65**.
11. Depress the ball valve and pump the piston up and down until no more air bubbles are visible. Remove wire.
12. Take tensioner to dealer. Have him install remaining parts (12-17 in **Figure 66**) and bleed the upper reservoir with Porsche tool P214.

Camshaft Chain Replacement

1. Disassemble crankcase as described in this chapter.
2. Reassemble crankcase with new chain(s).

VALVES AND VALVE SEATS

Exhaust valve seats made of a material with improved wear properties are used on

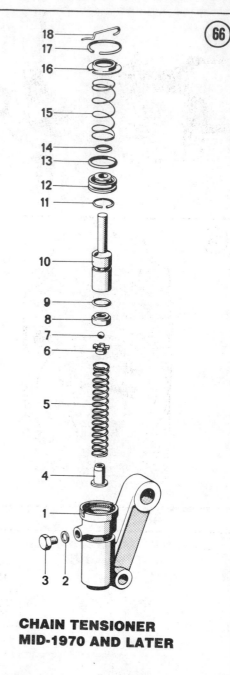

CHAIN TENSIONER MID-1970 AND LATER

1. Housing
2. Copper washer
3. Bleeder screw
4. Spring guide
5. Piston spring
6. Ball retainer
7. Ball (5 mm dia.)
8. Intermediate piece
9. O-ring
10. Piston
11. C-ring
12. Oil retainer
13. O-ring
14. O-ring
15. Oil retainer spring
16. Spring retainer
17. C-ring
18. Clamp (supplied only with new chain tensioners to help installation)

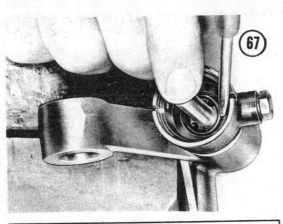

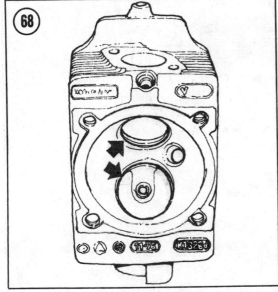

1978 and later engines. The new seats are identified with grooves (**Figure 68**). If exhaust valve seat replacement is required on 1978-on engines, make sure the replacements are of the new type.

Valve Removal

Refer to **Figure 69** for the following procedure.
1. Remove cylinder head.
2. Compress springs with a valve spring compression tool. Remove valve cotters and release compression.
3. Remove valve spring caps, springs and valves.

CAUTION
Remove any burrs from valve stem grooves before removing valves otherwise valve guides will be damaged.

4. Remove valve guide seals from valve guides.
5. Remove spacer washers and spring supports under springs.

Inspection

1. Clean valves with a wire brush and solvent. Discard burned, warped or cracked valves. If any valves are to be refaced, refer to **Figure 70** (1965-1976) or **Figure 71** (1977-on) for critical dimensions.

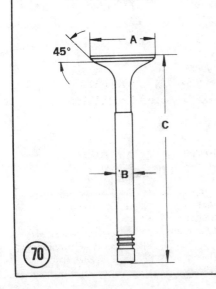

INTAKE VALVES

YEAR	A	B	C
1965 to 1969	1.535 ± 0.0039 in.	0.353—0.00047 in. (8.97—0.012mm)	4.315 ± 0.00197 in. (111.15 ± 0.05mm)
1970 to 1976	(46.0 ± 0.1mm)	(8.97—0.012mm)	(114.0 ± 0.1mm)

EXHAUST VALVES

YEAR	A	B	C
1965 to 1969	1.3779 ± 0.0039 in. (35.0 ± 0.1mm)	0.3523—0.00047 in. (8.95—0.012mm)	4.3996 ± 0.00197 in. (111.75 ± 0.05mm)
1970 to 1976	(40.0 ± 0.1mm)	(8.95—0.012mm)	(113.5 ± 0.1mm)

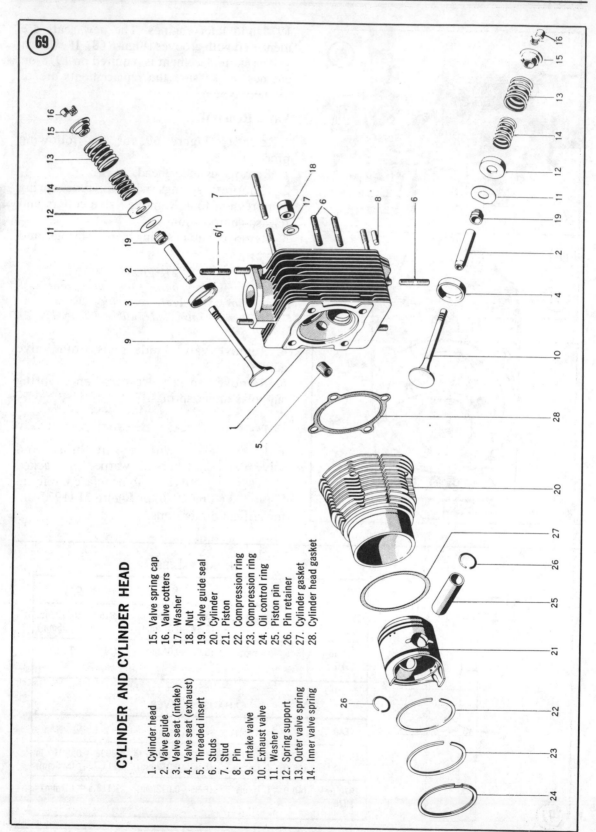

69

CYLINDER AND CYLINDER HEAD

1. Cylinder head
2. Valve guide
3. Valve seat (intake)
4. Valve seat (exhaust)
5. Threaded insert
6. Studs
7. Stud
8. Pin
9. Intake valve
10. Exhaust valve
11. Washer
12. Spring support
13. Outer valve spring
14. Inner valve spring
15. Valve spring cap
16. Valve cotters
17. Washer
18. Nut
19. Valve guide seal
20. Cylinder
21. Piston
22. Compression ring
23. Compression ring
24. Oil control ring
25. Piston pin
26. Pin retainer
27. Cylinder gasket
28. Cylinder head gasket

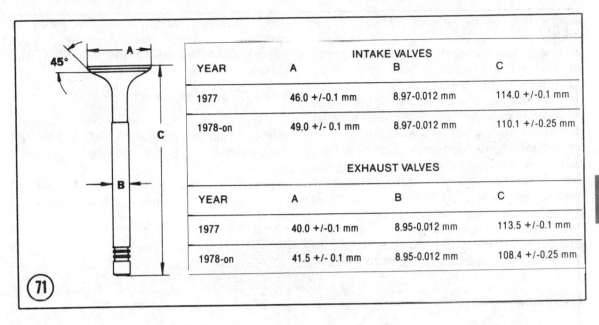

	INTAKE VALVES		
YEAR	A	B	C
1977	46.0 +/-0.1 mm	8.97-0.012 mm	114.0 +/-0.1 mm
1978-on	49.0 +/- 0.1 mm	8.97-0.012 mm	110.1 +/-0.25 mm
	EXHAUST VALVES		
YEAR	A	B	C
1977	40.0 +/-0.1 mm	8.95-0.012 mm	113.5 +/-0.1 mm
1978-on	41.5 +/- 0.1 mm	8.95-0.012 mm	108.4 +/-0.25 mm

⑦

4

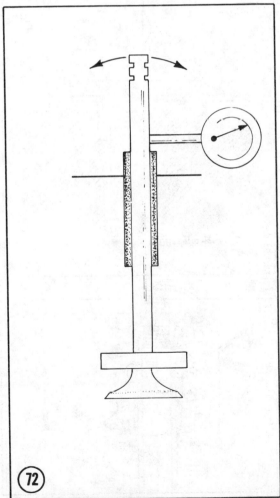

⑦

2. Check valve stems for wear, bends and traces of seizure. Check end for excessive wear (ridge formation). Valves with stem damage must be replaced; valve stems cannot be reground or straightened.

3. Remove all carbon and varnish from valve guides with a stiff spiral wire brush.

4. Insert valves in guides.

5. Rig a dial indicator so that it bears on the valve stem just above the valve guide. See **Figure 72**.

6. Lift the valve about 1/16 in. off its seat and rock the valve stem back and forth. Play indicated on the dial indicator should be 0.0012-0.0022 in. (0.030-0.057 mm) on the inlet valve and 0.002-0.003 in (0.050-0.077 mm) on the exhaust valve. If play is excessive, the valve guide and/or valve stem is worn. See *Valve Guide Replacement* later in this section.

7. Measure valve spring heights. All should be of equal height (up to 5% variation permissible), with no bends or other distortion. Replace defective springs. Inner and outer spring must be replaced as a set.

NOTE
Intake and exhaust springs are identical.

8. Take inner and outer valve springs, along with spring supports and valve caps, to your

dealer for testing. **Figure 73** shows one method.

9. Check valve cotters. Press them together on the end of the valve. The valve should turn freely within the cotters.

10. Inspect valve seats. If worn, burned or loose, they must be reconditioned by a dealer or other competent machine shop. The procedure is provided later in this section. Seats and valves in near perfect condition can be reconditioned by lapping with fine carborundum paste. Lapping, however, is always inferior to precision grinding.

11. Check valve seating with Prussian (machinist's) blue as described in Steps 4-7, *Valve Seat Reconditioning*.

Installation

1. Coat valve stems with molybdenum disulfide paste and insert them into cylinder head.

2. On engines manufactured from May 6, 1965, with 17 mm bore spacer washers, fit valve guide seals over end of valves and push seals down until the base contacts the top of the guide. See **Figure 74**.

3. Install 2 washers and spring support over each valve guide.

4. Install springs with close-pitched coils next to the cylinder head.

5. Install valve spring caps, compress springs with compression tool and install valve cotters.

6. Measure installed length of all valve springs (A, **Figure 75**). Disassemble and adjust number of washers if necessary so installed length is correct. See **Table 1**.

7. On engines prior to May 6, 1965 with 14 mm bore washers, disassemble spring, install valve guide seal (Step 2), and reinstall valve spring.

Valve Guide Replacement

Valve guide replacement is a very exacting job requiring several special tools and skills. Inexperienced and/or poorly equipped mechanics can quickly ruin these very expensive cylinder heads. Take the job to your dealer or competent machine shop. The

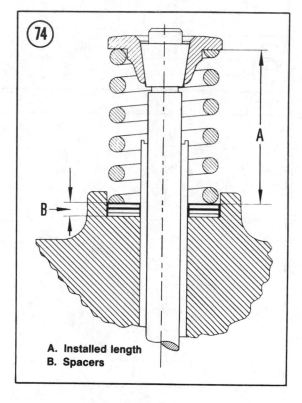

A. Installed length
B. Spacers

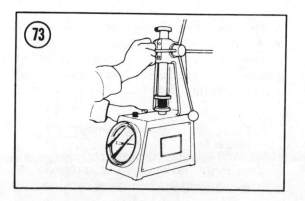

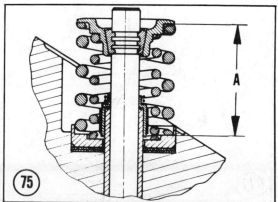

following procedure is for use by properly equipped machine shops unfamiliar with Porsches. For specifications, refer to **Table 2**.

1. Drill out the old guide from the camshaft side with an 11 mm drill. See **Figure 76**. Be sure the head is firmly clamped at the proper angle.

2. Hammer the guide out with a drift from the camshaft side.

3. Accurately measure the valve guide bore.

NOTE
Driving the old guide out increases the bore.

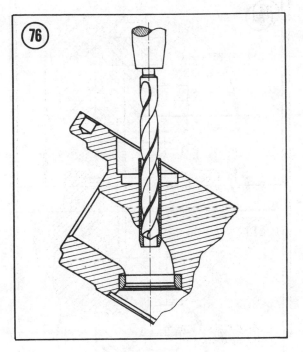

4. Turn oversize valve guide down to 0.001-0.002 in. (0.03-0.06 mm) larger than the measured bore. **Table 2** lists available oversizes.

5. Lubricate valve guide with Lubriplate and press it into cylinder head from camshaft side. Guide should protrude *exactly* 0.515 +0.012 in. (13.2 ±0.3 mm) above recess in head (**Figure 77**).

NOTE
Chill valve guides in a freezer if possible to shrink them and make insertion easier.

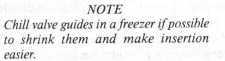

6. Ream the guides with a broach or fine boring mill to 0.3543-0.3549 in. (9.000-9.0125 mm).

Valve Seat Reconditioning

This job is best left to your dealer or local machine shop. They have the special equipment and knowledge required for this exacting job. The following procedure is provided in the event you are not near a dealer and the local machine shop is not familiar with Porsches. For specifications, refer to **Table 2**.

Valve seats are shrunk into the cylinder heads. Damaged or burned seats may be reconditioned as long as the proper 45 degree seat width can be maintained (**Table 1**) and dimension A, **Figure 78**, is within specifications.

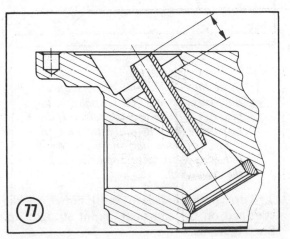

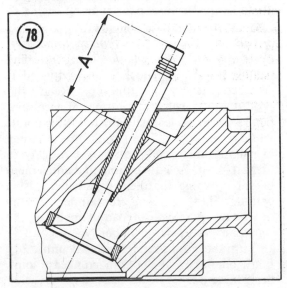

NOTE
Dimension A is 47.50 mm for 1977
models and 46.00 mm for 1978 and
later models.

When the seats can no longer be reconditioned, replace the cylinder heads; seats cannot be replaced with standard machine shop tools.

1. Using a 45° valve seat cutter or special stone, cut the 45° face. Don't take off any more metal than necessary to provide a clean, concentric seat. See **Figure 79**.

2. Slightly chamfer the bottom of the 45° seat with a 75° cutter or stone. See **Figure 80**.

3. Narrow the width of the 45° seat by cutting the top of the seat with a 30° cutter or stone. See **Figure 81**. Refer to **Table 1**, at the end of this chapter, for proper intake and exhaust valve seat widths.

4. Coat the corresponding valve face with Prussian blue.

5. Insert the valve into the guide.

6. Rotate the valve under light pressure approximately 1/4 turn.

7. Lift the valve out. If the valve seats properly, the blue will transfer to the valve seat evenly.

VALVE TIMING

Whenever a chain has been removed from either camshaft sprocket, such as when removing the camshaft, valve timing must be checked and adjusted. Penalty for failing to do so ranges from a poor running engine to very expensive engine damage.

This procedure is extremely important, especially on 1978 and later engines. The timing should be checked and adjusted if required at every tune-up. Read the procedure through several times, if necessary, before you start. Look for the following points while reading. The relation between camshafts and crankshaft is set roughly in Steps 1-4. Steps 5-10 permit fine adjustment of valve timing for the left camshaft, using cylinder No. 1. The remainder of the procedure permits fine adjustment of the right camshaft using cylinder No. 4.

1. Turn the crankshaft very slowly until "Z1" mark on pulley aligns with crankcase joint. See **Figure 82**.

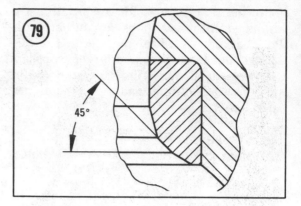

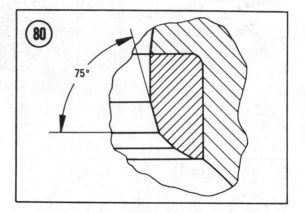

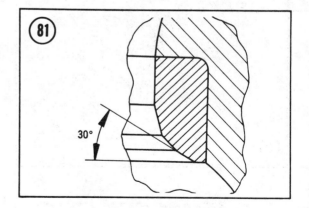

CAUTION
Since the camshaft and crankshaft are not synchronized, it is possible for the pistons to collide with the valves. If any resistance is felt while turning the crankshaft, stop and move the valves out of the way, then continue turning the crankshaft.

2. Turn both camshafts until punch marks stamped on the camshafts point straight up. See **Figure 82**.

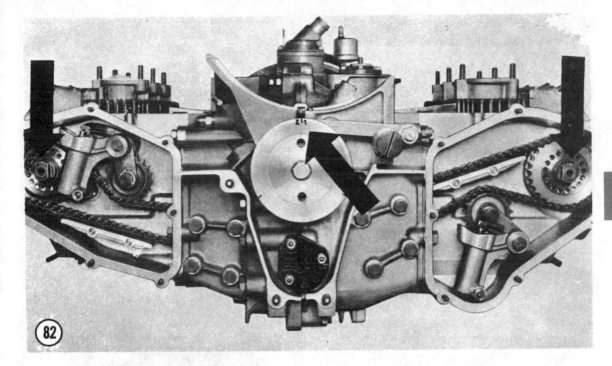

(82)

4

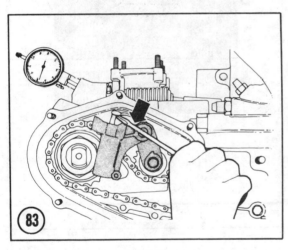

(83)

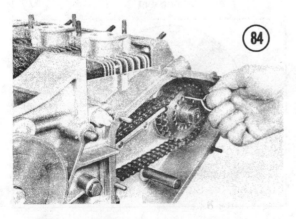

(84)

3. Find the hole (only one) in each camshaft sprocket which lines up with a hole in each sprocket flange. Insert dowel pin into each hole.

4. Install lockwashers and sprocket retaining nuts. Tighten to 72 ft.-lb. (10 mkg).

5. Adjust cylinder No. 1 intake valve clearance to 0.004 in. (0.1 mm).

6. Install dial gauge so it bears on the edge of the valve spring retaining collar. Adjust dial gauge for a preload of 0.4 in. (10 mm).

7. Depress chain tensioner with a screwdriver (**Figure 83**) and block it in this position. Turn crankshaft 360° so that "Z1" again aligns with crankcase seam.

8. Dial gauge reading should be the same as indicated in **Table 3** or **Table 4** for your engine.

9. If dial gauge reading is higher or lower than specified for your engine, remove camshaft sprocket nut and remove dowel pin (**Figure 84**). Turn camshaft (**Figure 85**) until dial gauge reading is proper for your engine. One, and only one, hole in the sprocket will align with the sprocket flange hole. Reinsert dowel pin in this hole. Install lockwasher and sprocket retaining nut. Torque to 72 ft.-lb. (10 mkg).

10. Turn crankshaft 2 complete turns (720°) clockwise and observe dial gauge again. If reading agrees with **Table 3** or **Table 4** (as appropriate), go to next step. If reading does not agree, repeat entire procedure again.

11. If you have followed the procedure exactly to this point, piston No. 4 is at TDC on its compression stroke. Repeat Steps 5-10 for cylinder No. 4.

12. When the valve timing is correct, remove blocks used on chain tensioners. See Step 7.

CYLINDERS

Removal

1. Remove cylinder heads either individually or in groups of 3, as described earlier.

2. Remove air deflector plates below cylinders.

3. Mark cylinder numbers on each cylinder (**Figure 86**) and carefully lift them off.

Inspection and Cleaning

1. Carefully clean the cylinder inside and out. Brush out all dirt between the fins. Clean away dirt on the cylinder sealing surfaces and remove old gasket on the crankcase end.

2. Check wear pattern in cylinder bore. If uneven, the corresponding connecting rod/piston may be out of alignment. Remove and inspect connecting rods as described in this chapter.

3. Check cylinder bore for excessive wear. See *Piston Clearance*. If worn, replace with a *matched* cylinder and piston of the same diameter, piston weight and cylinder height. See **Table 5** and **Table 6**.

4. Check cylinder inside and out for cracks. Replace cylinder and piston if necessary.

Installation

1. Install a new gasket on the crankcase end of each cylinder.

2. Rotate the crankshaft slowly until the desired piston is out as far as possible.

> *CAUTION*
> *While rotating the crankshaft, watch that skirts of exposed pistons do not catch on the crankcase. This will crack the piston.*

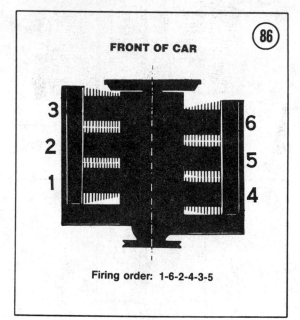

FRONT OF CAR

Firing order: 1-6-2-4-3-5

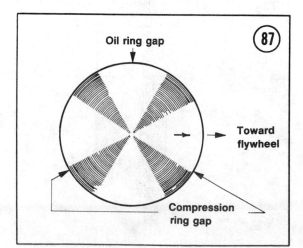

Oil ring gap

Toward flywheel

Compression ring gap

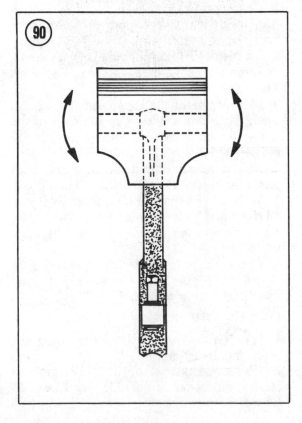

3. Apply a heavy coat of assembly lubricant to the piston.

4. Make sure that the oil ring gap is straight up. The other 2 ring gaps should be evenly spaced 120° apart. See **Figure 87**. Compress the rings with a 2-piece breakaway type ring compresser.

5. Liberally oil the cylinder bore and slide the cylinder over the piston. See **Figure 88**. Be careful not to break any cooling fins against the studs.

6. Repeat Steps 2-5 for the remaining cylinders.

7. Rotate the cylinder back and forth to ensure that there is clearance between the studs and the holes in the cylinder. Position the cylinders so that the studs do not touch the cylinders. If this is not possible, check for bent studs and straighten or replace them.

8. Install air deflectors around cylinders and secure with clips. See **Figure 89**.

9. Install cylinder heads as described previously.

PISTONS, PINS AND RINGS

Piston Removal

1. Remove cylinder heads and cylinders as described previously.

2. Mark piston crown to make sure it is reinstalled in the same direction and in the same cylinder. See **Figure 86** for numbering.

3. Rotate crankshaft slowly until desired piston is out as far as it goes.

CAUTION
While rotating the crankshaft, watch that skirts of any exposed pistons do not catch on the crankcase. This will damage the piston.

4. Before removing the piston pin, hold the connecting rod tightly and rock the piston as shown in **Figure 90**. Any rocking movement (do not confuse with sliding motion) indicates wear in the piston pin, rod bushing, piston pin bore, or, more likely, a combination of all three. Mark the piston, pin and rod for further examination later.

CAUTION
Proper marking is important. There are 2 indentations on the crown of older

pistons; one for the intake and one for the exhaust valve. Installing these pistons backwards can cause serious piston and/or valve damage. If the piston is symmetrical and does not have the 2 indentations on the crown, it may be installed in either direction on the rod.

5. Remove the snap rings at each end of the piston pin.

6. Turn the engine so that the crankshaft is vertical and place wet rags around the oily area of the crankcase.

7. Heat the piston and pin with a small butane torch. The piston pin will probably drop right out but may need coaxing with a metal rod. Heat the piston to 176° F (80° C) or until it is too warm to touch but not excessively hot.

Inspection

1. Clean piston thoroughly in solvent. Scrape carbon deposits from the top of the piston and ring grooves. Do not damage the piston.

2. Examine each ring for burrs, dented edges and side wear. Pay particular attention to the top compression ring groove as it usually wears more than the others.

3. Weigh each piston. The difference in weight between any 2 pistons in the same engine must not exceed 10 grams.

4. If damage, wear or weight suggest replacement, replace with a size and weight comparable to others in the engine. If the associated cylinder shows no wear or damage, it may be possible to replace the piston alone with one in the same size group. See **Table 5** or **Table 6**. Otherwise, replace piston and cylinder.

5. Measure any parts marked in Step 4, *Piston Removal*, with a micrometer to determine which part or parts are worn. Any machinist can do this for you if you do not have micrometers.

6. When replacing a piston pin, select a size compatible with the piston pin bore. Proper piston pin size is indicated by a color code marking inside the piston on the piston pin boss. Match new piston pin color code (**Table 7**) with the piston color code.

Piston Clearance

Porsche discourages using a feeler gauge to check piston clearance and therefore does not provide specifications to do so. The following procedure is the "hard way" but it is adequate.

1. Make sure that the piston and cylinder walls are clean and dry.

2. Measure the inside diameter of the cylinder bore at a point 1.2 in. (30 mm) from the bottom edge. See **Figure 91**.

3. Measure outside diameter of piston skirt at the bottom of the skirt. See **Figure 92**.

4. If the difference in the 2 readings is near 0.004 in. (0.1 mm), the piston/cylinder combination requires overhaul. If the cylinder bore is excessive, replace the cylinder *and* piston. If the piston is worn or damaged, you may replace the piston only. Choose one which is the correct size and weight. See **Table 6** to select correct components. Also see *Cylinder Inspection* procedure earlier in this chapter.

Piston Ring Fit and Installation

1. Check ring gap of each ring. To check a ring, insert it in the bottom of the cylinder bore and square it with the wall by tapping with a piston. The ring should be in about 0.2 in. Insert a feeler gauge as shown in **Figure 93**. The gap should be 0.012-0.018 in. (0.30-0.45mm). If the gap is smaller, hold a small flat file in a vise, grip the ends of the ring with your fingers and enlarge the gap. See **Figure 94**.

2. Roll each ring around its piston groove as shown in **Figure 95** to check for binding.

3. With a ring expander tool, carefully install oil ring, then 2 compression rings (**Figure 96**). The compression ring side marked TOP *must* be up.

4. Check the side clearance of the ring as shown in **Figure 97**. Compare with the specifications for your engine.

Piston Installation

1. Install rings on all 6 pistons using the preceding procedure.

2. Rotate crankshaft until connecting rod No.1 is out as far as possible. See **Figure 86** for numbering.

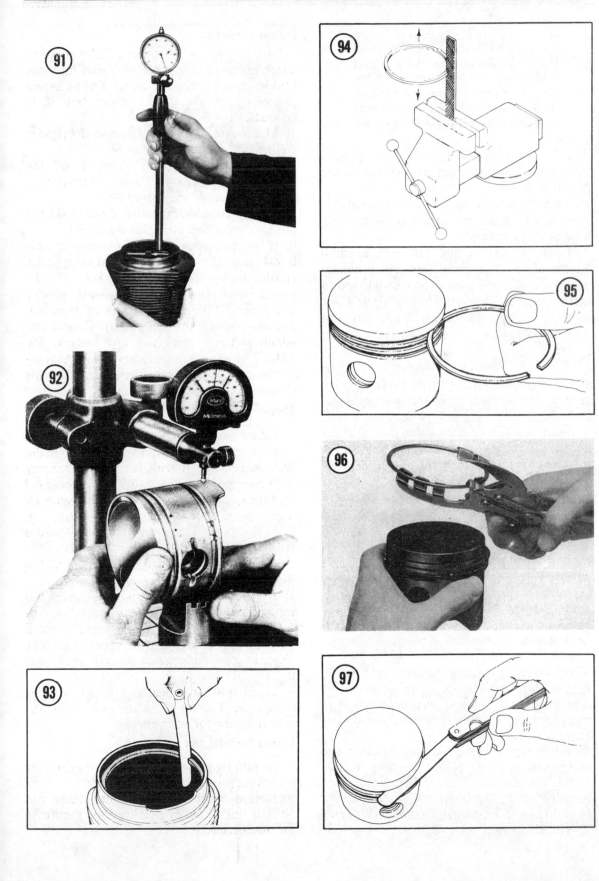

CAUTION
While rotating crankshaft, watch that skirts of any exposed pistons do not catch on the crankcase. This will crack the piston.

3. Install a snap ring in one end of piston No. 1.
4. Coat the connecting rod bushing, piston pin and piston holes with assembly lubricant.
5. Align the piston over the connecting rod in the direction marked in Step 2, *Piston Removal*. Make sure that piston and rod marks made in Step 4, *Piston Removal* align.

CAUTION
There are 2 indentations on the crown of older pistons; one for the intake and one for the exhaust valve. Installing these pistons backwards can cause serious piston and/or valve damage. New pistons are symmetrical and may be installed in either direction on the rod.

6. Heat the piston to about 176° F (80° C) as in Step 7 of *Piston Removal*. Push the piston pin through the piston and connecting rod until it touches the snap ring.
7. Install the other snap ring.
8. Rotate crankshaft slowly until connecting rod No. 2 is out as far as possible.

CAUTION
While rotating crankshaft, watch that skirts of any exposed pistons do no catch on the crankcase. This will crack the piston.

9. Repeat Steps 3-8 for the remaining pistons.

FLYWHEEL

A new flywheel attached with 9 bolts instead of the former 6 bolts is used on 1978 and later models. No lockwashers are used. See **Figure 98**.

Removal

1. Remove clutch pressure plate and disc as described in Chapter Eight.
2. Remove Allen bolts securing flywheel to crankshaft.

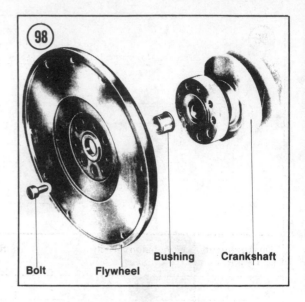

3. Remove flywheel and washer.

Inspection

1. Check flywheel teeth for wear or damage. If teeth are damaged only slightly, remachine and rechamfer as described in procedure below.
2. Check surface which contacts clutch disc. Slight refacing is possible. See procedure below.
3. Check drive shaft bushing in flywheel for wear. See specifications. Replace bushing if necessary.

Remachining

Figure 99 and **Figure 100** show critical flywheel dimensions and tolerances for 1972 and earlier models. Only dimension (b) can be remachined to any extent and should be done in stages as shown in the figures. Dimensions (a) and (c) may be slightly refaced (use extra hard tool steel), but neither dimension should be reduced below that shown in the figures. See **Figure 101** for 1973 and later models.

Flywheel/Pilot Bearing (1980-on)

A redesigned pilot bearing is used on 1980 and later models. The new pilot bearing uses a collar in which the bushing, needle bearing and seal form a complete unit. See **Figure 98**

Measurement point	Dimensions when new	Re-machining stages inch (mm)				Tolerances
		1	2	3	4	
a	.886″ (22.5mm)	.886 (22.5)	—	—	—	.0078″ (+ 0.2)
b	1.7559″ (44.6mm)	1.7401 (44.2)	1.5039 (38.2)	1.4881 (37.8)	1.4724 (37.4)	.0078″ (+ 0.2)
c	Wear (reject) .4330″ (11.000mm)					

Measurement point	Dimensions when new	Re-machining stages inch (mm)				Tolerances
		1	2	3	4	
a	.886″ (22.5mm)	.886 (22.5)	—	—	—	.0078″ (+ 0.2)
b	1.5354″ (39.0mm)	1.5196 (38.6)	1.5039 (38.2)	1.4881 (37.8)	1.4724 (37.4)	.0078″ (+ 0.2)
c	Wear (reject) .4330″ (11.000mm)					

⑩¹

REMACHINING:
The flywheel may be machined on a lathe to remove
heavy scoring or heat spots.
   1. Wear limit of flywheel thickness 0.337 in. (8.5 mm).
   2. Keep lathe cut as small as possible.
   3. Maximum runout 0.04 in. (0.1 mm).
   4. Lathe mounting points.

1   2   3

4

for the old design and **Figure 102** for the new one. The pilot bearing is installed to the crankshaft with three M6 x 12 Allen head bolts. Oil bolts lightly before installation. Tighten to 7.2 ft.-lb. (10 N•m).

Drive Shaft Bushing Replacement

1. Drive out old bushing with a press as shown in **Figure 103**.
2. Press in new bushing as shown in **Figure 104**.

Installation

1. Ensure that flywheel washer and crankshaft mating surfaces are smooth and absolutely clean.
2. Lightly oil threads of mounting bolts. Fit flywheel and washer over crankshaft. Insert mounting bolts and tighten finger tight.

> *NOTE*
> *The original crankshaft and flywheel are balanced as a unit. Mounting holes for flywheel are staggered so that the flywheel can be installed only one way. Replacement crankshafts and flywheels are perfectly balanced so they are individually replaceable.*

3. Tighten diagonally opposite bolts evenly and progessively until all are tightened to 108.5 ft.-lb. (15 mkg).

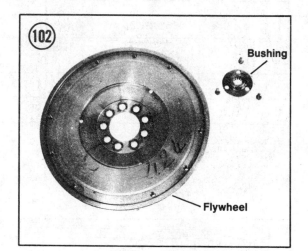

⑩² Bushing

Flywheel

⑩³

SPORTOMATIC

The drive plate is attached to the crankshaft in the same manner as a flywheel except much shorter bolts are required.

A special retaining ring shown in **Figure 105** is required to hold the drive plate while removing the mounting bolts. Rather than improvise a retaining ring and risk warping the drive plate, take the entire engine to a Porsche dealer and let him remove it. Later, when the engine is reassembled, let the dealer reinstall the drive plate.

CRANKSHAFT

A new crankshaft is used on 1978 and later models. It has larger counterweights, strengthened journals and a larger flywheel flange. Larger diameter and narrower width connecting rod journals are used. Specifications are found in **Table 1**. If replacement is indicated, make sure the proper part is obtained. Maximum allowable crankshaft runout is 0.0015 in. (0.04 mm).

> *NOTE*
> *Crankshafts on 1978 and later models are surface hardened. For this reason, it is not possible to remachine crankshaft journals. Refer all crankshaft service to a Porsche dealer.*

Removal

1. When the right half of the crankcase has been removed (see *Crankcase Disassembly*), lift the crankshaft out.
2. Remove bearing inserts from crankcase halves. Mark each on its back as it is removed so that it may be reinstalled in the same position. Set them aside where they won't be damaged.

Inspection

If inspection of the distributor drive gear indicates a need for replacement on 1978 and later crankshafts, make sure the proper replacement part is obtained. The teeth of the 1978-on drive gear are cut to provide counterclockwise rotation of the distributor shaft. The previous gears provided clockwise rotation. See **Figure 106**.

When replacing the distributor drive gear or any time the crankshaft is removed from the engine, check the distributor drive gear axial play. Maximum allowable axial play is 0 mm. If any axial play is felt at the drive gear, a different thickness circlip should be used. Circlips are available in thicknesses of 2.4, 2.3, 2.2 and 2.1 mm. See **Figure 107**.

1. Check connecting rod play, then remove all connecting rods. Both procedures are described under *Connecting Rod Removal* below.

2. Clean the crankshaft thoroughly with solvent. Clean the oil holes with rifle cleaning

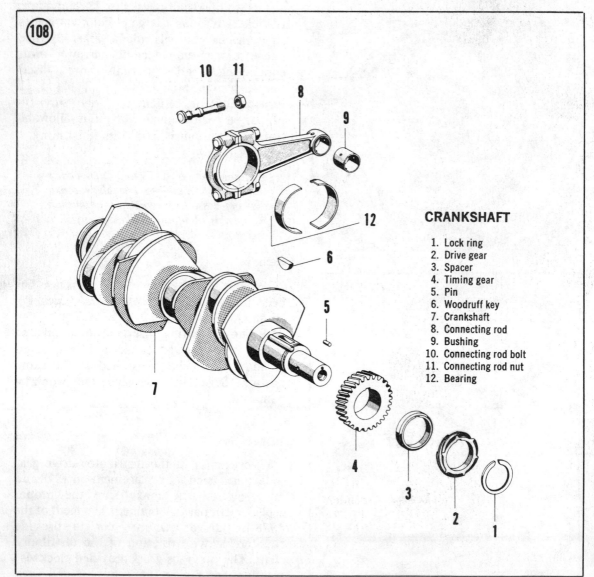

CRANKSHAFT

1. Lock ring
2. Drive gear
3. Spacer
4. Timing gear
5. Pin
6. Woodruff key
7. Crankshaft
8. Connecting rod
9. Bushing
10. Connecting rod bolt
11. Connecting rod nut
12. Bearing

brushes; flush thoroughly and blow dry with air. Lightly oil all journal surfaces immediately to prevent rust.

3. Carefully inspect each journal for scratches, ridges, scoring, nicks, etc. Very small nicks and scratches may be removed with crocus cloth. More serious damage must be removed by grinding which is a job for a machine shop.

4. If the surface finish on all journals is satisfactory, take the crankshaft to your dealer or local machine shop. They can check for out-of-roundness, taper and wear on the journals. They will also check crankshaft alignment and inspect for cracks.

5. Check condition of distributor drive and timing gears. Replace if worn.

Gear and Bearing Disassembly

Refer to **Figure 108** for the following procedure.

1. Remove snap ring on rear of crankshaft. See **Figure 109**.

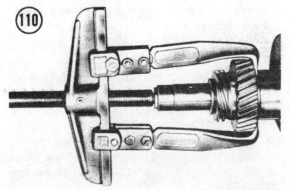

2. With a large gear puller, pull on the bottom of the innermost (timing) gear. See **Figure 110**. Remove the distributor drive spacer and timing gears. Save the Woodruff key.

Gear and Bearing Assembly

Refer to **Figure 108** for the following procedure.

1. Lay the crankshaft vertically on a piece of wood with the flywheel end down.

2. Insert Woodruff key in crankshaft slot. It must be flat, not canted in the slot.

3. Heat timing gear to approximately 300° F in an oven. Push it onto the crankshaft with the shoulder facing toward the flywheel. See **Figure 111**.

> *WARNING*
> *Handle gear very carefully with asbestos gloves or cloth. It is hot enough to cause severe burns.*

4. Install spacer over Woodruff key.

5. Heat distributor drive gear to about 212° F (100° C) and push it onto the crankshaft.

6. Install snap ring.

Installation

Installation is simply a matter of setting the crankshaft into place while assembling crankcase. See *Crankcase Assembly*.

CONNECTING RODS

The connecting rods used on 1978 and later models differ from those previously used. If rods are to be replaced, make sure the proper ones are obtained.

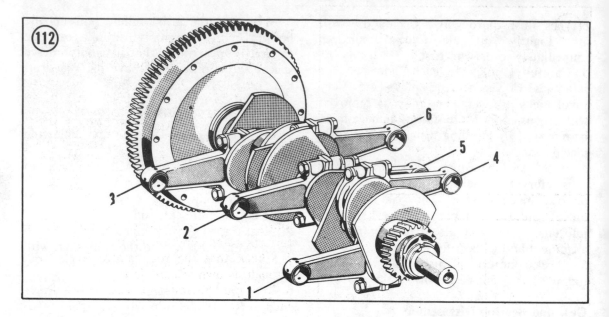

Removal

1. Remove crankshaft from engine. Clamp it down or have someone hold it.

2. File very small marks on each rod to indicate its position for reassembly. For example, make one mark on rod No. 1, two marks on rod No. 2, etc. Rods are numbered as shown in **Figure 112**.

3. Insert a feeler gauge between the side of each rod and the crank throw (**Figure 113**). If this gap (connecting rod end play) is greater than 0.016 in. (0.4 mm), mark the rod for replacement.

4. Remove connecting rod bolts and pull off rod caps and rod.

5. Remove bearing inserts from rods and caps. Mark insert with rod numbers for later inspection and reassembly. Do not mix up bearings.

6. Loosely install caps on rods to keep them together.

Inspection

1. Discard any rods with excessive end play. See Step 3, above.

2. Clean all parts thoroughly in solvent.

3. Check each rod for obvious damage such as cracks or burns.

4. Check piston pin bushing for wear or scoring. At room temperature, a piston pin should slide through with light finger pressue.

5. Discard all rod bolts and nuts. Replace with new ones.

NOTE
Bolts on 1970 and later engines are longer than earlier bolts. They are not interchangeable with shorter bolts.

6. Take rods to a machine shop and have their alignment checked for twisting and bending.

7. On a scale, weigh each rod with new nuts and bolts, but without bearing inserts. They should be within 9 grams of each other. Replacement rods are available in various weights in 9 gram increments. See **Table 8**.

8. Examine bearing inserts for wear, scoring or burning. They are reusable if in good condition. Make a note of bearing size, if any, stamped on the back if a bearing is to be discarded; a previous owner may have used undersized bearings.

Installation

1. Carefully match the number on the side of each rod to its associated rod cap.

2. Install bearing inserts in the rods and caps. Press the bearings in with your thumbs on the ends of the bearing. Do not press down on the middle of the bearing. Be sure that the tangs on the bearings fit into the notches on the caps.

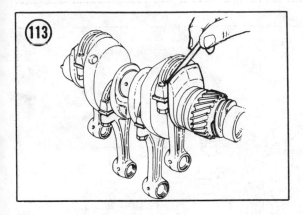

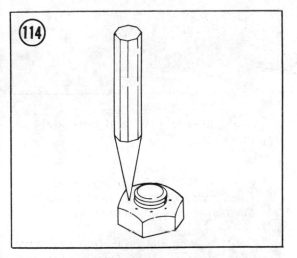

CAUTION
Bearing ends will extend slightly above the cap or rod. Do not file any part of the rod, cap or bearing for a different fit.

3. Oil the nuts and rod cap bolts lightly.

4. Cut a piece of Plastigage the width of the rod bearing. Assemble the rod cap on the crank throw for cylinder No. 3 (the one closest to the flywheel) with the Plastigage inserted between the rod cap and the crank throw. Tighten the nuts to 36 ft.-lb. (5 mkg).

5. Remove the bearing cap and measure the width of the flattened Plastigage wire following the manufacturer's instructions. This is the bearing clearance. Compare it to the specifications for your engine. If it is not right, make sure that you have installed the proper bearings.

6. Remove the strip of Plastigage, coat the bearing and crank throw with assembly lubricant and reassemble the rod on the corresponding crank throw.

7. Check that the rod rotates freely 180° through its own weight alone.

8. Measure the rod end play with a feeler gauge (*Removal*, Step 3). Compare with specifications.

9. Repeat Steps 4-9 for each rod. Be sure you assemble each rod on the crank throw originally used for that rod. Also ensure that the rod and cap number are aligned.

10. Peen the nut around the rod bolts with a center punch to lock them in place (**Figure 114**).

OIL PUMP (ENGINE)

The engine must be removed to perform these procedures.

Removal

1. Separate crankcase halves as described under *Crankcase Disassembly*.

2. Remove the bolts securing the oil pump (**Figure 115**).

3. Lift out oil pump, intermediate shaft and connecting shaft.

4. Separate pump from shafts.

Inspection

The oil pump cannot be disassembled or repaired. When defective, replace the entire pump.

1. Clean pump in solvent and blow dry with compressed air.

2. Turn shaft. Pump gears should turn smoothly and quietly.

3. Examine the sealing surfaces at all oil inlets and outlets.

Installation

1. Insert new seal in right crankcase half oil passage. See **Figure 116**.
2. Insert oil pump, intermediate shaft, connecting shaft and drive chains in right crankcase half. See **Figure 117**. Make sure that seals remain in place.
3. Secure pump with new tabbed lockwashers and nuts. Bend tabs up.
4. Reassemble crankcase.

OIL PUMP (TORQUE CONVERTER)

The left camshaft drives the Sportomatic torque converter oil pump. The oil pump can be removed and installed with the engine in the car.

Removal/Installation

1. Raise rear of car on jackstands and remove left rear wheel.
2. Remove left heat exchanger. See Chapter Five.
3. Disconnect oil pressure and suction lines from oil pump. See **Figure 118**.
4. Remove 3 bolts or nuts securing pump to engine and remove pump.
5. Installation is the reverse of these steps. Use a new paper gasket. Make sure that the roll pins in the end of the crankshaft are oriented as in **Figure 119** so that the oil pump dowel pin does not contact the slot in either roll pin. See **Figure 120**.

Disassembly/Assembly

1. Lift off oil pump cover. See **Figure 121**.
2. Remove drive pin out of rotor shaft and remove rotors.
3. Remove nuts from pressure relief valve cover. See **Figure 122**. Remove cover, spring and control piston.
4. Clean all parts in solvents.
5. Inspect all parts for wear or damage. Replace if necessary.

> *NOTE*
> *Inner and outer rotor with shaft must be replaced as a unit.*

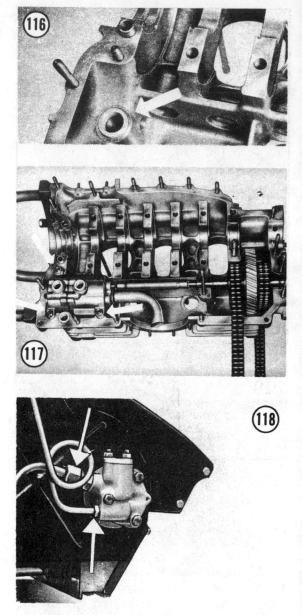

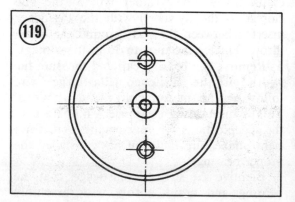

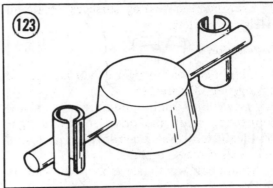

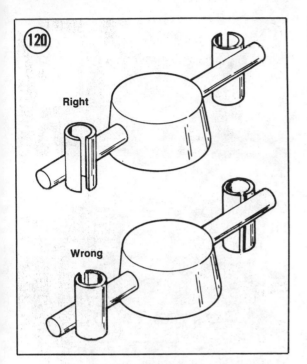

6. Lubricate oil pressure relief piston and insert it in pump body. Install spring and cover with new O-ring. Tighten nuts equally.

7. Lubricate inner and outer rotors thoroughly with SAE 30 engine oil.

8. Install inner rotor in rotor housing.

9. Install rotor shaft dowel pin so that it is centered in shaft. See **Figure 123**.

10. Install outer rotor with beveled edge toward rotor housing. See **Figure 124**.

11. Fit oil pump cover to rotor housing with new paper gasket.

INTERMEDIATE SHAFT

Removal

1. Separate crankcase halves as described under *Crankcase Disassembly*.

2. Remove the bolts securing oil pump (**Figure 115**).

3. Lift out oil pump, intermediate shaft, connecting shaft and inserts if used.

4. Separate pump from shafts.

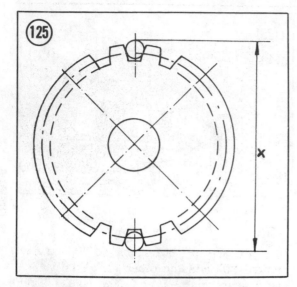

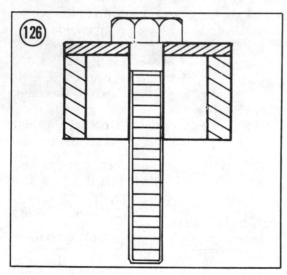

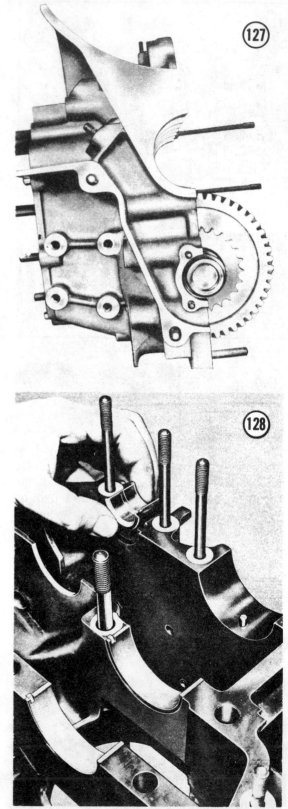

Inspection

1. Clean shaft thoroughly in solvent.

2. Check shaft bearing surfaces for wear or scoring.

3. Check chain sprockets and gear for wear and broken or cracked teeth.

4. Insert two 4.5 mm diameter steel balls between teeth 180° from each other. See **Figure 125**. Measure dimension (X) which should be 135.6 mm for gears marked "0" and 136.55 mm for gears marked "1." If (X) is smaller, gear is worn; replace it.

5. If engine was torn down for general overhaul and/or bearing replacement, the aluminum plug in the intermediate shaft

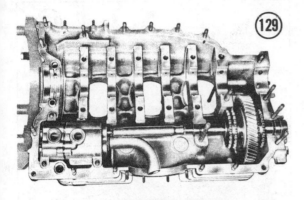

should be removed so that the oilway can be throroughly cleaned. Drill and tap the plug for a 5/16 x 2 in. bolt. Cut a one inch length of pipe to bear on end of shaft with an inside diameter large enough to clear the plug. Fit a steel washer over the pipe and install bolt. Finished puller is shown in **Figure 126**. Tighten the bolt and pull the plug out.

6. Clean oilway in shaft when aluminum plug is out. Press in a new plug.

Installation

Crankcases have been manufactured with 2 different distances between crankshaft and intermediate shaft centers. A number (0 or 1) stamped on the left crankcase half below the alternator mounting point (**Figure 127**) identifies the crankcase size. A similar number is stamped onto the intermediate shaft gear and the crankshaft gear.

The numbers on the crankcase and gears must be matched according to **Table 9**. For example, if you have a crankcase stamped

"0," you may use gears marked "0," or one marked "0" and the other "1." You cannot use 2 gears marked "1." The last column indicates the gear backlash you will get by using each gear/crankcase combination.

1. Install intermediate shaft bearing shells (if any) in crankcase halves. See **Figure 128**.
2. Coat bearing surfaces of connecting shaft and intermediate shaft with assembly lubricant.
3. Install intermediate shaft, connecting shaft and oil pump without camshaft chains. See **Figure 129**.
4. Turn intermediate shaft and ensure that it runs smoothly.
5. Lift out intermediate shaft, connecting shaft and oil pump.
6. Insert new seals in right crankcase half oil passage. See **Figure 130**.
7. Insert oil pump, intermediate shaft, connecting shaft and camshaft chains in right crankcase half. See **Figure 131**. Make sure that seals remain in place.
8. Secure pump with new lock tabs and nuts. Bend tabs up.
9. Reassemble crankcase as described in *Crankcase Assembly*.
10. Adjust intermediate shaft end play.

End Play Adjustment

Intermediate shaft end play need be adjusted only on early shafts without bearing shells. The bearing shells used for later shafts have shoulders to take the thrust and determine end play. See **Figure 128**.

Intermediate shaft end play must be adjusted after reassembling the crankcase halves but before installing the chain housings.

1. Install intermediate shaft cover with a new paper gasket. See **Figure 132**.

2. Attach dial indicator so that it bears on the shaft through the small hole in the cover.

3. Move the shaft back and forth with a screwdriver (**Figure 133**) and record end play on dial indicator.

4. Proper end play is 0.0031-0.0047 in. (0.08-0.012 mm); if end play is less, install shims under cover as necessary.

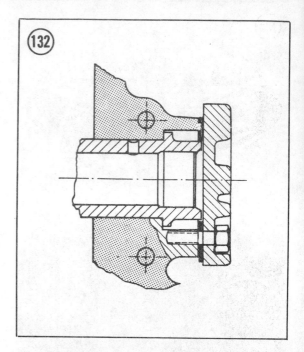

CRANKCASE

Disassembly

1. Perform Steps 1-5 of *General Overhaul Sequence* described earlier in chapter.

2. Remove oil pressure relief and bypass valves.

3. Remove crankcase breather outlet. See **Figure 134**.

4. Remove cover over intermediate shaft. See **Figure 135**.

5. Remove all M8 nuts around outer edges of crankcase.

6. Remove acorn nuts shown in **Figure 136**.

7. Remove large through bolts.

8. Remove nut shown in **Figure 137**.

9. Check very carefully all around crankcase for any remaining nuts and bolts.

10. Loosen the left crankcase half by tapping with a rubber mallet or block of wood. Keep pulling upward on the crankcase half and tapping until the left half is free.

11. Lift out the crankshaft.

12. Remove engine oil pump with intermediate shaft and chains as described in *Intermediate Shaft Removal*.

13. Bend up tabs on oil screens and remove them. See **Figure 138**.

14. Remove bearing inserts for crankshaft and intermediate shaft.

Inspection

1. Clean and flush both halves of crankcase with solvent. Blow out oil passages with air. Remove all traces of old sealing compound on mating surfaces.

2. Check both crankcase halves for cracks and other damage. Mating and sealing

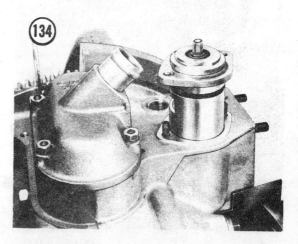

surfaces should be free of nicks and scratches or they will leak.

3. Check all studs in the crankcase for looseness. If any cannot be tightened, have a machinist install a Heli-coil insert.

4. Inspect all bearing bores for burrs. Remove very carefully with a file. Flush out any metal particles.

Assembly

1. Install oil screens and bend tabs over. See **Figure 138**.

2. Install intermediate shaft, oil pump and camshaft chains exactly as described in *Intermediate Shaft Installation* in this chapter.

3. Install main bearing No. 2-No. 7 shells in both crankcase halves. See **Figure 139**.

4. Install main bearing No. 1 shells. See **Figure 140**.

5. Install O-ring and oil seal on main bearing. Mark position of dowel hole with a pencil. See **Figure 141**. Coat inside of bearing with assembly lubricant and slide onto rear of crankshaft.

6. Coat main bearings and crankshaft journals with assembly lubricant.

7. Lift crankshaft assembly by connecting rods No. 1 and No. 3. Hold No. 2 up. Place crankshaft on the main bearings. Make absolutely certain that dowel hole, indicated by pencil mark, fits over dowel. If the oil hole fits over the dowel instead, the bearing will appear to be properly seated, but will not receive any oil when the engine is run. Also connecting rods No. 4, No. 5 and No. 6 must protrude through corresponding cylinder holes.

8. Install two oil seal rings in oil pump and one oil seal ring in the right crankcase half. See **Figure 142**.

9. Coat outer perimeter of front oil seal with gasket compound and install it in the right crankcase half.

10. Spread a thin layer of gasket compound on crankcase mating surfaces.

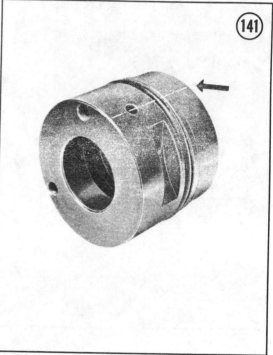

CAUTION
Do not get any gasket compound on bearings or in oil passages.

11. Hold up connecting rods No. 1, No. 2 and No. 3. Place left crankcase half over right.

12. Fit a double chamfered washer over each long through bolt. The smoothest side of the washer should face the crankcase. Slide a rubber O-ring in place over each bolt.

13. Install through bolts. Slide a rubber O-ring over the threaded end of each bolt. Install a double chamfered washer over each bolt with smoothest side next to crankcase. Install cap nuts finger-tight. Completed assembly of each bolt should look like **Figure 143**.

14. Slide on O-ring and double chamfered washer (smooth side down) over the 2 studs

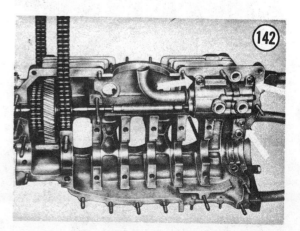

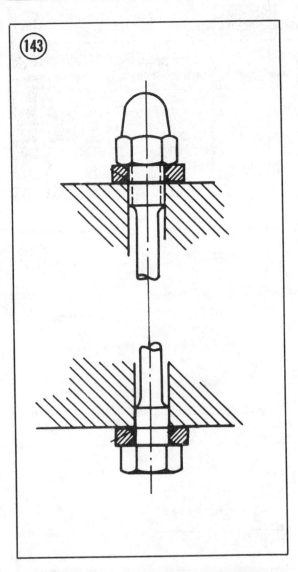

shown in **Figure 144**. Install cap nuts finger-tight.

15. Install a steel washer and nut on stud shown in **Figure 145**. Tighten finger-tight.

CAUTION
Throughout the tightening process in the next 2 steps, turn the crankshaft occasionally. If there is any binding, stop, take the case apart and find out the trouble.

16. Tighten all through bolts and 3 studs to 25 ft.-lb. (3.5 mkg). Tighten finger-tight.

17. Install lockwashers and nuts on remaining crankcase studs. Tighten to 16-18 ft.-lb. (2.2-2.5 mkg).

18. Adjust intermediate shaft end play and install cover over intermediate shaft. See *Intermediate Shaft* procedures.

19. Install oil pressure relief and bypass valves.

20. Perform Steps 1-15 of *General Overhaul Sequence* in reverse order.

Table 1   911 ENGINE SPECIFICATIONS

	2.0 LITER ENGINE TOLERANCE (NEW)	WEAR LIMIT	2.2 LITER ENGINE TOLERANCE (NEW)	WEAR LIMIT
GENERAL				
Number of cylinders	6		6	
Bore, inch (mm)	3.15 (80)		3.307 (84)	
Stroke, inch (mm)	2.60 (66)		2.60 (66)	
Displacement, cu. in. (cc)	121.5 (1991)		133.9 (2195)	
Compression ratio	9.0[1], 8.6[2], 9.9[3]		8.6[4], 9.1[5], 9.8[6]	
Firing order	1-6-2-4-3-5		1-6-2-4-3-5	
Output (SAE) bhp @ rpm				
	148 @ 6100[1]		142 @ 5800[4]	
	125 @ 5800[2]		175 @ 6200[5]	
	180 @ 6600[3]		200 @ 6500[6]	
Torque (SAE) foot-pounds @ rpm				
	129 @ 4200[1]		148 @ 4200[4]	
	131 @ 4200[2]		160 @ 4500[5]	
	132 @ 5200[3]		164 @ 5200[6]	
CYLINDERS				
Bore, inch (mm)	**See Table 5**		**See Table 5**	
Cylinder/piston clearance, inch (mm)	0.0021-0.0029 (0.055-0.075)	0.0007 (0.0180)	0.0021-0.0029 (0.055-0.075)	0.0007 (0.0180)
Out-of-round, inch (mm)		0.0008 (0.0020)		0.0008 (0.020)
PISTONS				
Material	light alloy		light alloy	
Permissable weight deviation	3 grams		3 grams	
Diameter	**See Table 5**		**See Table 5**	
PISTON RINGS				
Number per piston				
Compression	2		2	
Oil control	1		1	
Ring end gap	0.0118-0.0177 (0.30-0.45)	0.394 (1.000)	0.0118-0.177 (0.30-0.45)	0.394 (1.000)
Ring side clearance				
Top compression	0.0035-0.0039 (9.085-0.095)	0.0078 (0.20)	0.0035-0.0039 (0.085-0.095)	0.0078 (0.20)
Bottom compression	0.0022-0.0027 (0.057-0.060)	0.0078 (0.20)	0.0022-0.0027 (0.057-0.060)	0.0078 (0.20)
Oil control	0.0013-0.0015 (0.037-0.040)	0.0078 (0.20)	0.0013-0.0015 (0.037-0.040)	0.0078 (0.20)
PISTON PINS				
Diameter	0.8657-0.8661 (21.994-22.000)		0.8657-0.8661 (21.994-22.000)	
Clearance in rod bushing, inch (mm)	0.0007-0.0015 (0.020-0.039)	0.0021 (0.055)	0.0007-0.0015 (0.020-0.039)	0.0021 (0.055)

1. 2000 Engine   4. 911T-C
2. 2000T Engine   5. 911E-C
3. 2000S Engine   6. 911S-C

NOTE: All dimensions are given in inches (mm) unless otherwise stated.

(continued)

Table 1 911 ENGINE SPECIFICATIONS (continued)

	2.0 Liter Engine Tolerance (New)	Wear Limit	2.2 Liter Engine Tolerance (New)	Wear Limit
CRANKSHAFT				
Number of main bearings	8		8	
Main bearing journal diameter				
Bearing journals 1-7	2.242-2.243 (56.971-56.990)	2.241 (56.960)	2.242-2.243 (56.971-56.990)	2.241 (56.960)
Bearing journal 8	1.219-1.220 (30.980-30.993)	1.218 (30.970)	1.219-1.220 (30.980-30.993)	1.218 (30.970)
Connecting rod journal diameter	2.242-2.243 (56.971-56.990)	2.241 (56.960)	2.242-2.243 (56.971-56.990)	2.241 (56.960)
Main bearing clearances				
Bearings 1-7	0.002-0.003 (0.049-0.069)		0.002-0.003 (0.049-0.069)	
Bearing 8	0.003-0.004 (0.061-0.091)		0.003-0.004 (0.061-0.091)	
End play	0.0043-0.0076 (0.110-0.195)		0.0043-0.0076 (0.110-0.195)	
CONNECTING RODS				
Weight deviation in same engine	9 grams		9 grams	
Side clearance	0.007-0.015 (0.200-0.400)		0.007-0.015 (0.200-0.400)	
Connecting rod bearing clearance	0.0011-0.0034 (0.30-0.088)		0.0011-0.0034 (0.30-0.088)	
Piston pin bushing inside diameter	0.8668-0.8673 (22.020-22.033)		0.8668-0.8673 (22.020-22.033)	
CAMSHAFT				
Number of camshafts	2		2	
Bearings per camshaft	3		3	
Journal diameter	1.8474-1.8481 (46.926-46.942)		1.8474-0.8481 (46.926-46.942)	
Bearing clearance	0.0009-0.0025 (0.025-0.066)	0.0039 (0.10)	0.0009-0.0025 (0.025-0.066)	0.0039 (0.10)
End play	0.0059-0.0078 (0.150-0.200)	0.0157 (0.40)	0.0059-0.0078 (0.150-0.200)	0.0157 (0.40)
Run-out		0.0007 (0.02)		0.0007 (0.02)
VALVES — INTAKE				
Valve guide inside diameter	0.3543-0.3548 (9.000-9.015)		0.3543-0.3548 (9.000-9.015)	
Valve face angle	45°		45°	
Valve seat angle	45°		45°	
Valve seat width	0.0492±0.0059 (1.25±0.15)		0.0492±0.0059 (1.25±0.15)	
VALVES — EXHAUST				
Valve guide inside diameter	0.3518-0.3523 (8.938-8.950)		0.3518-0.3523 (8.938-8.950)	
Valve face angle	45°		45°	
Valve seat angle	45°		45°	
Valve seat width	0.0610±0.0059 (1.55±0.15)		0.0610±0.0059 (1.55±0.15)	
VALVE SPRINGS				
Installed length, intake	1.417±0.012 (63±0.3)[1] 1.614±0.020 (41.0±0.5)[2] 1.398±0.020 (35.5±0.5)[3]		1.417±0.012 (36±0.3)[4,5] 1.398±0.020 (35.5±0.5)[6]	
Installed length, exhaust	1.417±0.012 (63±0.3)[1] 1.614±0.020 (41.0±0.5)[2] 1.378±0.012 (35±0.3)[3]		1.417±0.012 (36±0.3)[4] 1.378±0.012 (35±0.3)[5] 1.3593±0.012 (34.5±0.3)[6]	

(continued)

Table 1   911 ENGINE SPECIFICATIONS (continued)

2.4 LITER ENGINE

NOTE: All dimensions are given in **Inches (Millimeters)** unless otherwise stated.	Tolerance (New)	Wear Limit
General		
Number of cylinders	6	
Bore	3.31 (84)	
Stroke	2.77 (70.4)	
Displacement, cu. in. (cc)	142.8 (2.341)	
Compression ratio	7.5①, 8.0②, 8.5③	
Firing order	1-6-2-4-3-5	
Output (SAE) bhp @ rpm	157 @ 5,600①	
	185 @ 6,200②	
	210 @ 6,500③	
Torque (SAE) foot-pounds @ rpm	166 @ 4,000①	
	174 @ 4,500②	
	181 @ 5,200③	
Cylinders		
Bore	**See Table 5**	
Cylinder/piston clearance	0.0021-0.0029 (0.055-0.075)	0.0007 (0.02)
Out-of-round		0.0008 (0.02)
Pistons		
Material	Light alloy	
Permissible weight deviation	3 grams	
Diameter	**See Table 5**	
Piston Rings		
Number per piston		
Compression	2	
Oil control	1	
Ring end gap	0.0118-0.0177 (0.30-0.45)	0.394 (1.000)
Ring side clearance		
Top compression		0.0078 (0.20)
Bottom compression		0.0078 (0.20)
Oil control		0.0078 (0.20)
Piston Pins		
Diameter	0.8657-0.8661 (21.994-22.000)	
Clearance in rod bushing	0.0007-0.0015 (0.020-0.039)	0.0021 (0.055)

(continued)

Table 1   911 ENGINE SPECIFICATIONS (continued)

2.4 LITER ENGINE		
	Tolerance (New)	**Wear Limit**
Crankshaft		
Number of main bearings	8	
Main bearing journal diameter		
Bearing journal 1-7	2.242-2.243 (56.971-56.990)	2.241 (56.960)
Bearing journal 8	1.219-1.220 (30.980-30.993)	1.218 (30.970)
Connecting rod journal diameter	2.242-2.243 (56.971-56.990)	2.241 (56.960)
Main bearing clearances		
Bearings 1-7	0.002-0.003 (0.049-0.069)	
Bearing 8	0.003-0.004 (0.061-0.091)	
End play	0.0043-0.0076 (0.110-0.195)	
Connecting Rods		
Weight deviation in same engine	9 grams	
Side clearance	0.007-0.015 (0.200-0.400)	
Connecting rod bearing clearance	0.0011-0.0034 (0.030-0.088)	
Piston pin bushing inside diameter	0.8668-0.8673 (22.020-22.033)	
Camshaft		
Number of camshafts	2	
Bearings per camshaft	3	
Journal diameter	1.8474-1.8481 (46.926-46.942)	
Bearing clearance	0.0009-0.0025 (0.025-0.066)	0.0039 (0.10)
End play	0.0059-0.0078 (0.150-0.200)	0.016 (0.40)
Runout		0.0007 (0.02)
Valves — Intake		
Valve guide inside diameter	0.3543-0.3548 (9.000-9.015)	
Valve face angle	45°	
Valve seat angle	45°	
Valve seat width	0.0492 ± 0.0059 (1.25 ± 0.15)	
Valves — Exhaust		
Valve guide inside diameter	0.3518-0.3523 (8.938-8.950)	
Valve face angle	45°	
Valve seat angle	45°	
Valve seat width	0.0610 ± 0.0059 (1.55 ± 0.15)	
Valve Springs		
Installed length, intake	1.417 ± 0.012 (36 ± 0.3)①②	
	1.398 ± 0.020 (35.5 ± 0.5)③	
Installed length, exhaust	1.417 ± 0.012 (36 ± 0.3)①	
	1.378 ± 0.012 (35 ± 0.3)②	
	1.3593 ± 0.012 (34.5 ± 0.3)③	

① 911T-C   ② 911E-C   ③ 911S-C

(continued)

Table 1 911 ENGINE SPECIFICATIONS (continued)

2.7 LITER ENGINE

NOTE: All dimensions are given in **Inches (Millimeters)** unless otherwise stated.	Tolerance (New)	Wear Limit
General		
Number of cylinders	6	
Bore	3.54 (90)	
Stroke	2.77 (70.4)	
Displacement, cu. in. (cc)	164 (2,687)	
Compression ratio	8.5:1	
Firing order	1-6-2-4-3-5	
Output (SAE) bhp @ rpm	157 @ 5,800	
Torque (SAE) foot-pounds @ rpm	168 @ 4,000	
Cylinders		
Bore	**See Table 5**	
Cylinder/piston clearance	0.0010-0.0018 (0.025-0.045)	0.0031 (0.08)
Out-of-round		0.0016 (0.04)
Pistons		
Material	Light alloy	
Permissible weight deviation per set	6 grams	
Piston Rings		
Number per piston		
Compression	2	
Oil	1	
Ring end gap	0.0059-0.0177 (0.15-0.45)	0.394 (1.0)
Ring side clearance		
Top compression	0.0028-0.0040 (0.070-0.102)	0.0078 (0.20)
Bottom compression	0.0020-0.0032 (0.050-0.082)	0.0078 (0.20)
Oil control	0.0008-0.0020 (0.020-0.052)	0.0078 (0.20)
Piston Pins		
Diameter	0.8659-0.8661 (21.996-22.000)	
Clearance in rod bushing	0.0007-0.0015 (0.02-0.039)	0.0021 (0.05)

(continued)

Table 1   911 ENGINE SPECIFICATIONS (continued)

2.7 LITER ENGINE		
	Tolerance (New)	Wear Limit
Crankshaft		
Number of main bearings	8	
Main bearing journal diameter		
Bearing journals 1-7	2.242-2.243 (56.971-56.990)	2.241 (56.960)
Bearing journal 8	1.219-1.220 (30.980-30.993)	1.218 (30.970)
Connecting rod journal diameter	2.046-2.047 (51.971-51.990)	2.046 (51.960)
Main bearing clearances		
Bearing 1-7	0.0004-0.0028 (0.010-0.072)	
Bearing 8	0.0019-0.0040 (0.048-0.104)	
End play	0.0043-0.0077 (0.110-0.195)	0.0118 (0.30)
Connecting Rods		
Weight deviation in same engine	9 grams	
Side clearance	0.007-0.015 (0.200-0.400)	
Bearing clearance	0.0011-0.0034 (0.030-0.088)	
Piston pin bushing inside diameter	0.8668-0.8673 (22.020-22.033)	
Camshaft		
Number of camshafts	2	
Bearings per camshaft	3	
Journal diameter	1.8474-1.8481 (46.926-46.942)	
Bearing clearance	0.0009-0.0025 (0.025-0.066)	0.0039 (0.10)
End play	0.0059-0.0078 (0.150-0.200)	0.16 (0.40)
Runout		0.0007 (0.02)
Valves — Intake		
Valve guide inside diameter	0.3543-0.3548 (9.000-9.015)	
Valve face angle	45°	
Valve seat angle	45°	
Valve seat width	0.0591 ± 0.0059 (1.50 ± 0.15)	
Valves — Exhaust		
Valve guide inside diameter	0.3518-0.3523 (8.938-8.950)	
Valve face angle	45°	
Valve seat angle	45°	
Valve seat width	0.0591 ± 0.0059 (1.50 ± 0.15)	
Valve Springs		
Installed length, intake	1.3780 ± 0.0118 (35.0 ± 0.30)	
Installed length, exhaust	1.3976 ± 0.0118 (35.5 ± 0.30)	

(continued)

4

Table 1 ENGINE SPECIFICATIONS (continued)

Note: All dimensions are given in inches (mm) unless otherwise stated.	3.0 Liter Engine Tolerance (New)	Wear Limit
General		
Number of cylinders	6	
Bore	3.74 (95.0)	
Stroke	2.77 (70.4)	
Displacement, cu. in. (cc)	182.7 (2,994)	
Compression ratio	8.5:1	
Firing order	1-6-2-4-3-5	
Output (SAE) bhp @ rpm	180 @ 5,500	
Torque (SAE) foot-pounds @ rpm	175 @ 4,200	
Valves - Intake		
Head diameter	1.925-1.933 (48.9-49.1)	
Stem diameter	0.353-0.0005 (8.97-0.012)	
Valve guide inside diameter	0.3543-0.3548 (9.000-9.015)	
Valve face angle	45°	
Valve seat angle	45°	
Valve seat width	0.0591 ± 0.0059 (1.50 ± 0.15)	
Valves - Exhaust		
Head diameter	1.630-1.638 (41.4-41.6)	
Stem diameter	0.353-0.0005 (8.97-0.012)	
Valve guide inside diameter	0.3543-0.3548 (9.000-9.015)	
Valve face angle	45°	
Valve seat angle	45°	
Valve seat width	0.0591 ± 0.0059 (1.50 ± 0.15)	
Valve Springs		
Installed length, intake	1.358 ± 0.0118 (34.5 ± 0.3)	
Installed length, exhaust	1.358 ± 0.0118 (34.5 ± 0.3)	
Camshaft		
Number of camshafts	**2**	
Bearings per camshaft	**4**	
Journal diameter	**1.8474-1.8481 (46.926-46.942)**	
Bearing clearance	**0.0009-0.0025 (0.025-0.066)**	**0.0039 (0.10)**
End play	**0.0059-0.0078 (0.150-0.200)**	**0.016 (0.40)**
Runout		**0.0007 (0.02)**
Cylinders		
Bore	See text	
Cylinder/piston clearance	0.0009-0.0017 (0.023-0.044)	0.0031 (0.08)
Out-of-round		0.0016 (0.04)
Pistons		
Material	Light alloy	
Permissible weight deviation	6 grams	
Diameter	See text	

(continued)

Table 1 ENGINE SPECIFICATIONS (continued)

Note: All dimensions are given in inches (mm) unless otherwise stated.	3.0 LITER ENGINE Tolerance (New)	Wear Limit
Piston Rings		
Number per piston		
Compression	2	
Oil	1	
Compression ring end gap	0.0039-0.0079 (0.1-0.2)	0.031 (0.8)
Oil ring end gap	0.0059-0.0118 (0.15-0.30)	0.039 (1.0)
Ring side clearance		
Top compression	0.0028-0.0040 (0.070-0.102)	0.0078 (0.20)
Bottom compression	0.0016-0.0027 (0.040-0.072)	0.0078 (0.20)
Oil control	0.0008-0.0015 (0.020-0.052)	0.039 (0.10)
Piston Pins		
Diameter	0.8659-0.8661 (21.996-22.000)	
Clearance in rod bushing	0.0007-0.0015 (0.02-0.039)	0.0021 (0.05)
Crankshaft		
Number of main bearings	8	
Main bearing journal diameter		
Bearing journals 1-7	2.361-2.362 (59.971-59.990)	2.361 (59.960)
Bearing journal 8	1.219-1.220 (30.980-30.993)	1.218 (30.970)
Connecting rod journal diameter	2.085-2.086 (52.960-52.990)	2.085 (52.960)
Main bearing clearances		
Bearings 1-7	0.0004-0.0028 (0.010-0.072)	
Bearing 8	0.0019-0.0040 (0.048-0.104)	
End play	0.0043-0.0077 (0.110-0.195)	0.0118 (0.30)
Connecting Rods		
Weight deviation in same engine	9 grams	
Weight	645-727 grams	
Side clearance	0.007-0.015 (0.200-0.400)	
Bearing clearance	0.0011-0.0034 (0.030-0.088)	
Piston pin bushing inside diameter	0.8668-0.8673 (22.020-22.033)	

Table 2   VALVE GUIDES AND SEATS

	Standard	1st Oversize	2nd Oversize
1965-1969			
Valve seat, d_1			
Intake	1.66-1.6599 in. (42.180-42.164mm)	1.6732-1.6724 in. (42.500-42.484mm)	——
Exhaust	1.5039-1.5033 in. (38.200-38.184mm)	1.5259-1.5253 in. (38.760-38.744mm)	——
1965-1969			
Valve seat bore, D_1			
Intake	1.6535-1.6545 in. (42.000-42.025mm)	1.6661-1.6670 in. (42.320-42.345mm)	——
Exhaust	1.4960-1.4970 in. (38.000-38.025mm)	1.5180-1.5190 in. (38.560-38.585mm)	——

(continued)

Table 2 VALVE GUIDES AND SEATS (continued)

	Standard	1st Oversize	2nd Oversize
1970-1976			
Valve seat, d_1			
Intake	1.8968-1.8962 in. (88.180-48.164mm)	1.9094-1.9088 (48.500-48.484mm)	——
Exhaust	1.6614-1.6607 in. (42.200-42.184mm)	1.6835-1.6828 in. (42.760-42.744mm)	——
1970-1976			
Valve seat bore, D_1			
Intake	1.8898-1.8907 in. (48.000-48.025mm)	1.9024-1.9033 in. (48.320-48.345mm)	——
Exhaust	1.6535-1.6545 in. (42.000-42.025mm)	1.6756-1.6766 in. (42.560-42.585mm)	——
1965-1976			
Valve guide, d2	0.5141-0.5137 in. (13.060-13.049 mm)	Machine 1st or 2nd oversize to fit bore in cylinder head. Press fit: 0.002-0.004 in. (0.06-0.09 mm)	——
Valve guide bore, D2	0.5118-0.5125 in. (13.000-13.018 mm)		——
Valve guide bore, g	0.3545-0.3549 in. (9.000-9.015 mm)		——
1977-on			
Valve seat, d1			
Intake	2.034-2.035 in. (51.661-51.680 mm)	2.046-2.047 in. (51.980-52.000 mm)	——
Exhaust	1.739-1.740 in. (44.184-44.200 mm)	1.761-1.762 in. (44.744-44.760 mm)	——
Valve seat bore, D1			
Intake	2.028-2.029 in. (51.500-51.530 mm)	2.040-2.041 in. (51.820-51.850 mm)	——
Exhaust	1.732-1.733 in. (44.000-44.025 mm)	(1.754-1.755 in. (44.560-44.585 mm)	——
Valve guide, d2	0.5141-0.5137 in. (13.060-13.049 mm)	0.5220-0.5216 in. (1) (13.260-13.249 mm)	——
Valve guide bore, D2	0.5118-0.5125 in. (13.000-13.018 mm)	0.5196-0.5203 in. (2) (13.200-13.218 mm)	——
Valve guide bore, g	0.3545-0.3549 in. (9.000-9.015 mm)		——

Table 3 VALVE OVERLAP (1965-1976)

See text, under Valve Timing		
Engine	Acceptable Overlap Range	Preferred Overlap
2000 (up to Engine No. 909927)	0.165-0.181 in. (4.2-4.6mm)	0.169 in. (4.3mm)
2000 (from Engine No. 909927)	0.118-0.130 in. (3.0-3.3mm)	0.124 in. (3.15mm)
2000S	0.197-0.213 in. (5.0-5.4mm)	0.205 in. (5.2mm)
2000T	0.091-0.106 in. (2.3-2.7mm)	0.098 in. (2.5mm)
911T-C	0.091-0.106 in. (2.3-2.7mm)	0.098 in. (2.5mm)
911E-C	0.118-0.130 in. (3.0-3.3mm)	0.124 in. (3.15mm)
911S-C	0.197-0.213 in. (5.0-5.4mm)	0.205 in. (5.2mm)
911 2.7 CIS	0.028-0.035 in. (0.7-0.9mm)	0.032 in (0.8mm)
911S 2.7 CIS	**0.016-0.024 in. (0.4-0.6mm)**	0.020 in. (0.5mm)

Table 4 VALVE OVERLAP (1977-ON)

See text, under Valve Timing	
Year	Overlap
1977	0.019 in. (0.47 mm)
1978-1979	0.039 in. (1.0 mm)
1980-on	0.055-0.067 in. (1.4-1.7 mm)

Table 5 STANDARD CYLINDER AND PISTON DIAMETERS*

	Minus 1	0	Plus 1	Plus 2	Plus 3
Cylinders					
1965-1967	79.990-80.000	80.000-80.010	80.010-80.020	-	-
1968-1969	-	80.000-80.010	80.010-80.020	80.020-80.030	-
1970-1973	-	84.000-84.010	84.010-84.020	84.020-84.030	-
1974-1977	-	90.000-90.010	90.010-90.020	90.020-90.030	-
1978-on	-	95.000-95.007	95.007-95.014	95.014-95.021	95.021-95.028
Pistons					
1965-1967	-	79.925-79.935	79.935-79.945	79.945-79.955	-
1968 911S	-	79.945-79.955	79.955-79.965	79.965-79.975	-
1968 911L	-	79.955-79.965	79.965-79.075	79.985-79.995	-
1968-1969					
911T (Mahle)	-	79.965-79.975	79.975-79.985	79.985-79.995	-
911T (Schmidt)	-	79.955-79.965	79.965-79.975	79.975-79.985	-
1969 911E	-	79.945-79.955	79.955-79.965	79.965-79.975	-
1969 911S	-	79.935-79.945	79.945-79.955	79.955-79.965	-
1970-1973					
911T (Mahle)	-	83.952-83.967	83.962-83.977	83.972-83.987	-
911T (Schmidt)	-	83.965-83.975	83.975-83.985	83.985-83.995	-
911E	-	83.955-83.965	83.965-83.975	83.975-83.985	-
911S	-	83.945-83.955	83.955-83.965	83.965-83.975	-
1974-1977					
911, 911S					
Nikasil cyl.	-	89.965-89.975	89.975-89.985	89.985-89.995	-
Alusil cyl.	-	89.952-89.967	89.962-89.977	89.972-89.987	-
1978-on	-	94.463-94.977	94.970-94.984	94.977-94.991	94.984-94.998
* All dimensions are in millimeters.					

Table 6 OVERSIZE CYLINDER AND PISTON DIAMETERS

Note: All Dimensions are in Millimeters				
	−1KD1	0KD1	1KD1	2KD1
CYLINDERS				
1965-1967	80.490-80.500	80.500-80.510	80.510-80.520	—
1968-1969	—	80.500-80.510	80.510-80.520	80.520-80.530
1970-1973	—	84.250-84.260	84.260-84.270	84.270-84.280
PISTONS				
1965-1967	80.425-80.435	80.435-80.445	80.445-80.455	—
1968 911S	—	80.445-80.455	80.455-80.465	80.465-80.475
1968 911L	—	80.455-80.465	80.465-80.475	80.475-80.485
1968-1969				
911T (Mahle)	—	80.865-80.875	80.875-80.885	80.885-80.895
911T (Schmidt)	—	80.455-80.465	80.465-80.475	804.75-80.485
1969 911E	—	80.445-80.455	80.455-80.465	80.465-80.475
1969 911S	—	80.435-80.845	80.445-80.455	80.455-80.465
1970-1973				
911T (Mahle)	—	84.202-84.217	80.212-84.227	84.222-84.237
911T (Schmidt)	—	84.215-84.225	84.225-84.235	84.235-84.245
911E	—	84.205-84.215	84.215-84.225	84.225-84.235
911S	—	84.195-84.205	84.205-84.215	84.215-84.225

Table 7 PISTON PIN SIZES

Color Code	Piston Pin Diameter	Bushing Diameter
White	21.996-22.000mm	21.995-22.000mm
Black	21.997-22.006mm	21.997-22.006mm

Table 8 CONNECTING ROD WEIGHTS

Engine	Weights Available①
2.0 liter	551-659
2.2 liter	700-772
2.4 liter	645-717
2.7, 3.0 liter	**645-717**

① In 9 gram increments from first weight given

Table 9 CRANKCASE SIZES

Crankcase Number	Crankshaft Gear Number	Intermediate Gear Number	Gear Backlash
0	0	0	0.00114-0.00193″ (0.029-0.049mm)
	1	0	0.00063-0.00165″ (0.016-0.42mm)
	0	1	0.00067-0.00169″ (0.017-0.043mm)
	1	1	Not possible
1	0	0	Not possible
	1	1	0.00047-0.00161″ (0.012-0.041mm)
	0	1	0.00098-0.00193″ (0.025-0.049mm)
	1	0	0.00098-0.00189″ (0.025-0.048mm)

COOLING, HEATING AND EXHAUST SYSTEMS

The engine cooling, heating and exhaust systems on a Porsche are closely related. A large fan directs fresh air to the engine for cooling. In addition, fresh air from the fan passes through heat exchangers where it is heated by the engine exhaust for use in the passenger area.

Figure 1 and **Figure 2** show a typical complete passenger compartment heating system. The cooling fan draws fresh outside air into the engine compartment to cool the engine. A duct (3) directs a portion of the fan output to the heat exchangers (4). Exhaust gases from the cylinders pass through the heat exchangers to the muffler and heat the fresh air. The heated air from the heat exchangers passes though heater control boxes (8), sound mufflers (10) and into the passenger area.

A steady fresh air flow passes through the heat exchangers. Varying the heater control lever in the passenger area directs either more or less of this air flow into the passenger area. Some of the flow is directed to defrost the rear window (12, **Figure 1**; 1965-1967 models only) and the remainder discharges into the outside air.

An auxiliary gasoline powered heater is installed as an option. A fan in the heater draws air through the vent in the rear of the passenger area (**Figure 3**). This air passes through the gasoline fired heat exchanger and back into the passenger area through the fresh air outlets. Air required for combustion in the heater is drawn from the right wheel well and heater exhaust gases pass through a muffler to the outside air.

The exhaust system on all models is straightforward, with all exhaust passing through the heat exchangers to the muffler.

COOLING SYSTEM

Models through 1977 use an 11-blade 242 mm cooling fan. The fan size is reduced to 226 mm on 1978-1979 models and increased in size to 245 mm on 1980 and later models. The 245 mm fan requires a 9.5 x 710 mm drive belt.

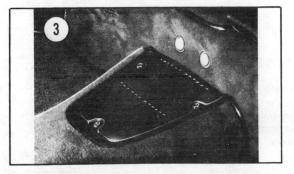

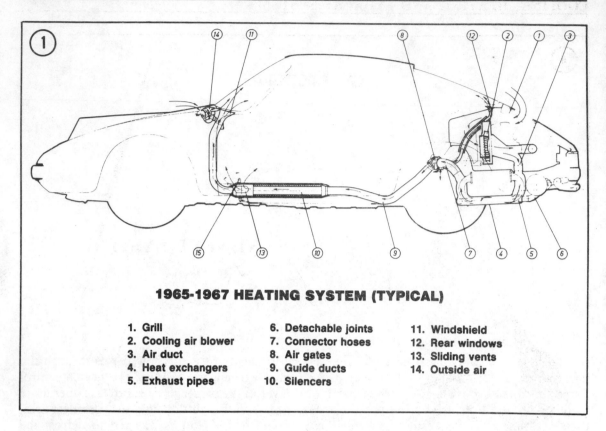

1965-1967 HEATING SYSTEM (TYPICAL)

1. Grill
2. Cooling air blower
3. Air duct
4. Heat exchangers
5. Exhaust pipes
6. Detachable joints
7. Connector hoses
8. Air gates
9. Guide ducts
10. Silencers
11. Windshield
12. Rear windows
13. Sliding vents
14. Outside air

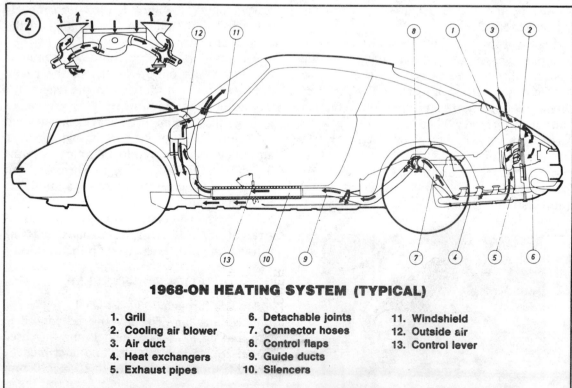

1968-ON HEATING SYSTEM (TYPICAL)

1. Grill
2. Cooling air blower
3. Air duct
4. Heat exchangers
5. Exhaust pipes
6. Detachable joints
7. Connector hoses
8. Control flaps
9. Guide ducts
10. Silencers
11. Windshield
12. Outside air
13. Control lever

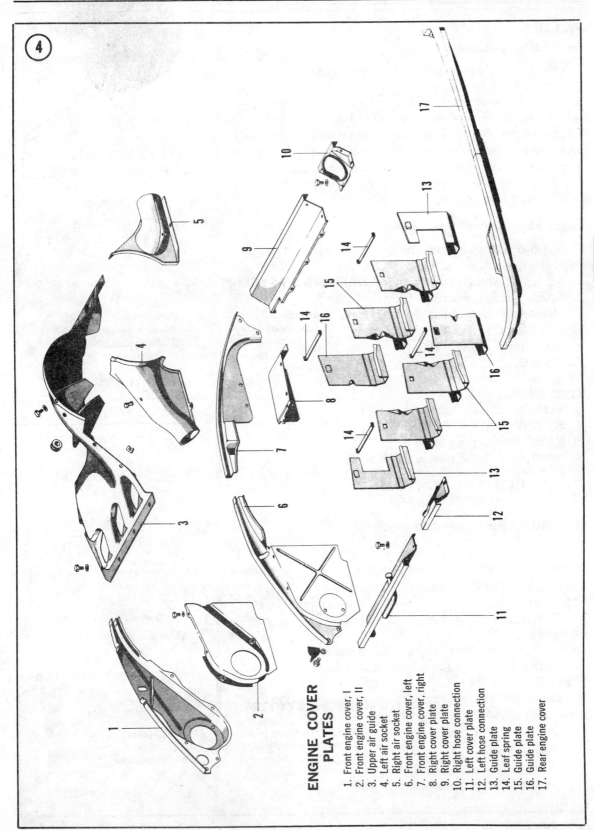

ENGINE COVER PLATES

1. Front engine cover, I
2. Front engine cover, II
3. Upper air guide
4. Left air socket
5. Right air socket
6. Front engine cover, left
7. Front engine cover, right
8. Right cover plate
9. Right cover plate
10. Right hose connection
11. Left cover plate
12. Left hose connection
13. Guide plate
14. Leaf spring
15. Guide plate
16. Guide plate
17. Rear engine cover

Cooling Fan
Removal/Installation

This procedure is possible while the engine is installed. The cooling fan and alternator must be removed as an assembly. To do this, follow the alternator removal procedure in Chapter Eight. Once this is done, remove nuts securing the alternator/fan to the fan housing and remove the fan housing. Installation is the reverse. Be sure that you adjust the fan belt tension as described in Chapter Three.

Cover Plate Removal/Installation

This procedure assumes that the engine has been removed. Refer to **Figure 4**.
1. Remove carburetors and intake manifolds.
2. Remove rear cover plate. See (1), **Figure 5**.
3. Disconnect fuel lines passing over fan housing. See (2), **Figure 5**.
4. Disconnect both air hoses to heat exchangers.
5. Remove all screws attaching fiberglass upper air channel.
6. Remove left and right heater ducts.
7. Remove front cover plates.
8. Remove side cover plate.
9. Installation is the reverse of these steps.

EXHAUST POWERED
HEATING SYSTEM

Heat Exchanger Removal/Installation

1. Remove muffler as described in this chapter.
2. Disconnect hot air outlet hose from front of heat exchanger.
3. Disconnect fresh air hose from side of heat exchanger.
4. Remove 3 lower mounting bolts as shown in **Figure 6**. Remove 6 flange nuts as shown in **Figure 7**.
5. Check carefully for leaks in the exhaust pipe running through the exchanger.

> *WARNING*
> *Exhaust leaks can allow poisonous fumes to enter passenger area. Replace defective heat exchangers immediately.*

6. Installation is the reverse of these steps. Use new gaskets.

Heater Control Cable Replacement

1. Disconnect cable ends from heat control boxes. See **Figure 8**.
2. Remove gearshift housing as described in Chapter Ten.
3. Lift heater control lever slightly and disconnect cable. See **Figure 9**.
4. Pull cable out of tunnel from either end.
5. Connect end of new cable to lever.

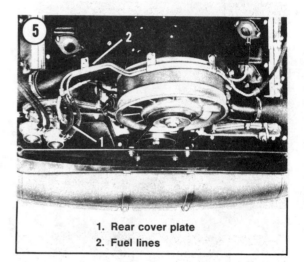

1. Rear cover plate
2. Fuel lines

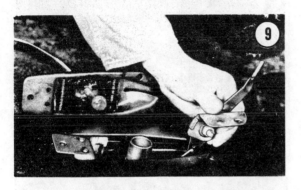

1. Heater hose	3. Glow plug
2. Clamp	4. Series resistor

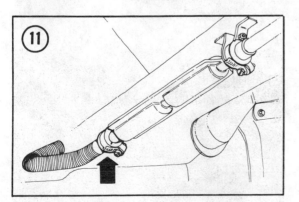

6. Insert heater control box end into guide tube. Make sure that the ends are not entangled.

7. Install gearshift housing as described in Chapter Ten.

8. Push heat control lever all the way forward.

9. Connect cables to heater control boxes.

10. Operate the lever and ensure that both control boxes work smoothly.

GASOLINE HEATER
(OPTIONAL)

The gasoline heater is accessible through the front luggage compartment. A defective heater should be repaired by a Porsche dealer.

Removal/Installation

1. Disconnect battery ground cable(s).

2. Remove front luggage compartment carpet.

3. Open heater compartment.

4. Disconnect heater hose. See **Figure 10**.

5. Remove 3 bolts securing heater fuel pump bracket.

6. Lift pump out and disconnect all hoses and wires.

7. Loosen front clamp on heater exhaust muffler. Disconnect exhaust pipe and bend it down. See **Figure 11**.

8. Remove clamp (**Figure 10**) and slide white collar onto heater.

9. Disconnect wire at glow plug and all wires from series resistor. See **Figure 10**.

10. Carefully lift heater out.

11. Remove protective cover from terminal block. Remove and mark all wires from terminal block.

12. Installation is the reverse of these steps.

Glow Plug Check/Replacement

1. Disconnect battery ground cable(s).

2. Remove front luggage compartment carpet.

3. Open heater comparment.

4. Disconnect glow plug wires. See **Figure 10**.

5. Unscrew glow plug from heater.

5

6. Connect glow plug as shown in **Figure 12**. Voltmeter must read 3.8-4.5 volts.

7. Glow plug must get red hot within 7 seconds. If necessary, replace with BERO 129 G 4, 4-volt glow plug.

8. Install by reversing Steps 1-5 above.

EXHAUST SYSTEM

Muffler Replacement

Figure 13 shows the 911 engine exhaust system.

1. Remove bolts joining muffler to heat exchangers. See **Figure 14**.

2. Remove bolts on mounting bands.

3. Remove muffler.

4. Installation is the reverse of these steps. Use new gaskets.

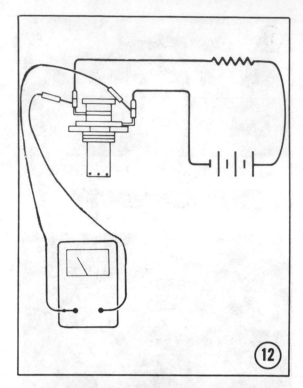

THERMAL REACTORS

All 1975-1977 911 models originally sold in California are equipped with thermal reactors. This device essentially consists of 2 cylinders, one inside the other. See **Figure 15**. The inner cylinder (2, **Figure 15**) contains the combustion chamber. The outside wall of the outer cylinder (1) is covered with an insulating material. The inner cylinder is perforated with a series of holes (5). The hot exhaust gas, which is mixed with air supplied by the secondary air injection pump, enters the combustion chamber (3), via the exhaust pipe (4). Gas is expelled through the holes into the outer chamber space (6), and exits through the outlet port (7). The arrangement of the holes in the wall of the inner chamber slows the flow of gas, allowing the after-burning process to take place. This reduces the emission of pollutants.

CATALYTIC CONVERTER

A catalytic converter is used on all 1978 and later models. The converter is installed in place of the primary muffler (**Figure 16**). If converter service is required, see your Porsche dealer.

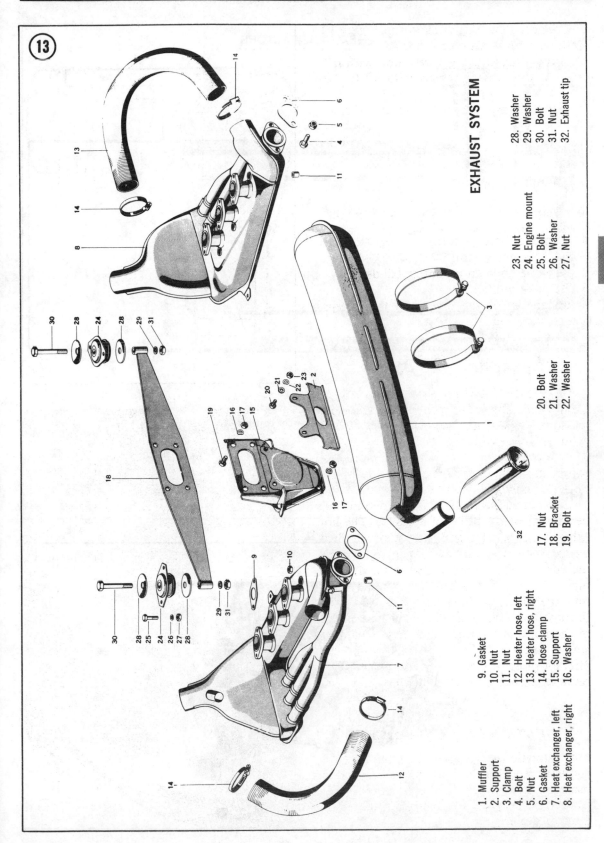

EXHAUST SYSTEM

1. Muffler
2. Support
3. Clamp
4. Bolt
5. Nut
6. Gasket
7. Heat exchanger, left
8. Heat exchanger, right
9. Gasket
10. Nut
11. Nut
12. Heater hose, left
13. Heater hose, right
14. Hose clamp
15. Support
16. Washer
17. Nut
18. Bracket
19. Bolt
20. Bolt
21. Washer
22. Washer
23. Nut
24. Engine mount
25. Bolt
26. Washer
27. Nut
28. Washer
29. Washer
30. Bolt
31. Nut
32. Exhaust tip

5

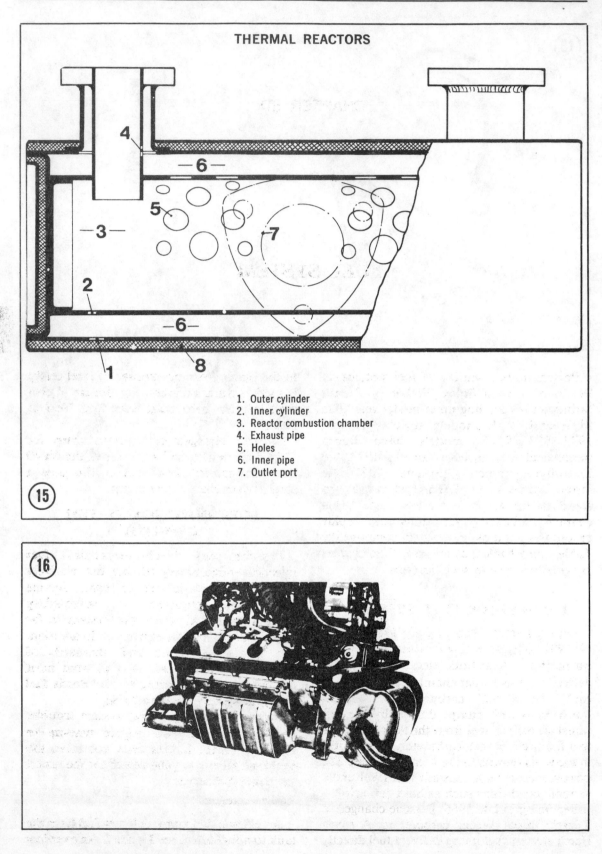

THERMAL REACTORS

1. Outer cylinder
2. Inner cylinder
3. Reactor combustion chamber
4. Exhaust pipe
5. Holes
6. Inner pipe
7. Outlet port

⑮

⑯

FUEL SYSTEM

Porsche uses a variety of fuel systems. A 911 may have a Solex, Weber or Zenith carburetor, depending upon model year. The 911E and 911S models since 1969 and 1972-1973 911T models have Bosch mechanical fuel injection. In mid-1973, the Continuous Injection System (CIS) was introduced on the 911T. This system has been standard on all 911 models since. This chapter includes descriptions and repair procedures for most fuel system components. **Table 1** and **Table 2** at the end of the chapter provide fuel system specifications.

CARBURETOR FUEL SYSTEMS

Porsches from 1965 to early 1966 (engine No. 907.000) use 6 single throat Solex 40 PI carburetors. A Bendix electric fuel pump delivers fuel to a float chamber at the base of each bank of carburetors. Tandem mechanical fuel pumps driven by the left camshaft deliver fuel from the float chambers to a fuel well in each carburetor. Surplus fuel in the wells returns to the float chambers. The system maintains a constant fuel level under extreme conditions such as hard cornering.

Beginning in late 1966, Porsche changed to 2 triple throat Weber carburetors. A single Hardi electric fuel pump delivers fuel directly to the carburetors; no mechanical fuel pump is used. Several different, but similar, Weber models have been used from late 1966 to 1969.

Porsche changed carburetors again for 1970-1972 models to 2 triple throat Zenith 40 TIN carburetors. This system also uses a single Hardi electric fuel pump.

FUEL INJECTION SYSTEM
(1969-1973)

Porsche uses Bosch mechanical fuel injection which is very reliable, but relatively complicated and delicate to repair. Service information required to successfully troubleshoot and repair the system is far beyond the scope of this manual. In addition, the specialized tools and standards of cleanliness required are beyond what most owners possess. Fortunately, the Bosch fuel injection system is very reliable.

Before suspecting a fuel system trouble, perform the *complete* engine tune-up in Chapter Three. If this does not solve the problem, take it to your dealer for the expert attention it deserves.

Basic Principles

An electric fuel pump delivers fuel from the tank to a fuel filter. See **Figure 1**. An overflow

FUEL INJECTION SYSTEM (1969-1973)

1. Fuel delivery pump
2. Fuel tank
3. Fuel Filter
4. Solenoid for cold starting unit

5. Injection valve
6. Injection line
7. Injection pump

valve in the fuel filter establishes 12 psi fuel pressure to the injection pump. A bypass valve in the fuel filter returns fuel to the tank if pressure attempts to exceed 14 psi.

A double row 6-plunger injection pump, driven by the left engine camshaft, delivers fuel at carefully timed intervals to the cylinders. The plungers admit fuel through equal length lines to injection valves in the cylinder heads. These valves maintain injection fuel pressure at 213-256 psi. The fuel injects behind each intake valve just as it opens.

A number of factors determine the actual quantity of fuel injected. See **Figure 2**. A centrifugal governor moves a contoured cam axially according to engine speed. Throttle linkage transmits accelerator position by rotating the cam on its axis. A sensor rides on the contoured cam and transfers combined engine speed/load information via the control rack to the plungers to vary their fuel output.

Outside atmospheric pressure also affects injected fuel volume. A barometric cell which operates in the same manner as an aneroid barometer transmits barometric pressure through levers to the control rack. At higher pressures, more fuel is injected; at lower pressures, less fuel is injected.

A thermostat on the injection pump varies the fuel volume injected depending on engine cooling air temperature. A portion of the cooling air from a heat exchanger is ducted to the thermostat through a hose. When the engine is cold, the thermostat moves the control rack to its richest position. As the engine warms, the thermostat reduces enrichment. At 113° F (1965-1969) or 127° F (1970-1973), the thermostat has no further effect on enrichment.

A solenoid moves the control rack so that fuel delivery is shut off when the engine is coasting. A microswitch on the intake stack senses when the throttle is closed. An rpm transducer connected to the ignition coil senses engine speed. When the throttle is closed *and* engine speed is above 1,500 rpm, the shut-off solenoid energizes and shuts off fuel delivery. When engine speed drops below 1,300 rpm, regardless of throttle position, the shut-off solenoid releases and fuel delivery

resumes to produce a smooth transition to idle.

For cold starts on 2 liter engines, an enrichment solenoid increases the fuel volume injected. A time-limit relay operates the solenoid for 2 seconds at each start, regardless of temperature. A thermoswitch keeps the solenoid energized for a longer period when the air temperature in the crankcase is between -14° F and 50° F (-25° C and 10° C). When air temperature in the crankcase is between -22° F and 14° F (-30° C and -10° C) another thermoswitch operates a cold start valve on the fuel filter which sprays fuel directly into the intake stacks. For cold starts on 2.2 liter engines, a thermoswitch in the breather cover operates the cold start valve. This valve operates when crankcase air temperature is below 113° F (45° C).

CIS FUEL INJECTION
(1973-ON)

The continuous injection system (CIS), introduced in 1973 on the 911T and standard on all 1974-on 911 models, is a relatively simple system (**Figure 3**). Fuel is delivered from the fuel tank to the fuel distributor by an electric fuel pump via a fuel accumulator and a fuel filter. The fuel accumulator improves hot starting by maintaining fuel line pressure after the engine is shut off, thus avoiding fuel vaporization and vapor lock. Air enters the engine via the air venturi, and the quantity of air required is measured by the air flow sensor. The fuel distributor then meters fuel to each cylinder in accordance with the amount of air flow. Cold starting is assisted by the cold start valve, which injects additional fuel into the intake manifold, a control pressure regulator which also provides additional fuel when the engine is cold, and the auxiliary air regulator which supplies additional air during the warm-up phase. A pressure relief valve limits the pressure in the system to a predetermined value and allows excess fuel to flow back to the fuel tank.

Service of the CIS elements, other than changing fuel filters, requires special tools and/or knowledge and should be performed by a dealer.

6

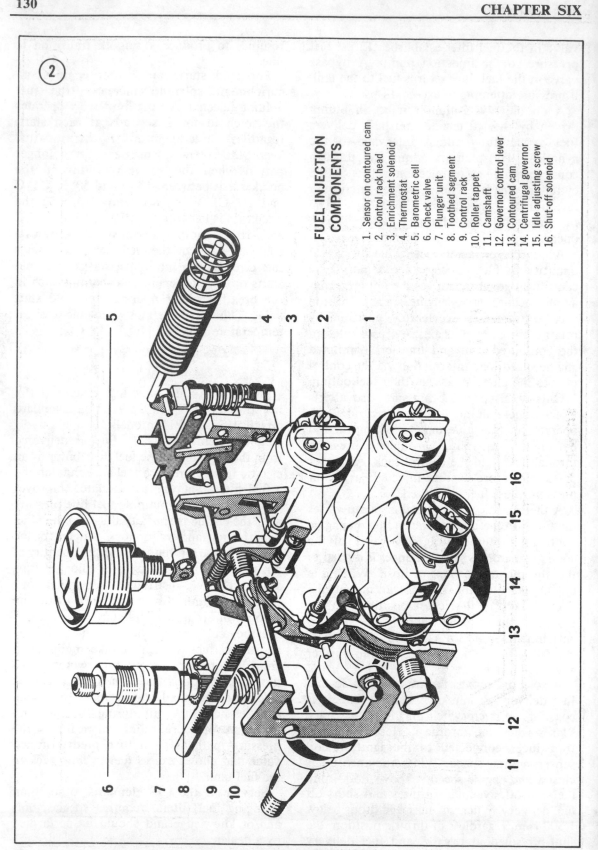

②

FUEL INJECTION COMPONENTS

1. Sensor on contoured cam
2. Control rack head
3. Enrichment solenoid
4. Thermostat
5. Barometric cell
6. Check valve
7. Plunger unit
8. Toothed segment
9. Control rack
10. Roller tappet
11. Camshaft
12. Governor control lever
13. Contoured cam
14. Centrifugal governor
15. Idle adjusting screw
16. Shut-off solenoid

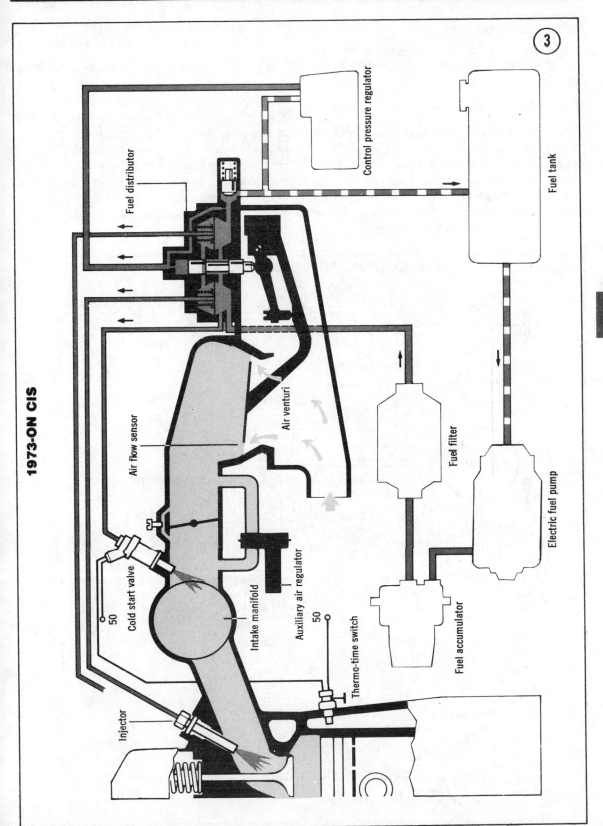

1973-ON CIS

Idle Speed Adjustment

Idle speed is adjusted by turning the idle speed screw located on the throttle valve housing.

Carbon Monoxide Value

An exhaust analyzer that reads out in percentage of carbon monoxide (CO) is required. Follow manufacturer's instructions for set-up and operation of analyzer. The CO content of the exhaust is adjusted by turning a CO adjustment screw which is located under a rubber plug in the fuel distributor.

FUEL EVAPORATIVE CONTROL SYSTEM

All 1970-on Porsches are equipped with a fuel evaporative control system to prevent the release of fuel vapor into the atmosphere.

Refer to **Figure 4**. Fuel vapor from the fuel tank passes through the expansion tank to the activated charcoal filter. When the engine runs, cool air from the fan housing forces the fuel vapor into the air cleaner. Instead of being released into the atmosphere, the fuel vapor takes part in the normal combustion process.

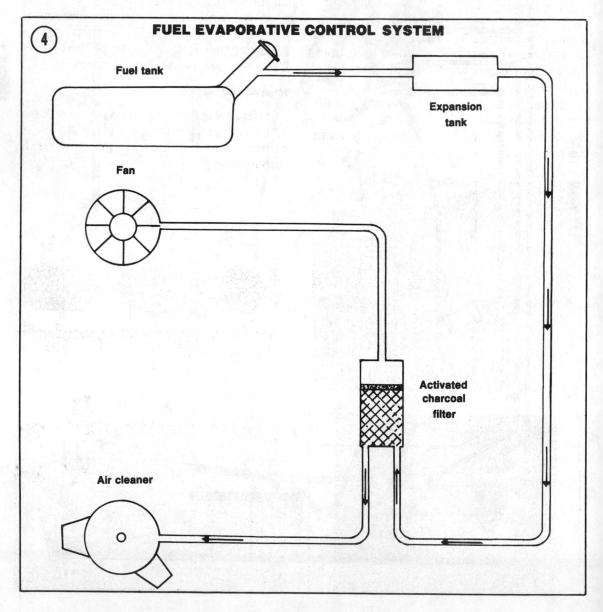

FUEL EVAPORATIVE CONTROL SYSTEM

④ Fuel tank
Expansion tank
Fan
Activated charcoal filter
Air cleaner

There is no preventive maintenance other than checking the tightness and condition of the lines connecting parts of the system. The expansion tank and activated charcoal filter are located in the front luggage compartment.

AIR CLEANER

All 911 models use a disposable paper cartridge. See Chapter Three for replacement.

Removal/Installation

This procedure describes the entire air cleaner housing's removal and installation.

1. Disconnect preheater hose from air cleaner. See **Figure 5**.

2. Disconnect crankcase breather hose from back of air cleaner. See **Figure 6**. Clean flame arrester as described in Chapter Three.

3. Unsnap 4 clips at each carburetor and lift air cleaner off.

4. Remove nuts securing air cleaner bases to carburetors. Lift bases off.

5. Installation is the reverse of these steps. Ensure that gaskets are in good condition.

SOLEX 40 PI CARBURETOR

Removal/Installation

1. Remove hot air duct from air cleaner.

2. Loosen clamps and remove air cleaner.

3. Disconnect throttle linkage from carburetor.

4. Pull float bowl vent hose off.

5. Remove retaining nuts (**Figure 7**) and lift air horns off.

6. Remove carburetor retaining nuts and lift carburetor off. See **Figure 8**.

7. Cover carburetor and intake openings to prevent entry of dirt and loose parts.

8. Installation is the reverse of these steps. Use a new gasket. Adjust idle speed.

Disassembly

Refer to **Figure 9** for following procedures.

1. Clean away all dirt on outside of carburetor body. Do not get any inside carburetor.

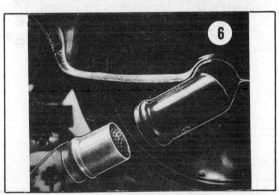

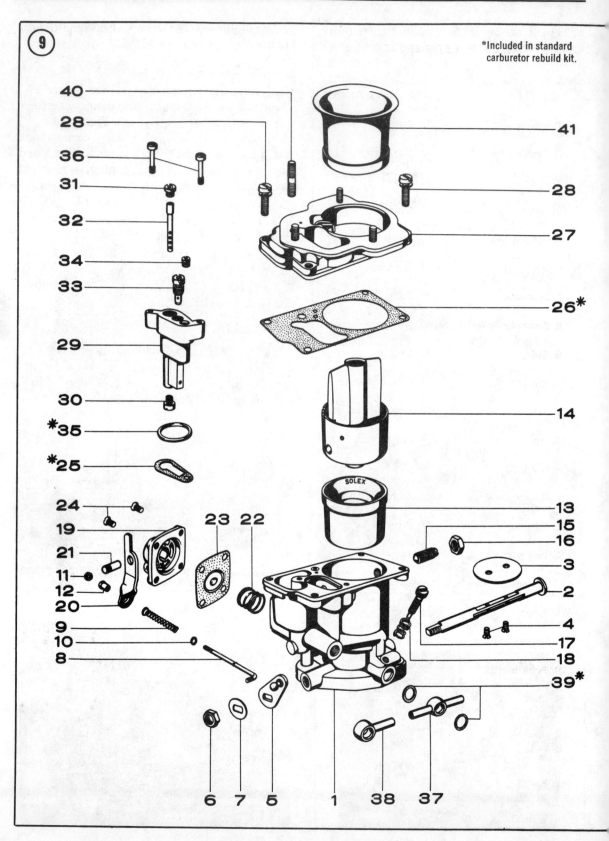

⑨

*Included in standard
carburetor rebuild kit.

SOLEX PI CARBURETOR

1. Housing	22. Spring
2. Throttle shaft	23. Diaphragm
4. Screw	24. Screw
5. Throttle arm	25. Gasket
3. Butterfly valve	26. Gasket
6. Nut	27. Top cover
7. Lockwasher	28. Screw
8. Accelerator linkage	29. Jet carrier
9. Spring	30. Main jet
10. Washer	31. Air correction jet
11. Nut	32. Emulsion tube
12. Nut	33. Idle metering jet
13. Nut	34. Idle air jet
14. Pre-atomizer	35. O-ring
15. Setscrew	36. Screw
16. Lock nut	37. Banjo
17. Idle mixture screw	38. Banjo
18. Spring	39. Seal
19. Accelerator pump cover	40. Stud
20. Pump lever	41. Velocity stock
21. Shaft	

2. Remove cover screws (**Figure 10**) and remove cover (**Figure 11**).
3. Remove screws securing jet carrier and remove carrier. See **Figure 12**.
4. Unscrew idle metering jet. See **Figure 13**.
5. Remove air correction jet and carefully shake out emulsion tube. See **Figure 13**.
6. Remove idle air jet on early carburetors. See **Figure 13**. Later carburetors have a bleed jet bored in carrier and a plug is inserted where the jet used to be.
7. Remove main jet. See **Figure 13**.

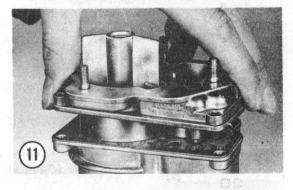

8. Remove idle mixture adjustment (**Figure 14**).

9. Loosen locknut and screw and remove preatomizer. See **Figure 15**.

10. Remove venturi.

11. Remove accelerator pump adjusting nuts. See **Figure 16**.

12. Unscrew screws securing accelerator pump cover and remove it. See **Figure 17**

13. Remove the accelerator pump diaphragm and spring.

Cleaning

1. Clean all parts in solvent.

2. Clean jets and drillings in the carburetor body with compressed air. Do not clean them with pins or pieces of wire; you might enlarge the holes.

Inspection and Reassembly

Refer to **Figure 9** for following procedure.

> *NOTE*
> *Use all new parts included in a standard rebuild kit, Porsche Part No. 901.108.945.00; this kit includes parts for all 6 carburetors. Asterisks identify these parts on **Figure 9**.*

1. Check throttle shaft for wear.

2. Hold carburetor up to light, close throttle. No light should be visible around throttle valve.

3. Install diaphragm and spring for accelerator pump.

4. Examine idle mixture adjustment screw. If not bent or scored, install it with spring in carburetor body.

5. Install venturi and preatomizer in carburetor body. Secure with locknut and screw.

6. Install main jet, idle air jet (if removable), idle metering jet, emulsion tube and air correction jet in jet carrier.

7. Install jet carrier with new O-ring and gasket. Tighten screws finger-tight, then tighten alternately 1/4 turn at a time until they are tight.

> *NOTE*
> *Uneven tightening can damage gasket and lead to high fuel consumption.*

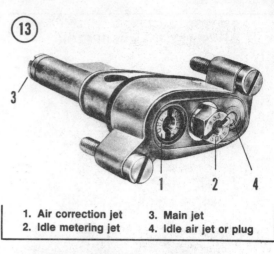

1. Air correction jet	3. Main jet
2. Idle metering jet	4. Idle air jet or plug

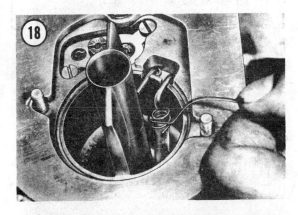

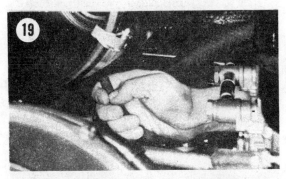

Accelerator Pump Adjustment

This procedure requires use of an auxiliary electric fuel pump in place of the mechanical fuel pump. If you cannot get one, let your dealer do this job.

1. Remove air cleaner assembly.
2. Disconnect throttle linkage.
3. Disconnect fuel lines from mechanical fuel pump and connect an electric fuel pump in its place. Connect the electric pump to terminal 15 on the coil.
4. Switch ignition on but do not start engine. Ensure that fuel pump works.
5. Hold a very small graduate below the injector nozzle. See **Figure 18**.
6. Operate the throttle twice through its entire range. The pump should deliver: 0.40-0.50 cc during summer; 0.55-0.65 cc during winter.
7. Loosen locknut and adjust length of rod as necessary. See **Figure 16**.

NOTE
If you run out of threads and cannot make adjustment, add small shims under nut.

8. Check and adjust all 6 accelerator pumps so they deliver the same fuel quantity.
9. Reconnect mechanical fuel pump and throttle linkage. Install air cleaner.

WEBER CARBURETORS

Removal/Installation

1. Disconnect the condensation hose from the air cleaner. See **Figure 19**.
2. Unsnap air cleaner cover and remove air cleaner element.
3. Unsnap the air cleaner ducts from the top of the carburetors.
4. Disconnect fuel lines from carburetors.
5. Disconnect throttle linkage from carburetors. See **Figure 20**.
6. Remove the retaining nuts and lift the carburetor(s) off.

CAUTION
Do not let lockwashers or other loose parts fall into intake manifolds.

7. Cover intake manifolds (**Figure 21**) to prevent entry of dirt and loose parts.

8. Installation is the reverse of these steps. Clean carburetor base and manifold surfaces and use new gaskets. Adjust idle speed.

Disassembly

Each Weber carburetor consists of 3 nearly identical throats. To aid reassembly, keep parts from the 3 throats in 3 separate containers. Keep parts common to all throats in a fourth container.

Refer to **Figure 22** for the following procedure.

1. Remove 10 nuts securing top of carburetor and lift top off. See **Figure 23**.

2. Remove hollow bolts securing fuel line to top of carburetor. See **Figure 24**.

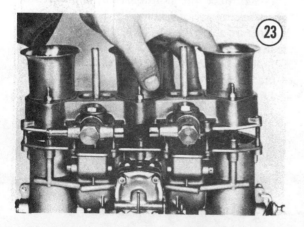

(22)

WEBER CARBURETOR

1. Cover	40. Screw
2. Stud	41. Lever
3. Velocity stack	42. Linkage
4. Nut	43. O-ring
5. Needle valve	44. Shear pin
6. Seal	45. Throttle valves
7. Plug	46. Screw
8. Seal	47. Nut
9. T-fitting	48. Spacer
10. Banjo	49. Lever (left)
11. Seal	50. Lever (right)
12. Filter	51. Spacer
13. Seal	52. Spring
14. Plug	53. Spring
15. Float	54. Adjustment screw
16. Stud	55. Inspection screw
17. Seal	56. Nut
18. Float pin	57. Adjustment screw
19. Spring	58. Setscrew
20. Throttle shaft (40 IDT)	59. Seal
21. Throttle shaft (40 IDT)	60. Main jet
22. Stud	61. Jet support
23. Stud	62. Idle screw
24. Spring	63. Gasket
25. Valve	64. Plug
26. Inner diaphragm	65. Idle jet
27. Pump body	66. Jet support
28. Spring	67. Venturi
29. Outer diaphragm	68. Pre-atomizer
30. Accelerator pump cover (left)	69. Gasket
31. Accelerator pump cover (right)	70. Pump jet
32. Lockwasher	71. Pressure valve
33. Nut	72. Suction valve
34. Linkage	73. Emulsion tube
35. U-joint	74. Air correction jet
36. Screw	75. Gasket
37. Spacer	76. Stud
38. Throttle shaft	77. Bracket
39. Cotter pin	78. Bushing

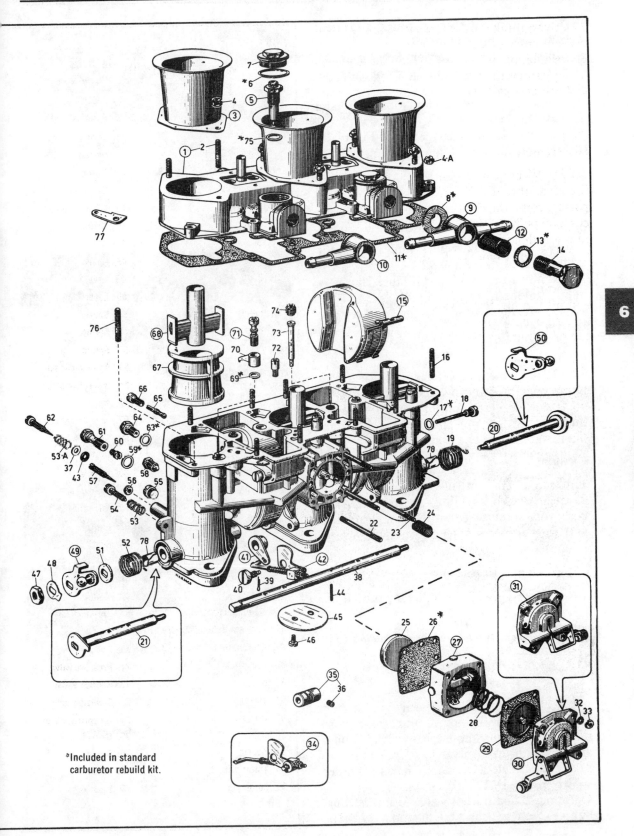

*Included in standard
carburetor rebuild kit.

3. Remove needle valve plugs and float needle valves. See **Figure 25**.

4. Remove main jet carrier. See **Figure 26**. Unscrew main jet from back of each jet carrier. See **Figure 27**.

5. Remove air adjustment locknuts and screws. See **Figure 26**.

6. Remove idle metering jets. See **Figure 26**.

7. Remove idle speed adjustment screw. See **Figure 26**.

8. Remove idle mixture screws. See **Figure 26**.

9. Remove air correction jets and shake out emulsion tubes.

10. Remove check valves and accelerator pump nozzles. See **Figure 28**.

11. Remove preatomizers; if stuck, tap very lightly to loosen. See **Figure 28**.

12. Loosen the venturi setscrews and remove the venturis.

13. Unscrew float pins (**Figure 29**) and lift out the floats.

14. Remove the nuts securing the accelerator pump cover and remove the cover.

15. Remove accelerator pump outer diaphragm, spring, pump body, inner diaphragm, valve and spring.

Cleaning

1. Clean all parts in solvent.

2. Clean jets and drillings in the carburetor body with compressed air. Do not clean them with pins or pieces of wire; you might enlarge the holes.

Inspection and Reassembly

Refer to **Figure 22** for following procedure.

NOTE
Use all parts included in a standard rebuild kit, Porsche Part No. 901.108.948.00; asterisks identify these parts on Figure 22.

1. Check throttle shaft for wear.

2. Hold carburetor up to light and close throttle. No light should be visible around any of the throttle valves.

3. Install accelerator pump parts in order shown in **Figure 22**.

4. Immerse float in hot water. If it is leaking, bubbles will appear and the float must be

(24)

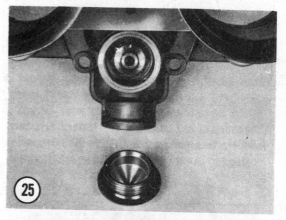

(25)

1. Idle speed adjustment screw
2. Idle mixture screw
3. Air adjusting screw
4. Main jet carrier

(26)

replaced. Do not attempt to solder the hole. This increases float weight and causes high fuel level.

5. Install floats and secure with float pins.

6. Install venturis and secure with setscrews. Safety-wire setscrews.

7. Install preatomizers.

8. Install the pressure valves and accelerator pump nozzles.

9. Install emulsion tubes and air correction jets.

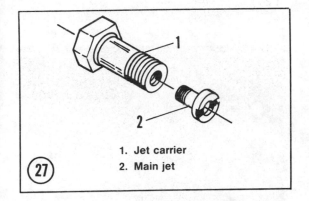

1. Jet carrier
2. Main jet

10. Install idle mixture screws. Make sure they are not bent or scored; replace if necessary.

11. Install idle speed adjustment screw.

12. Install idle metering jets.

13. Install air adjustment locknuts and screws.

14. Install main jets in jet carriers. Install carriers in carburetor.

15. Install top of carburetor on body.

16. Install float needle valves and plugs.

17. Check float needle valve and seat for wear. To do this, install it in top cover, hold the valve in lightly with your finger and blow in the fuel inlet. If it leaks, install a new needle valve.

18. Install fuel lines with hollow bolts and fuel screens.

ZENITH 40 TIN CARBURETOR

Removal/Installation

1. Disconnect carburetor preheating hose from air cleaner. See **Figure 19**.

2. Unsnap air cleaner cover and remove air cleaner element.

3. Unsnap the air cleaner ducts from the top of the carburetors.

4. Disconnect fuel lines from carburetors.

5. Disconnect throttle linkage from carburetors. See **Figure 20**.

6. Remove the retaining nuts and lift the carburetor(s) off.

> *CAUTION*
> *Do not let lockwashers or other loose parts fall into intake manifolds.*

7. Cover intake manifolds to prevent entry of dirt and loose parts.

8. Installation is the reverse of these steps. Clean carburetor base and manifold surfaces and use new gaskets. Adjust idle speed.

Disassembly

The Zenith carburetor consists of 3 nearly identical throats. To aid reassembly, keep parts from the 3 throats in 3 separate containers. Keep parts common to all in a fourth container.

Refer to **Figure 30** for the following procedure.

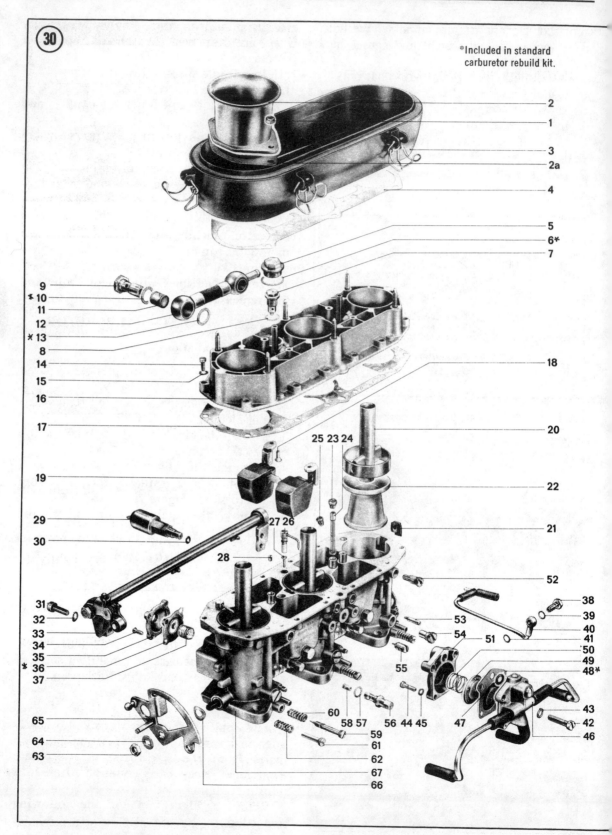

*Included in standard
carburetor rebuild kit.

ZENITH 40 TIN CARBURETOR

Self-locking nut	34. Round head screw
Velocity stack	35. Accelerator pump cover
Gasket	36. Diaphragm
Clamp pan	37. Pump spring
Gasket	38. Hollow bolt
Threaded plug	39. Gasket
Ring gasket	40. Fuel line, complete
Float needle valve	41. Gasket
Gasket	42. Fillister head screw
Hollow bolt	43. Lockwasher
Gasket	44. Fillister head screw
Filtering screen	45. Lockwasher
Connector	46. Auxiliary enrichment valve cover
Gasket	47. O-ring
Fillister head screw	48. Diaphragm
Lockwasher	49. Diaphragm plunger
Carburetor cover	50. Spring
Gasket	51. Enrichment valve bottom
Round head screw	52. Idle jet
Float, complete	53. Air bypass control screw
Pre-atomizer	54. Threaded plug
Retaining clip	55. Auxiliary mixture control screw
Venturi	
Air correction jet	56. Jet housing
Emulsion tube	57. Gasket
Pump inlet valve	58. Main jet
Injection tube	59. Idle mixture control screw
Plug	60. Spring
Fuel jet for enrichment valve	61. Idle speed adjusting screw
Enrichment solenoid	62. Spring
Gasket	63. Nut
Fillister head screw	64. Lock plate
Lockwasher	65. Cam track
Pump shaft	66. Spring washer
	67. Carburetor housing

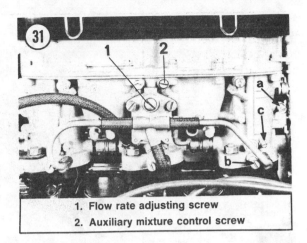

1. Flow rate adjusting screw
2. Auxiliary mixture control screw

1. Remove 12 screws securing top of carburetor and lift top off.
2. Remove hollow bolts securing fuel line to top of carburetor.
3. Remove 4 screws securing floats and remove floats.
4. Remove needle valve plugs and remove float needle valves.
5. Remove main jet carriers. Unscrew main jet from back of each housing. See **Figure 27**.
6. Remove air adjustment screw and air bypass control screw. See **Figure 31**.
7. Remove idle metering jets.
8. Remove idle mixture screws.
9. Remove air connection jets and shake out emulsion tubes.
10. Remove accelerator pump nozzles.
11. Remove retaining clips and remove preatomizer; if stuck, tap very lightly to loosen.
12. Remove venturis.
13. Remove accelerator pump covers. Remove accelerator pump parts.
14. Remove auxiliary enrichment pump cover. Remove internal pump parts.
15. Remove enrichment solenoid.

Cleaning

1. Clean all parts in solvent.
2. Clean jets and drillings in the carburetor body with compressed air. Do not clean them with pins or pieces of wire; you might enlarge the holes.

Inspection and Reassembly

Refer to **Figure 30** for following procedure.

6

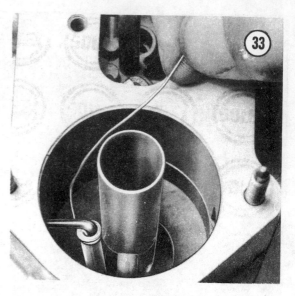

NOTE
*Use all new parts included in a standard rebuild kit, Porsche Part No. 911.108.948.00. Asterisks identify these parts on **Figure 30**.*

1. Check throttle shaft for wear.
2. Hold carburetor up to light and close throttle. No light should be visible around any of the throttle valves.
3. Install accelerator pump parts in the order shown in **Figure 30**.
4. Install auxiliary enrichment pump parts as shown in **Figure 30**.
5. Install venturis and preatomizers. Hold with retaining clips.
6. Install accelerator pump nozzles.
7. Install emulsion tubes and air correction jets.
8. Install idle metering jets.
9. Install idle mixture screws.
10. Install air adjustment and air bypass control screws.
11. Install main jets in jet carriers. Install carriers in carburetor.
12. Install float needle valves with plugs.
13. Check float needle valve and seat for wear. To do this, install it in top cover, hold the valve in lightly with your finger and blow in the fuel inlet. If it leaks, install a new needle valve.
14. Immerse float in hot water. If it is leaking, bubbles will appear and the float

must be replaced. Do not attempt to solder the hole. This increases float weight and causes high fuel level.
15. Install floats.
16. Install top of carburetor on body.
17. Install fuel lines with hollow bolts and screens.
18. Install enrichment solenoid.

Accelerator Pump Adjustment

Perform this adjustment when engine is cold.
1. Remove air cleaner assembly.
2. Turn screw (a, **Figure 32**) until tabs on shaft are vertical.
3. Hold a very small graduate below injector nozzle for cylinder No. 1. See **Figure 33**.
4. Operate the throttle through its entire range. The pump should deliver 0.4-0.6 cc of fuel per stroke.
5. Loosen locknut (b, **Figure 32**) and adjust screw until injection quantity is proper.
6. Repeat Steps 3-5 for each throat.
7. Install air cleaner assembly.

INTAKE MANIFOLD
**Removal/Installation
(Carburetted 911 Models)**

1. Remove air cleaner assembly.
2. Disconnect throttle linkage.
3. Disconnect fuel lines from float chamber (Solex carburetors) and carburetors.

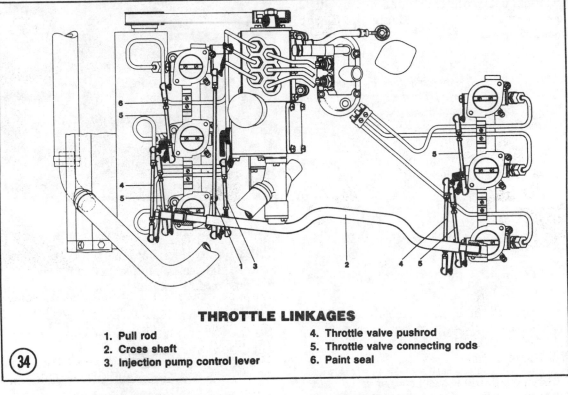

THROTTLE LINKAGES

1. Pull rod
2. Cross shaft
3. Injection pump control lever
4. Throttle valve pushrod
5. Throttle valve connecting rods
6. Paint seal

(34)

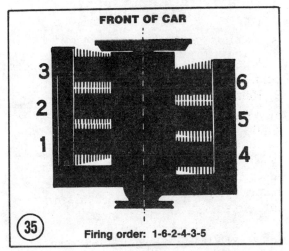

FRONT OF CAR

Firing order: 1-6-2-4-3-5

(35)

4. Remove intake manifold retaining nuts. Lift intake manifold off complete with carburetors.

CAUTION
Keep intake ports covered to prevent entry of dirt and other foreign material.

5. Remove carburetor from intake manifold.
6. Installation is the reverse of these steps. Use new gaskets.

Removal/Installation
(Fuel Injected 911)

While removing and installing the intake manifolds and throttle valve assemblies is in itself a simple matter, subsequent adjustments, if needed, are not possible without special tools and skills. Be extremely careful not to bend or loosen the throttle linkage while performing this procedure. Take the car to a dealer for adjustment as soon as possible after completion; tell him what you have done and he will be sure to check it thoroughly.

1. Remove air cleaner assembly including bases on top of intake manifolds.

2. Disconnect 4 linkage rods marked 1, 3 and 4 in **Figure 34**.

3. Remove nut, bellcrank, spring and washers from left end of cross shaft.

4. Remove retaining nuts from both intake manifolds. Lift them out simultaneously with the cross shaft. Do not bend the shaft.

5. Mark fuel injection lines with cylinder number. See **Figure 35** for numbering.

6. Disconnect both ends of each line with 2 wrenches as shown in **Figure 36**. Leave injectors in head.

CAUTION
Cover the hole in the injectors and both ends of the lines to prevent entry of dust and dirt. Even minute particles can clog the injectors.

7. Remove nuts securing throttle valve assemblies and lift them off.

CAUTION
Keep intake ports covered to prevent entry of dirt and other foreign material.

8. Installation is the reverse of these steps. Use new gaskets.

MECHANICAL FUEL PUMP

Fuel Pump Test

If the fuel pump is suspected of being faulty (see *Troubleshooting*, Chapter Two), check the line connections to make sure they are tight. Also make certain the mounting bolts and the fuel pump body screws are tight. If these checks prove okay, perform the following test.
1. Disconnect the fuel outlet line from one of the fuel pumps. Connect one end of a 25.6 in. (650 mm) length hose to the pump and place the other end in a graduated vessel. The hose must be placed vertically to ensure accurate readings. See **Figure 37**.
2. Attach the disconnected fuel outlet line to the opposite fuel pump outlet line with a 3-way connector as shown in **Figure 37**.
3. Start the engine, run it for one minute at 3,000 rpm and then shut it off.
4. If the pump is operating correctly, there should be at least 800 cc of fuel in the graduated vessel. If there is appreciably less, the pump should be replaced.
5. Repeat Steps 1-4 for the opposite pump.
6. Fuel pump delivery pressure can be checked as described in Chapter Two. Specifications are found in **Table 2** (end of chapter).

Removal/Installation

1. Disconnect fuel lines from pump. Mark them so they can be reinstalled properly.
2. Remove nuts securing pump to engine and pull pump off.
3. Installation is the reverse of these steps. Use a new gasket and make sure that all connections are tight.

ELECTRIC FUEL PUMPS

Fuel Pump Test

Test specifications for electric fuel pumps used on the vehicles covered in this manual are found in **Table 2**. If you suspect the pump is faulty, check the line connections to make sure they are tight. Also make certain the mounting bolts and the fuel pump body screws are tight. If fuel pump operation cannot be corrected by performing these checks and other damage is not readily apparent, refer testing and further service to your Porsche service department.

Removal (Hardi)

1. Disconnect battery ground cable.
2. Disconnect fuel lines at pump. Clamp them to prevent fuel leakage.
3. Remove bolts securing pump and disconnect ground cable.
4. Disconnect the positive lead from the pump terminal.
5. Installation is the reverse of these steps. Use new seals at banjo fittings and replace mounting grommets if deteriorated.

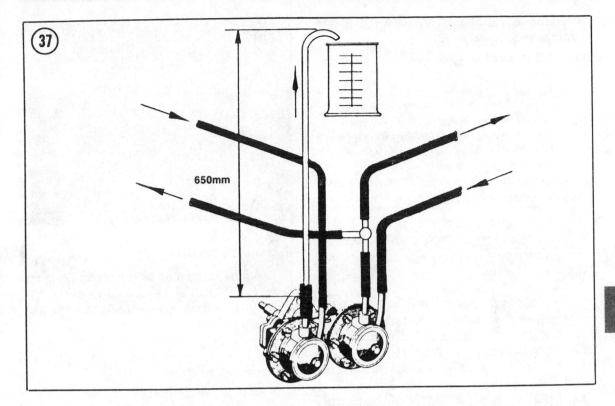

650mm

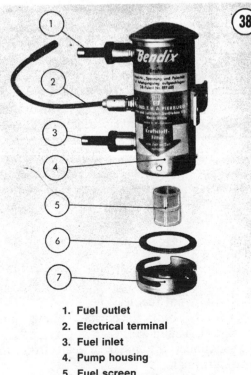

1. Fuel outlet
2. Electrical terminal
3. Fuel inlet
4. Pump housing
5. Fuel screen
6. Gasket
7. Cover with filtering magnet

Removal/Installation (Bendix)

Refer to **Figure 38** for following procedure.
1. Disconnect electric cable from pump.
2. Disconnect fuel lines.
3. Remove mounting screws and remove fuel pump.
4. Installation is the reverse of these steps.

FUEL TANK

The fuel tank is accessible through the front luggage compartment.

Removal

WARNING
Always disconnect battery before starting tank removal. The tank can brush against electrical connections during removal. If power is connected, sparks can cause a gasoline fire. It has happened many times.

1. Set fire extinguisher nearby.
2. Disconnect battery ground cable.
3. Warn others nearby not to smoke or use any open flames while you are working.

4. Remove drain plug and drain fuel into container. See **Figure 39**.

> *NOTE*
> *If there is a lot of fuel in the tank, take the car to a service station. Let them drain the fuel, then refill with just enough to get home (1 or 2 gallons). They have facilities for disposing of fuel. You probably have no safe way of disposing of or storing more than a gallon or so.*

5. Disconnect both fuel lines from tank.
6. Open front luggage compartment. Remove the compartment padding, the spare tire and the spare tire pad.
7. Disconnect vent hose.
8. Disconnect fuel gauge wire from sender.
9. Remove 3 Allen bolts securing tank.
10. Loosen hose clamp and disconnect fuel filter from tank.
11. Lift the fuel tank out through the luggage compartment.
12. Installation is the reverse of these steps. Replace the tank support gasket if damaged.

Table 1 CARBURETOR SPECIFICATIONS

	Solex 40 PI	Weber 40 IDAP/ 3C/3C1	Zenith 40 TIN[1] 1970-1971	Zenith 40 TIN[2] 1971	Zenith 40 TIN[3] 1971
Venturi	30	30	27.5	27.5	27.5
Main jet	125	125	115	115	115
Air correction jet	180	180	185	195	110
Idle metering jet	55	52	47.5	47.5	47.5
Idle air bleed	1.0	110	140	165	47.5p
Accelerator pump jet	0.5 mm	50	50	50	50
Emulsion tube	8	F26	4 mm	4.3 mm	170
Float needle valve	2.0	1.75	P1.5		
Float weight (grams)	7	15.5	15.7		

1. 911T engine No. 6105001-6108563 without Sportomatic and engine No. 6108001-6108267 with Sportomatic.
2. 911T from engine No. 6108564 without Sportomatic.
3. 911T from engine No. 5119553 with Sportomatic.

Table 2 FUEL PUMP SPECIFICATIONS

Twin mechanical	
Delivery pressure per pump	2.65-3.23 psi (0.18-0.22 atm)
Delivery capacity per pump	27 oz. (800 cc) @ 3,000 rpm
Bendix electric	
Delivery pressure	3.23-4.41 psi (0.22-0.30 atm)
Delivery capacity	Not specified
Bosch	
Electric (1974-1975 CIS)	
Delivery pressure	72 psi (5.57 atm)
Delivery capacity	50.7 oz. (1,500 cc) per minute
Others	
Delivery pressure	4.3 psi (0.3 atm)
Delivery capacity	45 oz. (1,332 cc) per minute
Hardi Electric	
Delivery pressure	3.6-4.3 psi (0.25-0.30 atm)
Delivery capacity	30 oz. (900 cc) per minute

6

EMISSION CONTROL SYSTEMS

Harmful emissions from the Porsche are minimized by 5 systems:

a. Crankcase ventilation.
b. Exhaust emission control (air injection pump).
c. Fuel evaporative emission control.
d. Thermal reactor system (described in Chapter Five).
e. Exhaust gas recirculation (EGR) system.

This chapter includes a description of each system and procedures for the maintenance and repair of each. Improper operation of any of these systems not only causes dangerous and illegal emissions but reduces engine performance as well.

CRANKCASE VENTILATION

The crankcase ventilation system scavenges emissions (e.g., piston blow-by) from the crankcase and directs them to the air cleaner. Eventually they can be reburned in the normal combustion process.

Figure 1 shows the 911 system. Vapors from the crankcase collect in the oil tank. The induction system draws the vapors from the oil tank through the air cleaner. There is a flame arrestor in the air cleaner connection but no PCV valve is used.

Engine blow-by and other fumes are channeled from the crankcase to the oil tank by a hose on all 1977 and later models. An additional hose then directs the fumes to the intake air system. On 1977 and earlier models, this hose was connected to the air cleaner, as shown in **Figure 2**. On 1978 and later models, the hose is connected to the rubber boot between the air flow sensor and the throttle housing as shown in **Figure 3**. The angled connector (6, **Figure 4**) of the 1978-on hose contains a 6.5 mm orifice, which restricts the crankcase vacuum under all operating conditions.

EXHAUST EMISSION CONTROLS

The exhaust emission control system uses air injection to produce additional burning *outside* the combustion chambers. See **Figure 5**. The air pump supplies clean air from its own air cleaner, through a control valve, to the cylinder head exhaust ports. The injected air burns (oxidizes) the hydrocarbons and carbon monoxide present in the exhaust and converts them to harmless gases such as carbon dioxide.

The control valve contains a pressure relief valve and a check valve for each cylinder

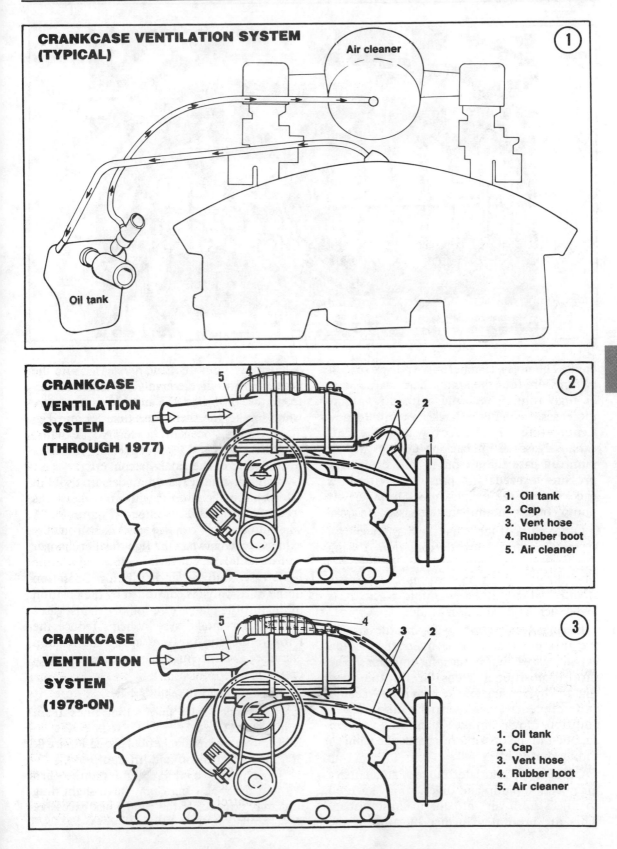

CRANKCASE VENTILATION SYSTEM (TYPICAL)

Air cleaner

Oil tank

①

CRANKCASE VENTILATION SYSTEM (THROUGH 1977)

②

1. Oil tank
2. Cap
3. Vent hose
4. Rubber boot
5. Air cleaner

7

CRANKCASE VENTILATION SYSTEM (1978-ON)

③

1. Oil tank
2. Cap
3. Vent hose
4. Rubber boot
5. Air cleaner

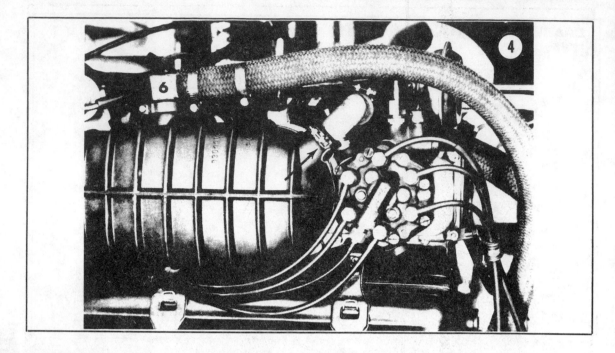

bank. The pressure relief valve releases excess air pressure into the atmosphere, particularly at high rpm, where the extra air volume increases exhaust back pressure and temperature. The check valve prevents exhaust gases from backing up into the air pump in case the air pump fails or exhaust pressure exceeds air pressure. Without a check valve, the exhaust gases from the air pump could contaminate the passenger area.

Other parts of the exhaust emission control system control throttle position during deceleration and ignition timing during idle. The throttle positioner opens the throttle slightly when intake manifold vacuum is high, such as during deceleration.

During deceleration, with throttle closed, the mixture tends to be overrich and the exhaust gases high in harmful emissions. The throttle positioner keeps the throttle open slightly by sensing intake manifold vacuum and prevents the overrich mixture. In addition, high intake manifold vacuum supplied to the distributor retards the ignition timing during idle.

On all 1977 and later models, an auxiliary air injection pump and diverter valve is used to inject fresh air into the exhaust system. This air promotes further burning of the exhaust gases before they are released into the open air. The diverter valve switches the air from the pump to the outside atmosphere when intake vacuum is less than 80 mm Hg. This helps prevent excessive exhaust backpressure and (on 1978-on models), overheating of the catalytic converter.

In addition, all 1978-on models first sold in California are equipped with an exhaust gas recirculation (EGR) system (**Figure 6**). A small amount of exhaust gas taken from the exhaust pipe between the right heat exchanger and the catalytic converter is injected via the EGR valve into the air distributor. Operation of the EGR valve is controlled by the position of the throttle plate. Injection of exhaust gases into the air intake system helps reduce the temperature and pressure in the combustion chamber, which in turn reduces harmful emissions.

Air Pump Removal/Installation

1. Disconnect inlet and outlet lines from pump. See **Figure 7**.
2. Remove pump bracket bolts. See **Figure 8**.
3. Pull drive belt off and lift pump out.
4. Turn pulley by hand. Old pumps turn without drag; new ones may have slight drag and may squeak. If the pump has excessive drag, replace it.

7

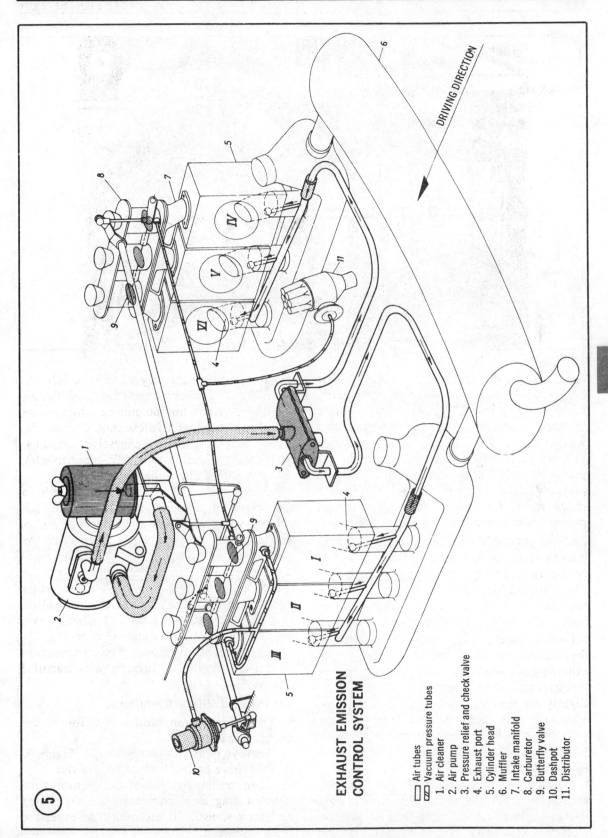

DRIVING DIRECTION

**EXHAUST EMISSION
CONTROL SYSTEM**

▭ Air tubes
▨ Vacuum pressure tubes
1. Air cleaner
2. Air pump
3. Pressure relief and check valve
4. Exhaust port
5. Cylinder head
6. Muffler
7. Intake manifold
8. Carburetor
9. Butterfly valve
10. Dashpot
11. Distributor

⑤

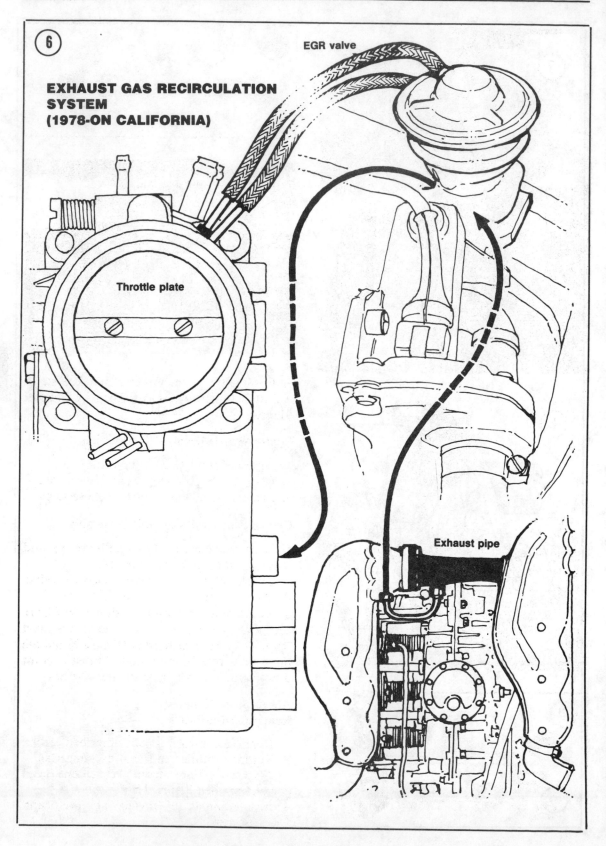

⑥

EXHAUST GAS RECIRCULATION SYSTEM (1978-ON CALIFORNIA)

EGR valve

Throttle plate

Exhaust pipe

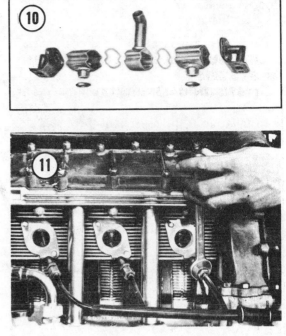

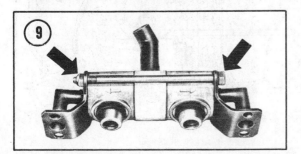

7

5. Installation is the reverse of these steps. Adjust belt tension as described in Chapter Three.

Control Valve Removal/Installation

1. Disconnect air lines from valve.
2. Remove 4 retaining bolts and lift valve off.
3. Installation is the reverse of these steps.

Control Valve Disassembly/Assembly

1. Remove through bolts (**Figure 9**) and separate all parts. See **Figure 10**.
2. Check rubber diaphragm in check valve. Replace it if cracked or torn.
3. Reassemble in the order shown in **Figure 10**. Note that the arrows on the valves must point away from each other (**Figure 9**) and the pressure relief openings must point downward. Use new gaskets and O-rings.

**Air Injection Line
Removal/Installation**

1. Remove control valve as described earlier.
2. Remove muffler and heat exchanger(s).
3. Unscrew line from cylinder head connection. See **Figure 11**.
4. Installation is the reverse of these steps. Use new gaskets.

Throttle Positioner
Removal/Installation

1. Disconnect vacuum line from positioner.
2. Disconnect linkage ball-joint on positioner.
3. Remove bolts securing positioners to bracket.
4. Installation is the reverse of these steps.
5. Check and adjust positioner (Chapter Three).

FUEL EVAPORATIVE CONTROL SYSTEM

All 1970-1973 Porsches sold in California are equipped with a fuel evaporative control system which prevents release of fuel vapor into the atmosphere.

Refer to **Figure 12** and **Figure 13**. Fuel vapor from the fuel tank passes through the expansion tank to the activated charcoal filter. When the engine runs, cool air from the fan housing forces the fuel vapor into the air cleaner. Instead of being released into the atmosphere, the fuel vapor takes part in the normal combustion process.

A slightly changed system was used on 1974-1977 models (**Figure 14**) and was further modified for use on 1978 and later models (**Figure 15**), although both function in a manner similar to the earlier system. Note

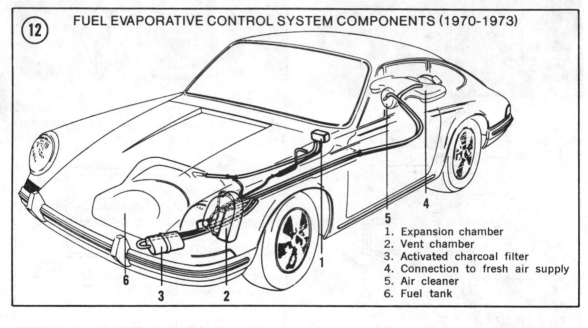

FUEL EVAPORATIVE CONTROL SYSTEM COMPONENTS (1970-1973)

1. Expansion chamber
2. Vent chamber
3. Activated charcoal filter
4. Connection to fresh air supply
5. Air cleaner
6. Fuel tank

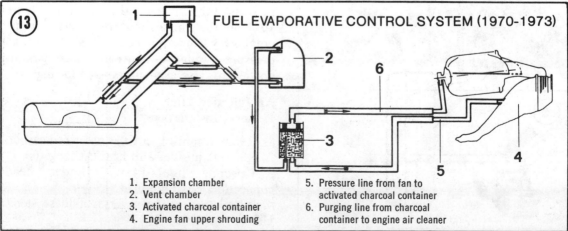

FUEL EVAPORATIVE CONTROL SYSTEM (1970-1973)

1. Expansion chamber
2. Vent chamber
3. Activated charcoal container
4. Engine fan upper shrouding
5. Pressure line from fan to activated charcoal container
6. Purging line from charcoal container to engine air cleaner

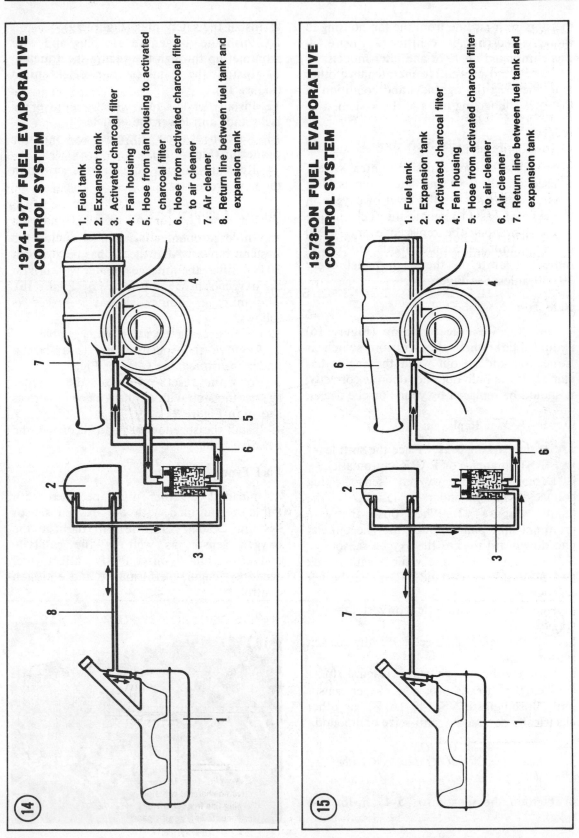

1974-1977 FUEL EVAPORATIVE CONTROL SYSTEM

1. Fuel tank
2. Expansion tank
3. Activated charcoal filter
4. Fan housing
5. Hose from fan housing to activated charcoal filter
6. Hose from activated charcoal filter to air cleaner
7. Air cleaner
8. Return line between fuel tank and expansion tank

1978-ON FUEL EVAPORATIVE CONTROL SYSTEM

1. Fuel tank
2. Expansion tank
3. Activated charcoal filter
4. Fan housing
5. Hose from activated charcoal filter to air cleaner
6. Air cleaner
7. Return line between fuel tank and expansion tank

7

that the fresh air line from the fan housing to the activated charcoal canister (5, **Figure 14**) was eliminated on 1978 and later models.

There is no preventive maintenance other than checking the tightness and condition of the lines connecting parts of the system.

OXYGEN SENSOR

An oxygen sensor emission control system is used on all 1980 and later models. The oxygen sensor detects the level of oxygen in the exhaust gas to regulate the fuel mixture control. It should be replaced every 30,000 miles. A mileage counter lights an "OXS" indicator lamp on the dash panel every 30,000 miles. See **Figure 16**.

Bulb Test

The "OXS" indicator lamp (**Figure 16**) should light when the ignition switch is turned on and go out when the engine has started. If the bulb does not operate correctly, it should be replaced by your Porsche dealer.

Oxygen Sensor Replacement

1. Set the parking brake. Place the shift lever in FIRST (manual) or PARK (automatic).
2. Disconnect the oxygen sensor plug connector located under the left side of the engine (**Figure 17**). Then push the wire grommet and plug through the sheet metal and downward toward the oxygen sensor.
3. Raise the rear of the vehicle with a jack and place it on jackstands. Remove the left rear wheel.
4. Remove the catalytic converter shield (**Figure 18**).
5. Pull the safety connector off the oxygen sensor (**Figure 19**).
6. Unscrew the oxygen sensor (**Figure 20**).
7. Coat the threads of a new oxygen sensor with Bosch paste VS 140 16 FT or other electrically conductive anti-seize compound.

CAUTION
Keep the paste out of the oxygen sensor slot.

8. Tighten the sensor to 35-45 ft.-lb. (5-6 mkg).

9. Install the safety plug (**Figure 19**).
10. Push the oxygen sensor plug and wire grommet up through the engine sheet metal.
11. Install the catalytic converter shield (**Figure 18**).
12. Install the left rear wheel. Remove the jackstands and lower the vehicle.
13. Reconnect the oxygen sensor wire connector (**Figure 17**).
14. Reset the mileage counter as described in the next procedure.

Mileage Counter Reset

A mileage counter is installed behind the fresh air blower. After the car has been driven 30,000 miles, the mileage counter will turn on the oxygen sensor indicator lamp (**Figure 16**). The mileage counter should be reset as follows:
1. Disconnect the negative battery cable.
2. Remove the speedometer as described under *Instruments* in Chapter Eight.
3. Press the reset button on the counter against the stop with a 3 mm piece of wire as shown in **Figure 21**.
4. Install the speedometer and reconnect the negative battery cable.

Fuel Type

Unleaded gasoline must be used with vehicles equipped with the oxygen sensor system. Leaded gasoline will damage the oxygen sensor as well as the catalytic converter and consequently affect fuel economy, engine performance and emission control.

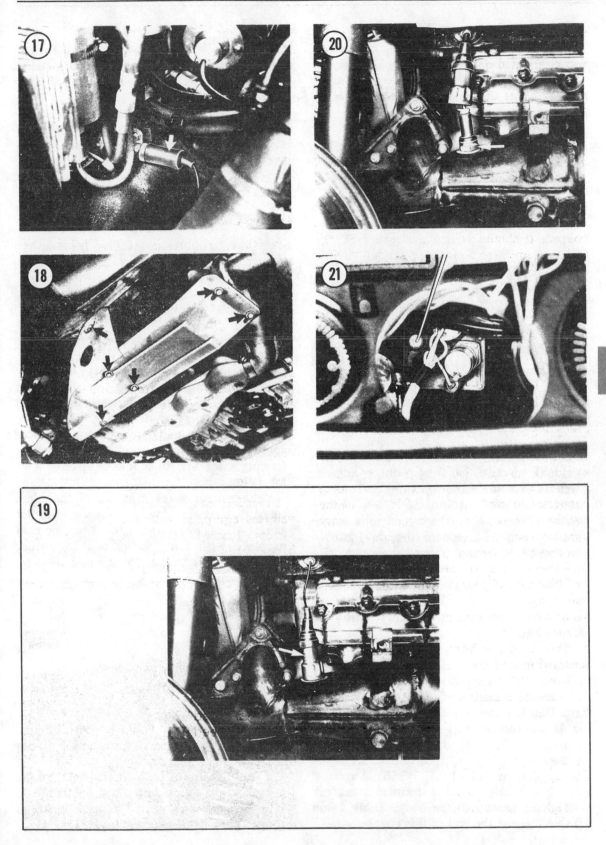

ELECTRICAL SYSTEM

Porsche 911 electrical systems are quite similar on all models. All use an alternator-based charging system. Differences occur mainly as small design changes in the alternator, regulator, starter, distributor, fuse and lighting arrangements.

When trouble is experienced in the electrical system, Chapter Two can serve as a valuable guide to isolating problem areas as well as explaining the functions and uses of electrical test equipment. Very often, electrical trouble can be traced to a simple cause, such as a blown fuse, a loose or corroded connection, a loose alternator drive belt or a frayed wire. But, while these problems are easily correctable and of seemingly no major importance, they can quickly lead to serious difficulty if they are allowed to go uncorrected.

If you plan to do much of your own electrical work, a multimeter (described in Chapter Two) combining the functions of an ohmmeter, ammeter and voltmeter, is essential to locating and sorting out problems.

Above all, electrical system repair requires a patient, thorough approach to find true causes of trouble and then correct all of the faults that are involved. Wiring diagrams, which can help to trace troubled areas, are found at the end of the book. **Table 1** and **Table 2** are at the end of this chapter.

SERVICE NOTE

Replacement and/or repair of many electrical components will require the resoldering of wiring connections. Should resoldering become necessary, rosin core solder–never use acid core solder on electrical connections–must always be used when splicing wires. Splices should be covered with insulating tape.

Replacement wires must be of the same gauge as the replaced wire–never use a smaller gauge. All harnesses and wires should be held in place with clips, cable ties and other holding devices so that chafing and abrasion can be avoided.

BATTERY

Battery specifications are given in **Table 1** at the end of the chapter.

Care and Inspection

1. Open front luggage compartment.
2. Remove battery hold down clamps. Disconnect battery cables from both batteries and remove the batteries.
3. Clean the top of the batteries with baking soda solution. Scrub with a stiff bristle brush. Wipe clean with a cloth moistened in ammonia or baking soda solution.

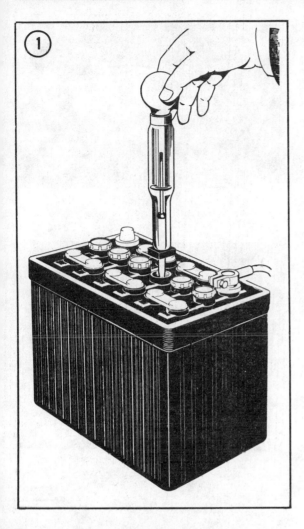

numbered graduations from 1.100 to 1.300 rather than one with color coded bands. To use the hydrometer, squeeze the rubber ball, insert the tip in the cell and release the ball (**Figure 1**). Draw enough electrolyte to float the weighted float inside the hydrometer. Note the number in line with the surface of the electrolyte; this is the specific gravity for this cell. Return the electrolyte to the cell from which it came.

The specific gravity of the electrolyte in each battery cell is an excellent indication of that cell's condition. A fully charged cell will read 1.275-1.380, while a cell in good condition may read from 1.250-1.280. A cell in fair condition reads from 1.225-1.250 and anything below 1.225 is practically dead.

If the cells test in the poor range, the battery requires recharging. The hydrometer is useful for checking the progress of the charging operation. A reading from 1.200 to about 1.225 indicates a half charge; 1.275-1.380 indicates a full charge.

NOTE
For every 10° above 80° F electrolyte temperature, add 0.004 to specific gravity reading. For every 10° below 80° F, subtract 0.004 from specific gravity reading.

CAUTION
Always disconnect both battery connections before connecting charging equipment. Make certain there are no open flames, electrical sparks or people smoking near a battery being charged. Highly explosive hydrogen gas is released during the process.

BOSCH/MOTOROLA ALTERNATORS

These alternators generate alternating current (AC) which is converted to direct current (DC) by 6 internal silicon diodes. The alternator consists of the rotor, stator, end plate, housing and drive pulley. Refer to **Table 1** for specifications.

Removal/Installation

1. Disconnect the battery ground cable(s).
2. Open the engine compartment lid.

CAUTION
Keep cleaning solution out of battery cells or the electrolyte will be seriously weakened.

4. Clean battery terminals with a stiff wire brush or one of the many tools made for this purpose.
5. Examine battery cases for cracks.
6. Install batteries and reconnect battery cables. Observe polarity.
7. Coat battery connections with light mineral grease or Vaseline after tightening.
8. Check the electrolyte level and top up if necessary.

Testing

Hydrometer testing is the best way to check battery condition. Use a hydrometer with

3. Remove the air cleaner assembly.

4. Remove the upper shroud bolts. See **Figure 2**.

5. Remove alternator pulley nut while holding fan with special tool included with owner's tool kit. See **Figure 3**. Remove fan belt.

6. Remove blower housing strap bolts. See **Figure 4**.

7. Pull blower/alternator assembly out toward the rear.

8. Disconnect and mark alternator wires. See **Figure 5**.

9. Installation is the reverse of these steps. **Figure 6** shows proper wire connections to alternator.

10. Adjust the fan belt tension as described in Chapter Three.

Brush Replacement (Bosch)

1. Remove 4 screws securing brush plate assembly to back of alternator. See **Figure 7**.

2. Measure brush length as shown in **Figure 8**. Minimum length should be 0.55 in. (14 mm).

3. If brushes are too short, unsolder them (**Figure 9**) and insert new ones. When soldering, do not allow solder to flow up braided lead; the lead will lose its flexibility.

Brush Replacement (Motorola)

1. Remove 2 screws securing brush holder to back of alternator. Lift cover and holder off.

2. Measure brushes as shown in **Figure 10**. Minimum length should be 5/16 in. (8 mm). Replace brushes if necessary.

ALTERNATOR
VOLTAGE REGULATOR

Adjusting the alternator voltage regulator requires special equipment not ordinarily available to a home mechanic. If a trouble appears to be in the voltage regulator, take the job to your dealer or a competent garage.

You might also consider replacing the regulator with a new one. The cost of adjusting an old regulator may be many times that of buying a new one. There is even a chance the old regulator cannot be adjusted; so you'll end up buying a replacement anyway.

An integral regulator is used on 1982 and later models. This regulator is contained within the 75 amp Bosch alternator and should be serviced by a Porsche dealer if defective.

Removal/Installation (Through 1981)

The alternator voltage regulator is located near the ignition coil. See **Figure 11**.

1. Disconnect battery ground cable(s).

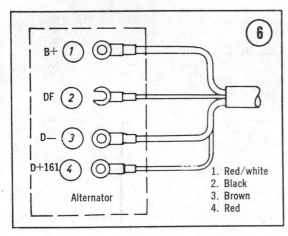

B+ (1)
DF (2)
D— (3)
D+161 (4)
Alternator

1. Red/white
2. Black
3. Brown
4. Red

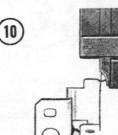

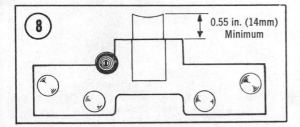

0.55 in. (14mm)
Minimum

8

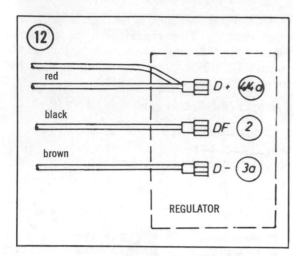

⑫

red — D+ 44a

black — DF 2

brown — D− 3a

REGULATOR

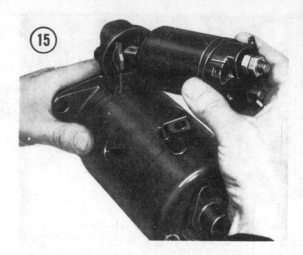

⑮

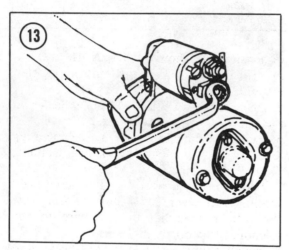

⑬

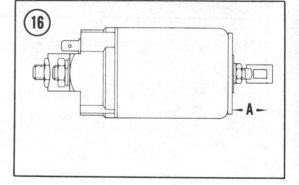

⑯

A

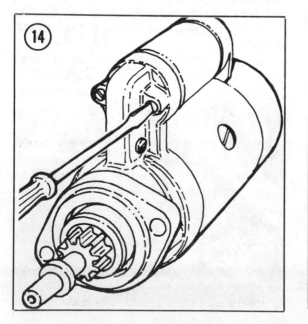

⑭

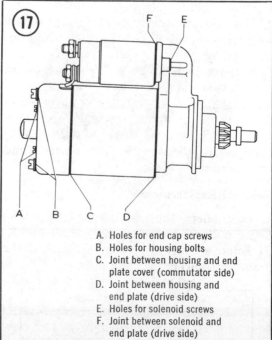

⑰

F E

A B C D

A. Holes for end cap screws
B. Holes for housing bolts
C. Joint between housing and end
   plate cover (commutator side)
D. Joint between housing and
   end plate (drive side)
E. Holes for solenoid screws
F. Joint between solenoid and
   end plate (drive side)

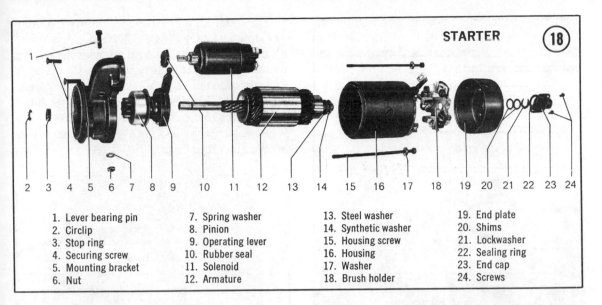

STARTER (18)

1. Lever bearing pin	7. Spring washer
2. Circlip	8. Pinion
3. Stop ring	9. Operating lever
4. Securing screw	10. Rubber seal
5. Mounting bracket	11. Solenoid
6. Nut	12. Armature

13. Steel washer	19. End plate
14. Synthetic washer	20. Shims
15. Housing screw	21. Lockwasher
16. Housing	22. Sealing ring
17. Washer	23. End cap
18. Brush holder	24. Screws

2. Sketch terminals of voltage regulator. Mark wires with terminal numbers. See **Figure 12**.

3. Remove screws securing voltage regulator and lift it out.

4. Installation is the reverse of these steps.

STARTER

Removal/Installation

1. Disconnect battery ground cable(s).

2. Disconnect battery cable from starter solenoid terminal 30 and the small wire from terminal 50.

3. Remove bolts securing the starter to the transmission case. Withdraw the starter.

4. Installation is the reverse of these steps. Before installing, apply universal grease to the starter shaft bushing. Use VW D1a Sealing Compound between the starter and transmission.

Solenoid Replacement

1. Disconnect the large connecting wire between starter and solenoid. See **Figure 13**.

2. Remove 2 screws securing solenoid to the mounting bracket. See **Figure 14**.

3. Lift solenoid pull rod free of the operating lever and remove solenoid (**Figure 15**).

4. Do not change pull rod adjustments if old solenoid is to be reinstalled. On new solenoids, loosen the locknut and adjust dimension "a" shown in **Figure 16** to 0.748 in. ±0.004 in. (19 ±0.1 mm). Tighten locknut.

5. Place a strip of VW D14 Plastic Sealer on the outer edge of solenoid face.

6. Pull the drive pinion to bring the operating lever back toward solenoid opening. Connect the pull rod to the operating lever.

7. Secure solenoid with mounting screws and reconnect large wire from starter. Ensure that the rubber grommet on the wire to the solenoid fits properly in the cover.

8. Install shims and lock ring. Check shaft end play, which should be 0.004-0.006 in. (0.1-0.15 mm). Adjust by adding or removing shims.

9. Install a new seal and install the end cap. Use sealing compound at (A) in **Figure 17**.

10. Reverse Steps 1-3 to install the solenoid.

Brush Inspection/Replacement

Brushes should be checked every 6,000 miles. Refer to **Figure 18** for this procedure. The starter must be partially disassembled to expose the brushes.

1. Remove the solenoid from the starter as described previously.

2. Remove the end cap (23) and sealing ring (22).

3. Pry out the lockwasher (21) and remove the shims (20).

4. Remove cover bolts (15) and end cap (19).

8

5. Remove the brush holder. See **Figure 19**.

6. Pull on the brush leads to check that they slide freely in their holders. Make sure the brushes are not worn; if the flexible lead is nearly touching the metal holder, all 4 brushes should be replaced.

NOTE
Step 7 describes brush replacement.

7. Unsolder all 4 brushes and remove. Solder in a new set of brushes using rosin core solder.

8. Examine the commutator before reassembling. If it is dirty or oily, clean it with a cloth moistened in solvent. If it is scored, burned or worn down to the mica strip, have your dealer overhaul the starter.

9. Reverse Steps 1-5 to assemble the brush holder into the starter.

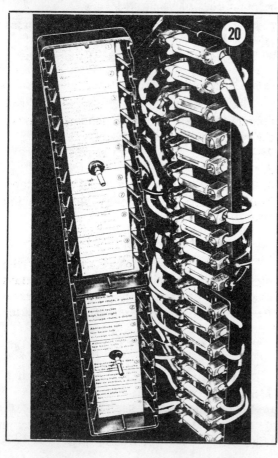

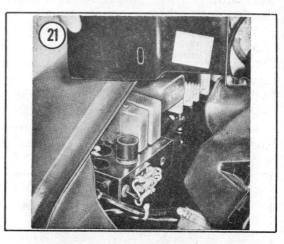

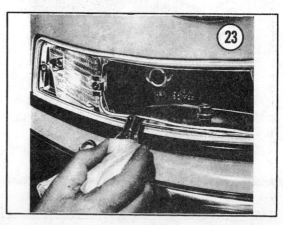

FUSES

The 2 main fuse boxes are located on the left side of the front luggage compartment. The function of each fuse is clearly marked inside the protective cover. See **Figure 20** and wiring diagrams.

Additional fuses on 1972-on models are located on the left side of the engine compartment behind the relay panel cover. See **Figure 21**.

Whenever a fuse blows, ascertain the reason for the failure before replacing the fuse. Usually the trouble is a short circuit in the wiring. This may be caused by worn-through insulation or a wire which works its way loose and shorts to ground.

Carry several spare fuses in the glove compartment.

CAUTION
Never substitute tinfoil or wire for a fuse. An overload could result in a fire and complete loss of the automobile.

HORN

If the horn works, but not loudly or not at the correct pitch, make sure it is not touching the body. Horn pitch and loudness can be adjusted by removing the seal on the rear of the horn and turning the adjusting screw underneath.

When the horn does not work at all, check the wiring to the horn and check the horn switch. To service the horn switch:

1. Disconnect the ground cables from both batteries.
2. Turn horn button to left and lift off. See **Figure 22**.
3. Remove contact pin.
4. Remove the steering wheel as described in Chapter Twelve.
5. Remove 2 screws securing contact ring. Disconnect wire from ring.
6. Clean contact points with fine crocus cloth.
7. Installation is the reverse of these steps.

Horn Replacement

1. The horns are located under the front fenders. Remove the front fenders. Remove the bolt securing the horn to its bracket.
2. Disconnect wire(s) from horn(s).
3. Remove the horn(s).
4. Installation is the reverse of these steps. Make sure that the horns do not touch the body.

LIGHTING SYSTEM

The following procedures describe replacement of lamps, switches, and relays associated with the lighting system. Refer to **Table 2** for the bulb used for each function.

CAUTION
*Handle bulbs with cloth (**Figure 23**); greasy fingerprints shorten bulb life.*

Headlight Replacement

1. Unscrew trim ring. See **Figure 24**.
2. Remove 3 screws identified by arrows in **Figure 25**. Remove retaining ring.

8

3. Lift sealed beam out and disconnect cable. See **Figure 26**.

4. Installation is the reverse of these steps.

5. Adjust headlights according to local traffic regulations. Adjusting screws are shown in **Figure 27**.

Headlight Switch Replacement

1. Disconnect battery ground cable(s).

2. Unscrew instrument panel knob.

3. Unscrew retaining ring with a special tool (Porsche P281) shown in **Figure 28**.

CAUTION
The retainer ring is usually plastic; be careful if you improvise a tool.

4. Remove switch.

5. Mark and disconnect wires from switch.

6. Installation is the reverse of these steps. Ensure that lights work properly.

Headlight Relay

The headlight relay is located under the left floorboard below the pedals.

1. Disconnect battery ground cables.

2. Remove left front carpet and floorboard.

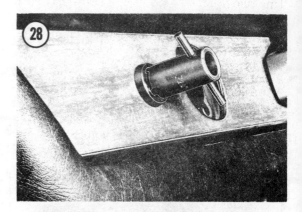

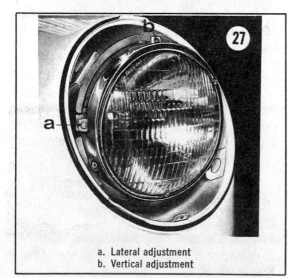

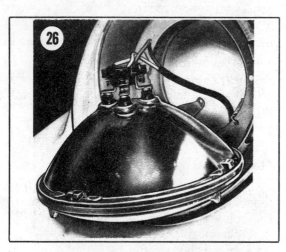

a. Lateral adjustment
b. Vertical adjustment

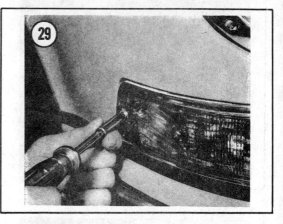

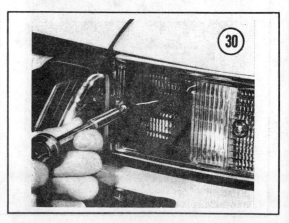

3. Mark and disconnect wires from relay.

4. Remove relay.

5. Install a new relay.

6. Install floorboards, carpeting and battery ground cable(s).

Taillights

To replace rear directional signal, brake and back-up lamps, remove screws securing lens and remove lens. See **Figure 29**. Push bulb inward, then twist counterclockwise. Install new bulb and lens. Do not overtighten the screws or the lens may crack.

Front Parking, Turn and Side Marker Lights

To replace these lamps, remove screws securing the lens and remove the lens. See **Figure 30**. Push bulb in, then twist counterclockwise. Install new bulb and lens.

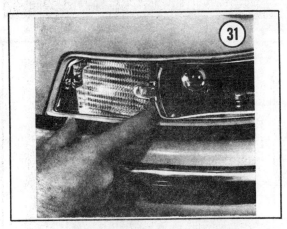

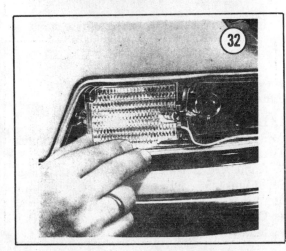

Do not overtighten the screws or the lens may crack.

Each side marker lamp is behind an additional lens. After removing the lens described above, lift out the side marker lens (**Figure 31**). After installing new bulb, insert lens as shown in **Figure 32**, then snap in place.

Interior Light

To replace the interior lamp, pull the entire assembly out of the roof member (**Figure 33**). Replace lamp and install holder back in the roof. Don't damage headliner.

Luggage Compartment Light

Remove lens and install a new 4-watt cartridge type bulb. Install lens.

License Plate Light

Remove both screws securing holder to engine compartment lid. Withdraw holder as a unit (**Figure 34**). Remove and replace bulb. Reinstall holder with attaching screws.

8

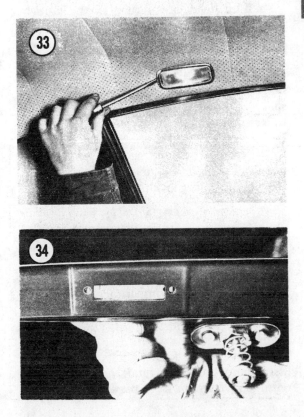

BACK-UP SWITCH

Back-up Lights

Back-up lights are located in the taillight assembly. See *Taillight* procedure.

Back-up Switch

The back-up switch is mounted on the right side of the transaxle. See **Figure 35** and **Figure 36**.

1. Remove rubber cap over terminals.
2. Disconnect electrical wires.
3. Unscrew switch and pull out pin.
4. Installation is the reverse of these steps. Long end of pin goes in first. See **Figure 36**.

INSTRUMENTS

Removal

All instruments are removed in the same manner.

1. Remove luggage compartment carpet.
2. Disconnect instrument electrical cables. On the speedometer, disconnect the mechanical cable.
3. Remove small knurled nuts securing the instrument, remove retaining clamp and remove instrument from passenger area.

4. Installation is the reverse of these steps.

Fuel Gauge Sender
Removal/Installation

1. Remove luggage compartment carpeting.
2. Disconnect cable to sender.
3. Remove bolts securing sender to fuel tank.

WARNING
Fuel in the tank is exposed when the sender is removed. Avoid open flames or cigarettes until sender is replaced.

4. Installation is the reverse of these steps.

DIRECTIONAL SIGNALS

Directional Switch
Removal/Installation (1965-1968)

1. Disconnect battery ground cable(s).
2. Remove the steering wheel. See Chapter Twelve.
3. Remove 2 screws from horn contact ring. See **Figure 37**. Disconnect horn wire and remove ring.
4. Disconnect wires from combination switch.

1. Cover cap
2. Backup light switch
3. Gasket
4. Actuating pin with spring retainer

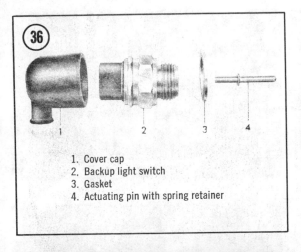

8

5. Remove nuts securing upper housing assembly and pull assembly off.
6. Remove left-hand switch mounting screws. Remove switch.
7. Installation is the reverse of these steps.

Directional Switch
Removal/Installation (1969-on)

1. Disconnect battery ground cable(s).
2. Remove the steering wheel. See Chapter Twelve.
3. Remove 2 screws from horn contact ring. See **Figure 37**. Disconnect wire and remove ring.
4. Remove screws holding upper and lower halves of switch housing. See **Figure 38** and **Figure 39**.
5. Disconnect wires from combination switch.
6. Remove switch mounting screws and lift switch out.

Flasher Relay Replacement

The flasher relay is located in the front luggage compartment near the steering column.
1. Open front luggage compartment and remove mat.
2. Unplug flasher relay.
3. Plug in new relay.
4. Install mat.

Lamp Replacement

Front directional signal lamps are behind same lens as parking lamps and side markers. See *Front Parking, Turn, and Side Marker Light* procedure given earlier.

Rear directional lamps are part of the brake lamps. See *Taillight* procedure given earlier.

WINDSHIELD WIPER SYSTEM

Wiper Motor Removal/Installation

1. Open front luggage compartment.

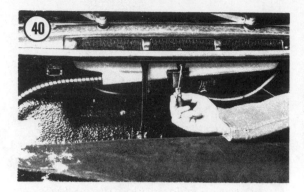

2. Pull back carpet.

3. Remove the forward ventilation case. See **Figure 40**.

4. Disconnect 5 wires from motor.

5. Remove wiper arms.

6. Pull rubber seals off wiper arm shafts. See **Figure 41**. Remove shaft retaining nuts.

7. Pull motor and linkage down and out.

8. Installation is the reverse of these steps.

Wiper Switch Removal/Installation

Perform *Directional Switch Removal* procedure except remove the right-hand switch instead of the left one.

IGNITION SYSTEM

The ignition system consists of the battery, ignition switch, ignition coil, capacitor-discharge system (some models), distributor, spark plugs and associated wiring. The following procedures describe replacement procedures.

Ignition Switch Replacement

1. Disconnect battery ground cable(s).

2. Remove switch cover on front panel.

3A. On models without steering lock, remove screws securing switch and drop it out the front of the panel.

3B. On models with steering lock, drill out the shear bolts and drop switch out the front of the panel. See **Figure 42**.

4. Mark and disconnect electrical wires from switch.

5. Install new switch. On models with steering lock, tighten new shear bolts uniformly until the heads break off.

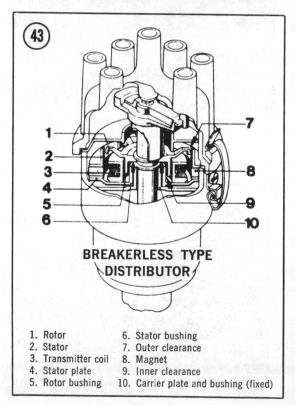

BREAKERLESS TYPE DISTRIBUTOR

1. Rotor	6. Stator bushing
2. Stator	7. Outer clearance
3. Transmitter coil	8. Magnet
4. Stator plate	9. Inner clearance
5. Rotor bushing	10. Carrier plate and bushing (fixed)

6. Install switch cover on front panel.

Ignition Coil Replacement

A defective ignition coil must be replaced. Disconnect primary and secondary wires from coil and remove coil from its bracket. Install new coil; connect wire.

Distributor

A breakerless distributor (**Figure 43**) is used on 1978 and later models. In this system, a pulse generator replaces the breaker points. The pulse generator produces current pulses, which are supplied to the pulse former in the control unit. A switching step sends the amplified pulses to a thyristor grid, which releases the pulses in synchronization with the control pulses. The control pulses are produced by an induction transmitter. Six control pulses are produced during one turn of the distributor rotor.

The distributor shaft turns counterclockwise. This makes the breakerless distributor unsuitable for use on earlier models which have drive gears designed for clockwise rotation.

A dual vacuum advance unit is used on 1980 and later distributors to provide vacuum retard and advance. The vacuum retard hose is colored blue; the advance hose is colored red.

Distributor service and repair requires special test equipment not available to the home mechanic. Such work should be referred to your Porsche dealer.

Removal

1. Turn engine crankshaft over until piston No. 1 is at TDC on a compression stroke. See Chapter Three, *Valve Adjustment*.
2. Remove distributor cap. Leave wires connected.
3. Disconnect primary lead from ignition coil terminal 1.
4. Disconnect vacuum line to advance unit if any.
5. Remove the distributor clamp nut. See **Figure 44**.
6. Lift distributor out.

Installation

1. Ensure that piston No. 1 is still at TDC on a compression stroke.
2. Insert the distributor. Rotor must point in approximate direction shown in **Figure 45**. Rotate distributor housing until notch lines up with rotor.
3. Tighten clamp nut.
4. Install distributor cap and adjust ignition timing as described in Chapter Three.

Capacitor Discharge Unit

The capacitor discharge unit cannot be repaired without special knowledge and equipment. If troubleshooting procedures in Chapter Three indicate trouble with the capacitor discharge unit, take the job to your dealer for repair or replacement.

Table 1 ELECTRICAL SPECIFICATIONS

Battery	
1965-1967	12 volt, 45 Ah
1968-1973	12 volt, 36 Ah (2 each)
1974-on	12 volt, 66 Ah
Alternator	
1965-1973	
Type	Bosch K1-14V or Motorola 26601
Voltage	14 volts
Maximum current	35 amps
Output power	490 watts
Nominal output speed	2,000 rpm
1974	
Type	Bosch 0120400
Voltage	14 volts
Maximum current	55 amps
Output power	770 watts
Nominal output speed	2,000 rpm
1975-1981	
Type	Bosch
Voltage	14 volts
Maximum current	70 amps
Output power	980 watts
Nominal output speed	2,000 rpm
1982	
Type	Bosch
Voltage	14 volts
Maximum current	75 amps
Starter	
Type	Bosch EB12v
Voltage	12 volts
Output	0.8 hp
Solenoid cut-in voltage	7 volts

Table 2   BULBS

Function	U.S. Replacement	Porsche Part No.
Headlights	6012	——
Front turn signals	1073	——
Front parking	1034	——
Side marker	1895	——
Stop/tail	1034	——
Rear turn signal	1034	——
License plate	——	999.631.104.91
Back-up	1003	——
Interior light	——	901.632.101.00
Instrument	——	900.631.102.90
Warning	——	900.631.102.90
Luggage compartment	——	900.631.115.90

CLUTCH

CLUTCH PEDAL ADJUSTMENTS

Three adjustments are required--clutch pedal travel, free play and cable length. All should be checked occasionally and adjusted if necessary, particularly after engine and transaxle removal, clutch replacement or clutch cable replacement.

All Porsche clutches are single plate, dry disc types mounted on the flywheel and incorporating a diaphragm spring. All are mechanically operated through an adjustable wire cable. **Figure 1** is typical.

All 1977-on models have an auxiliary spring on the transmission adjusting lever in addition to the clutch spring on the pedal assembly. See **Figure 2**. The auxiliary spring keeps the cable tight when the clutch is released.

Several different pressure plates and clutch discs are used on the various 911 models. To ensure proper replacements, always order by model, chassis number and engine number. See **Table 1** for specifications and torques at the end of chapter.

Pedal Free Play Adjustment (1965-1976)

Pedal free play adjustment involves taking up cable slack caused by cable stretch or lining wear. To check, depress clutch by hand until resistance is felt. Free play should be as given in **Table 1**. See **Figure 3**.

1. Jack up car on jackstands.
2. Loosen locknut at the end of cable. See **Figure 4**.
3. Adjust free play with adjusting nut. When free play is correct, tighten locknut.
4. Lower car.

Pedal Free Play Adjustment (1977-on)

Measurement of the clutch pedal free play is no longer made at the pedal. Instead, measure the distance between the adjusting bolt and positioning lever as shown in **Figure 2**. The correct clearance measurement is 0.040-0.043 in. (1.0-1.1 mm). Adjust, if required, by loosening the locknut on the screw. Turn the screw in or out as required. After adjustment, tighten the locknut.

9

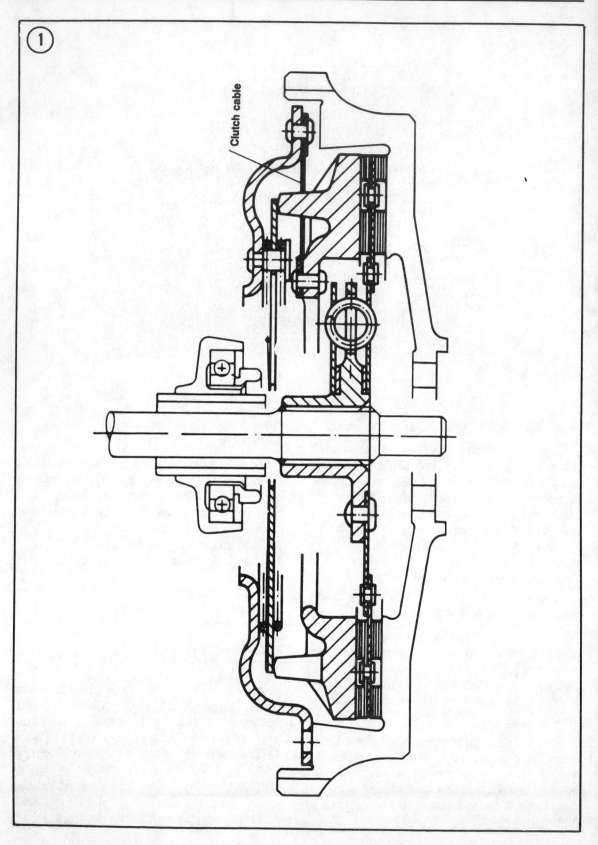

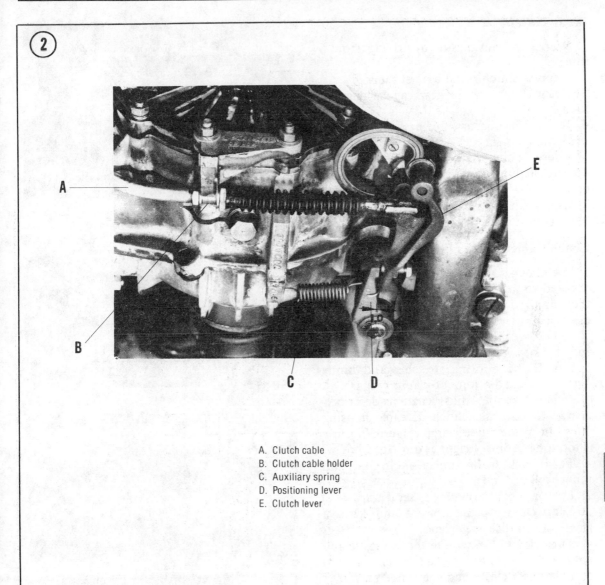

A. Clutch cable
B. Clutch cable holder
C. Auxiliary spring
D. Positioning lever
E. Clutch lever

9

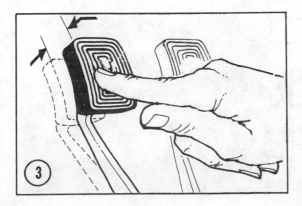

Pedal Travel

1. Warm up transmission by driving about 5 miles.
2. Depress clutch pedal against the stop.
3. Ensure that reverse gear can be engaged silently.
4. If gear clash occurs, fold back front rubber floor mat.
5. Loosen bolts securing stop and slide stop upward slightly. See **Figure 5**. Tighten bolts.
6. Retest by performing Steps 2 and 3.
7. Check that cable length is correct as described in next procedure.

Clutch Cable Length (1965-1975)

The clutch cable length must be carefully checked so that the release bearing can travel the required distance (about 15 mm) to disengage the clutch.

To check cable length, fully depress clutch and check the outer cable housing at the guide clamp. If the housing stretches and binds tightly against bottom of clamp (**Figure 6**), cable is too short. Adjust length as described below. Release the clutch. If cable housing pops out of the guide clamp (**Figure 7**), cable is too long. Adjust length as described below.

1. Fold back front rubber floor mat and tunnel cover.
2. Loosen locknut on clevis. See **Figure 8**.
3. Snap clevis spring upward and remove clevis pin to disengage cable.
4. Turn clevis clockwise to shorten cable and counterclockwise to lengthen cable.
5. Reconnect clevis and check free play.
6. Recheck clutch pedal travel adjustment as described previously.

Clutch Cable Adjustment (1976)

Adjust travel at lever (dimension A, **Figure 9**) to 0.85 in. (21.5 mm).

Clutch Cable Adjustment (1977-on)

1. Tighten the clutch cable at the cable holder (**Figure 2**) until play is reduced to 0.035-0.043 in. (0.9-1.1 mm) at point A in **Figure 10**.
2. Have an assistant depress and hold the clutch pedal.

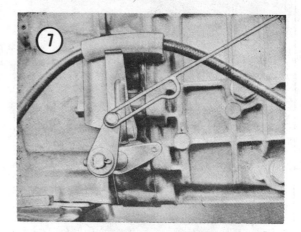

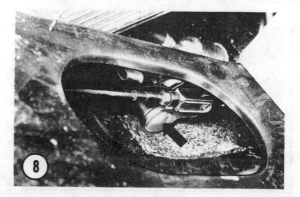

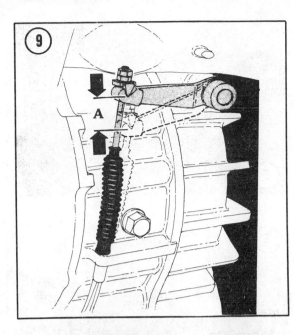

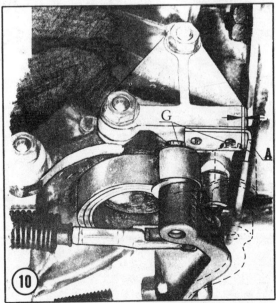

3. Measure the clutch cable as indicated in **Figure 11**. Correct cable release travel is 0.964-1.003 in. (24.5-25.5 mm). Correct travel can be obtained by adjusting the pedal floor plate stop bolt.

CLUTCH CABLE

Replacement

1. Fold back front rubber floor mat and tunnel cover.
2. Loosen the locknut on clevis. See **Figure 8**.
3. Snap retaining spring upward and remove clevis pin to disengage cable.
4. Screw clevis and locknut off cable.
5. Pull cable rearward and out.
6. Remove locknut and adjusting nut from rear end of cable.
7. Install locknut and adjusting nut on rear end of cable.
8. Lubricate cable with universal grease and thread it in from the rear.
9. Install clevis with locknut to front end of cable. Measure from the face of the threaded insert to the face of the locknut; adjust clevis position so that this measurement is 0.67-0.87 in. (17-22 mm).
10. Connect cable to clutch with clevis pin and retaining spring.
11. Hook rear end of cable on release lever. See **Figure 4**.
12. Adjust pedal free play travel and cable length as described earlier.

CLUTCH RELEASE LEVER (1978-ON)

Two counter springs are used to reduce clutch pedal effort. One spring is located on the clutch pedal and the other is located on the transmission and acts against the clutch release lever (**Figure 12**). If this assembly is disassembled, the bearing should be packed with waterproof lubricant before reassembly.

CLUTCH MECHANISM

Removal

1. Remove engine/transaxle and separate them as described in Chapter Four.
2. Using a sharp punch, mark the flywheel and the clutch cover for later reassembly in their same respective positions.

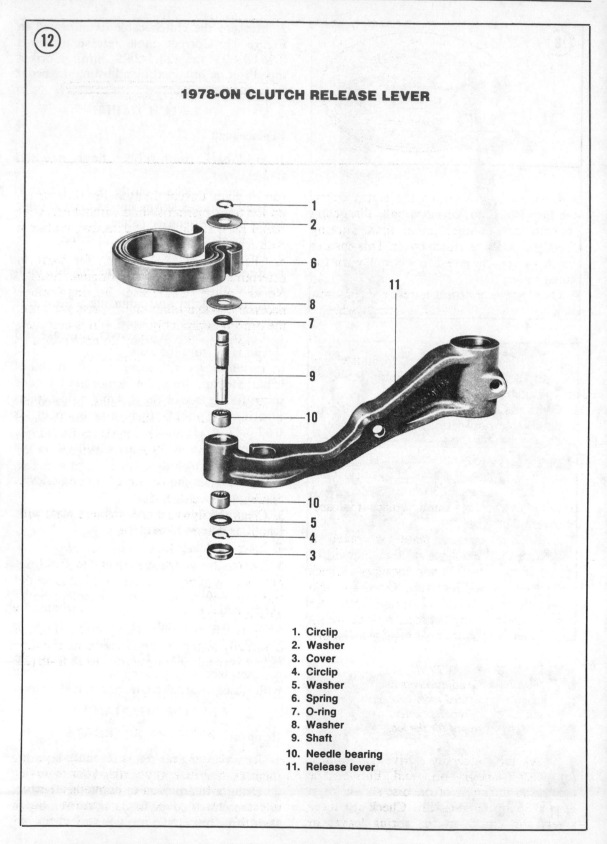

⑫

1978-ON CLUTCH RELEASE LEVER

1. Circlip
2. Washer
3. Cover
4. Circlip
5. Washer
6. Spring
7. O-ring
8. Washer
9. Shaft
10. Needle bearing
11. Release lever

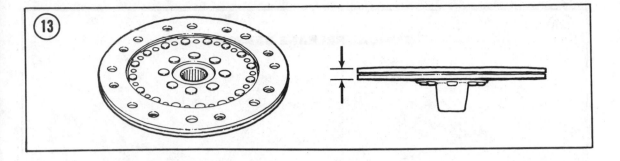

3. Unscrew bolts securing the clutch cover, one turn at a time. Unscrew bolts diagonally opposite one another rather than working directly around the clutch cover. This ensures that heavy spring pressure will not warp the clutch cover.

4. Once spring pressure is relieved, unscrew each bolt and remove clutch from flywheel.

Inspection

Never replace clutch parts without giving thought to the reason for failure. To do so only invites repeated troubles.

1. Clean the flywheel face and pressure plate assembly in a non-petroleum base cleaner.

2. Check the friction surface of the flywheel for cracks and grooves. Attach a dial indicator and check run-out. Maximum allowable run-out is 0.012 in. (0.30 mm). If necessary, have the flywheel reground; replace it in cases of severe damage.

3. Check the pressure plate for craked or broken springs, evidence of heat, cracked or scored friction surface and looseness. Check release lever ends for wear. On diaphragm spring clutches, check the spring fingers for wear. If there is any damage, replace with a professionally rebuilt pressure plate assembly.

CAUTION
Pressure plate adjustments and repairs require specialized tools and skills. Do not attempt repairs unless you are properly equipped for the job.

4. Check the clutch disc (drive plate) lining for wear, cracks, oil, and burns. The assembled thickness of the disc should be at least 0.36 in. (**Figure 13**). Check for loose rivets and cracks in the spring leaves or

carrier plate. Ensure that the disc slides freely on the transmission splines without excessive radial play. If the disc is defective, replace it with a new one.

5. Check the release bearing for wear to determine if it caused the original trouble. Never reuse a release bearing unless necessary. When other clutch parts are worn, the bearing is probably worn. If it is necessary to reinstall the old bearing, do not wash it in solvent; wipe it with a clean cloth.

Installation

1. Wash your hands *clean* before proceeding.

2. Sand the friction surface of the flywheel and pressure plate with a medium-fine emery cloth. Sand lightly across the surfaces, rather than around, until they are covered with fine scratches. This breaks the glaze and aids in seating a new clutch disc.

3. Clean the flywheel and pressure plate with a non-petroleum base cleaner.

4. Insert clutch disc.

5. Center the clutch disc over the gland nut hole with a pilot. An excellent pilot is an old transmission main shaft available from a wrecking yard.

6. Start all pressure plate bolts. Tighten diagonally opposite bolts a few turns at a time until all are tight. Torque bolts to 18 ft.-lb (2.5 mkg).

7. Remove the centering pilot.

RELEASE BEARING

The release bearing is mounted in the transaxle case and is accessible after removing the engine. In addition to checking a suspect release bearing, always remove clutch assembly from the flywheel and check for

9

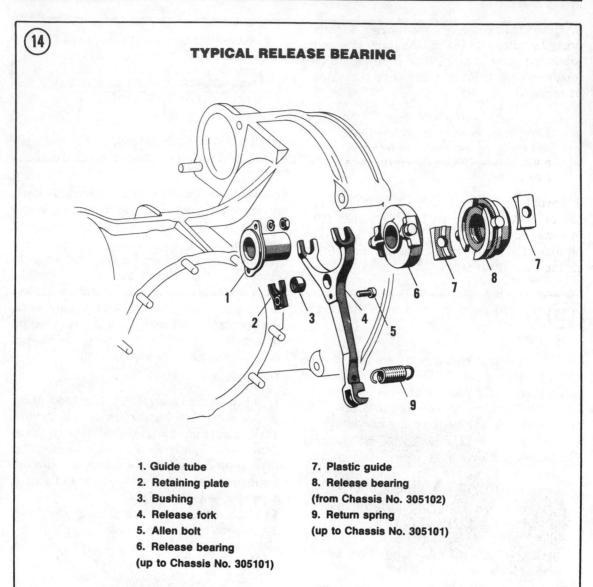

TYPICAL RELEASE BEARING

1. Guide tube
2. Retaining plate
3. Bushing
4. Release fork
5. Allen bolt
6. Release bearing
(up to Chassis No. 305101)

7. Plastic guide
8. Release bearing
(from Chassis No. 305102)
9. Return spring
(up to Chassis No. 305101)

damage as described earlier. Refer to **Figure 14** (typical).

1. Loosen Allen bolt securing release fork. See **Figure 15**.

2. Unhook the return spring (up to chassis No. 305.101) and withdraw the release bearing and fork.

NOTE
On 1976-on models, the guide tube for the release bearing is bolted to the gearbox and holds the main shaft seal in place (Figure 16).

3. Hold the inner race of the bearing. Lightly press the outer race against the inner race and rotate the outer race. If there is any noise or roughness, the bearing is defective and must be replaced.

CAUTION
The release bearing is prelubricated and sealed. Do not wash it in solvent or it will be ruined. Wipe the bearing with a clean cloth.

4. Install the release bearing with plastic guides in the release fork. Ensure that the bearing moves freely in the fork without binding. Dress the plastic guides with fine crocus cloth if necessary.

NOTE
Release bearings on the 911 prior to January 1967, have integral guides, not separate plastic guides. The new bearings with plastic guides may be installed in earlier models.

5. Lubricate all bearing surfaces of the release bearing and fork with molybdenum disulfide paste.

6. Install bearing and fork in transaxle and secure with Allen bolt. Tighten bolt to 7 ft.-lb. (1 mkg).

7. On models up to chassis No. 305 101, install return spring.

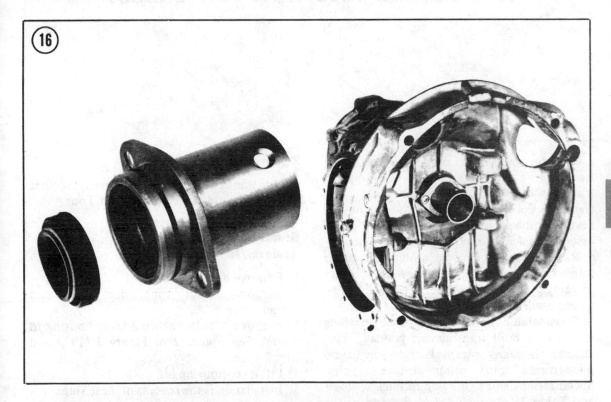

Table 1 CLUTCH SPECIFICATIONS AND TORQUES

Clutch type	Single-plate dry disc
Spring type	Diaphragm
Friction area	31.5 in.^{2} (203 cm^2)
Pedal free play	
1965-1975	0.75-1.0 in. (20-25 mm)
1976	0.40-0.75 in. (10-20 mm)
1977-on	0.040-0.043 in. (1.0-1.1 mm)
Pressure plate bolt torque	18 ft.-lb. (2.5 mkg)
Release fork Allen bolt torque	7 ft.-lb. (1 mkg)

MANUAL AND AUTOMATIC TRANSAXLES

Porsche transaxles consist of a single housing containing a 4- or 5-speed transmission and differential gears. The transaxle bolts to the front of the engine and several rubber mounts support the entire assembly. Each transaxle is described below.

Repair requiring disassembly of either transaxle are not possible for home mechanics or garage mechanics without special skills and a large assortment of special Porsche tools.

Considerable money can be saved installing a new or rebuilt transmission yourself. This chapter includes removal and installation procedures, plus other simple repairs. Specifications and tightening torques (**Table 1** and **Table 2**) are included at the end of the chapter. See Chapter Three for lubrication and preventive maintenance.

MANUAL TRANSAXLES

Two manual transaxles are available; a 4-speed and a 5-speed. The gears are in constant mesh and all forward speeds are fully synchronized. **Figure 1** shows a cutaway view of the engine transaxle.

Removal/Installation

The transaxle must be removed together with the engine. Refer to Chapter Four.

Gearshift Housing
Removal/Installation

1. Remove both front seats.
2. Remove heater knob, dust boot, and tunnel cover.
3. Remove 5 bolts securing lever housing to tunnel. See **Figure 2** or **Figure 3** (1973 and later 5-speed).
4. Lift lever housing off.
5. Installation is the reverse of these steps.

Gearshift Housing
Disassembly/Assembly

Refer to **Figure 4** for following procedure.
1. Pull plastic ball socket off bottom of lever.
2. Hold housing in a vise.
3. Remove C-rings on spring pins. See **Figure 5**.
4. Push one pin about halfway out.

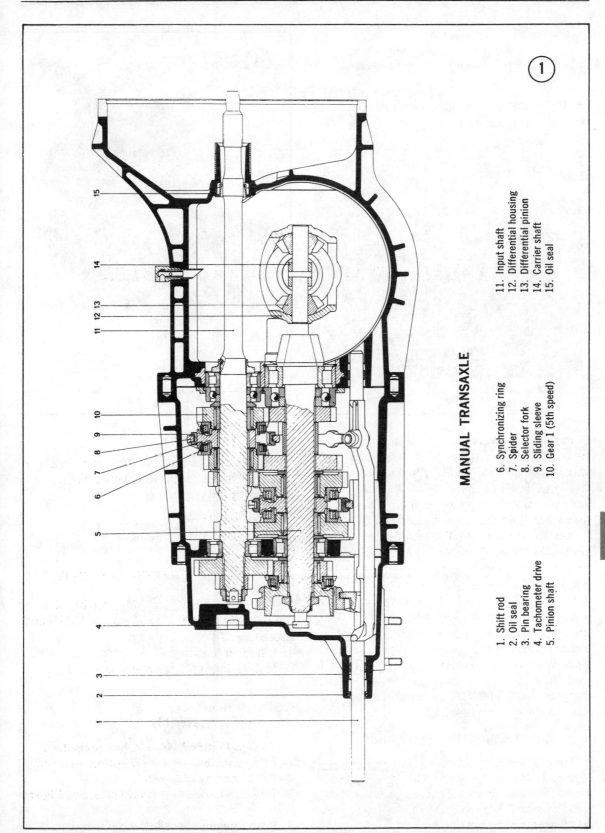

MANUAL TRANSAXLE

1. Shift rod
2. Oil seal
3. Pin bearing
4. Tachometer drive
5. Pinion shaft

6. Synchronizing ring
7. Spider
8. Selector fork
9. Sliding sleeve
10. Gear 1 (5th speed)

11. Input shaft
12. Differential housing
13. Differential pinion
14. Carrier shaft
15. Oil seal

10

WARNING
The spring could fly out of the housing.
Hold a rag around the housing to prevent
injury.

5. Keep the rag in place and pry the loose
spring out. See **Figure 6**.

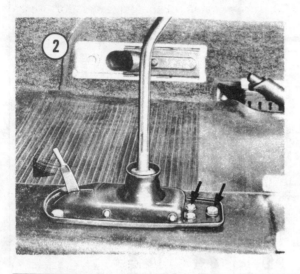

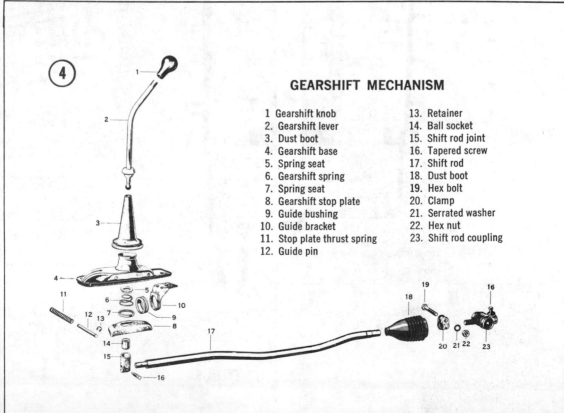

GEARSHIFT MECHANISM

1 Gearshift knob
2. Gearshift lever
3. Dust boot
4. Gearshift base
5. Spring seat
6. Gearshift spring
7. Spring seat
8. Gearshift stop plate
9. Guide bushing
10. Guide bracket
11. Stop plate thrust spring
12. Guide pin

13. Retainer
14. Ball socket
15. Shift rod joint
16. Tapered screw
17. Shift rod
18. Dust boot
19. Hex bolt
20. Clamp
21. Serrated washer
22. Hex nut
23. Shift rod coupling

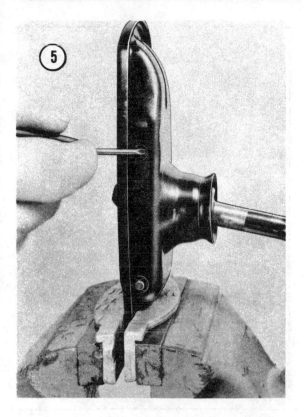

NOTE
The rag is not shown as it would hide the operation.

6. Remove the other spring in the same way.
7. Pull stop plate, spring, and spring seat out.
8. Remove gearshift lever.
9. Clean all parts in solvent.
10. Inspect stop plate and lever for wear. Replace if necessary.
11. Assembly is the reverse of these steps. Lubricate the bottom end of the lever with multipurpose (lithium) grease. When installing the springs, slip the pin in about halfway, then compress the spring with a modified screwdriver. See **Figure 7** and **Figure 8**.

10

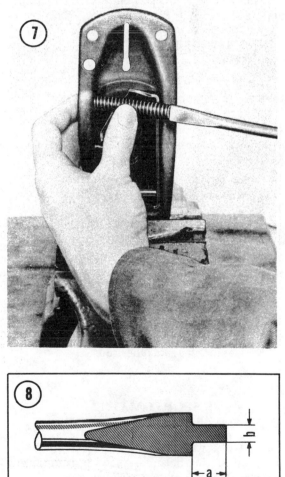

a = 12mm (approx. ½ inch)
b = 6mm (approx. ¼ inch)

Main Shaft Oil Seal Replacement

1. Remove engine/transaxle as described in Chapter Four.

2. Remove the clutch release bearing. See Chapter Nine.

3. Remove clutch release bearing guide. See **Figure 9**.

4. Clean dirt from outside of oil seal.

5. Pry oil seal out with a screwdriver.

CAUTION
Do not nick any metal surface.

6. Clean opening around main shaft.

7. Coat outer edge of seal with gasket compound. Oil main shaft and seal lip.

8. Slide oil seal on the main shaft and drive it into place. Use a special hollow drift or length of pipe as shown in **Figure 10**.

Determining Transmission Gear Ratios

Porsche has always offered a staggering number of optional gear ratios for the 4- and 5-speed manual transmission. Specifications are meaningless in this case. The safest way to determine gear ratios is by actual measurements.

1. Raise the rear of the car on jackstands.

2. Disconnect output of ignition coil.

3. Move the gearshift lever to the gear to be measured.

4. Make a chalk reference mark on one tire.

5. Count the number of crankshaft revolutions necessary to rotate the tire exactly one full turn.

6. Divide the engine revolutions in Step 5 by 4.429 (final drive ratio). The result is the gear ratio of the gear selected.

7. Repeat for all gears if desired.

SPORTOMATIC

The Sportomatic, introduced in 1968, consists of a torque converter, servo operated mechanical clutch, and 4-speed transmission. **Figure 11** is a detailed cutaway view of the transmission. **Figure 12** shows the hydraulic circuits and **Figure 13** shows the vacuum circuits in simplified form.

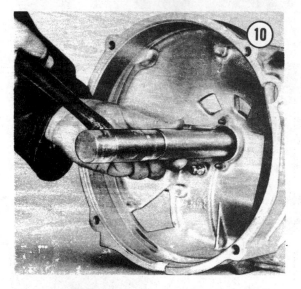

The Sportomatic has a conventional torque converter to provide smooth application of power over a wide range. But unlike full automatics, the Sportomatic requires a mechanical clutch to interrupt power flow for gear changes. Gear changes are entirely manual, not automatic.

The torque converter is capable of multiplying engine torque over 2:1 when the car moves from a complete stop. At this point, torque is maximum and slippage within the torque converter is also maximum. As slippage decreases, i.e., the speed difference between the turbine and impeller in the torque converter decreases, torque multiplication also decreases. When slippage decreases so that turbine speed is 84% of the impeller speed, there is no multiplication and

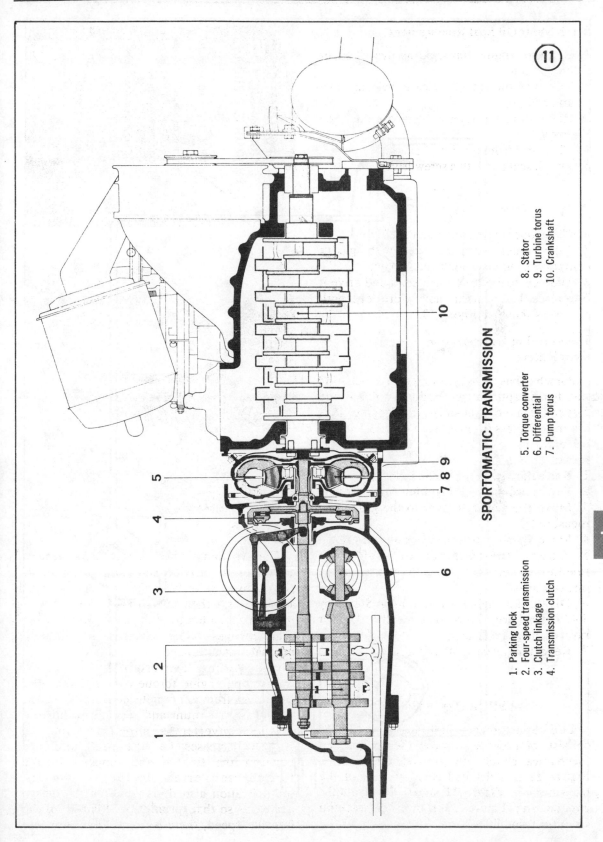

SPORTOMATIC TRANSMISSION

1. Parking lock
2. Four-speed transmission
3. Clutch linkage
4. Transmission clutch

5. Torque converter
6. Differential
7. Pump torus

8. Stator
9. Turbine torus
10. Crankshaft

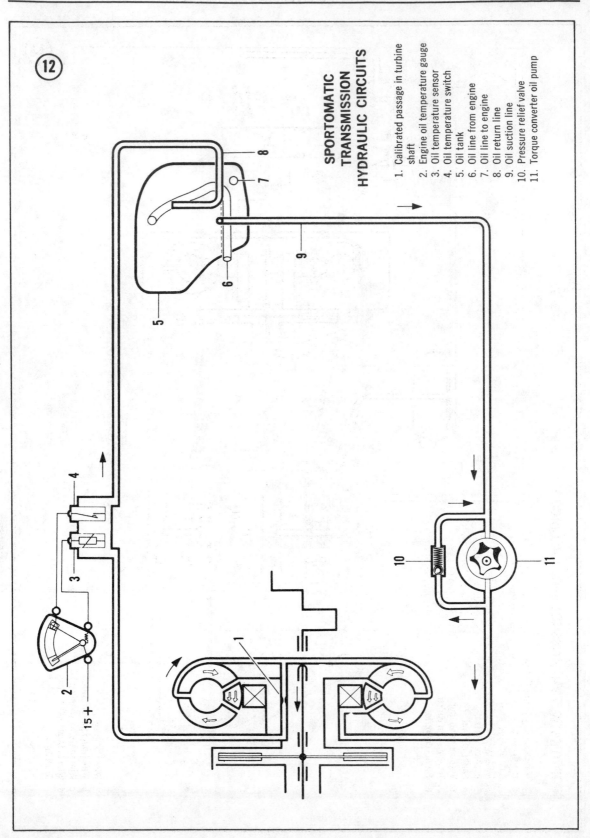

SPORTOMATIC TRANSMISSION HYDRAULIC CIRCUITS

1. Calibrated passage in turbine shaft
2. Engine oil temperature gauge
3. Oil temperature sensor
4. Oil temperature switch
5. Oil tank
6. Oil line from engine
7. Oil line to engine
8. Oil return line
9. Oil suction line
10. Pressure relief valve
11. Torque converter oil pump

SPORTOMATIC TRANSMISSION VACUUM CIRCUIT

1. Microswitch in gearshift lever
2. Bypass switch
3. Gear selector shaft
4. Backup light switch and park position contact
5. Shift rod P and R
6. Vacuum servo unit
7. Transmission clutch
8. Torque converter
9. Backup light
10. Crankshaft
11. Control valve
12. Adjusting screw
13. Vacuum reservoir
14. Electric solenoid switch
15. Cam and plunger
16. Intake manifold
17. Check valve

a. Wire from fuse 1
b. Wire from ignition switch
c. Wire to starter terminal 50
d. Wire to intermediate fuse 8/15 Amp

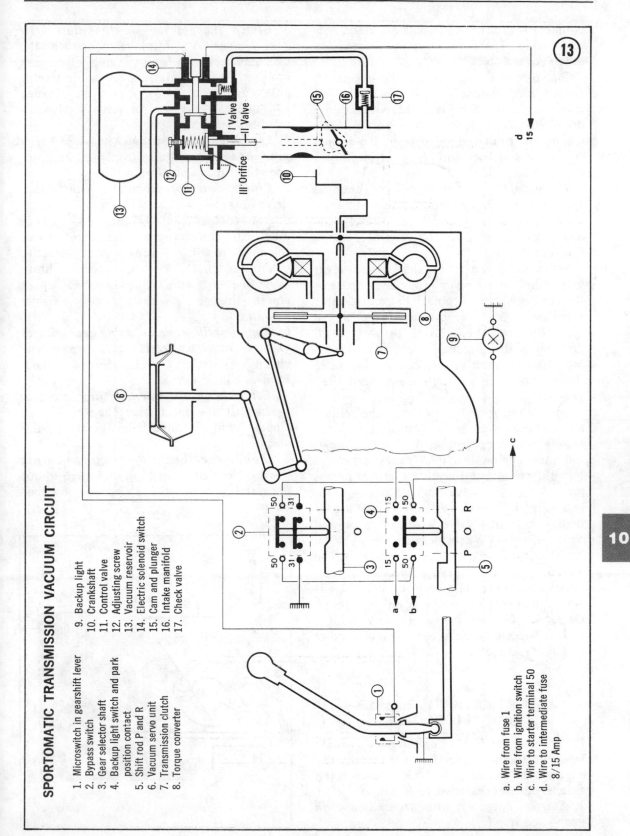

10

coupling is direct. The turbine can reach 96% of impeller speed—the maximum coupling efficiency possible.

The torque converter uses the engine oil supply independent of the rear axle and transmission oil. See **Figure 12**. An oil pump driven by the left engine camshaft delivers engine oil from the oil tank to the torque converter and back through a return line to the oil tank.

The torque converter drives a conventional 4-speed transmission through a single dry disc clutch. A vacuum operated servo disengages and engages the clutch in response to the control valve.

When the driver moves the gearshift lever longitudinally, a contact in the lever operates the control valve solenoid. The control valve supplies engine vacuum from the intake manifold to the clutch servo, which disengages the clutch. Since power flow is interrupted, the driver can continue to move the gearshift and manually select the desired gear.

The control valve engages the clutch automatically after an interval determined by engine load. A cam on the throttle valve shaft indicates engine load and opens or closes Valve II on the control valve. If engine load is low, the throttle valve is closed or nearly so, and Valve II remains closed. If engine load is high, the frontal valve is wholly open and Valve II opens. When the driver releases the gearshift, the solenoid closes Valve I. The vacuum in the servo "bleeds off" to atmospheric pressure quickly through Valve II which is open or slowly opening through Orifice III. The rate at which the servo returns to atmospheric pressure controls the speed of clutch engagement.

SPORTMATIC TRANSAXLE TROUBLESHOOTING

1. *Starter will not operate*—A starter inhibitor (neutral safety) switch permits the engine to be started in NEUTRAL only. If the switch becomes defective, replace it.

2. *Starter operates with transmission in gear*—See Step 1.

3. *Clutch engages too slowly (slips) after gear change*—A control valve operates the clutch. Check the control valve adjustment and hose connections between control valve and carburetor. Check clutch linkage adjustment. Leaky control valve diaphragms may also cause this.

4. *Clutch engages too quickly (jerks) after gear change*—A control valve adjustment sets operating time of clutch.

5. *Clutch does not disengage (can't select drive range)*—First check solenoid fuse in the engine compartment (**Figure 14**). Check electrical connections to control valve solenoid; you may even have a defective solenoid. Check all the vacuum hoses associated with the control valve. Check clutch linkage adjustments. See Chapter Eleven.

6. *Engine stalls when selecting gear*—Check vacuum hose between control valve and clutch servo. Check cluth servo for leaks. Replace both if necessary.

7. *Car jerks in idle when shifting into gear*—Readjust idle speed (see Chapter Three). Check control valve adjustment in this chapter.

8. *Poor acceleration (engine output good)*—Normally caused by defective torque converter. Check stall speed as described below.

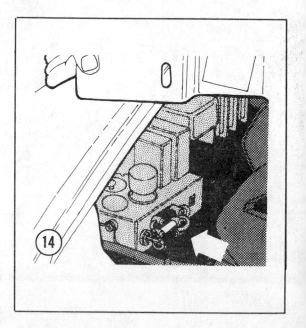

Torque Converter Stall Speed

This test permits rapid evaluation of the torque converter.

1. Connect an accurate tachometer to the engine. Start the engine, set the handbrake and warm up the engine.

2. Depress the footbrake firmly; shift the lever to DRIVE 4.

> *CAUTION*
> *This is a severe test and oil in torque converter heats very rapidly. Do not run the engine under full load any longer than necessary to read the tachometer (5-10 seconds).*

3. Depress accelerator briefly to full throttle while holding the car at a complete stop with handbrake and footbrake. Quickly read the engine speed reached on the tachometer.

4. If the stall speed is more than 600 rpm below the specifications (2,000-2,250 rpm), the torque converter is defective and must be replaced. A stall speed only a few hundred rpm below specifications indicates the engine is not delivering full power and probably needs a tune-up. A stall speed higher than specified indicates clutch slippage.

Removal/Installation

Remove engine/transaxle as a unit, then separate them. See Chapter Four for details.

Control Valve Replacement

The control valve is located on the right side of the left intake manifold. It cannot be repaired.

1. Disconnect battery ground cable(s).

2. Remove air cleaner assembly. See Chapter Six.

3. Pull rubber boot off control valve connector. Remove cotter pin and disconnect electrical connector. See **Figure 15**.

4. Disconnect vacuum lines from control valve.

5. Unbolt the control valve bracket from the carburetor.

6. Remove control valve from bracket.

7. Installation is the reverse of these steps. Smear multipurpose grease on the throttle cam where it contacts the control valve.

8. Adjust control valve as described below.

Control Valve Adjustment

This procedure assumes that the throttle linkage and idle speed are correctly adjusted. See Chapter Three.

To adjust for upshifts:

1. With throttle in idle position, insert feeler gauge under control valve cam follower. See **Figure 16**. Adjust length of follower so that clearance is 0.04-0.06 in. (1-1.5 mm).

2. Insert shim(s) 0.12 in. (3 mm) thick under left idle speed adjustment (**Figure 17**). Loosen Allen bolt on cam so that the drag spring (**Figure 18**) just touches the control valve cam follower.

3. Depress accelerator to full throttle. Ensure that the cam follower is not fully depressed. It should be possible to depress the follower an additional 0.012 in. (0.5 mm) by inserting a feeler gauge (**Figure 19**).

To adjust for downshift:

Adjust the control valve so that the clutch smoothly engages after a downshift without substantial time lag (0.3-0.5 seconds), yet does not cause rear wheels to lock and cause tire chirp.

1. Select "D" and drive at 4,500 rpm.
2. Take foot off throttle and shift to "L."
3. If clutch engages too fast or too slow, stop the car and remove the air cleaner. Remove the plastic cover over the control valve adjustment. See **Figure 20**. Turn screw clockwise if clutch engages too fast. Turn screw counterclockwise if clutch engages too slow.

> *NOTE*
> *Turn screw 1/4-1/2 turn, then repeat procedure.*

4. When adjustment is correct, reinstall plastic cover and air cleaner.

Temperature Sender and Switch Replacement

These switches screw into a housing mounted on top of the clutch housing. See **Figure 21**. The engine must be lowered to reach them, but need not be removed.

1. Raise rear of car on jackstands and open engine compartment lid.

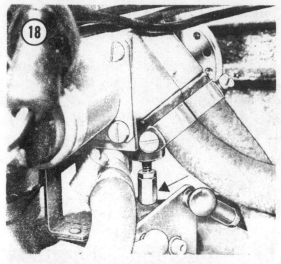

2. Disconnect battery ground cable.
3. Remove the air cleaner assembly. See Chapter Six.
4. On cars with exhaust emission control systems, disconnect hoses from air pump and unscrew air pump filters. See Chapter Seven.

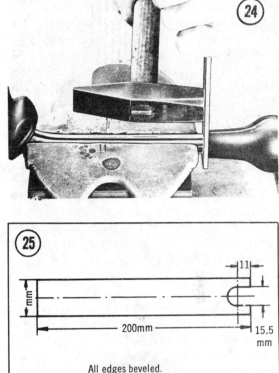

All edges beveled.
Flat steel stock, 6mm thick.

9. Carefully lower engine/transaxle assembly until the temperature switch and sender are accessible.

10. Disconnect wire from sender and/or switch and unscrew it.

11. Installation is the reverse of these steps. Torque switch or sender to 33-36 ft.-lb. (4.5-5.0 mkg). Torque engine mounting bolts to 69 ft.-lb. (9.5 mkg).

Gearshift Lever Microswitch Replacement

1. Push both front seats back as far as possible.

2. Remove center tunnel covering.

3. Remove 5 bolts securing gearshift base and lift base slightly. See **Figure 23**.

4. Disconnect microswitch wire and lift entire base out.

5. Hold lever in a vise with soft jaws and remove knob with a fork-shaped tool. See **Figure 24** and **Figure 25**. Pull locking sleeve out of knob.

5. Disconnect wires from ignition coil.

6. Disconnect hot air ducts from heat exchangers. See Chapter Five.

7. Place a floor jack under the center of the engine transaxle assembly. Raise the jack just enough to support weight of assembly.

8. Remove bolt from each engine mount. See **Figure 22**.

6. Pull dust boot and switch off lever.

7. Slide bottom of new microswitch onto lever with slit facing forward. See **Figure 26**.

8. Install top of switch and rubber boot.

9. Push new locking sleeve into knob. Hold lever in a vise with soft jaws and drive the knob on with a plastic or hardwood tool (**Figure 27**).

10. Reconnect microswitch wire in center tunnel and install base. The ground wire goes under the left front retaining bolt. Torque large bolts to 18 ft.-lb. (2.5 mkg) and small bolts to 7 ft.-lb. (1.0 mkg).

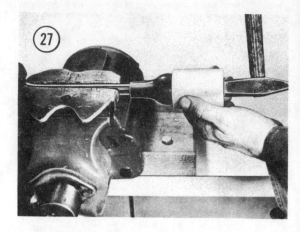

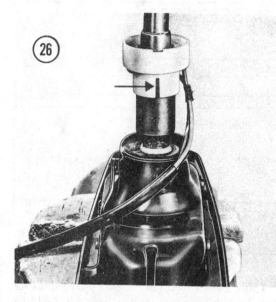

Table 1	SPECIFICATIONS
MANUAL TRANSAXLE	
Oil capacity	
with limited slip	3.17 quarts (3 liters)
without limited slip	2.6 quarts (2.5 liters)
Oil type	
with limited slip	SAE 90 (MIL-L-2105B)
without limited slip	SAE 90 hypoid gear oil
SPORTOMATIC	
Gear ratios	
1st	2.400
2nd	1.550
3rd	1.125
4th	0.858
Reverse	2.533
Final drive ratio	3.857
Oil capacity	2.6 quarts (2.5 liters)
Oil type	SAE 90 hypoid gear oil

Table 2	TIGHTENING TORQUES		
		foot-pounds	mkg
Transmission-to-frame bolts			
Sportomatic pressure plate bolts		10	1.4
Sportomatic transaxle-to-clutch			
housing bolts		14	2.0
Temperature switch or sender		33-36	4.5-5.0
Engine mounting bolts		69	9.5
Gearshift bolts (large)		18	2.5
Gearshift bolts (small)		7	1.0

REAR AXLE AND SUSPENSION

All 911 models have independent rear suspension with semi-trailing arms. See **Figure 1**. This gives more rear wheel camber change than a pure trailing arm system, but far less than a conventional swing axle system. The 2 trailing arms are sprung by separate torsion bars.

Double-articulated drive shafts drive the rear wheels. Nadella shafts with conventional universal joints (**Figure 2**) and Löbro shafts with constant velocity joints (**Figure 3**) are often used interchangeably without regard to year or model.

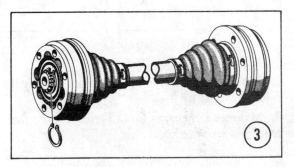

The trailing arm design changed slightly from 1969 on. Prior to 1969, a roller bearing and a ball bearing supported the wheel hub shaft. See **Figure 4**. Since 1969, a permanently lubricated and sealed double-row ball bearing is used. See **Figure 5**.

Table 1 provides tightening torque values for mounting hardware while **Table 2** includes specifications (both at end of chapter).

WHEEL ALIGNMENT

Wheel alignment on an independent rear suspension is as important to handling and tire wear as front wheel alignment. Rear axle height, camber and toe-in are adjustable and should be checked every 6,000 miles.

Rear Axle Height

This adjustment sets the basis for later rear suspension adjustments. The car should be on an alignment ramp or level floor. This procedure assumes radius arm angle is correct. See *Radius Arm Adjustment* in the *Torsion Arm* section of this chapter.

11

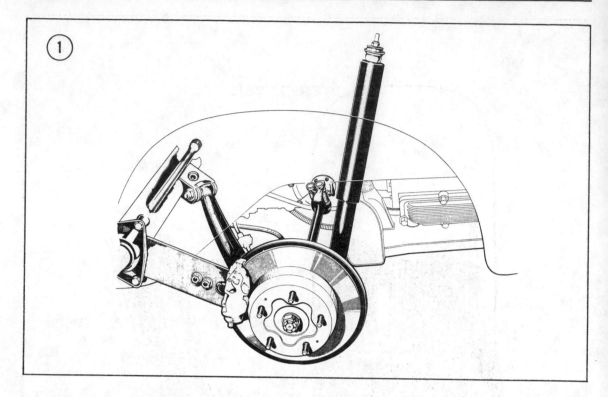

1. Remove wheel covers.

2. Depress rear of car several times and let it return to level by itself.

3. Measure dimension (a) in **Figure 6** from the axle center to the floor.

4. Measure dimension (b1) in Figure 6. Measure radius of torsion bar bushing cover. Add this figure to dimension (b1). Record this figure as dimension (b).

5. Subtract 12mm from dimension (b). See

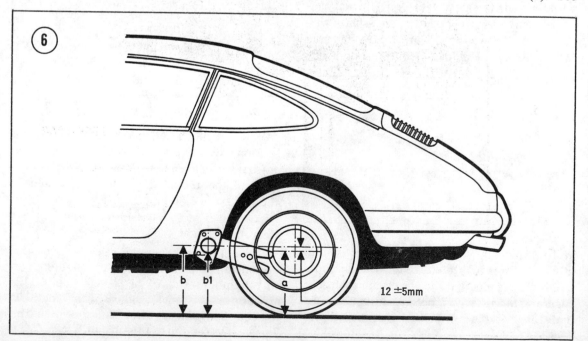

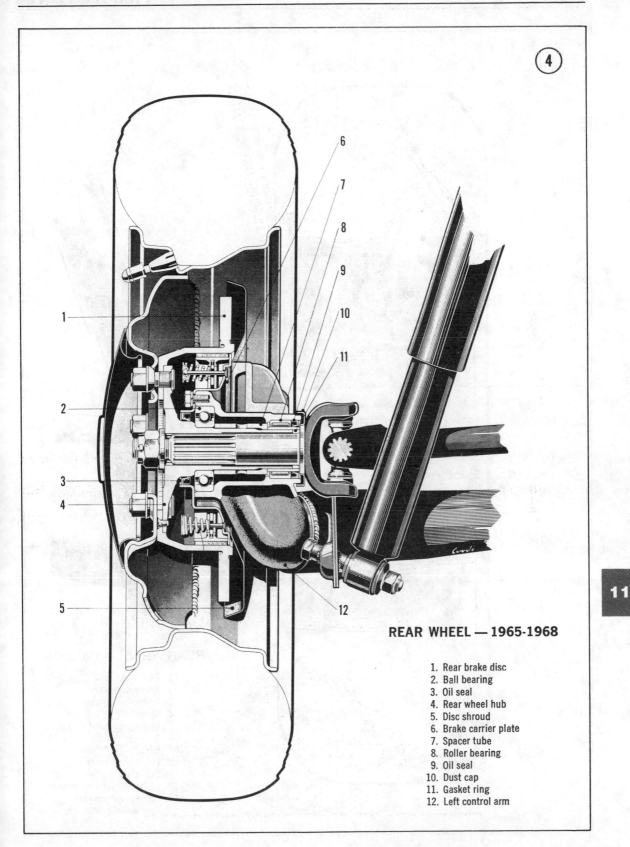

④

REAR WHEEL — 1965-1968

1. Rear brake disc
2. Ball bearing
3. Oil seal
4. Rear wheel hub
5. Disc shroud
6. Brake carrier plate
7. Spacer tube
8. Roller bearing
9. Oil seal
10. Dust cap
11. Gasket ring
12. Left control arm

11

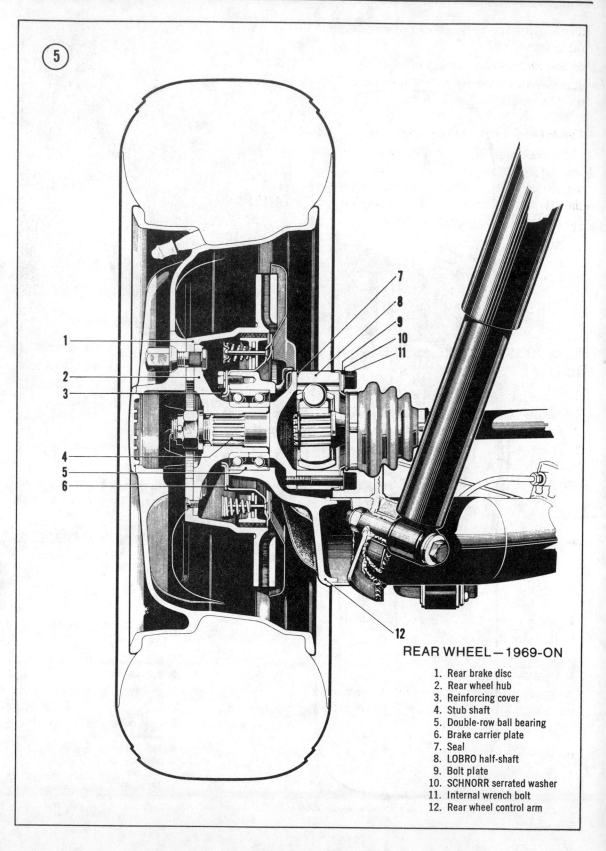

REAR WHEEL – 1969-ON

1. Rear brake disc
2. Rear wheel hub
3. Reinforcing cover
4. Stub shaft
5. Double-row ball bearing
6. Brake carrier plate
7. Seal
8. LOBRO half-shaft
9. Bolt plate
10. SCHNORR serrated washer
11. Internal wrench bolt
12. Rear wheel control arm

Step 4. This new figure should equal dimension (a) ±5mm.

6. Repeat procedure on the other axle.

7. Compare dimension (b1) of both axles. They must be within 8mm of each other.

Camber and Toe-in Adjustments

It is not possible to adjust camber or toe-in without an alignment ramp. If you have disassembled the torsion bars or trailing arms, take the car to your dealer or other suspension specialist immediately after reassembling.

CAUTION
Drive slowly and carefully as handling is affected. Don't drive too far as tires can wear extremely quickly when scrubbed sideways by a misaligned suspension.

DRIVE SHAFTS (NADELLA)

Removal

1. Put the transmission in gear and pull up the handbrake.

2. Loosen the wheel lug bolts.

3. Remove cotter key in castellated hub nut and loosen nut with a 36mm socket and a long breaker bar. The nut is torqued to 217 ft.-lb.

CAUTION
Never loosen the nut unless all 4 wheels are firmly on the ground. The force required to loosen the nut is sufficient to knock the car off the jackstands.

4. Raise the rear of the car on jackstands.

5. Remove the hub nut.

6. Remove Allen bolts from drive shaft flange at inner end. See **Figure 7**.

7. Knock inner end of the shaft loose from its seat and pull the outer end out of the wheel hub.

Inspection

1. Check universal joints for play. If worn, entire shaft must be replaced.

2. Check shaft for nicks and bends. Replace if necessary.

Installation

1. Install new seal over splined end of shaft.

2. Lightly oil splines and insert into wheel hub.

3. Connect flanged end of shaft to transaxle. Tighten Allen bolts to 34 ft.-lb. (4.7 mkg).

CAUTION
Be sure that flanged end is completely free of grease and oil.

4. Install washer and castellated nut on outer end of shaft. Tighten to 20-30 ft.-lb. (3-4 mkg).

5. Lower car.

6. Tighten castellated hub nut to 217-253 ft.-lb. (30-35 mkg). Secure with a new cotter pin.

DRIVE SHAFTS (LÖBRO)

Removal

1. Put the transmission in gear and pull up the handbrake.

2. Loosen the wheel lug bolts.

3. Remove cotter key in castellated hub nut and loosen nut with a 36mm socket and a long breaker bar. The nut is torqued to 217 ft.-lb.

CAUTION
Never loosen the nut unless all 4 wheels are firmly on the ground. The force required to loosen the nut is sufficient to knock the car off the jackstands.

11

4. Raise rear of car on jackstands.

5. Place jack under radius arm on same side as desired drive shaft. Raise radius arm enough to take tension off shock absorber.

CAUTION
The shock absorber limits wheel travel so that the spring tension must be supported by a jack or clamp when the shock is disconnected. **Figure 8** *shows Porsche tool P289 used for this purpose.*

6. Disconnect the lower end of shock absorber.

7. Remove the castellated hub nut.

8. Remove the Allen bolts at the inner flange. See **Figure 9**.

9. Knock inner end of shaft loose from its seat and pull the outer end out of the wheel hub.

Inspection

1. Check constant velocity joints for excessive play. If worn, entire shaft must be replaced.

2. Check shaft for nicks and bends. Replace if necessary.

3. Check rubber boots for deterioration. Replace as described below.

Installation

1. Lightly oil the splines and insert the shaft into wheel hub.

2. Connect inner end to transaxle. Make sure mating surfaces are thoroughly clean. Use a new gasket. Tighten the Allen bolts to 60 ft.-lb. (8.3 mkg).

3. Install washer and castellated nut on outer end of shaft. Tighten to 20-30 ft.-lb. (3-4 mkg).

4. Reconnect lower end of shock absorber. Remove jack from under spring plate.

5. Lower car.

6. Tighten castellated hub nut to 217-253 ft.-lb. (30-35 mkg). Secure with a new cotter pin.

REAR AXLE BOOTS
(LÖBRO SHAFTS)

Replacement

1. Remove drive shaft as described previously.

2. Remove hose clamps from boot.

3. Remove the lock ring from the end of the shaft (**Figure 10**) and press the constant velocity joint off. See **Figure 11**.

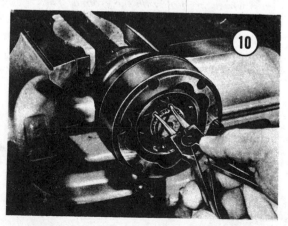

4. Remove rubber boots.

5. Clean all parts in solvent.

6. Slide new boot onto shaft.

7. Slide constant velocity joint onto shaft and secure with lock ring.

8. Pack about 2 1/2 ounces (70 grams) of multipurpose molybdenum disulfide grease into the inside of the constant velocity joint, boot, and inside flange area.

9. Clean area on constant velocity joint on which the rubber boot mounts.

10. Glue boot onto constant velocity joint with gasket compound.

11. Tighten hose clamps with pliers and bend tab over with small hammer. See **Figure 12**.

NOTE: *Two small holes must be drilled in clamps as shown in* **Figure 13** *in order to tighten with pliers.*

12. Install drive shaft.

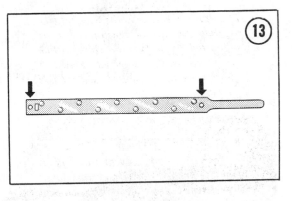

TORSION BARS

Removal

1. Jack up rear of car on jackstands.

2. Place jack under spring plate on same side as desired torsion bar. Raise radius arm enough to take tension off shock absorber.

CAUTION

The shock absorber limits wheel travel so that the spring tension must be supported by a jack or clamp when the shock is disconnected. Figure 8 shows Porsche tool P289 used for this purpose.

3. Disconnect lower end of shock absorber. See **Figure 14**.

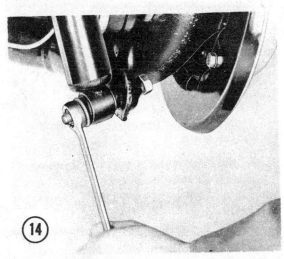

11

4. Remove 4 bolts securing radius arm to diagonal trailing arm. See **Figure 15**.

5. Remove retaining bolts from cover shown in **Figure 16**. Remove small spacer behind cover.

6. Pry radius arm cover off with 2 large screwdrivers.

7. Lower jack which is maintaining tension on the radius arm.

8. Remove plug from front lower edge of rear wheel well.

9. Pull radius arm off.

10. Withdraw torsion bar.

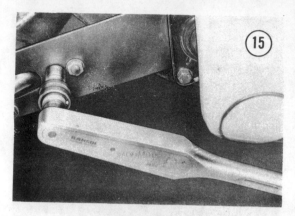

> *CAUTION*
> *A protective paint covers the torsion bars. Do not nick or scratch this paint. Even slight damage leads to corrosion and eventual fatigue fractures. Touch up with paint, if necessary.*

Removing Broken Torsion Bar

Following the procedure above will enable you to remove the outer piece of a broken torsion bar but the inner piece will remain. To remove the inner piece, remove the torsion bar on the opposite side also. Then push the broken piece out from the opposite side with a long rod.

Installation

1. Grease torsion bar splines with lithium grease and insert the bar.

> *NOTE*
> *Torsion bars are marked left (L) and (R); do not interchange them.*

2. Coat inner rubber bushing with glycerine paste or other lubricant made specifically for rubber.

> *CAUTION*
> *Do not use petroleum based lubricants such as oil or grease. These products attack the rubber.*

3. On early chassis with separate bushings, fit inner bushing over torsion bar. Later chassis have radius arms with integral bushings. See **Figure 17**.

4. Install radius arm and adjust it as described later.

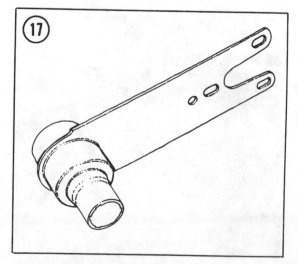

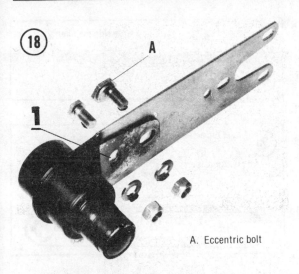

A. Eccentric bolt

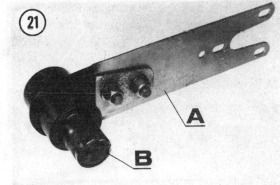

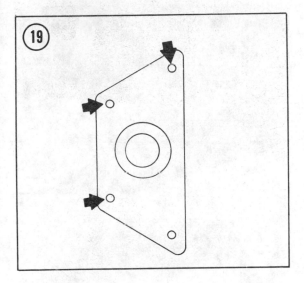

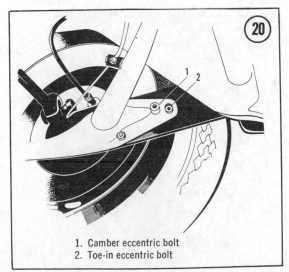

1. Camber eccentric bolt
2. Toe-in eccentric bolt

NOTE
During radius arm installation on 1977 and later models, make sure the hole in the spring plate is positioned at the top of the elongated hole in the hub (1, Figure 18). This assures complete range adjustment with the eccentric screw.

5. Coat outer rubber bushing with glycerine paste or equivalent.

6. Install radius arm cover with 3 bolts shown in **Figure 19**. Tighten finger-tight.

7. Raise radius arm with jack until fourth bolt (lower rear corner) and spacer can be installed.

8. Tighten all cover bolts to 34 ft.-lb. (4.7 mkg).

9. Install 2 bolts securing radius arm to trailing arm. Tighten to 65 ft.-lb. (9 mkg).

10. Install camber and toe-in eccentric bolts. See **Figure 20**. Tighten to 35 ft.-lb. (6 mkg) and 43 ft.-lb. (5 mkg), respectively.

NOTE
The toe-in eccentric bolt is the smaller of the two.

11. Connect the lower end of shock absorber. Tighten to 54 ft.-lb. (7.5 mkg).

12. Remove jack from under the radius arm and lower car.

13. Adjust rear wheel camber and tracking as described later in this chapter.

Radius Arm Adjustment

Two-part radius arms are used on 1977 and later models. The spring plate (A, **Figure 21**) and hub (B, **Figure 21**) are bolted together. To

11

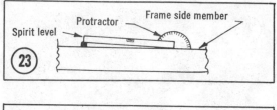

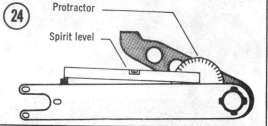

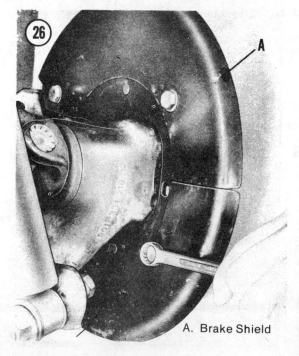

simplify height adjustments, the spring plate has been machined with an eccentric adjustment bolt. See **Figure 18**. Height adjustment is 1 1/4-1 21/32 in. (32-42 mm).

In order to obtain proper wheel alignment and adequate spring travel under all load conditions, the radius arm angle must be adjusted on the torsion bar. There are 40 splines on the inner end of the torsion bar and 44 splines on the outer end. Turning the inner end of the bar one spline alters the radius arm angle 9° 0'; turning the radius arm one spline on the bar alters the angle by 8° 10'. Therefore, it is possible to set the radius arm angle at any multiple of 50' by turning the splines in opposite directions.

Measurement of this angle is most easily done with a special tool made for this purpose. See **Figure 22**. Since this tool is expensive and not easily available, the following procedure allows adjustment with simple tools. No doubt other tools on hand can be used.

Always adjust both radius arms, even if only one was disassembled, especially if the car had high mileage.

1. Radius arm angle is measured in relation to the bottom of the door opening. See **Figure 22**. Since it is doubtful that this surface is level with the car jacked up, first determine the angle the car slants. **Figure 23** shows one method. Place a protractor on the door frame. Hold a spirit level against the protractor as shown in the figure; the bottom right corner of the level must touch the exact center of the protractor. Prop up the opposite end of the level until the spirit bubble is centered.

A. Brake Shield

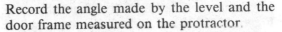

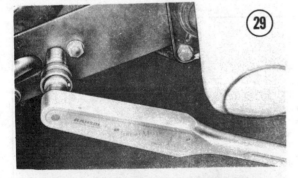

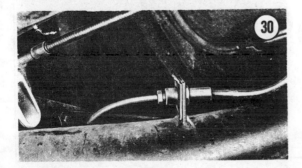

Record the angle made by the level and the door frame measured on the protractor.

2. Measure the radius arm angle as shown in **Figure 24**. Lift arm lightly to remove any play. Record this angle.

3. Subtract the angle measured in Step 1 from the angle in Step 2. The resulting angle should be the radius arm angle shown in the specifications for your model and year.

4. Move the torsion bar in its spline or move the radius arm on the torsion bar spline to correct the angle if necessary.

TRAILING ARM

Removal

1. On 1969-1972 models, remove the engine/transaxle. See Chapter Four. On 1973 and later models, it is not necessary to remove the engine/transaxle. On 1978 and later models, the stabilizer mounting is bolted to the rear trailing arm. See **Figure 25**.

2. Raise rear of car on jackstands and remove rear wheels.

3. Remove drive shaft as described later.

4. Remove brake shields as shown in **Figure 26**.

5. Remove brake caliper and brake disc as described in Chapter Thirteen.

6. Drive rear hub out with a punch (Porsche P297) as shown in **Figure 27**.

7. Remove cotter pin and castellated nut on handbrake handle. Pull cable out the back of the wheel hub.

8. Remove the brake carrier plate as shown in **Figure 28**.

9. Place jack under radius arm on same side as desired drive shaft. Raise radius arm enough to take tension off shock absorber.

> *CAUTION*
> *The shock absorber limits wheel travel so that the spring tension must be supported by a jack or clamp when the shock is disconnected. Figure 8 shows Porsche tool P289 used for this purpose.*

10. Disconnect lower end of shock absorber.

11. Remove 4 bolts securing radius arm to trailing arm. See **Figure 29**.

12. Disconnect the brake line from trailing arm. See **Figure 30**.

11

13. Remove mounting bolt and nut shown in **Figure 31** (1972 and earlier), or mounting bolt nuts as shown in **Figure 32** (1973 and later).

NOTE
On 1972 and earlier models you will have to drive bolt out with a punch. Do so carefully.

14. Remove trailing arm.

Disassembly (1965-1968)

Refer to **Figure 33** for following procedure.
1. Mount trailing arm in a vise with soft jaws.
2. Remove both oil seals.
3. Remove roller bearing inner race.
4. Carefully drive the ball bearing out as shown in **Figure 34**.
5. Remove spacer tube.
6. Press the roller bearing out as shown in **Figure 35**.

NOTE
If you do not have a press, take the trailing arm to your dealer or other competent machine shop.

Inspection (1965-1968)

1. Clean all parts in solvent.

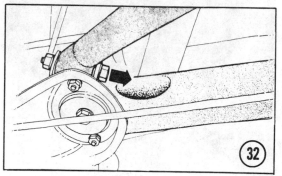

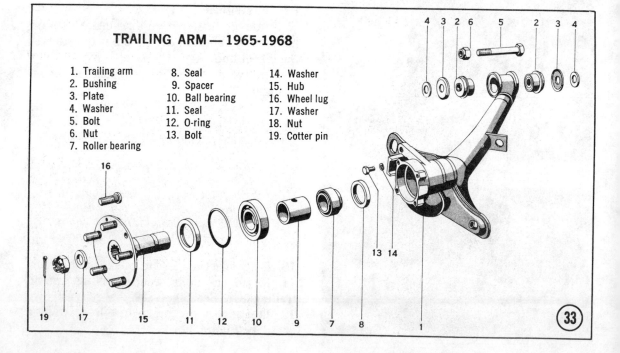

TRAILING ARM — 1965-1968

1. Trailing arm
2. Bushing
3. Plate
4. Washer
5. Bolt
6. Nut
7. Roller bearing
8. Seal
9. Spacer
10. Ball bearing
11. Seal
12. O-ring
13. Bolt
14. Washer
15. Hub
16. Wheel lug
17. Washer
18. Nut
19. Cotter pin

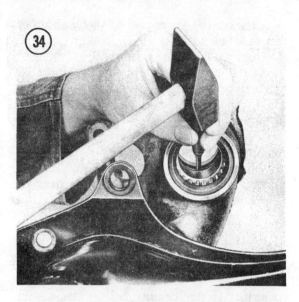

2. Check roller bearing and ball bearing for wear, scoring and evidence of excessive heat (bluish tint).

3. Check spacer tube for wear or scoring.

4. Take trailing arm to dealer and have alignment checked. This requires a special test jig.

5. Check condition of bushings where the trailing arm mounts to the body. Have your dealer replace them if necessary.

CAUTION
Do not attempt to remove these bushings unless they are to be replaced by new ones. Removal destroys the old ones.

Assembly (1965-1968)

1. Have dealer install bushings described in Step 5, *Inspection (1965-1968)*, if they were removed.

2. Have dealer install roller bearing in control arm.

3. Install new oil seal against outer end of roller bearing.

4. Install spacer tube so that end shown in **Figure 36** faces roller bearing.

5. Measure out about 1 1/2 ounces (40 grams) of multipurpose lithium grease. Work some of this into wheel bearings. Pack remainder into wheel hub opening.

6. Install ball bearing, new O-ring and new outer oil seal. See **Figure 37**.

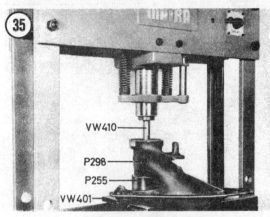

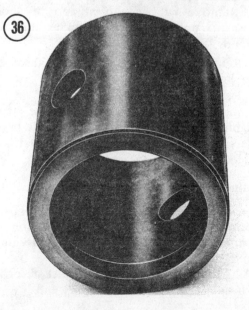

11

Disassembly (1969-on)

The 1969-on trailing arm has a double-row ball bearing with its own seals. This bearing cannot be removed without destroying it. If the bearing is defective, take the trailing arm to your dealer for replacement.

Inspection (1969-on)

1. Clean all parts in solvent.
2. Rotate inner race of double-row ball bearing by hand. If it is noisy or rough, have it replaced by your dealer.
3. Take trailing arm to dealer and have alignment checked. This requires a special test jig.
4. Check condition of bushings where the trailing arm mounts to the body. Have your dealer replace them if necessary.

> *CAUTION*
> *Do not attempt to remove these bushings unless they are to be replaced by new ones. Removal destroys the old ones.*

Assembly (1969-on)

1. Have dealer install bushings described in Step 4, *Inspection (1969–on)*, if they were removed.
2. Have dealer replace ball bearing if defective.

Installation

1. Secure trailing arm to frame bracket with bolt and self-locking nut. Use a washer under the bolt head and nut. Tighten finger-tight.

> *CAUTION*
> *The car must be resting on its rear wheels before final tightening of this bolt.*

2. Install 2 bolts securing radius arm to trailing arm. Tighten to 65 ft.-lb. (9 mkg).
3. Install camber and toe-in eccentric bolts. See **Figure 20**. Tighten to 36 ft.-lb. (6 mkg) and 43 ft.-lb. (5 mkg) respectively.

> *NOTE*
> *The toe-in eccentric bolt is the smaller of the two.*

4. Connect the lower end of shock absorber. Tighten bolt to 54 ft.-lb. (7.5 mkg).
5. Remove jack under radius arm.
6. Install brake carrier plate. See **Figure 28**. Tighten bolts to 18 ft.-lb. (2.5 mkg).
7. Install handbrake cable end as described in Chapter Thirteen.
8. Drive rear hub into trailing arm as far as possible with a plastic mallet.
9. While supporting the rear hub, drive the inner roller bearing race into place over the rear hub shaft.
10. Install drive shaft as described earlier.
11. Install brake shield, caliper and disc. See Chapter Thirteen.
12. Install rear wheels and lower car.
13. Adjust rear wheel camber and tracking as described in this chapter.
14. Tighten trailing arm-to-frame mounting nut to 87 ft.-lb. (12 mkg). See Step 1.

SHOCK ABSORBERS

> *CAUTION*
> *The shock absorbers limit rear wheel travel. Therefore, it is important that the wheels rest on the ground or the spring plates are clamped so that there is no stress on the shock absorbers.*

Removal/Installation

1. Leave car on the ground. There is no need to jack it up.
2. Remove rubber cap at top of shock absorber and remove self-locking nut. See **Figure 38**.
3. Remove bolt at bottom of shock absorber. See **Figure 39**.
4. Remove shock absorber.
5. Installation is the reverse of these steps. Tighten top nut until rubber bushings begin to compress. Tighten the lower bolt to 54 ft.-lb. (7.5 mkg).

Adjustment (Koni Shocks Only)

Koni adjustable shock absorber struts permit adjustment of damping action to compensate for wear or to suit individual driver requirements.
1A. To adjust damping when shock absorber is installed, disconnect the upper end.

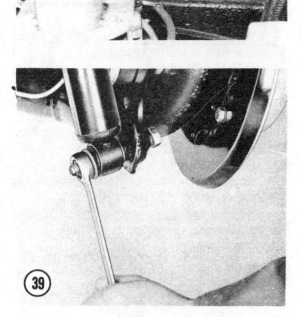

1B. To adjust damping before shock absorber is installed, hold bottom end in a vise with soft jaws. See **Figure 40**.

2. Compress the shock fully.

3. Turn upper tube clockwise (viewed from above) until you feel the internal adjusting lug engage. See **Figure 40**.

4. Make reference marks on the upper and lower tubes.

5. Turn the upper tube clockwise (viewed from above) with the adjusting lug engaged. Count the exact number of turns you are able to make. This indicates how much harder the shock was previously adjusted.

6. With the lug still engaged, turn the upper tube counterclockwise (viewed from above) until the original setting is reached.

7. Turn additionally counterclockwise 1/2 turn at a time until desired degree of damping is achieved.

NOTE
Maximum range of adjustment is 2 1/4 turns.

8. Adjust the other shock absorber to the same degree of damping.

REAR STABILIZER BAR

A stabilizer bar is standard or optional equipment depending on the year and model.

Removal/Installation

1. Pry upper end of stabilizer shackle off supporting ball on the trailing arm. See **Figure 41**.

2. Remove the mounting brackets and remove the stabilizer.

3. Check rubber bushings for wear. Replace if necessary. When replacing bushings, you may lubricate the shackle bushing with glycerine or other *rubber lubricant* but install the mounting bracket bushings dry.

4. Ensure that shackles are aligned on stabilizer as shown in **Figure 42**.

5. Lubricate upper end of shackles with molybdenum disulfide grease. Press the ends onto the supporting balls.

6. Install mounting brackets.

11

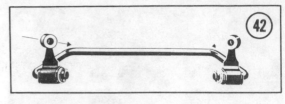

Table 1   TIGHTENING TORQUES

	foot-pounds	mkg
Castellated hub nut	217-253	30-35
Nadella drive shaft-to-transaxle bolts	34	4.7
Lobro drive shaft-to-transaxle bolts	60	8.3
Torsion bar cover bolts	34	4.7
Radius arm—trailing arm bolts	65	9
Camber bolt	36	6
Toe-in bolt	43	5
Brake carrier plate	18	2.5
Trailing arm-to-frame bolt	87	12
Upper shock absorber bolt	54	7.5
Lower shock absorber bolt	54	7.5

Table 2 REAR AXLE SPECIFICATIONS

Type	Independent double-jointed half axles
Springing	Torsion bars
Radius arm inclination	
1965-1967	36°
1968	39°
1969-1974	36° 30' to 37°
1975-1976	40° to 40° 30'
1976	
with Bilstein shock dampers	37'
normal	42°
1977-1979	
with Bilstein shocks	41°
1980-on Coupe	
Boge and Koni shocks	40°
Bilstein shocks	39°
1980-on Targa	
Boge and Koni shocks	41°
Bilstein shocks	40°
Wheel alignment	
Toe-in	
1965-1972	0° ±10'
1973-1976	0° ±20'
1977-on	+10° ±10'
Camber	
1965-1966	1° 15" ±20'
1967-1971	-50' ±20'
1972-1974	-1° ±10'
1975-on	0° ±10'
Rear track	
To chassis No. 305 101	51.85 in. (1,317 mm)
From chassis No. 305 101	52.03 in. (1,321 mm)
1973-1977	53.3 in. (1,354 mm)
1978-1979	53.8 in. (1,367 mm)
1980-on	54.29 in. (1,379 mm)

CHAPTER TWELVE

FRONT SUSPENSION AND STEERING

Porsche uses its version of a Mac Pherson strut suspension on all 911 models. The complete suspension is shown in **Figure 1** (1965-1968) and **Figure 2** (1969-on).

The front wheels are independently suspended on struts, each including a large shock absorber. The top of each strut is attached to the body through rubber mounts. The strut bottom consists of a steering knuckle which connects to a control arm (wishbone) through a ball-joint. The upper mount for the strut is adjustable for camber and caster. Each control arm is sprung by a torsion bar running longitudinally through the arm.

Self-leveling struts, instead of shock absorber struts, are used on some 911 models. These struts are standard on 1969-1973 911 models and optional on 1969-1973 911S and 911T models. When self-leveling struts are installed, torsion bar and stabilizer bar are not used. Shock absorbers are standard on all 1974-on cars.

The 1969-1973 911S comes standard with a 15 mm front stabilizer. As optional equipment, these cars may have an 11, 14, 15 or 16 mm bar. The 16 mm bar should be considered competition equipment only, and is not recommended for street use on these models. Diameter of the stabilizer was increased to 16 mm in 1974 and to 20 mm in 1976.

NOTE: *Some 1968 models did not have a factory installed stabilizer bar. To install one, you will need mounting hardware available from your dealer.*

Steering is by rack-and-pinion. The rack rides in replaceable bushings in the housing. The floating pinion carrier, located in the housing, supports the pinion which rotates within 2 bearings. Since a pressure block holds the pinion against the rack, there is no free play in the system.

The steering gear is filled with a permanent lubricant at the factory and requires no periodic maintenance. Drag induced by the steering gear may be adjusted, however.

Tables 1 and 2 at the end of this chapter give specifications and tightening torques for the front suspension.

FRONT WHEEL ALIGNMENT

Several front suspension dimensions affect running and steering of the front wheels. These variables must be properly aligned to maintain directional stability, ease of steering, and proper tire wear.

The dimensions involved define:

a. Caster   d. Steering axis inclination
b. Camber   e. Front axle height
c. Toe-in

12

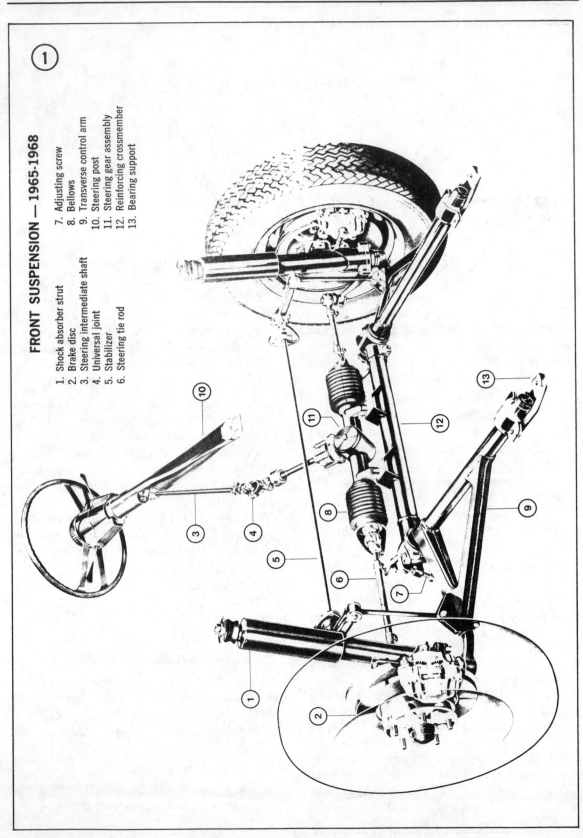

FRONT SUSPENSION — 1965-1968

1. Shock absorber strut
2. Brake disc
3. Steering intermediate shaft
4. Universal joint
5. Stabilizer
6. Steering tie rod
7. Adjusting screw
8. Bellows
9. Transverse control arm
10. Steering post
11. Steering gear assembly
12. Reinforcing crossmember
13. Bearing support

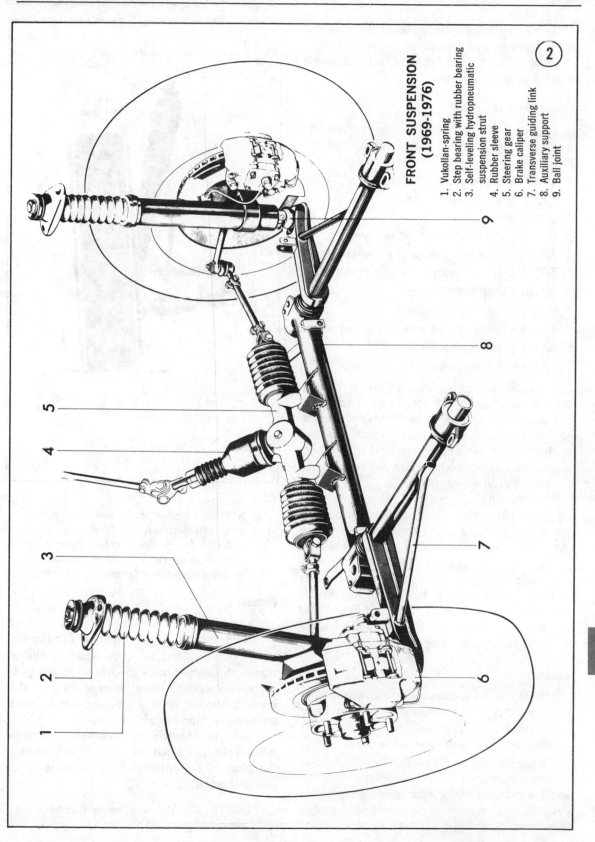

FRONT SUSPENSION (1969-1976)

1. Vukollan-spring
2. Step bearing with rubber bearing
3. Self-leveling hydropneumatic suspension strut
4. Rubber sleeve
5. Steering gear
6. Brake caliper
7. Transverse guiding link
8. Auxiliary support
9. Ball joint

12

All except steering axis inclination are adjustable. Since these adjustments are critical, they must be done by a competent front end alignment shop or your dealer.

Pre-alignment Check

Several factors influence the suspension angles, or steering. Before any adjustments are attempted, perform the following checks:

1. Check tire pressure and wear.

2. Check play in front wheel bearings. Adjust if necessary.

3. Check play in ball-joints or king pins.

4. Check for broken springs or torsion bars.

5. Remove any excessive load.

6. Check shock absorbers.

7. Check steering gear adjustments.

8. Check play in pitman arm and tie rod parts.

9. Check wheel balance.

10. Check *rear* suspension for looseness.

A proper inspection of front tire wear can point to several alignment problems. Tires worn primarily on one side show problems with toe-in. If toe-in is incorrect on one wheel, the car probably pulls to one side or the other. If toe-in is incorrect on both wheels, the car probably is hard to steer in either direction.

Incorrect camber may also cause tire wear on one side. Tire cupping (scalloped wear pattern) can result from worn shock absorbers, one wheel out of alignment, a bent spindle, or a combination of all. Tires worn in the middle, but not the edges, or worn nearly evenly on both edges, but not in the middle are probably over-inflated or under-inflated respectively. These conditions are not caused by suspension misaligment. See Chapter Two.

Camber

Camber is the inclination of the wheel from vertical as shown in **Figure 3**. Note that angle (a) is positive camber, i.e., the top of the tire inclines outward more than the bottom.

Camber is adjusted by loosening Allen bolts and moving the end of the suspension strut inward or outward to decrease or increase positive camber; 1mm movement equals about 6′ change in camber.

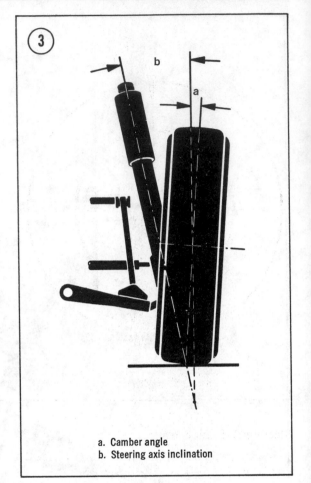

a. Camber angle
b. Steering axis inclination

NOTE: *Camber and caster are not adjustable on chassis No. up to 302.736. If camber or caster is incorrect on these chassis, check for bent or worn suspension parts.*

Caster

Caster is the inclination of the axis through the strut from vertical. See **Figure 4**. The Porsche has negative caster, i.e., the wheel is shifted rearward. Caster causes the wheels to return to a position straight ahead after a turn. It also prevents the car from wandering due to wind, potholes, or uneven road surfaces.

Caster is adjusted by loosening the same Allen bolts described for camber and moving the strut to the front or rear to decrease or increase caster.

NOTE: *See the note under* Camber, *above.*

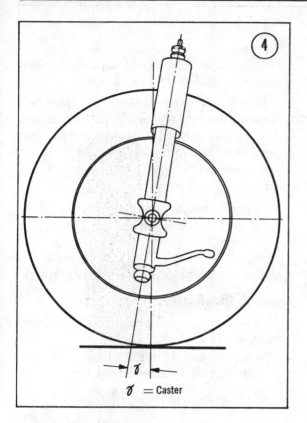

γ = Caster

Steering Axis Inclination

Steering axis inclination is shown in Figure 3 and is the inclination of the strut from vertical. This angle is not adjustable, but can be checked with proper front end racks to find bent suspension parts.

Toe-in

Camber and rolling resistance tend to force the front wheels outward at their forward edge. To compensate for this tendency, the front edges are turned slightly inward when the car is at rest. This is toe-in. See **Figure 5**.

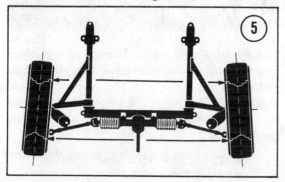

Toe-in is adjusted by lengthening or shortening the tic rods. Each tie rod is threaded so that the center section can be rotated to make the adjustment.

Front Axle Height

Before making any other suspension adjustments on cars with shock absorber suspension struts (not self-leveling struts), the front axle height must be checked and adjusted if necessary. The measurement requires a full tank of fuel, correct tire pressures (Chapter Three), spare tire in place, and no other loads. The car must be on an alignment ramp or level floor.

To check front axle height:

1. Mark dead center of dust caps of front wheels.

2. Depress front of car several times by pushing on the bumper guards. Release the guard when the car is down and let it bounce back up by itself.

3. Measure dimension (a, **Figure 6**) from floor to center of dust cover.

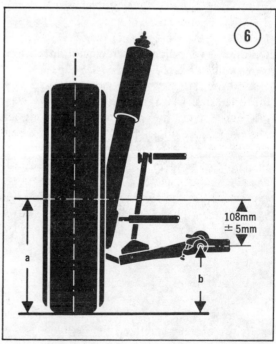

4. Subtract 108mm from dimension (a). This new dimension (b) shown in Figure 6 should be 207±5mm. Measure dimension (b) to the center of the torsion bar.

5. If dimension (b) on left side is within tolerance, measure (b) on right side in the same manner. Dimension (b) on right side must be within 5mm of dimension (b) on left side, but in no case can it be less than 202mm or greater than 212mm.

6. If dimension (b) on either side is not 207±5mm or if dimension (b) on either side is not within 5mm of the other dimension (b), the front axle height must be readjusted.

To adjust front axle height:

1. Remove dust cover over torsion bar adjusting lever. See **Figure 7**.

2. Adjust lever adjusting screw until dimension (b) on that side is 207±5mm. See **Figure 8**.

3. Recheck other side to be sure it is within 5mm of the first side. If not, adjust dimension (b) on second side in the same manner as the first side.

4. Install dust cover.

On cars with self-leveling suspension struts, the front must be jacked up to a specified height while on the alignment ramp. To do this:

1. Measure dimension (a) shown in Figure 6.

2. Lift the car at the front center with a jack until dimension (a) minus 180 equals dimension (b) and dimension (b) equals 207±5mm.

3. Perform other alignment checks and adjustments.

> NOTE: *Check dimension (b) frequently to ensure that the jack is not sinking.*

FRONT STABILIZER (ANTI-ROLL BAR)

Removal/Installation

1. Raise front of car on jackstands and remove both front wheels.

2. Loosen 2 clamp bolts on each lever arm and pull arms off stabilizer. See **Figure 9**.

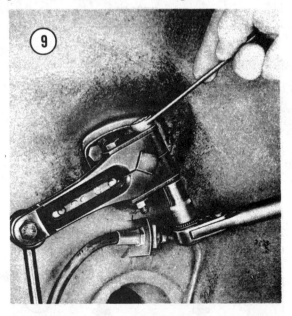

3. Remove 3 bolts at the left end of stabilizer securing the rubber bushing and support. See **Figure 10**.

4. Squirt penetrating oil on the rubber bushing and support. Pry the 2 parts apart, then remove them.

5. Remove 3 bolts at the right end of stabilizer.

6. Pull stabilizer out from the right side.

7. Remove rubber bushing and support from stabilizer.

8. Remove bolts securing stabilizer shackles to control arms. Remove shackles and lever arms.

9. Check all rubber bushings for deterioration and wear.

10. Coat rubber bushings with glycerine or similar rubber lubricant.

CAUTION
Do not use petroleum based lubricants. Petroleum based products attack rubber and cause rapid deterioration.

11. Bolt shackles with lever arms attached to the control arms.

12. Install rubber bushing and support on stabilizer.

13. Insert stabilizer from the right side. Install the 3 bolts finger-tight.

14. Install left rubber bushing and support. Install 3 bolts finger-tight.

15. Center the stabilizer and tighten all 6 bolts to 18 ft.-lb. (2.5 mkg).

16. Attach lever arms to stabilizer ends. About one millimeter should protrude past surface of lever arm. Tighten bolts to 18 ft.-lb. (2.5 mkg).

FRONT SUSPENSION STRUT (1965-1968)

These suspension struts have integral shock absorbers.

Removal/Installation

1. Raise front of car on jackstands and remove front wheels.

2. Remove brake caliper and disc as described in Chapter Fifteen.

3. Remove bolts securing caliper bracket to strut. See **Figure 11**.

4. Disconnect tie rods at struts as described in a later section.

5. Remove bolts in transverse control arm. See **Figure 12**.

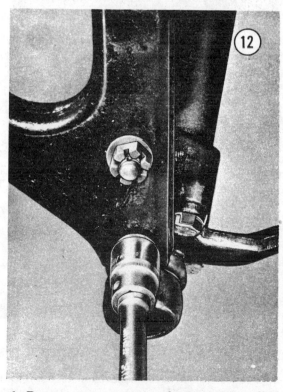

12

6. Remove nut at top of struts accessible through front luggage compartment. See **Figure 13**.

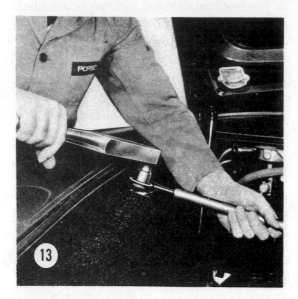

2. Pull upper tube off and remove rubber buffer.

3. Remove bolts securing steering lever. See **Figure 15**.

7. Remove strut.

8. Installation is the reverse of these steps. Torque nut at top of strut to 58 ft.-lb. (8 mkg). Torque 2 bottom nuts and bolts to 54 ft.-lb. (7.5 mkg); secure with cotter pin. Use new rubber bushings at top of strut.

Disassembly/Assembly

Refer to **Figure 14** for the following procedure.

1. Hold strut in a vise with soft jaws (copper or wood).

4. Examine spacer on spindle. If worn, drive it off by striking it all around the inner edge with a punch.

5. Check alignment of strut and steering lever. Since this requires special jigs, take the strut with steering lever/ball-joint assembly to your dealer. Ask him to check alignment condition of shock absorber and condition of ball-joint.

6. If spacer on spindle was removed, install new spacer with O-ring. Heat the ring to about 300°F (150°C) and push it on with a hollow punch (a piece of pipe will do).

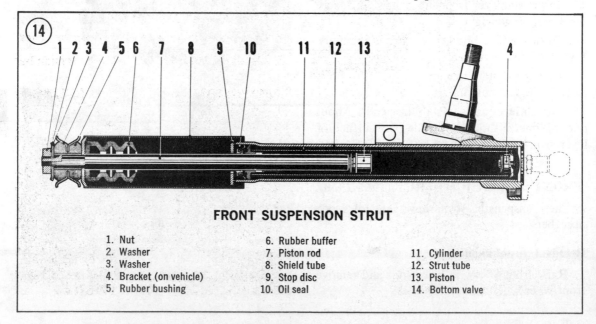

FRONT SUSPENSION STRUT

1. Nut
2. Washer
3. Washer
4. Bracket (on vehicle)
5. Rubber bushing
6. Rubber buffer
7. Piston rod
8. Shield tube
9. Stop disc
10. Oil seal
11. Cylinder
12. Strut tube
13. Piston
14. Bottom valve

7. Bolt steering lever assembly to strut. Tighten to 34 ft.-lb. (4.7 mkg). Use new lock plates.

8. Install new rubber buffer in strut. Do not apply any kind of lubricant.

9. Slide upper tube in place.

Adjustment (Koni Struts Only)

Koni adjustable shock absorber struts permit adjusment of damping action to compensate for wear or to suit individual driver requirements.

1a. To adjust damping when shock absorber is installed, disconnect the upper end.

1b. To adjust damping before shock absorber is installed, hold bottom end in a vise with soft jaws. See **Figure 16**.

2. Compress the shock fully.

3. Turn upper tube clockwise (viewed from above) until you feel the internal adjusting lug engage. See Figure 16.

4. Make reference marks on the upper and lower tubes.

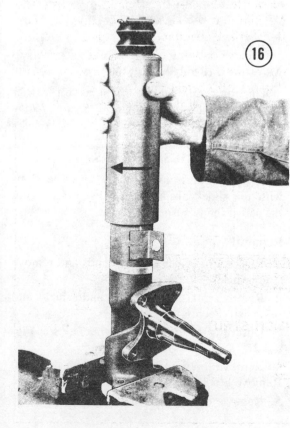

5. Turn the upper tube clockwise (viewed from above) with the adjusting lug engaged. Count the exact number of turns you are able to make. This indicates how much harder the shock was adjusted previously.

6. With the lug still engaged, turn the upper tube counterclockwise (viewed from above) until the original setting is reached.

7. Turn additionally counterclockwise ½ turn at a time until desired degree of damping is achieved.

NOTE: *Maximum range of adjustment is 2¼ turns.*

8. Adjust other shock absorber to the same degree of damping.

FRONT SUSPENSION STRUT (1969-ON)

Self-leveling suspension struts act as shock absorbers and also eliminate the need for torsion bars.

Removal/Installation

1. Raise front of car on jackstands and remove front wheels.

2. Remove brake caliper and disc as described in Chapter Thirteen.

3. Remove backing plate (**Figure 17**).

4. Disconnect tie rod at strut as described later.

5. On shock absorber struts, loosen torsion bar

12

adjusting screw and pull adjusting arm off. See **Figure 18**.

6. Loosen clamp bolt at bottom of strut. See **Figure 19**. Push control arm (wishbone) down until ball-joint is clear of the strut.

7. Remove nut at top of strut accessible through front luggage compartment. See **Figure 20**.

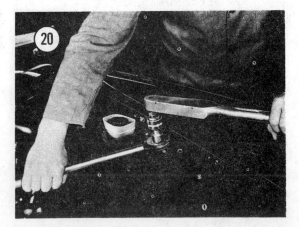

8. Remove strut.

9. Check alignment of strut and steering knuckle. Since this requires special jigs, take the strut to your dealer. Ask him to check alignment and condition of shock absorber (if applicable).

10. Installation is the reverse of these steps. Be sure to reinstall the steel washer on the ball-joint as shown in **Figure 21**. When installing the torsion bar adjusting lever, pry control arm downward with a tire iron or similar tool until it contacts its stop. See Table 2 for proper tightening torques.

Adjustment (Koni Shocks Only)

This procedure is the same as for earlier shocks. See *Front Suspension Strut (1965-1968)*.

TORSION BARS

This procedure applies only to suspensions with the shock absorber suspension strut, not the self-leveling suspension strut.

Removal

1. Raise front of car on jackstands and remove front wheel.

2. Remove nuts and bolts on undershield and remove it. See **Figure 22**.

3. Unscrew torsion bar adjustment. See **Figure 23**.

4. Remove bolts from control arm bracket. Remove bracket and cap. See **Figure 24**.

5. Remove torsion bar dust caps.

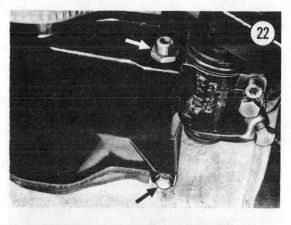

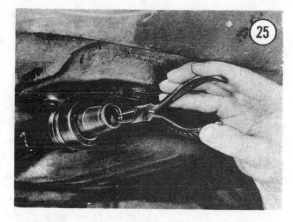

8. Drive torsion bar adjusting lever rearward and out of the control arm.

CAUTION

A protective paint covers the torsion bars. Do not nick or scratch this paint. Even slight damage leads to corrosion and eventual fatigue fractures. Touch up with paint if necessary.

Installation

1. Lightly grease torsion bars and particularly the splines with lithium grease.
2. Insert the torsion bar from the front.

NOTE: *Torsion bars are marked left (L) and right (R) and must not be interchanged. See* **Figure 26**.

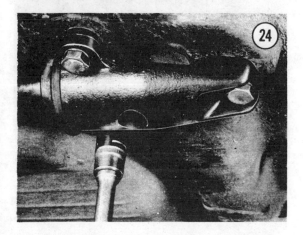

6. Remove lock ring at forward end of torsion bar. See **Figure 25**.

7. Drive torsion bar forward and out using an appropriate punch.

CAUTION

Do not damage torsion bar splines.

3. Coat the front rubber bushing with glycerine. Install bushing, bracket, and cap. Do not pinch rubber between bracket and cap. Torque bolts to 34 ft.-lb. (4.7 mkg).

4. Assuming the shock absorber strut is connected to the control arm, pry the control arm down until strut reaches its stop. See **Figure 27**.

12

5. Insert torsion bar adjusting lever into cross member and over torsion bar spline with adjusting screw backed off as far as possible. Leave as little clearance as possible between the end of the adjusting screw and the lever.

6. Tighten adjusting screw to take up any gap below the screw.

7. Install lock ring and dust cap at front of torsion bar.

8. Adjust front end height as described in this chapter.

9. Have the wheel alignment checked and adjusted by your dealer or other competent wheel alignment expert. Tell him what repairs you have made to help him do a thorough job.

WHEEL BEARINGS

Replacement

1. Raise front of car on jackstands and remove both front wheels.

2. Remove brake calipers as described in Chapter Thirteen.

3. Remove dust cap as shown in **Figure 28**.

4. Loosen Allen bolt in clamping nut. See **Figure 29**. Remove nut and thrust washer.

5. Remove wheel hub/brake disc assembly.

6. Remove wheel bearings. To do this, lay the wheel hub assembly over a clean cloth. Tap the lower bearing out from the inside with a hardwood stick and a hammer. Turn the wheel hub over. Tap the other bearing out in the same manner. Do not mix bearings up. Tag them if necessary to mark which wheel they were on.

NOTE: *In some cases it may be necessary to separate the hub from the disc to remove the bearings. Mark the relationship between the two, then remove the bolts joining them.*

7. Clean wheel bearings thoroughly in solvent and blow dry.

CAUTION
Although it is fascinating to watch the bearings rotate rapidly by compressed air, it will ruin a clean, unlubricated bearing in a very short time.

8. Clean bearing races in the wheel hub with solvent.

9. Check rollers for scores, wear, and evidence of overheating (bluish tint). Check bearing races also.

10. If a bearing or bearing race is damaged, the bearing and race must be replaced. Take the hub to your dealer. For a small bench fee, he will press the old race out and install new one.

CAUTION
Bearings made by Timken, SKF, and FAG may be used interchangeably on all models and years. Be certain, however, that the bearing and race are of the same manufacture.

11. Insert the inner bearing in the hub.

12. Press the oil seal in carefully and evenly until the seal is flush with the hub housing.

13. Assemble the hub to the disc if they were disassembled in Step 6. Torque bolts to 17 ft.-lb. (2.3 mkg).

14. On 1965-1968 models, pack the hub with about 1.6 ounces (50 grams) of lithium based multi-purpose grease. On 1969-on models, use 2.1 ounces (65 grams). Make sure that the bearings are thoroughly coated with grease. Work it in well between rollers. Pack some between the inner seal and bearing.

15. Install brake disc/wheel hub assembly as described in Chapter Thirteen.

16. Adjust wheel bearings as described below.

Adjustment

1. Raise front of car on jackstands.

2. Remove dust covers on hub. See Figure 28.

3. Loosen Allen bolt in clamping nut. See Figure 29.

4. Tighten clamp nut to about 11 ft.-lb. (1.5 mkg) while rotating the wheel. This takes all slack out of the bearings.

5. Loosen the clamping nut just to the point when the thrust washer can be moved when pried lightly with a screwdriver. See **Figure 30**.

6. Tighten Allen bolt in clamping nut. Do not move clamping nut while doing this.

7. Recheck adjustment and repeat if necessary.

8. Install dust cap. Do not fill it with grease.

9. Lower car.

STEERING WHEEL

Removal/Installation

1. Disconnect battery ground cable.

2. Twist horn button counterclockwise and remove it. See **Figure 31**.

3. Remove horn contact pin.

4. Remove steering wheel retaining nut. See **Figure 32**.

5. Mark relationship between steering wheel and steering shaft.

6. Pull steering wheel off.

12

7. Remove bearing support ring and spring. See **Figure 33**.

8. Ensure that wheels are straight ahead.

9. Install bearing support ring and spring.

10. Install steering wheel so that spokes are horizontal and marks made in Step 5 align. Tighten nut to 58 ft.-lb. (8 mkg).

11. Check that directional lever returns properly when steering wheel is turned.

12. Insert horn contact pin and install horn cap. Turn cap clockwise to lock.

TIE ROD REPLACEMENT

1. Raise car on jackstands and remove front wheels.

2. Remove cotter pins from castellated nuts on tie rod ends.

3. Remove nut on ball-joint at outer end of tie rod.

4. Loosen universal coupling nut and bolt at inner end of tie rod.

5. Press tie rod end out with a special tool as shown in **Figure 34**.

CAUTION
Do not damage rubber seals when removing tie rods.

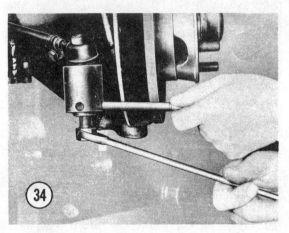

6. Check tie rods for bends and other damage. Bent tie rods must be replaced, not straightened.

7. Check tie rod pin. If there is any play or the pin is frozen, the tie rod end must be replaced.

8. Check rubber seals. Damaged seals must be replaced.

9. Installation is the reverse of these steps.

10. Adjust toe-in.

STEERING HOUSING

The steering housing contains the rack-and-pinion gears.

Removal/Installation

1. Remove carpeting in front luggage compartment.

2. Detach heater duct from steering column.

3. Open access door and remove cover over intermediate shaft. Pry up one of the 2 prongs in the spring clip with a screwdriver to aid removal. See **Figure 35**.

4. Remove 3 bolts on heater fuel pump bracket and lay pump to one side. See **Figure 36**.

5. Remove cotter pin from castellated clamp nut (arrow, **Figure 37**). Loosen nut and pull universal joint off steering shaft.

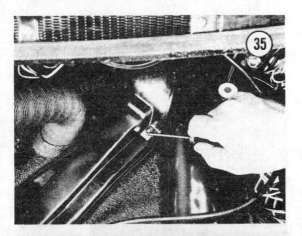

6. Remove Allen bolts from steering shaft bushing cap. See Figure 37. Pull bushing and dust boot off.

7. Unlock and remove steering coupling bolts. See **Figure 38**.

8. Remove dust cover shown in **Figure 39**.

9. Remove nuts at bottom of tie rod ball-joints. Disconnect tie rod with a special tool as shown in **Figure 40**.

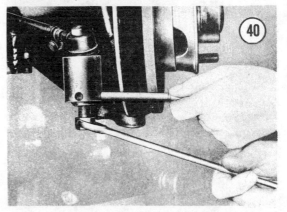

12

10. Remove steering housing retaining bolts. See **Figure 41**.

11. Remove reinforcing brace shown in **Figure 42**.

12. Withdraw steering housing assembly from the right side.

13. Unlock tie rod bolts and remove tie rods from housing.

14. Installation is the reverse of these steps. See Table 2 for proper tightening torques. Use new lock tabs and cotter pins when applicable.

Disassembly

Refer to **Figure 43** for following procedure.

1. Hold steering housing in a vise with soft jaws.

2. Remove base plate (**Figure 44**).

3. Unscrew adjusting nut. The base plate may be used as a wrench.

4. Remove pressure block and spring.

5. Turn housing 90° in the vise.

6. Remove cotter pin and castellated nut. See **Figure 45**.

7. Using a suitable puller (Porsche P293 shown), remove the coupling flange. See **Figure 46**.

8. Carefully pry oil seal out.

9. Remove C-ring and shim(s). See **Figure 47**.

10. With a suitable puller (Porsche P282 shown), remove pinion.

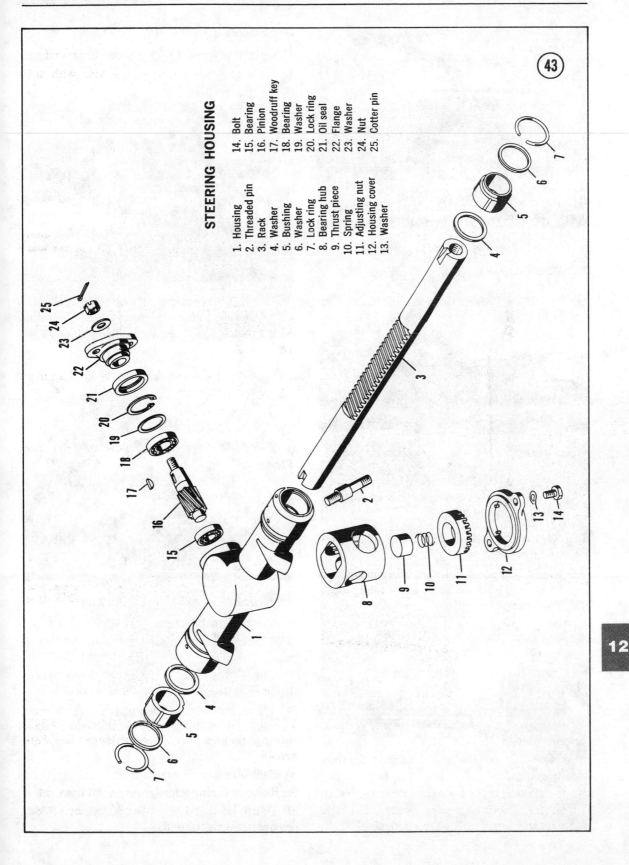

STEERING HOUSING

1. Housing
2. Threaded pin
3. Rack
4. Washer
5. Bushing
6. Washer
7. Lock ring
8. Bearing hub
9. Thrust piece
10. Spring
11. Adjusting nut
12. Housing cover
13. Washer
14. Bolt
15. Bearing
16. Pinion
17. Woodruff key
18. Bearing
19. Washer
20. Lock ring
21. Oil seal
22. Flange
23. Washer
24. Nut
25. Cotter pin

12

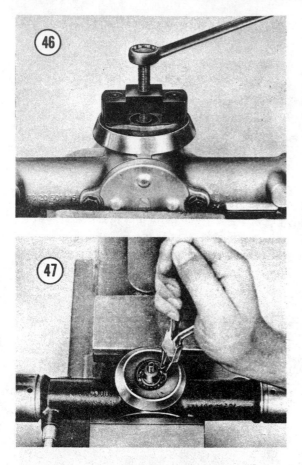

13. Remove pinion carrier. See **Figure 49**.

14. Press ball bearing out of pinion carrier.

15. Remove snap rings from ends of housing with a punch and screwdriver. See **Figure 50**.

16. Remove support rings.

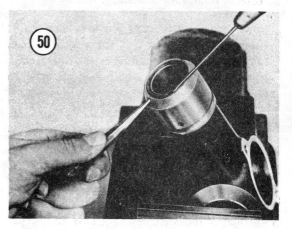

CAUTION

Make sure that ball bearing does not bind against housing.

11. Remove Woodruff key from pinion and press bearing off.

12. Mark race so that it can be reinstalled in exactly the same way. Slide it out of the housing. See **Figure 48**.

Inspection

1. Clean all parts in solvent.

2. Check rack and pinion for wear or broken teeth.

3. Check bearings for worn or scored balls. Replace if necessary.

4. Check bushings in ends of housing for wear or scoring. If necessary, have your dealer replace the bushings.

Assembly

1. Install bushing support rings and snap rings.

2. Press bearing into pinion carrier. Work grease between the balls.

3. Coat pinion carrier with multipurpose grease containing molybdenum disulfide and insert in housing. See **Figure 49**.

NOTE
The steering housing is packed with 40 grams (1 1/3 ounces) of multi-purpose molybdenum disulfide (MoS²) grease during the remaining steps. Measure out this quantity beforehand.

4. Coat the rack thoroughly using a portion of the total 40 grams of grease mentioned above.

5. Slide the rack into the housing. If reinstalling old rack, install according to marks made during *Disassembly*, Step 12.

6. Press bearing onto pinion. Work some grease between the balls. Insert Woodruff key into pinion.

7. Pack the remainder of the 40 grams of grease into the steering housing.

8. Insert pinion into housing. Push down until it rests on its seat.

9. Install shim(s) and C-ring. Check end play of pinion. Change shim(s) if necessary to achieve zero end play.

NOTE: *Shims are available in the following thisknesses: 0.1, 0.12, 0.15, and 0.30mm.*

10. Install the pinion oil seal with the sealing lip facing inward.

11a. On early steering housings with a Woodruff key on the pinion, install the flange, coat both sides of the washer with grease and install catellated nut. Tighten nut to 18 ft.-lb. (2.5 mkg) and secure with new cotter pin.

11b. On later steering housings with a splined pinion, install the rubber O-ring, then the flange, and secure with self-locking nut. Tighten nut to 34 ft.-lb. (4.7 mkg).

12. Install pressure block and spring.

13. Install the adjusting nut and adjust as described below.

14. Install cover plate with new paper gasket. Tighten cover bolts to 11 ft.-lb. (1.5 mkg).

Adjustment

1. If steering housing is in car, raise front of car on jackstands, disconnect tie rods and steering damper from steering housing.

2. Remove cover plate. See Figure 44 or 41.

3. Tighten adjusting nut (clockwise) until it seats firmly. Use the cover plate as a wrench.

4. Back the adjusting nut off (counterclockwise) 3 teeth.

5a. If steering housing is installed in car, check drag at steering wheel nut over the entire range of rack. See **Figure 51**. Adjust steering adjusting nut as necessary if drag exceeds 8.5 in.-lb. (10 cmkg). Do not tighten nut if drag is less than this.

5b. If steering housing is not installed, check drag at coupling flange nut over entire range of rack. See **Figure 52**. Adjust steering adjusting nut as necessary if drag exceeds 7 in.-lb. (8 cmkg). Do not tighten nut if drag is less than this.

6. Install cover plate with new paper gasket.

CAUTION
The 4 pins in the cover must fit between adjusting nut teeth. If necessary, move the nut slightly so the pins fit properly.

Steering Intermediate Shaft
Removal/Installation

1. Disconnect battery ground cable.

12

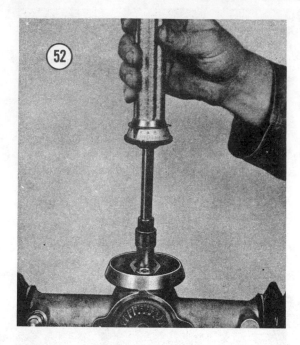

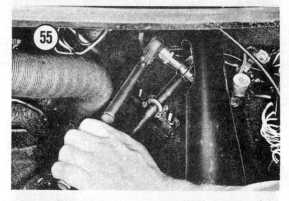

2. Remove carpeting from front luggage compartment and open access door.

3. Disconnect auxiliary heater duct from steering post and bend duct to one side.

4. Remove cover over intermediate shaft. Pry up one of the 2 prongs in the spring clip with a screwdriver to aid removal. See **Figure 53**.

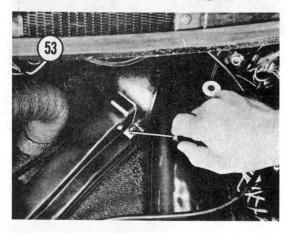

5. Remove 3 bolts on heater fuel pump bracket. See **Figure 54**. Lay pump to one side.

6. Remove cotter pin from lower clamping bolt in each of the 2 universal joints. Loosen the retaining nuts. See **Figure 55**.

7. Remove Allen bolts from steering shaft bushing cap. See **Figure 56**. Remove cap.

8. Pull lower universal joint off the steering housing.

9. Drive intermediate shaft out of upper universal joint. See **Figure 57**.

10. Installation is the reverse of these steps. Tighten clamp bolts to 18 ft.-lb. (2.5 mkg).

STEERING SWITCH ASSEMBLY

Removal/Installation

1. Remove steering wheel as described earlier.

2. Remove steering intermediate shaft as described earlier.

3. Remove steering lock cover (if car is so equipped). Drill out shear bolts and remove lock. See **Figure 58**. Do not disconnect electrical cables.

4. With a special tool (Porsche P281), remove light switch and let it hang on its connecting wires.

5. Loosen Allen bolt in switch assembly clamp. See **Figure 59**.

6. Turn clamp down and pull out locking pin with pliers. See **Figure 60**.

7. Disconnect electrical cables to switch assembly at connectors. Mark cables for later reassembly.

8. Withdraw switch assembly with upper steering shaft and universal joint. Guide electrical wires through space in instrument panel.

9. Installation is the reverse of these steps. Tighten switch assembly clamp bolt to 18 ft.-lb. (2.5 mkg). Leave a 2mm gap between the switch assembly and the instrument panel. When installing the steering lock, alternately tighten the bolts until the heads shear off.

12

Table 1 FRONT SUSPENSION SPECIFICATIONS

	1965	1966	1967-1969
Toe-in	15-20'	5-20'	0°
Caster	7° 45'	7° 45'	6° 45'
Camber	4'	0 ±20'	0 ±20'
Steering axis inclination	10° 56'	10° 56'	10° 56'
Steering gear ratio	16.5	16.5	17.78

	1970-1974	1975-on	
Toe-in	0°	0°	
Caster	6° 5' ±15'	6° 5' ±15'	
Camber	0 ±20'	plus 30' ±10'	
Steering axis inclination	10° 56'	10° 56'	
Steering gear ratio	17.78	17.78	

Table 2   TIGHTENING TORQUES

	foot-pounds	mkg		foot-pounds	mkg
Steering coupling bolts	18	2.5	Tie rod nut	32.5	4.5
Steering universal clamp nut	34	4.7	Strut clamp bolt (1969-1972)	47	6.5
Reinforcing brace nut	47	6.5	Strut mounting bolts (1965-1968)	54	7.5
Reinforcing brace bolt	34	4.7	Upper strut nut	58	8.0
Steering housing mounting bolts	34	4.7	Brake backing plate bolts	18	2.5
Steering bushing cap Allen bolts	18	2.5	Steering lever-to-strut (1965-1968)	34	4.7

BRAKES

Porsche uses fixed caliper disc brakes on all 4 wheels. Models from 1965-1967 have a single circuit hydraulic system which operates front and rear brakes. Models from 1968 sold in the U.S. have a dual circuit hydraulic system; one circuit operates front brakes while the other operates rear brakes. Both systems operate in a similar manner.

When the driver depresses the brake pedal, he operates a master cylinder piston through a pushrod. See **Figure 1**. Hydraulic pressure developed in the master cylinder expands the caliper pistons at each wheel, forcing brake pads against the brake disc.

The dual circuit brakes shown in **Figure 2** work similarly. The master cylinder has 2 independent pressure circuits. When the driver depresses the pedal, pressure in the front half of the master cylinder operates both front brakes; pressure from the rear half operates both rear brakes. If one circuit should fail, the other remains intact, permitting a safe stop with 2 wheels. A warning circuit incorporated in 1968 and later master cylinders indicates that pressure in one circuit is low. Increased pedal travel and decreased braking also indicate trouble.

The brake light switch is mechanically coupled to the master cylinder pushrod. It is not operated by hydraulic pressure.

Cable operated mechanical handbrakes act on the rear wheels. When the hand lever is drawn up, special brake shoes expand against the hub of each rear brake disc. The hub is formed like a brake drum in a conventional drum brake system.

This chapter describes repair procedures for all parts of the brake system. **Table 1** and **Table 2** at the end of the chapter list specifications and tightening torques.

Porsche used a large variety of calipers and discs from 1965 to the present. For this reason *always* order brake parts by chassis number and compare new parts to old before installation.

MASTER CYLINDER

Two different master cylinders are used from 1965-1972. All 1965-1967 models use a single circuit master cylinder. All 1968 and later models sold in the U.S. use a dual circuit master cylinder with a special system to warn the driver of a failure in either circuit.

Removal

1. Raise front of car on jackstands.

2. Pull accelerator pedal back to disengage it. Remove left front floor mat.

3. Remove retaining nut and floorboard. See **Figure 3**.

13

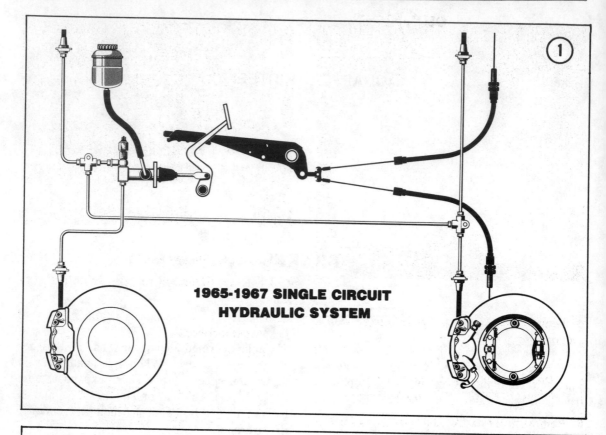

**1965-1967 SINGLE CIRCUIT
HYDRAULIC SYSTEM**

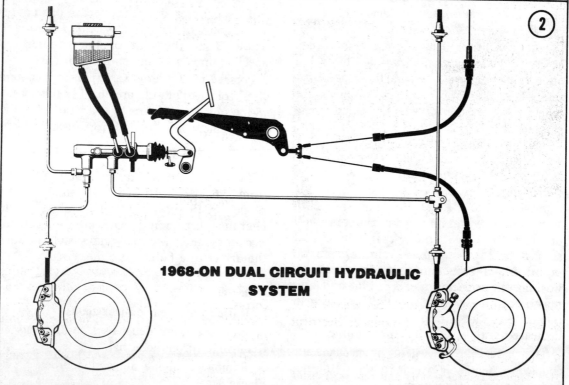

**1968-ON DUAL CIRCUIT HYDRAULIC
SYSTEM**

4. Draw brake fluid out of reservoir(s) with a suction pump.

WARNING
Do not siphon by sucking on a length of tubing. Brake fluid is highly poisonous.

5. Remove front axle shield over master cylinder. See **Figure 4**.

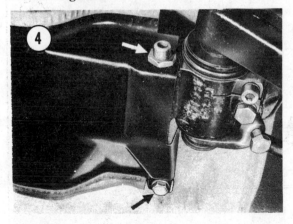

6. Pull the lines leading from the reservoir out of the master cylinder. Be careful that brake fluid doesn't drip in your face.

7. Disconnect hydraulic lines. See **Figure 5**.

8. On 1968-on models, disconnect electrical wires to circuit failure switch.

9. Pull rubber boot free of master cylinder.

10. Remove retaining nuts and remove master cylinder.

Disassembly (Single Circuit)

Refer to **Figure 6** for the following procedure.

1. Scrape off all outside dirt and wash with denatured alcohol.

2. Remove the rubber boot.

3. Remove the lock ring.

4. Remove the stop washer and piston. If the piston is stuck, seal the brake line holes with plugs, insert the rubber grommet in the top of the master cylinder, and force the piston out with compressed air. Even a bicycle tire pump develops sufficient pressure.

5. Remove the piston washer, primary cup, and return spring with check valve.

Inspection (Single Circuit)

1. Clean all parts in denatured alcohol or clean brake fluid.

CAUTION
Never use gasoline, kerosene, or any solvent other than alcohol for rubber brake parts. You may wash metal parts in other solvents if you blow them dry, rinse several times in clean alcohol, and blow dry again.

2. Inspect the cylinder bore for scoring, pitting or heavy corrosion. Very light scratches and corrosion may be removed with *crocus cloth*. Discard the master cylinder if damage is more severe.

3. Run a small, smooth copper wire through the compensating and intake ports. See **Figure 7**. Don't use steel or rough wire which

13

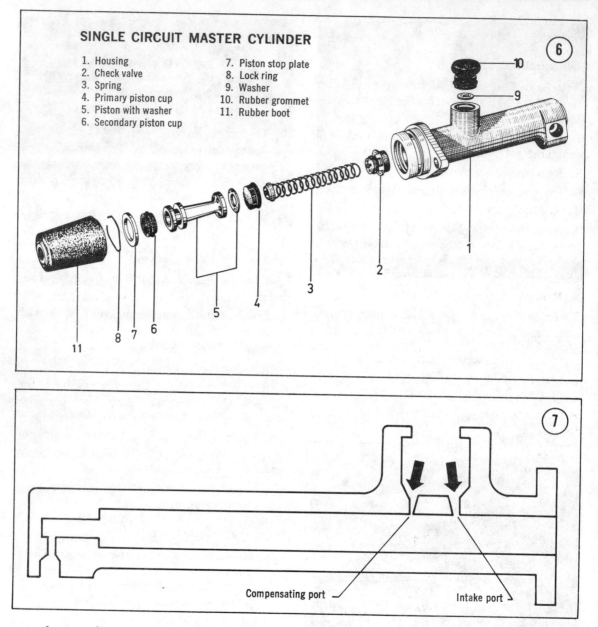

SINGLE CIRCUIT MASTER CYLINDER

1. Housing
2. Check valve
3. Spring
4. Primary piston cup
5. Piston with washer
6. Secondary piston cup
7. Piston stop plate
8. Lock ring
9. Washer
10. Rubber grommet
11. Rubber boot

Compensating port

Intake port

may damage the ports. Ensure that no burrs exist at the bottom of these ports which may cut the primary cup.

Assembly (Single Circuit)

When assembling the master cylinder, use parts from standard Porsche repair kit, part No. 695.355.930. Never reuse old parts.

1. Clean all parts in alcohol or brake fluid. Blow dry if you use alcohol.

2. Lubricate the cylinder walls and all internal parts with brake fluid.

NOTE: *Volkswagen developed a special brake cylinder paste which may be used to lubricate brake parts. This paste does not attack rubber brake parts, but mineral oil and grease will.*

3. Insert check valve and return spring.

4. Insert the primary cup in the direction shown.

5. Insert the piston washer and piston.

6. Insert the stopwasher and install the lock ring.

Disassembly (Dual Circuit)

Refer to **Figure 8** for the following procedure. Save *all parts* until master cylinder is reassembled.

1. Scrape off all outside dirt and wash with denatured alcohol.

2. Remove rubber boot.

3. Pry out lock ring with a small screwdriver.

4. Remove stop washer.

5. Remove primary piston and stroke limiter parts (items 3-6 and 8-10). Unscrew stroke limiter screw and remove limiter parts from piston.

6. Remove stop bolt and gasket.

7. Tamp the open end of the master cylinder on a wooden bench or block and the secondary piston will slide out. If it sticks in the bore, plug all holes except the grommeted hole for the secondary circuit (**Figure 9**). Inject compressed air through the grommet to force the piston out. A bicycle tire pump develops sufficient pressure for this.

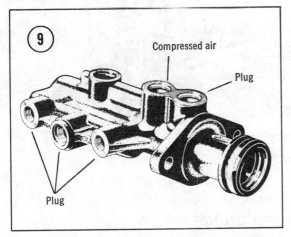

8. Remove spring.

9. Remove circuit failure switch.

10. Unscrew plug and remove 2 springs and pistons for the circuit failure system.

Inspection (Dual Circuit)

1. Clean all parts in denatured alcohol or clean brake fluid.

CAUTION
Never use gasoline, kerosene, or any solvent other than alcohol for rubber brake parts. You may wash metal parts in other solvents if you blow them dry, rinse several times in clean alcohol, and blow dry again.

2. Inspect the cylinder bore for scoring, pitting or heavy corrosion. Very light scratches and corrosion may be removed with *crocus cloth*. Discard the master cylinder if damage is more severe.

3. Run a small, smooth copper wire through the compensating ports and intake ports. See Figure 7. Note that dual master cylinders have 4 ports in all. Do not use steel or rough wire which may damage the port. Ensure that no burrs exist at the bottom of these ports which may cut the primary cup.

Assembly (Dual Circuit)

When assembling the master cylinder, use parts from a standard Porsche repair kit, Part No. 901.355.930.00. Parts included in this kit are indicated in Figure 8 by an asterisk. Never reuse old parts.

1. Clean all parts in alcohol or brake fluid. Blow dry if you use alcohol.

2. Lubricate the cylinder walls and all internal parts with brake fluid.

NOTE: *VW developed a special brake cylinder paste which may be used to lubricate brake parts. This paste does not attack rubber brake parts, but mineral oil or grease will.*

3. Install new cups on secondary piston. The closed ends should face each other.

4. Assemble the cup washer, primary cup, support washer, spring seat, and spring on secondary piston. Open end of primary cup should face spring.

5. Hold the master cylinder vertically with the open end down. Insert the secondary piston assembly up into the cylinder bore. If you try to install these parts horizontally, they will fall off the piston.

13

⑧

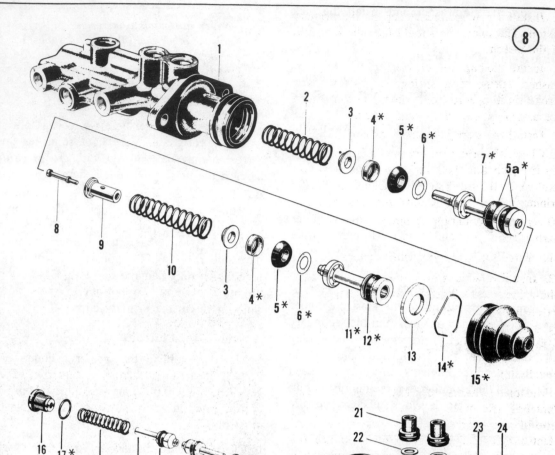

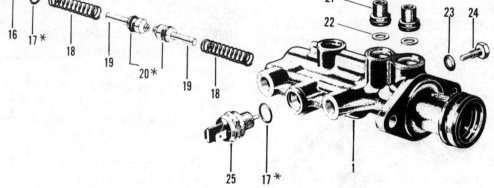

DUAL CIRCUIT MASTER CYLINDER

1. Housing
2. Secondary piston return spring
3. Spring seat
4. Supporting washer
5. Primary cup
5a. Secondary cups
6. Cup washer
7. Secondary piston

8. Stroke limiting screw
9. Stop sleeve
10. Primary piston return spring
11. Primary piston
12. Secondary cup
13. Stop plate
14. Lock ring
15. Dust boot
16. Plug

17. O-ring
18. Spring
19. Piston
20. Piston cup
21. Grommet
22. Washer
23. Gasket
24. Stop bolt
25. Circuit failure switch

* Replaceable parts included in brake rebuild kit

6. Install a new secondary cup on the primary piston. The open end should face the long end of the piston.

7. Install the cup washer, primary cup support washer, spring seat, spring, stop sleeve, and stroke limiting screw on primary piston. Insert the assembly into the cylinder bore.

8. Install the stop plate and lock ring.

9. Check that the primary piston is not blocking the stop bolt hole and insert the stop bolt and seal. If the hole is blocked, push the primary piston inward until the hole is clear.

10. Install the circuit failure switch with an O-ring.

11. Install top grommets with washers.

12. Install new cups on circuit failure pistons. These are *not* included in standard repair kit; order them separately.

13. Install springs and pistons in order shown in Figure 8. Install plug with O-ring.

Installation

Master cylinders for disc brake equipped Porsches are marked by a blue vinyl band around the body of the master cylinder. Master cylinders without this band are for drum brake systems. While outwardly they may look identical, they must not be interchanged.

1. Coat the master cylinder mounting flange with sealing compound to prevent entry of water.

2. Slip a new rubber boot over the pedal-mounted pushrod.

3. Mount the master cylinder from underneath while an assistant guides the pushrod into the master cylinder.

4. Secure the master cylinder with the retaining nuts and new lockwashers. Tighten nuts to 18 ft.-lb. (2.5 mkg).

5. Connect hydraulic lines, reservoir line(s), and circuit failure switch wires (1968-on models).

6. Adjust the pushrod length so that there is about 0.040 in. (1mm) clearance between pushrod and piston. See **Figure 10**. Rock the pedal back and forth by hand; only slight movement should be felt. If movement is excessive, or no

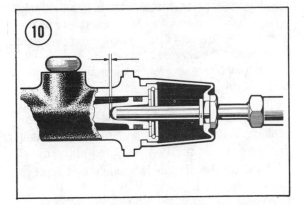

movement is detectable, loosen the locknut on the pushrod and turn the rod to lengthen or shorten as required. See **Figure 11**.

7. Check vent in reservoir cap. Clean it out if clogged.

8. Refill system with brake fluid.

> WARNING
> *Brake fluid must be clearly marked SAE 70R3, SAE J1703, DOT 3, or DOT 4. Do not use SAE 70R1 or any other brake fluid which can vaporize in disc brake systems.*

9. Bleed brakes as described later in this chapter.

10. Check brake light operation.

11. Install front axle shield.

BRAKE PAD REPLACEMENT

Brake pads on all 4 wheels should be inspected every 6,000 miles as described in Chapter Three. Replace brake pads on both

13

front wheels or both rear wheels if pad thickness is 0.08 in. (2mm) or less. It is rarely necessary to bleed the brake system after a single brake pad replacement.

Porsche offers several replacement brake pad sets for the various years and models. Each consists of 4 brake pads, 4 pin retainers, and 2 expander springs for both front or both rear brakes. When ordering, specify year, model, and presence of solid or ventilated brake discs.

1. Jack up the car on jackstands and remove the wheels.

2. Withdraw pin retainers. See **Figure 12**.

3. Push pins towards the center of the car while depressing the expander spring. See **Figure 13**.

4. Mark original positions of pads which are to be reused.

5. Pull brake pads out as shown in **Figure 14**.

6. Carefully clean out the cavity which holds the brake pads. Do not use solvents other than denatured alcohol and do not use sharp tools.

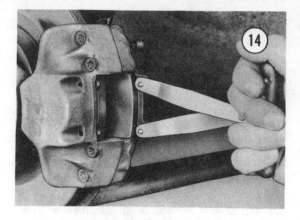

7. Inspect rubber dust covers; if they are damaged, replace them. If dirt has penetrated the cylinders due to a damaged cover, recondition the brake unit as described later.

8. Draw some brake fluid out of the reservoir to prevent overflow while performing the next step. Use a suction pump used exclusively for brake fluid.

9. Before installing new brake pads, push the pistons in as shown in **Figure 15**. If a special tool is not available, pry the pistons back with a hardwood block. Do not use metal tools for prying or the piston may be damaged.

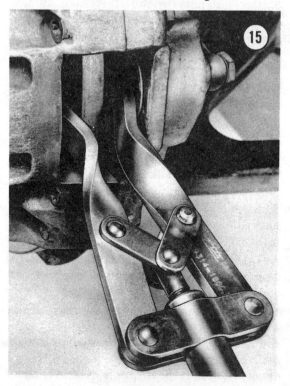

10. Clean brake discs with fine emery cloth.

11. Install new brake pads on both front wheels or both rear wheels. Old brake pads which are not excessively worn should be reinstalled only when the other 3 front (or rear) pads are serviceable. Even then, pads should be returned to their original position.

12. Install expander spring, pins, and pin retainers.

13. Depress the brake pedal several times before driving the car to force the pistons against the pads and correctly align the pads against the disc.

14. Check level in brake fluid reservoir and top up if necessary.

FRONT BRAKE CALIPERS

Removal/Installation

1. Raise car on jackstands and remove wheels.

2. Remove brake pads as described under *Brake Pad Replacement*.

3. Depress brake pedal about one inch and hold it there to prevent complete loss of brake fluid in next step. Porsche dealers use a special tool shown in **Figure 16**.

4. Disconnect hydraulic line at banjo fitting on brake caliper. Wrap fitting to prevent entry of dirt.

5. Remove caliper retaining bolts and lift caliper off. See **Figure 17** (typical).

6. Installation is the reverse of these steps. Use new lockwashers on caliper retaining bolts; tighten them to 50 ft.-lb. (7 mkg).

Reconditioning

Four different calipers are used. Gasket kits required for reconditioning are available for front or rear wheels for "L", "M", "S", and "A" calipers. Each kit does one caliper.

Order gasket kits by year, model, and disc type (solid or ventilated).

CAUTION
Do not disassemble the caliper any further than described below. If the caliper leaks, take it to your dealer for repair. Alignment of housing parts is very critical.

1. Remove caliper as described earlier.

2. Remove brake pads as described previously.

3. Loosen bleeder valve(s) and blow brake fluid out of caliper.

4. Clamp the caliper in a vise with soft jaws.

5. On 1965-1968 models, remove the dust cap shield over the outside piston.

6. Pry out retaining ring and rubber boot. See **Figure 18**.

7. Clamp one piston in place as shown in **Figure 19**. Hold a piece of ¼ in. thick wood in the housing and force the other piston against it with compressed air.

NOTE: *Once one piston is removed, pressure cannot be built up to force the other out. Therefore, completely rebuild one side before working on the other.*

13

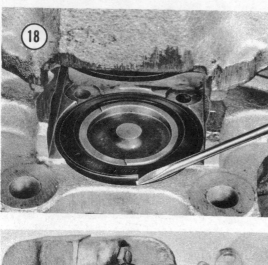

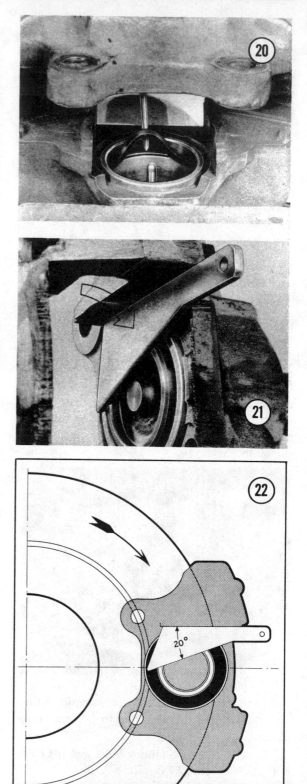

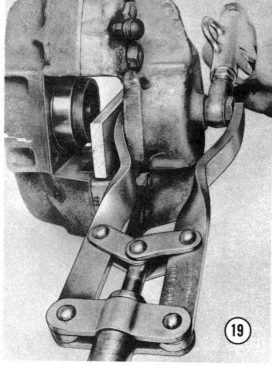

8. Remove rubber seal with a plastic or rubber rod to prevent damage to the housing. See **Figure 20**.

9. Clean all parts in alcohol or clean brake fluid.

10. Check parts for wear. If a cylinder is worn or damaged, the complete caliper must be replaced.

11. Coat the new rubber piston seal with brake cylinder paste. Install the seal and piston. Align the piston in the bore with the tool shown in **Figures 21 and 22** while pressing it in.

CAUTION
The piston must be installed carefully so that it doesn't tilt when pressed in and jam. The piston depressor shown in Figure 19 may be used to press the piston in. If you don't have the proper tools, consider taking the caliper to your dealer.

12. Wipe brake cylinder paste (if any) from piston ridge and install new rubber boot without lubricating it in any way. Secure the boot with a new retaining ring.

13. Repeat Steps 4-11 for the other piston/cylinder.

REAR BRAKE CALIPERS

Removal/Installation

1. Raise car on jackstands and remove wheels.

2. Remove brake pads as described under *Brake Pad Replacement.*

3. Remove bolts securing disc shrouds and remove the shrouds. See **Figure 23**.

4. Depress brake pedal about one inch and hold it there to prevent complete loss of brake fluid

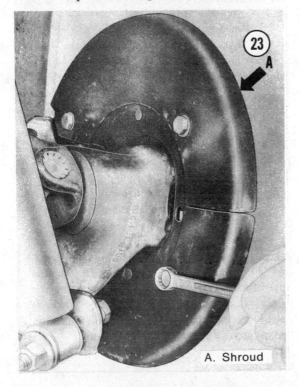

A. Shroud

during next step. Porsche dealers use a special tool shown in Figure 16.

5. Disconnect hydraulic line at caliper and plug the line to prevent entry of dirt.

6. Remove caliper retaining bolts and lift caliper off. See **Figure 24**.

7. Installation is the reverse of these steps. Use new lockwashers on caliper retaining bolts; tighten bolts to 43 ft.-lb. (6 mkg).

Reconditioning

See *Front Brake Calipers, Reconditioning.*

FRONT BRAKE DISCS

Inspection

The brake discs may be inspected with the caliper mounted, but the front of the car must be raised on jackstands and wheels removed. Small marks on the disc are not important, but radial scratches reduce braking effectiveness and increase pad wear.

Before checking disc runout, check wheel bearing adjustment as described in Chapter Fourteen. Mount a dial gauge as shown in **Figure 25**; about 0.4-0.6 in. (10-15mm) from the edge of the disc. Rotate the disc; runout should not exceed 0.008 in. (0.2mm). In critical

13

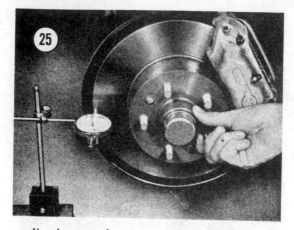

applications, such as competition, check runout on both sides of disc.

Check disc thickness with a micrometer. Make about 12 measurements around the disc about one inch from the outer edge. Measurements should not vary more than 0.0012 in. (0.03mm).

If the disc has excessively deep radial scratches, excessive runout, or variation in thickness, renew or replace the disc. See procedure later in this section.

Removal

1. Remove caliper as described earlier.

2. Remove dust cap as shown in **Figure 26**.

3. Loosen Allen bolt on wheel bearing clamp bolt (**Figure 27**). Remove clamp nut and thrust washer.

4. Pull brake disc off hub by hand. If necessary, use a standard puller.

CAUTION
Never hit a stubborn disc with anything to remove it.

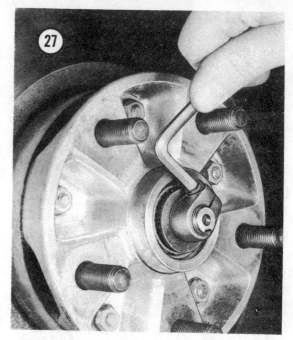

Resurfacing

Brake discs should be resurfaced only when absolutely necessary. **Figure 28** shows a disc with rounded ridges on the surface; this disc does *not* require resurfacing. The disc in **Figure 29**, however, has sharp ridges and should be resurfaced or replaced.

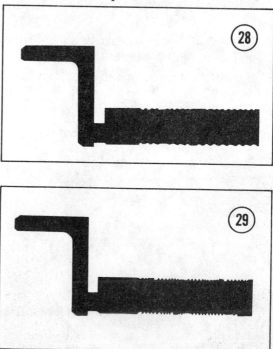

If a disc requires resurfacing, take it to your dealer. He will confirm the need for resurfacing and remove the required metal symmetrically from both sides of the disc.

Installation

1. Check condition of inner and outer wheel bearings in wheel hub. Replace if necessary as described in Chapter Twelve.

2. Pack wheel bearings with lithium grease.

3. Install brake disc on hub.

4. Install thrust washer and wheel bearing clamp nut. Adjust wheel bearings as described in Chapter Twelve.

5. Install dust cap.

6. Install brake caliper as described earlier.

REAR BRAKE DISCS

Inspection

Inspect rear brake discs in exactly the same manner as front brake discs. See earlier procedure.

Removal/Installation

1. Remove rear brake caliper as described earlier.

2. Remove 2 screws securing brake disc (**Figure 30**) and pull disc off.

3. Installation is the reverse of these steps.

Resurfacing

See *Front Brake Discs, Resurfacing.*

BRAKE BLEEDING

Brakes require bleeding whenever air enters the system, as this lowers the effective braking pressure. Air can enter when the master cylinder or wheel cylinders are serviced, or if the fluid in the reservoir runs dry. Air can also enter through a leaky brake line or hose. Find the leaky line and replace it before bleeding.

Whenever handling brake fluid, do not get any on the brake pads or body paint. Brake pads will be permanently damaged, requiring replacement. Body paint can be damaged also unless you wipe the area with a clean cloth, then wash it with a soapy solution immediately.

1. Ensure that the brake fluid reservoir is full and that the vent in the cap is open.

2. Connect a plastic or rubber tube to the bleeder valve on the right rear wheel. Suspend the other end of the tube in a jar or bottle filled with a few inches of clean brake fluid. See **Figure 31**. During the remaining steps, keep this end submerged at all times and never let the level in the brake fluid reservoir drop below ½ full.

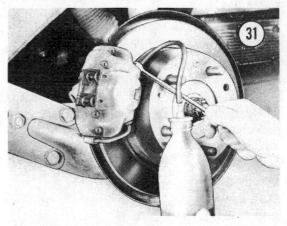

3. Have an assistant pump the brake pedal quickly several times, then hold the pedal down. Open the outer bleeder valve on the left rear caliper ½ to ¾ turn. Push pedal all the way down quickly. Close the bleeder valve and let the pedal up. Repeat this step as many times as necessary, i.e., until fluid with no air bubbles issues from the tube.

4. Bleed the remaining valves in the same manner described in the preceding steps. Follow the sequence shown in **Figure 32**. Note that the

13

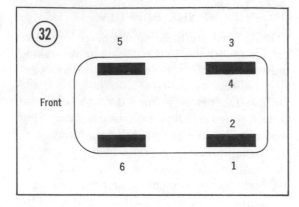

rear calipers have an inner and outer bleeder valve. Keep checking the brake fluid reservoir to be sure it doesn't run out of fluid or you will have to start all over again.

5. When all wheels are bled, discard the brake fluid in the jar or bottle; never reuse such fluid. Top up the brake fluid reservoir with clean brake fluid. See Step 8, *Master Cylinder Installation*.

HANDBRAKE

Cable Replacement

Separate cables connected to a common handbrake lever operate the rear wheel drum brakes.

1. Remove rear caliper and brake disc as described previously.

2. Remove cotter pin, castellated nut, and washer from brake cable (**Figure 33**) and pull cable out back of backing plate.

3. Remove tunnel cover and handbrake lever dust boot.

4. Remove 3 retaining bolts on handbrake lever housing. See **Figure 34**.

5. Lift handbrake lever housing and unhook cable from cable equalizer. See **Figure 35**. Pull cable out through front.

6. Coat the new cable with lithium grease and feed it into the guide tube in the tunnel.

7. Hook the cable on the equalizer. Have an assistant pull gently on the rear of the cable so that it doesn't unhook itself. Install handbrake lever housing.

8. Maintain tension on the cable, slide the spacer tube over the cable, then feed it into

the backing plate. Slip a washer over the end and install the castellated nut. Tighten the nut and secure with a cotter pin.

9. Adjust handbrake as described later.

Handbrake Shoe Replacement

1. Remove rear calipers and brake discs as described previously.

2. Remove cotter pin, castellated nut, and washer on cable (Figure 33) and pull cable out back of wheel.

3. Remove mechanical expander and spring. See Figure 33.

4. Remove spring retainer from upper brake shoe hold-down pin. See **Figure 36**. Remove the spring and pin.

5. Pry upper shoe upward with a screwdriver. Remove starwheel and unhook rear return spring. See **Figure 37**.

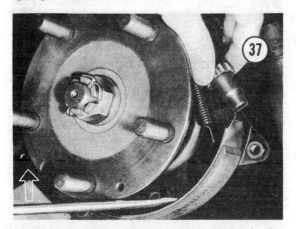

6. Remove spring retainer from lower brake shoe hold-down pin. Remove spring and pin.

7. Pull brake shoes apart to clear the axle and

lift off toward the front of the car. Unhook them from the front return spring.

8. Check brake linings and surrounding area for evidence of oil leaks. Replace axle shaft oil seals (Chapter Ten) if necessary. Replace oil-soaked brake linings regardless of wear.

9. Insert brake cable from behind and slide washer and inner part of expander onto cable.

10. Hook brake shoes together with front return spring.

11. Pull brake shoes apart to hold return spring in place. Fit shoes in place from the front.

12. Secure brake shoes to backing plate with hold-down pins, springs, and retainers.

13. Insert inner expander between brake shoe seats.

14. Install starwheel assembly between brake shoes.

15. Install second return spring. Note orientation of both springs in **Figure 38**.

16. Install expander spring, top half of expander, washer, and castellated nut. Then, tighten the nut just far enough to secure it with a new cotter pin.

17. Install rear brake discs and calipers. Tighten caliper retaining bolts to 43 ft.-lb. (6 mkg).

18. Bleed brakes.

19. Adjust handbrake as described later.

13

BRAKE ADJUSTMENT

Foot Brake Adjustment

A self-adjusting device in the brake pistons automatically maintains the proper brake pad-to-brake disc clearance. Therefore, no foot brake adjustment is necessary.

Handbrake Adjustment

The handbrake must be adjusted periodically to compensate for cable stretch and lining wear.

1. Raise rear of car on jackstands and remove rear wheels.

2. Release handbrake.

3. Push brake pads back so discs revolve freely.

4. Loosen cable adjusting nuts on left wheel (**Figure 39**) to slacken cable.

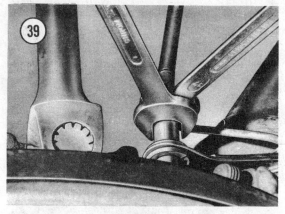

5. Insert screwdriver in left wheel adjusting hole and turn starwheel until brake disc cannot be turned. See **Figures 40 and 41**.

6. Repeat Steps 4 and 5 for right wheel.

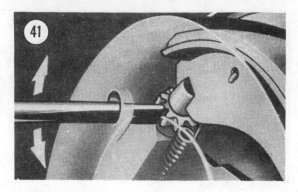

7. Tighten cable adjusting nuts to remove slack from both cables.

8. Pull tunnel cover and handbrake boot up at the rear. Pull up on handbrake lever as if setting the brake. Look through inspection holes and ensure that the cable equalizer is perpendicular to the car's longitudinal axis. See **Figures 42 and 43**. If uneven, readjust cable adjusting nuts (Figure 39).

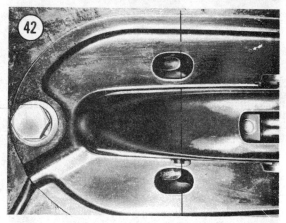

9. Release the handbrake lever.

10. Back off starwheel in each wheel (Figures 40 and 41) about 4 or 5 teeth so that the discs rotate freely.

11. Check that the handbrake is set when pulled up 4 notches.

12. Depress the brake pedal several times as far as possible to return brake pistons to proper position. Check fluid level in reservoir.

WARNING
If pistons are not returned in this manner, excessive pad-to-disc clearance will prevent stopping on the first or second brake application.

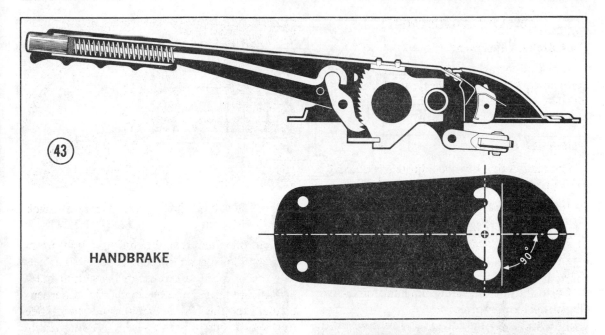

HANDBRAKE

Brake Light Adjustment

1. Pull accelerator pedal back to disengage it. Remove left front floor mat.

2. Remove retaining nut and floorboard. See **Figure 44**.

3. Place a 5/32 in. (4mm) metal gauge between the brake pedal and its stop. See **Figure 45**.

4. Loosen locknut on brake light switch. See **Figure 46**.

5. Move switch until brake lights go out, then back where they just go on. Tighten locknut.

6. Remove metal gauge and replace floorboard, nut, and accelerator pedal.

13

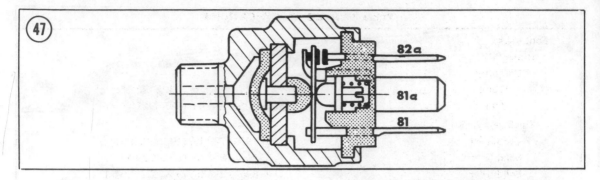

Handbrake Warning Light Adjustment

1. Pull tunnel cover and handbrake lever boot up at the rear.
2. Release handbrake, then pull it up one notch.
3. Loosen switch screw on handbrake lever housing 1 or 2 turns.
4. Move screw in slot to the point where the warning light just comes on. Tighten the screw in this position.

BRAKE LIGHT WARNING SWITCH

All 1968 and later master cylinders have a warning light switch for each brake circuit. See **Figure 47**. The switch is constructed with 3 connections with the following terminal designations:

  a. 81–stop light.
  b. 81a–instrument panel indicator light.
  c. 82a–voltage from terminal 15.

If either brake circuit should fail, its warning switch will turn to the OFF position. The working brake circuit will then apply current to terminal 81 of the failed switch so that the instrument panel brake warning light will come on when the brakes are applied.

1. Reservoir 2. Master cylinder 3. Brake booster
4. Warning switch (1) 5. Warning switch (2)

BRAKE BOOSTER

All 1977 and later models are equipped with a brake booster. The booster is located in the luggage compartment (**Figure 48**) and is bolted to a bracket together with the master cylinder and brake fluid reservoir (**Figure 49**). The vacuum check valve is located on the booster housing (**Figure 50**). Brake pedal free play with the brake booster is 13/32 in. (10 mm). Refer all brake booster service to your Porsche dealer.

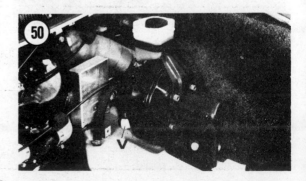

Table 1 BRAKE SPECIFICATIONS

Foot Brake	
Brake disc	
Diameter	
Front	11.11-11.12 in. (282.2-282.5mm)
Rear	11.25-11.41 in. (285.7-290.0mm)
Thickness (new)	
Ventilated	0.780-0.787 in. (19.8-20.0mm)
Solid, front	0.492-0.500 in. (12.5-12.7mm)
Solid, rear	0.386-0.394 in. (9.8-10.0mm)
	or
	0.406-0.413 in. (10.3-10.5mm)
Minimum thickness	
Ventilated	0.71 in. (18mm)
Solid, front	0.43 in. (11mm)
Solid, rear	0.33 in. (8.5mm)
Thickness variation	0.0012 in. (0.03mm)
Lateral run-out (maximum)	0.008 in. (0.2mm)
Brake calipers	
Cylinder diameter	
Front	1.890 in. (48mm)
Rear	1.378 in. (35mm)①, 1.496 in. (38mm)②
Brake pads	
Thickness (new)	0.590 in. (15mm)⑤, 0.394 in. (10mm)⑥
Minimum thickness	0.079 in. (2mm)
Area per wheel	
Front in.² (cm²)	8.14 in. (52.5mm), 11.78 in. (76mm)③
Rear in.² (cm²)	6.20 in. (40.0mm)①, 8.14 in. (52.5mm)②
Master cylinder	
Bore	0.750 in.(19.05mm), 0.813 in. (20.64)④
Handbrake	
Drum diameter	7.087 in. (180mm)
Brake lining width	1.181 in. (30mm)①, 0.984 in. (25mm)②
Brake lining area (2 wheels)	32.55 in. (210mm)①, 26.35 in. (170mm)②

① 1965-1968	④ 1969 911E, S
② 1969-1976	⑤ 1965-1973
③ 1969-1976 911E, S	⑥ 1974-on

13

Table 2 TIGHTENING TORQUES

	Ft.-lb.	Mkg
Master cylinder mounting nuts	18	2.5
Brake disc-to-wheel hub nut	16.6	2.3
Front caliper bolt	50.6	7.0
Rear caliper bolt	43.4	6.0
Castellated hub nut	217-253	30.35

INDEX

14

14

WIRING DIAGRAMS

COLOR CODE	
Blue	Bl
Black	BLK
Brown	BRN
Grey	Gr
Green	Grn
Light green	Lt Grn
Olive	Ol
Purple	Pur
Red	R
Violet	V
White	W
Yellow	Y

ELECTRICAL SYMBOLS

Heating resistor (element)		Antenna	
Danger! High Voltage		Dipole antenna	
Spark gap		Direct current	
Condenser		Alternating current	
Feedthrough (suppressor) condenser		Three-phase current	
Coil, iron core		Generator	
Transformer, iron core		Battery cell	
Diode		Motor	
Zener diode		Measuring gauge	
Transistor		Voltmeter	
Thyristor		Ammeter	
Mechanical connection of components		Wiring	
Mechanical connection, spring loaded contact		Wire cross section in mm²	
Time switch		Wire junction, fixed	
Manually operated switch		Wire connector, separable	
Mechanically operated switch		Wire junction, separable	
Motor operated switch		Suppression wire	
Relay coil		Wire crossing	
Solenoid coil		Ground	
Relay, electrothermal		Switch position, open	
Relay, electromagnetic		Switch position, closed	
Electromagnetic valve (jet)		Multiple contact switch	
Boundary line for an assembly		Fuse	
Horn		Light bulb	
Loudspeaker		Glow lamp	
		Resistor	
		Potentiometer	
		Tapped resistor	
		Thermal resistor, automatically regulating	

15

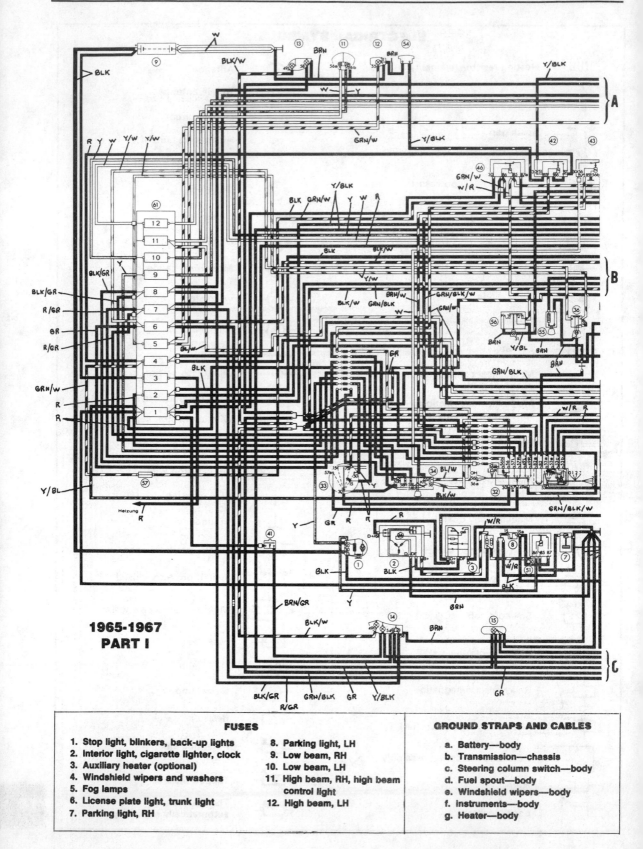

1965-1967 PART I

FUSES		GROUND STRAPS AND CABLES
1. Stop light, blinkers, back-up lights	8. Parking light, LH	a. Battery—body
2. Interior light, cigarette lighter, clock	9. Low beam, RH	b. Transmission—chassis
3. Auxiliary heater (optional)	10. Low beam, LH	c. Steering column switch—body
4. Windshield wipers and washers	11. High beam, RH, high beam control light	d. Fuel spout—body
5. Fog lamps	12. High beam, LH	e. Windshield wipers—body
6. License plate light, trunk light		f. instruments—body
7. Parking light, RH		g. Heater—body

1965-1967
PART II

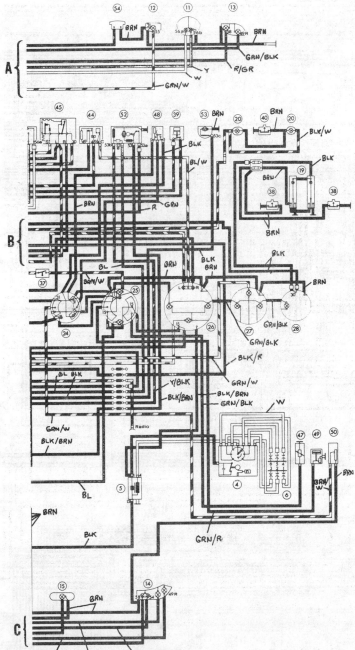

CIRCLED NUMBERS

1. Starter motor
2. Alternator
3. Voltage regulator
4. Ignition distributor
5. Ignition coil
6. Spark plugs
7. Fuel pump
8. Resistor
9. Battery
11. Headlamps
12. Fog lamps
13. Blinker/parking lights
14. Tail/stop/blinker/back-up lights
15. License plate light
19. Interior light
20. Trunk light
24. Fuel/oil level gauge cluster
25. Oil temp./press. gauge cluster
26. Transistorized tachometer
27. Speedometer
28. Clock
32. Blinker/dimmer/signal/wiper/washer switch with signal knob on steering wheel
33. Starter/ignition switch
34. Light switch
36. Fog lamp switch with control light
37. Handbrake control light switch
38. Door contact switch
39. Brake light switch
40. Trunk light switch
41. Back-up light switch
42. Horn relay
43. Headlamp flasher relay
44. Directional signal flasher
45. Hazard light flasher
46. Hazard light relay
47. Oil temperature sender
48. Fuel tank unit
49. Oil pressure sender
50. Oil level sender
51. Resistor relay
52. Windshield wiper motor
53. Windshield washer pump
54. Horn
55. Cigarette lighter
56. Hazard light switch
57. Hazard light fuse
61. Fuse box
62. Heater
63. Radio

WIRING DIAGRAMS

1968-1972*
PART I

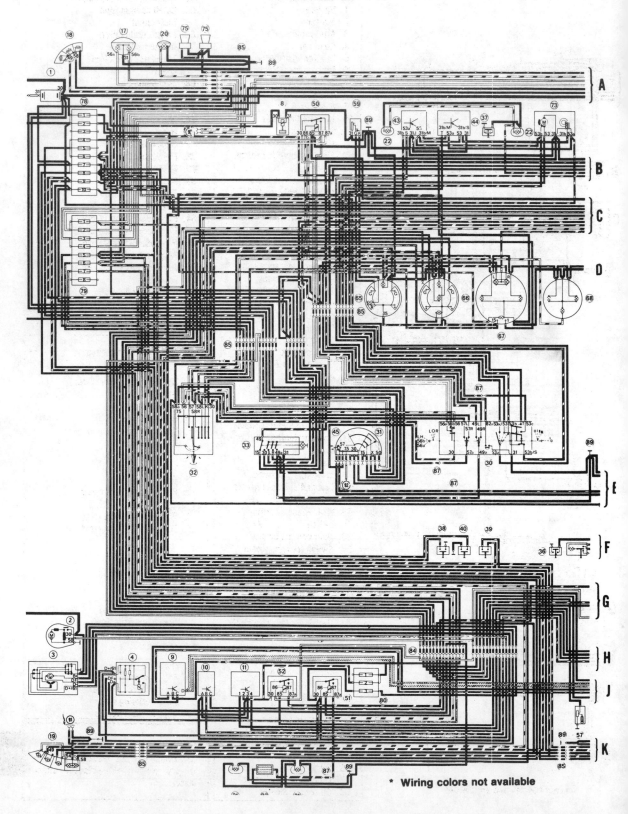

* Wiring colors not available

1968-1972*
PART II

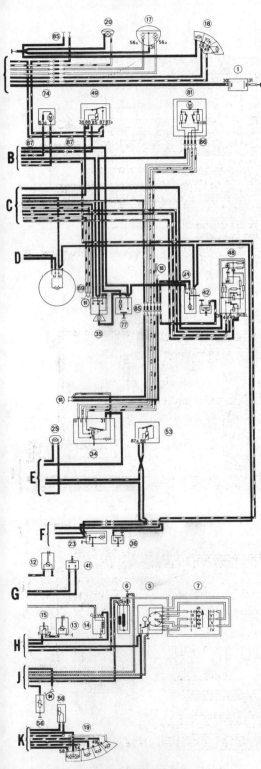

CIRCLED NUMBERS

1. Battery
2. Starter
3. Alternator
4. Governor
5. Ignition distributor
6. Ignition transformer
7. Spark plugs
8. Gasoline pump
9. BHKZ unit
10. Intermediate unit
11. Speed switch
    (E and S only)
12. Electromagnetic control
    valve
13. Lifting magnet (stop)
    (E and S only, on 911 T
    USA solenoid valve)
14. Temperature time switch
15. Microswitch
    (E and S only)
17. Headlamps
18. Blinker, clearance and
    side marker lamps
19. Tail, brake, blinker, side
    marker and backup lamps
20. Fog lamp (optional)
21. License plate lamp
22. Trunk lamp
23. Interior lamp
24. Glovebox lamp
25. Ashtray lamp
30. Blinker, dimming, head-
    lamp flasher, wiper-
    washer switch with signal
    button in steering wheel
31. Steering ignition starter
    switch
32. Light switch
33. Warning light switch
34. Fan and separate heater
    switch
35. Rear window heater
    switch
36. Door contact switch
37. Switch for trunk room
    light
38. Hand brake contact
39. Brake light switch
40. Brake warning switch
41. Back-up light switch
42. Switch for glovebox light
43. Interval switch
44. Wiper follow-up switch
45. Buzzer contact
48. Direction warning
    blinker indicator
49. Horn relay
50. Headlight flasher
    changeover relay
51. Rear window heater relay
52. Auxiliary starting relay
53. Buzzer
56. Oil temperature indicator
57. Oil pressure indicator
58. Oil level indicator

59. Indicator for fuel gauge
65. Small combination
    instrument
66. Large combination
    instrument
67. Transistor revolution
    counter
68. Speedometer
69. Electric time clock
73. Wiper motor
74. Washer pump
75. Horn
77. Cigarette lighter
78. Fuse box I 10-pole
79. Fuse box II 8-pole
80. Fuse box III 3-pole
81. Fan motor
82. Heated pane
84. Plug connection 14-pole
85. Plug connection 6-pole
86. Plug connection 4-pole
87. Plug connection 1-pole
89. Ground connection - body
90. Fog light
91. Fog light indicator
92. Radio
93. Auxiliary heater
94. Oil temperature switch

FUSES
Fusebox I
1. Interior light, time clock,
   trunk light
2. Warning light
3. (Window lifter)
4. Cigarette lighter
5. (Slide roof)
6. Windshield wiper,
   washer pump
7. Fresh air fan
8. Brake, blinker, back-up
   lights
9. Blinker light front left
10. Blinker light front right

Fusebox II
1. High beam left
2. High beam right
3. Dimmer left
4. Dimmer right
5. Clearance light left
6. Clearance light right
7. License plate light
8. (Fog lights)

Fusebox III
1. (Sportomatic)
2. Stop magnet, solenoid
   valve, starting valve
3. Rear window heater

CAUTION
Disconnecting the battery with the
engine running will ruin the alternator.

15

* Wiring colors not available

1973 911T, E, S, CARRERA 2.7
KEY

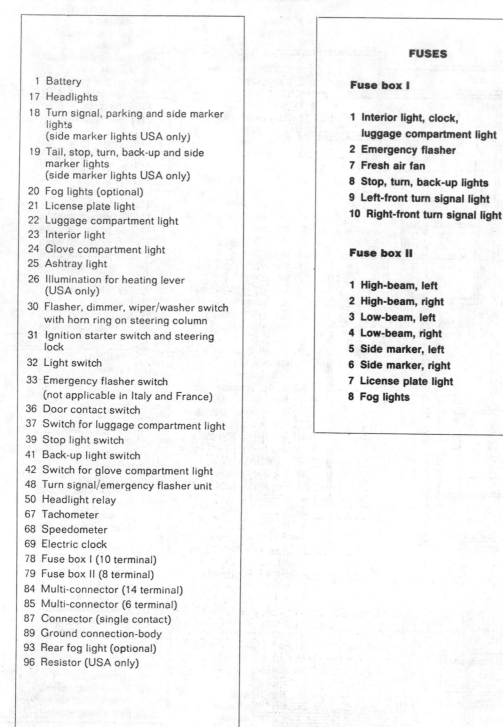

1 Battery
17 Headlights
18 Turn signal, parking and side marker
   lights
   (side marker lights USA only)
19 Tail, stop, turn, back-up and side
   marker lights
   (side marker lights USA only)
20 Fog lights (optional)
21 License plate light
22 Luggage compartment light
23 Interior light
24 Glove compartment light
25 Ashtray light
26 Illumination for heating lever
   (USA only)
30 Flasher, dimmer, wiper/washer switch
   with horn ring on steering column
31 Ignition starter switch and steering
   lock
32 Light switch
33 Emergency flasher switch
   (not applicable in Italy and France)
36 Door contact switch
37 Switch for luggage compartment light
39 Stop light switch
41 Back-up light switch
42 Switch for glove compartment light
48 Turn signal/emergency flasher unit
50 Headlight relay
67 Tachometer
68 Speedometer
69 Electric clock
78 Fuse box I (10 terminal)
79 Fuse box II (8 terminal)
84 Multi-connector (14 terminal)
85 Multi-connector (6 terminal)
87 Connector (single contact)
89 Ground connection-body
93 Rear fog light (optional)
96 Resistor (USA only)

FUSES

Fuse box I

1 Interior light, clock,
  luggage compartment light
2 Emergency flasher
7 Fresh air fan
8 Stop, turn, back-up lights
9 Left-front turn signal light
10 Right-front turn signal light

Fuse box II

1 High-beam, left
2 High-beam, right
3 Low-beam, left
4 Low-beam, right
5 Side marker, left
6 Side marker, right
7 License plate light
8 Fog lights

1973 911T, E, S, CARRERA 2.7
PART I

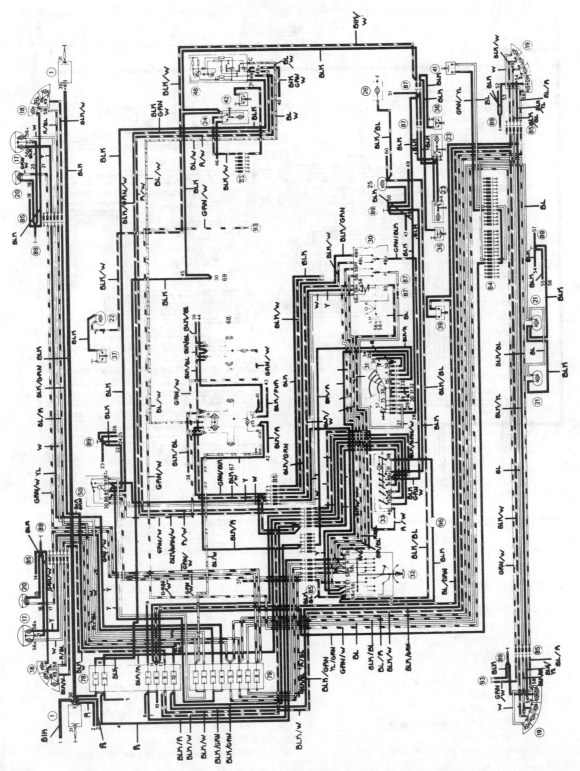

15

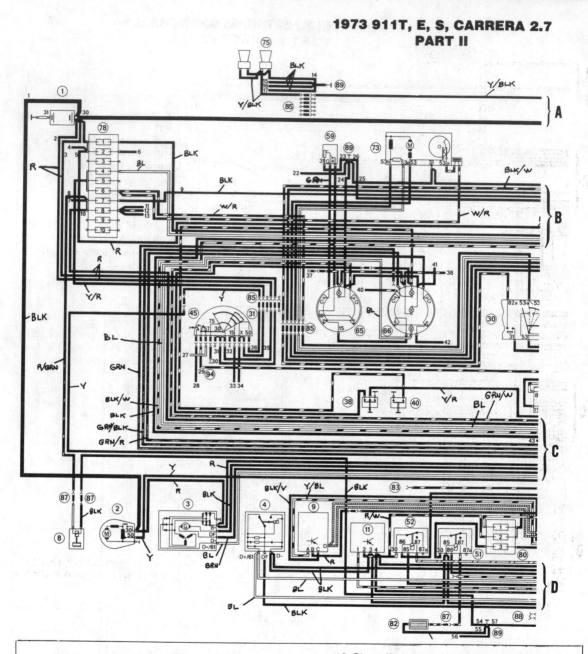

1973 911T, E, S, CARRERA 2.7 PART II

1 Battery	13 Shut-off solenoid (911 TV: solenoid valve)
2 Starter	14 Thermo-time switch (except 911 TV)
3 Alternator	15 Micro switch
4 Governor	30 Flasher, dimmer, wiper/washer switch with horn ring on steering column
5 Distributor	
6 Ignition transformer	31 Ignition starter switch and steering lock
7 Spark plugs	
8 Fuel pump	34 Switch for fan and auxiliary heater
9 High tension ignition unit	35 Rear window defogger switch
11 Speed switch	38 Parking brake contact
12 Cold start solenoid (except 911 TV)	40 Brake warning light switch (USA only)

1973 911T, E, S, CARRERA 2.7
PART III

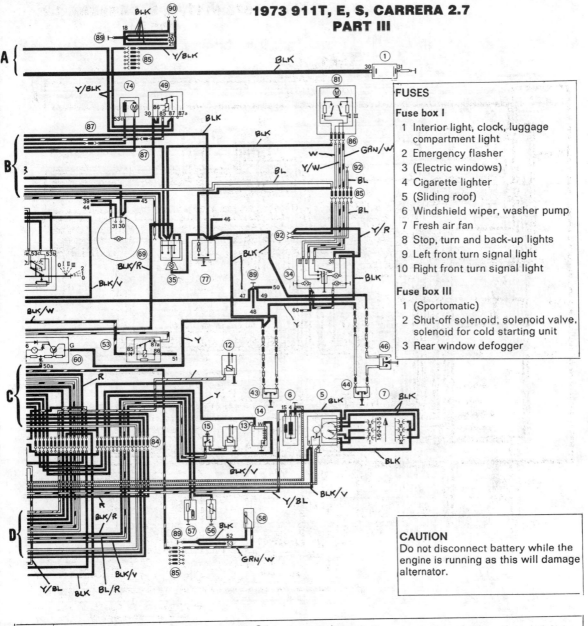

FUSES

Fuse box I

1 Interior light, clock, luggage compartment light
2 Emergency flasher
3 (Electric windows)
4 Cigarette lighter
5 (Sliding roof)
6 Windshield wiper, washer pump
7 Fresh air fan
8 Stop, turn and back-up lights
9 Left front turn signal light
10 Right front turn signal light

Fuse box III

1 (Sportomatic)
2 Shut-off solenoid, solenoid valve, solenoid for cold starting unit
3 Rear window defogger

CAUTION
Do not disconnect battery while the engine is running as this will damage alternator.

43 Safety belt contact, driver side (USA only)	57 Oil pressure indicator	81 Fan motor
44 Safety belt contact, passenger side (USA only)	58 Oil level indicator	82 Rear window defogger element
	59 Indicator for fuel gauge	83 Sportomatic (optional)
45 Buzzer contact (USA only)	60 Safety belt warning light	84 Multi-connector (14 terminal)
46 Seat contact, passenger side (USA only)	65 Fuel gauge dial	85 Multi-connector (6 terminal)
	66 Oil temperature gauge dial	86 Multi-connector (4 terminal)
49 Horn relay	69 Electric clock	87 Connector (single contact)
51 Rear window defogger relay	73 Wiper motor	88 Gear lever contact SPM
52 Auxiliary starting relay (except 911 TV)	74 Washer pump	89 Ground connection-body
	75 Horns	90 Optional horn
53 Buzzer (USA only)	77 Cigarette lighter	92 Auxiliary combustion heater
56 Oil temperature indicator	78 Fuse box I (10 terminal)	94 Radio (optional)
	80 Fuse box III (3 terminal)	

15

1973 911T, FUEL INJECTED
PART I

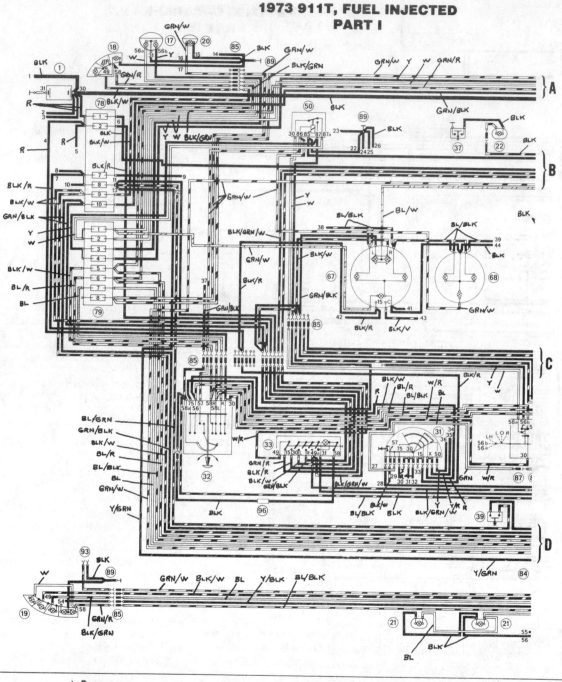

1 Battery
17 Headlights
18 Turn signal, parking and side marker lights
(side marker lights USA only)
19 Tail, stop, turn, back-up and side marker lights
(side marker lights USA only)
20 Fog lights (optional)

21 License plate light
22 Luggage compartment light
23 Interior light
24 Glove compartment light
25 Ashtray light
26 Illumination for heating lever (USA only)
30 Flasher, dimmer, wiper/washer switch with horn ring on steering column

1973 911T, FUEL INJECTED
PART II

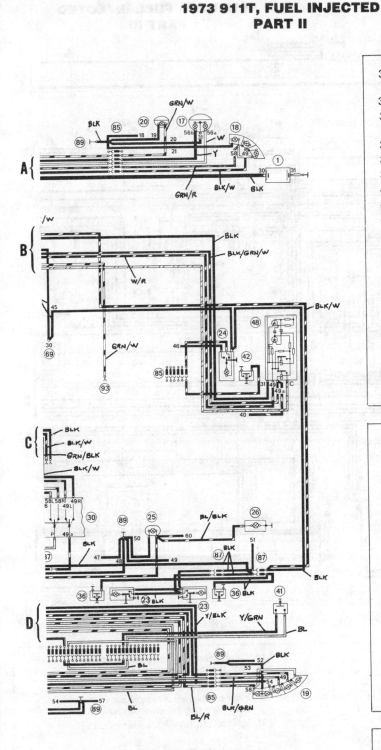

31 Ignition starter switch and steering lock
32 Light switch
33 Emergency flasher switch
   (not applicable in Italy and France)
36 Door contact switch
37 Switch for luggage compartment light
39 Stop light switch
41 Back-up light switch
42 Switch for glove compartment light
48 Turn signal/emergency flasher unit
50 Headlight relay
67 Tachometer
68 Speedometer
69 Electric clock
78 Fuse box I (10 terminal)
79 Fuse box II (8 terminal)
84 Multi-connector (14 terminal)
85 Multi-connector (6 terminal)
87 Connector (single contact)
89 Ground connection-body
93 Rear fog light (optional)
96 Resistor (USA only)

FUSES

Fuse box I:

1 Interior light, clock, luggage compartment light
2 Emergency flasher
7 Fresh air fan
8 Stop, turn and back-up lights
9 Left front turn signal light
10 Right front turn signal light

Fuse box II

1 High beam, left
2 High beam, right
3 Low beam, left
4 Low beam, right
5 Side marker, left
6 Side marker, right
7 License plate light
8 (Fog lights)

CAUTION

Do not disconnect battery while the engine is running as this will damage the alternator.

15

**1973 911T, FUEL INJECTED
PART III**

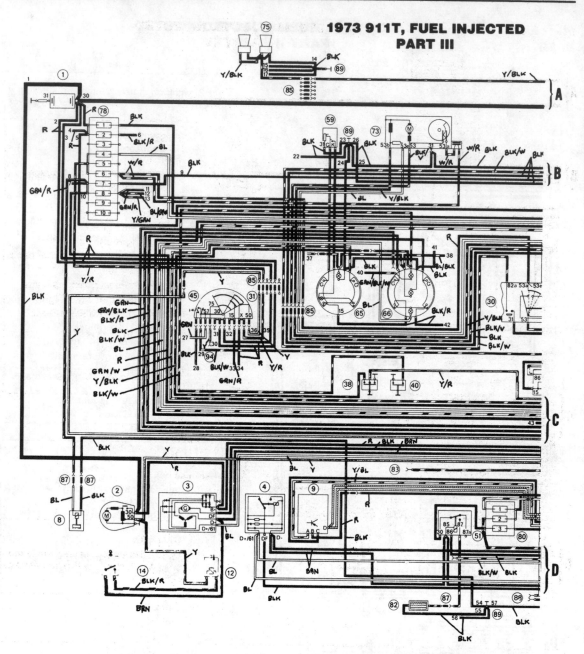

1 Battery	13 Control pressure regulating valve with warm-up compensation
2 Starter	14 Micro switch
3 Alternator	30 Flasher, dimmer, wiper/washer switch with horn ring on steering column
4 Governor	
5 Distributor	31 Ignition starter switch and steering lock
6 Ignition transformer	
7 Spark plugs	34 Switch for fan and auxiliary heater
8 Fuel pump	35 Rear window defogger switch
9 High tension ignition unit	38 Parking brake contact
12 Cold start solenoid	40 Brake warning light switch (USA only)

1973 911T, FUEL INJECTED
PART IV

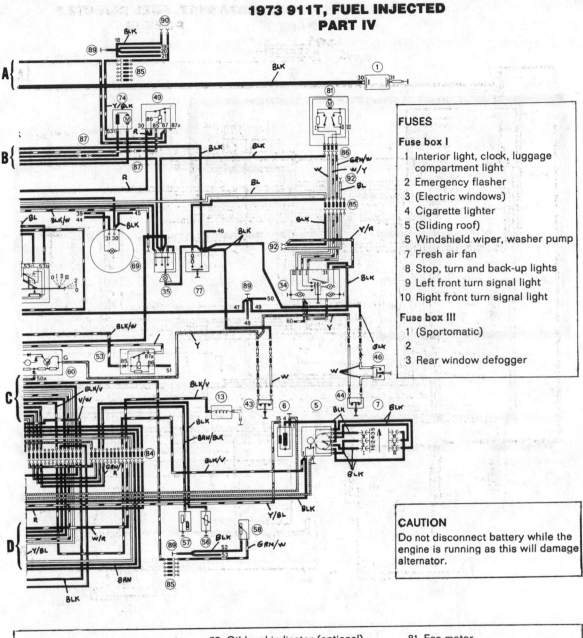

FUSES

Fuse box I

1 Interior light, clock, luggage compartment light
2 Emergency flasher
3 (Electric windows)
4 Cigarette lighter
5 (Sliding roof)
6 Windshield wiper, washer pump
7 Fresh air fan
8 Stop, turn and back-up lights
9 Left front turn signal light
10 Right front turn signal light

Fuse box III

1 (Sportomatic)
2
3 Rear window defogger

CAUTION

Do not disconnect battery while the engine is running as this will damage alternator.

43 Safety belt contact, driver side (USA only)
44 Safety belt contact, passenger side (USA only)
45 Buzzer contact (USA only)
46 Seat contact, passenger side (USA only)
49 Horn relay
51 Rear window defogger relay
53 Buzzer (USA only)
56 Oil temperature indicator
57 Oil pressure indicator (optional)

58 Oil level indicator (optional)
59 Indicator for fuel gauge
60 Safety belt warning light (USA only)
65 Fuel gauge dial
66 Oil temperature gauge dial
69 Electric clock
73 Wiper motor
74 Washer pump
75 Horns
77 Cigarette lighter
78 Fuse box I (10 terminal)
80 Fuse box III (3 terminal)

81 Fan motor
82 Rear window defogger element
83 Sportomatic (optional)
84 Multi-connector (14 terminal)
85 Multi-connector (6 terminal)
86 Multi-connector (4 terminal)
87 Connector (single contact)
88 Gear lever contact SPM
89 Ground connection-body
90 Optional horn
92 Auxiliary combustion heater
94 Radio (optional)

15

1973 911T, FUEL INJECTED
PART V

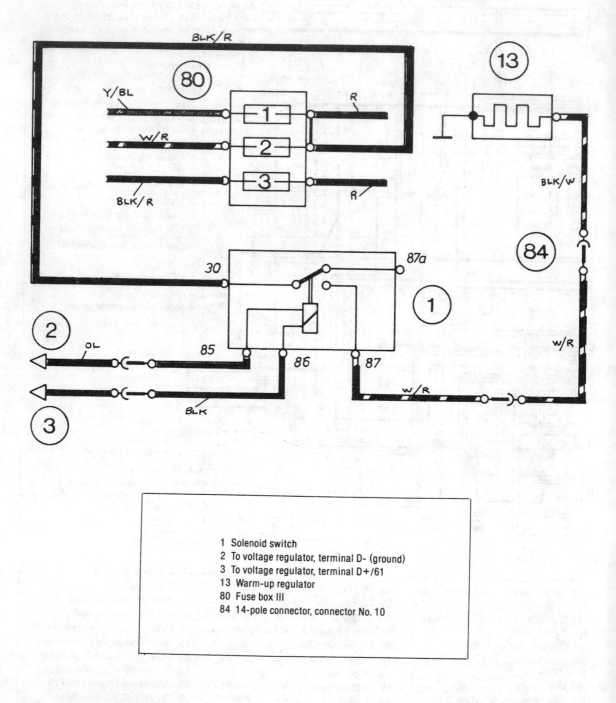

1   Solenoid switch
2   To voltage regulator, terminal D- (ground)
3   To voltage regulator, terminal D+/61
13   Warm-up regulator
80   Fuse box III
84   14-pole connector, connector No. 10

HOW TO READ 1974-ON WIRING DIAGRAMS

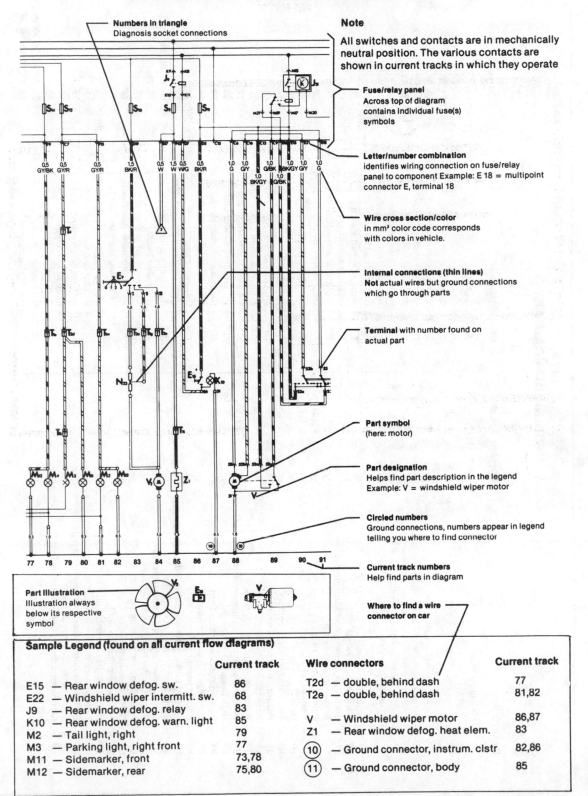

Numbers in triangle
Diagnosis socket connections

Note

All switches and contacts are in mechanically neutral position. The various contacts are shown in current tracks in which they operate

Fuse/relay panel
Across top of diagram contains individual fuse(s) symbols

Letter/number combination
identifies wiring connection on fuse/relay panel to component Example: E 18 = multipoint connector E, terminal 18

Wire cross section/color
in mm² color code corresponds with colors in vehicle.

Internal connections (thin lines)
Not actual wires but ground connections which go through parts

Terminal with number found on actual part

Part symbol
(here: motor)

Part designation
Helps find part description in the legend
Example: V = windshield wiper motor

Circled numbers
Ground connections, numbers appear in legend telling you where to find connector

Current track numbers
Help find parts in diagram

Part Illustration
Illustration always below its respective symbol

Where to find a wire connector on car

Sample Legend (found on all current flow diagrams)

		Current track			Current track
E15	— Rear window defog. sw.	86	T2d	— double, behind dash	77
E22	— Windshield wiper intermitt. sw.	68	T2e	— double, behind dash	81,82
J9	— Rear window defog. relay	83			
K10	— Rear window defog. warn. light	85	V	— Windshield wiper motor	86,87
M2	— Tail light, right	79	Z1	— Rear window defog. heat elem.	83
M3	— Parking light, right front	77	(10)	— Ground connector, instrum. clstr	82,86
M11	— Sidemarker, front	73,78	(11)	— Ground connector, body	85
M12	— Sidemarker, rear	75,80			

15

1974
WIRING DIAGRAM KEY

Description	Current Track
E¹ — Headlight switch	6, 8, 9, 11, 15, 20
E² — Turn signal switch	28
E³ — Emergency flasher switch	24, 25, 28, 31, 34
E⁴ — Dimmer switch	6, 39
E⁵ — Headlight flasher switch	4
E¹⁹ — Parking light switch	13
E²⁰ — Instrument panel illumination potentiometer	20
E²⁶ — Switch for glove compartment light	41
F — Stop light switch	50
F² — Left door switch	45
F³ — Right door switch	46
F⁴ — Back-up light switch	48
F⁵ — Switch for luggage compartment light	42
F⁶ — Brake warning switch	34
F⁹ — Parking brake switch	33
H — Horn switch	39
H² — Horns	36, 38
H⁶ — Key warning buzzer contact	43
J¹ — Hazard / turn signal flasher	33, 34, 35
J⁴ — Horn relay	36, 37
J²⁵ — Headlight relay	4, 5
J²⁷ — Diode for seat belt warning system	46
K¹ — High beam indicator light	2
K⁴ — Parking lights indicator light	1
K⁵ — Turn signal indicator light	27, 29
K⁶ — Hazard flasher indicator light	24
K⁷ — Parking brake / brake warning indicator light	34
L¹ — Sealed beam unit, left headlight	3, 7
L² — Sealed beam unit, right headlight	4, 8
L⁶ — Speedometer illumination light	22
L⁷ — Fuel gauge illumination light	22
L⁸ — Clock illumination light	22
L¹⁵ — Ashtray illumination light	20
L¹⁶ — Heater control assembly illumination light	19
L²¹ — Temperature control lever illumination light	21
L²⁴ — Oil temperature indicator illumination light	22
L²⁶ — Tachometer illumination light	22
L²⁷ — Oil pressure indicator illumination light	22

Description	Current Track
A — Battery	89
B — Starter	86, 87
C — Generator	81, 82, 83, 84
C² — Voltage regulator	81, 82, 83
D — Ignition / starter switch	68, 69, 70, 71, 72
E — Windshield wiper switch	63, 64, 65
E⁹ — Fresh air blower switch	60
E¹⁵ — Rear window defogger switch	55, 56
E²⁴ — Left seat belt switch	69
E²⁵ — Right seat belt switch	71
E³¹ — Left seat sensor switch	69
E³² — Right seat sensor switch	71
F¹ — Oil pressure switch	79
G — Fuel sender unit	75
G¹ — Fuel gauge	76
G⁵ — Tachometer	78
G⁶ — Fuel pump	54
G⁸ — Oil temperature sender unit	77
G⁹ — Oil temperature indicator	77
G¹⁰ — Oil pressure sender unit	80
G¹¹ — Oil pressure indicator	78
G¹² — Oil level sender unit	74
G¹³ — Oil level gauge	74
J⁹ — Rear window defogger relay	56, 57
J³⁴ — Seat belt warning system relay with integrated buzzer	66, 67, 68, 69, 70, 71, 72, 73
K² — Generator charge indicator light	77
K³ — Oil pressure indicator light	78
K⁸ — Blower indicator light	61
K¹⁰ — Rear window defogger indicator light	55
K¹⁶ — Low fuel warning light	75
K¹⁹ — Seat belt warning light	74
N — Ignition transformer	90
N¹⁵ — High tension ignition unit	90
O — Distributor	91, 92, 93, 94, 95, 96, 97
P — Spark plug connector	92, 93, 94, 95, 96, 97

1974 KEY (Continued)

Description	Current Track
M^2 — Right stop / rear light	17, 50
M^4 — Left stop / rear light	13, 51
M^5 — Left front turn signal / parking light	11, 25
M^6 — Left rear turn signal	26
M^7 — Right front turn signal / parking light	15, 31
M^8 — Right rear turn signal	30
M^{11} — Front side marker light	12, 16
M^{12} — Rear side marker light	14, 18
M^{16} — Left back-up light	48
M^{17} — Right back-up light	49
N^6 — Resistor	23
S^2 — Fuses	9, 15, 11
to — on the	8, 7, 4
S^{11} — on the	3, 31, 25, 48
S^{17} — fuse box	34
S^{18} —	40
T^1 — Cable connector, single	14
a — near regulator panel	11, 25
b — behind sealed beam unit, left	15, 31
c — behind sealed beam unit, right	37
d — behind fuse box	22, 42, 44, 45, 46
e — on luggage compartment floor	6, 22, 24, 28
f — behind instrument panel	24
h — near left rear lights	
T^6 — Cable connector, sixfold	
a — in the engine compartment, rear left	9, 13, 24, 26, 48, 51
b — in the engine compartment, rear right	10, 17, 30, 49, 50
d — below instrument panel	4, 6, 26, 30, 39
e — below instrument panel	25, 31, 32, 34
g — below instrument panel	8, 9, 11, 15, 22
h — below instrument panel	41
T^{14} — Cable connector, fourteenfold	
a — on regulator panel, front	48
b — on regulator panel, rear	48
W — Interior light	45, 46
W^3 — Luggage compartment light	42
W^6 — Glove compartment light	41
X — License plate light	9, 10
Y — Clock	40

Description	Current Track
Q — Spark plug	92, 93, 94, 95, 96, 97
S^{12} — Fuses	55, 63
to — on the	62
S^{15} — fuse box	61
S^{22} — Fuses on the	99
S^{24} — rear fuse box (regulator panel)	57
T^1 — Cable connector, single	
a — near regulator panel	56, 57, 58, 79, 83, 99
d — behind fuse box	65
e — on luggage compartment floor	60, 72, 73, 100
f — behind instrument panel	58, 60, 61, 69, 70
g — below shift lever housing	99
T^2 — Cable connector, double	
a — below regulator panel	99
b — in engine compartment, left	54
c — near left seat	69
d — below left seat	69
e — near left seat	69
f — near right seat	71
g — below right seat	71
h — near right seat	71
T^6 — Cable connector, sixfold	
b — in engine compartment, right	74
c — below instrument panel	63, 64, 65
f — below instrument panel	66, 67, 72, 88, 89
h — below instrument panel	60, 61
T^{14} — Cable connector, fourteenfold	
a — on regulator panel, front	56, 58, 73, 77, 80, 85, 98, 99, 100
b — on regulator panel, rear	57, 77, 80, 81, 83, 85, 98, 100
U^1 — Cigar lighter	62
V — Windshield wiper motor	63, 64
V^2 — Blower motor	60
V^5 — Washer pump	65
Z^1 — Rear window defogger	57

1974
PART I

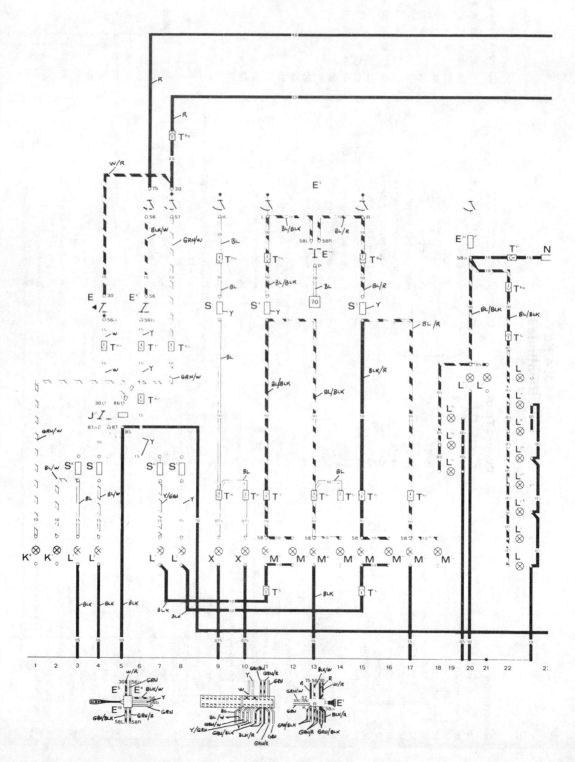

1974
PART II

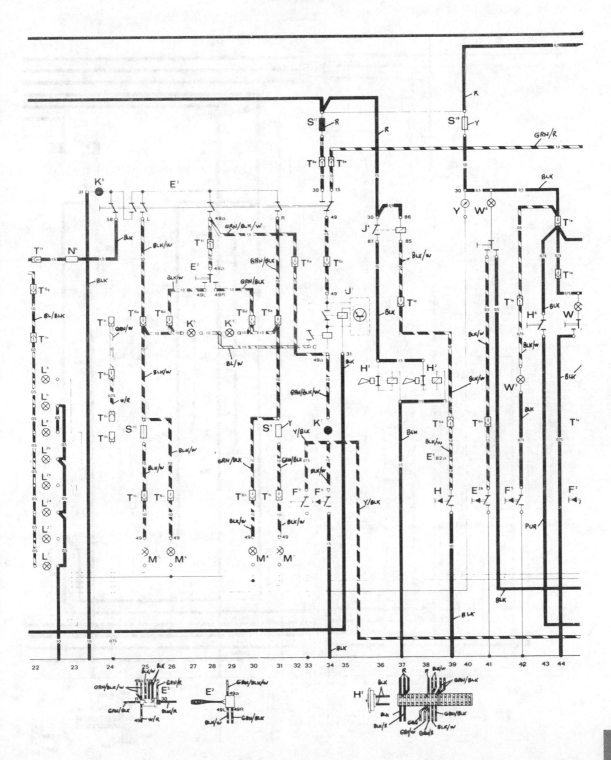

1974
PART III

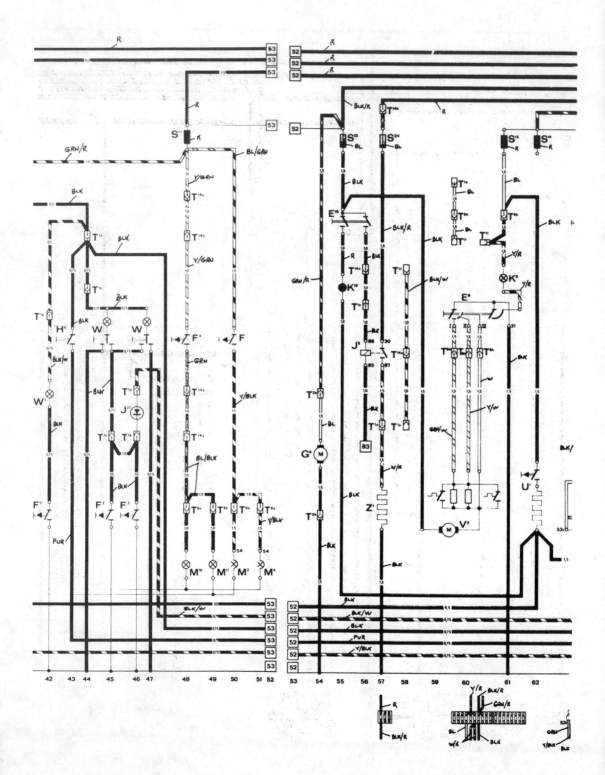

1974
PART IV

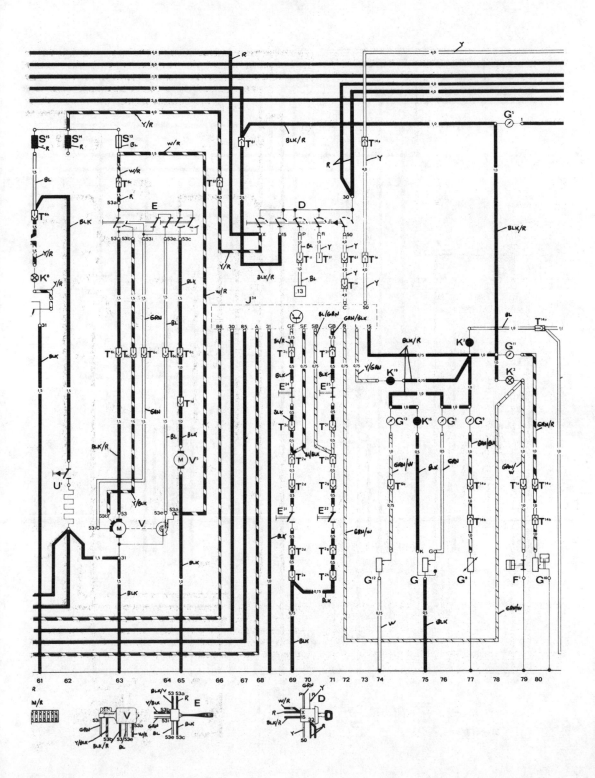

1974
PART V

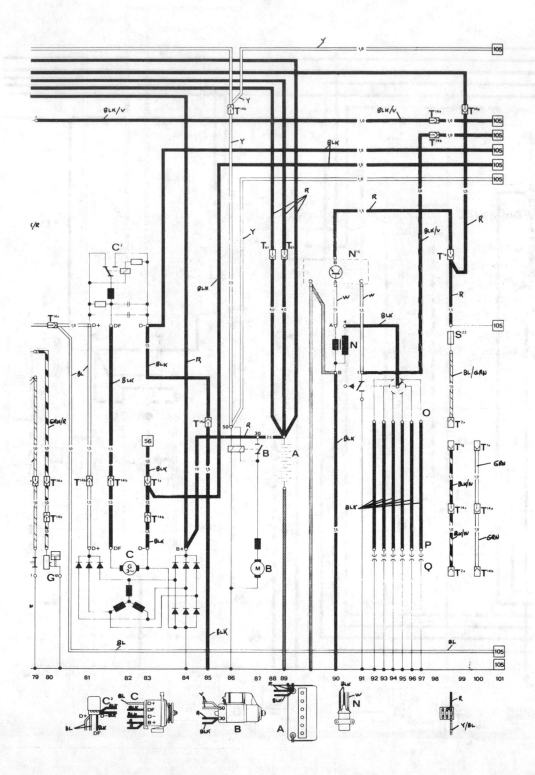

1974 CIS (SUPPLEMENT)

Description		Current Track
F25	– Throttle valve switch	109
F26	– Thermo-switch for cold start valve	109
J15	– Relay for warm-up regulator	107, 108
N9	– Warm-up regulator	107
N17	– Cold start valve	110
S23	– Fuse on the rear fuse box	106
T14b	– Cable connector, fourteenfold on regulator panel, rear	107

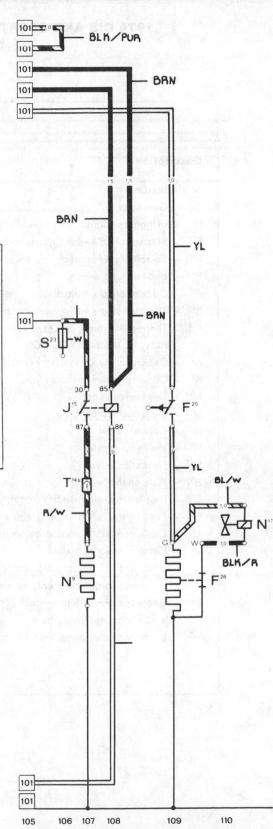

1974 CIS AND SPORTOMATIC (SUPPLEMENT)
KEY

Description	Current Track
B – Starter	114, 115
C – Generator	110, 111
D – to ignition / starter switch	115
E^{17} – Starter cutout switch (bypass switch)	111, 112
E^{21} – Selector lever contact	109
F^4 – Back-up light switch	115, 116
F^{13} – Oil temperature switch	118
F^{25} – Throttle valve switch (micro switch)	112
F^{26} – Thermo-switch for cold start valve	112
J^{15} – Relay for warm-up regulator	106, 107
K^2 – Generator charge indicator light	118
K^9 – Oil temperature indicator light	118
M^{16} – Left back-up light	116
M^{17} – Right back-up light	117
N^7 – Control valve	109
N^9 – Warm-up regulator	107
N^{17} – Cold start valve	113
S^{11} – Fuse on the fuse box	116
S^{22} – Fuse on the rear fuse box (regulator panel)	109
S^{23} – Fuse on the rear fuse box (regulator panel)	108
T^2 – Cable connector, double, below regulator panel	109
T^6 – Cable connector, sixfold	
a – in engine compartment, rear left	116
b – in engine compartment, rear right	117
T^{14} – Cable connector, fourteenfold	
a – on regulator panel, front	109, 116, 118
b – on regulator panel, rear	107, 115, 116, 118

1974 CIS AND SPORTOMATIC (SUPPLEMENT)

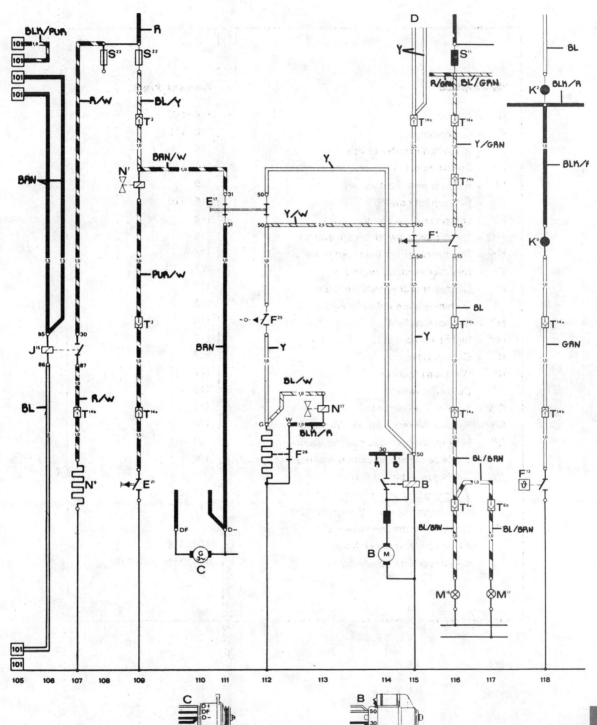

1975

WIRING DIAGRAM KEY

Description	Current Track
A — Battery	96
B — Starter	93, 94
C — Generator	81, 82, 83, 84
C² — Voltage regulator	81, 82, 83
D — Ignition / starter switch	68, 69, 70, 71, 72
E — Windshield wiper switch	63, 64, 65
E⁹ — Fresh air blower switch	60
E¹⁵ — Rear window defogger switch	55, 56
E²⁴ — Left seat belt switch	69
E²⁵ — Right seat belt switch	71
E³¹ — Left seat sensor switch	69
E³² — Right seat sensor switch	71
F¹ — Oil pressure switch	79
F²⁵ — Throttle valve switch	91
F²⁶ — Thermo-switch for cold start valve	91
G — Fuel sender unit	75
G¹ — Fuel gauge	76
G⁵ — Tachometer	78
G⁶ — Fuel pump	54
G⁸ — Oil temperature sender unit	77
G⁹ — Oil temperature indicator	77
G¹⁰ — Oil pressure sender unit	80
G¹¹ — Oil pressure indicator	78
G¹² — Oil level sender unit	74
G¹³ — Oil level gauge	74
J⁹ — Rear window defogger relay	56, 57
J¹⁴ — Relay for heater blower	87, 88
J¹⁵ — Relay for warm-up regulator	89, 90
J³⁴ — Seat belt warning system relay with integrated buzzer	66, 67, 68, 69, 70, 71, 72, 73
K² — Generator charge indicator light	77
K³ — Oil pressure indicator light	78
K⁸ — Blower indicator light	61
K¹⁰ — Rear window defogger indicator light	55
K¹⁶ — Low fuel warning light	75
K¹⁹ — Seat belt warning light	74
N — Ignition transformer	97
N⁹ — Warm-up regulator	90
N¹⁵ — High tension ignition unit	97

Description	Current Track
E¹ — Headlight switch	6, 8, 9, 11, 15, 20
E² — Turn signal switch	28
E³ — Emergency flasher switch	24, 25, 28, 31, 34
E⁴ — Dimmer switch	6, 39
E⁵ — Headlight flasher switch	4
E¹⁹ — Parking light switch	13
E²⁰ — Instrument panel illumination potentiometer	20
E²⁶ — Switch for glove compartment light	41
F — Stop light switch	50
F² — Left door switch	45
F³ — Right door switch	46
F⁴ — Back-up light switch	48
F⁵ — Switch for luggage compartment light	42
F⁶ — Brake warning switch	34
F⁹ — Parking brake switch	33
H — Horn switch	39
H² — Horns	36, 38
H⁶ — Key warning buzzer contact	43
J¹ — Hazard / turn signal flasher	33, 34, 35
J⁴ — Horn relay	36, 37
J²⁵ — Headlight relay	4, 5
J²⁷ — Diode for seat belt warning system	46
K¹ — High beam indicator light	2
K⁴ — Parking lights indicator light	1
K⁵ — Turn signal indicator light	27, 29
K⁶ — Hazard flasher indicator light	24
K⁷ — Parking brake / brake warning indicator light	34
L¹ — Sealed beam unit, left headlight	3, 7
L² — Sealed beam unit, right headlight	4, 8
L⁶ — Speedometer illumination light	22
L⁷ — Fuel gauge illumination light	22
L⁸ — Clock illumination light	22
L¹⁵ — Ashtray illumination light	22
L¹⁶ — Heater control assembly illumination light	20
L²¹ — Temperature control lever illumination light	19
L²⁴ — Oil temperature indicator illumination light	21
L²⁶ — Tachometer illumination light	22
L²⁷ — Oil pressure indicator illumination light	22

1975 KEY (Continued)

Description	Current Track
N^{17} — Cold start valve	92
O — Distributor	98—104
P — Spark plug connector	99—104
Q — Spark plug	99—104
S^{12} — Fuses	55, 63
to — on the	62
S^{15} — fuse box	61
S^{22} — Fuses on the	105
bis — rear fuse box (regulator panel)	87
S^{24}	57
T^{1} — Cable connector, single	
a — near regulator panel	56, 57, 58, 85, 88
d — behind fuse box	65
e — on luggage compartment floor	60, 72, 73
f — behind instrument panel	58, 60, 61, 69, 70
g — below shift lever housing	105
T^{2} — Cable connector, double	
a — below regulator panel	104, 105
b — in engine compartment, left	54
c — near left seat	69
d — below left seat	69
e — near left seat	69
f — near right seat	71
g — below right seat	71
h — near right seat	71
T^{6} — Cable connector, sixfold	
b — in engine compartment, right	74
c — below instrument panel	63, 64, 65
f — below instrument panel	66, 67, 72, 95, 96
h — below instrument panel	60, 61
T^{14} — Cable connector, fourteenfold	77, 79, 80, 84, 85, 87,
on regulator panel	90, 93, 105, 106
U^{1} — Cigar lighter	62
V — Windshield wiper motor	63, 64
V^{2} — Blower motor	60
V^{4} — Heater blower	87
V^{5} — Washer pump	65
Z^{1} — Rear window defogger	57

Description	Current Track
M^{2} — Right stop / rear light	17, 50
M^{4} — Left stop / rear light	13, 51
M^{5} — Left front turn signal // parking light	11, 25
M^{6} — Left rear turn signal	26
M^{7} — Right front turn signal // parking light	15, 31
M^{8} — Right rear turn signal	30
M^{11} — Front side marker light	12, 16
M^{12} — Rear side marker light	14, 18
M^{16} — Left back-up light	48
M^{17} — Right back-up light	49
N^{6} — Resistor	23
S^{2} — Fuses	9, 15, 11
to — on the	8, 7, 4
S^{11} — fuse box	3, 31, 25, 48
S^{17}	34
S^{18} — fuse box	40
T^{1} — Cable connector, single	
a — near regulator panel	14
b — behind sealed beam unit, left	11, 25
c — behind sealed beam unit, right	15, 31
d — behind fuse box	37
e — on luggage compartment floor	22, 42, 44, 45, 46
f — behind instrument panel	6, 22, 24, 28
h — near left rear lights	24
T^{6} — Cable connector, sixfold	
a — in the engine compartment, rear left	9, 13, 24, 26, 48, 51
b — in the engine compartment, rear right	10, 17, 30, 49, 50
d — below instrument panel	4, 6, 26, 30, 39
e — below instrument panel	25, 31, 32, 34
g — below instrument panel	8, 9, 11, 15, 22
h — below instrument panel	41
T^{14} — Cable connector, fourteenfold	
on regulator panel	48
W — Interior light	45, 46
W^{3} — Luggage compartment light	42
W^{6} — Glove compartment light	41
X — License plate light	9, 10
Y — Clock	40

1975
PART I

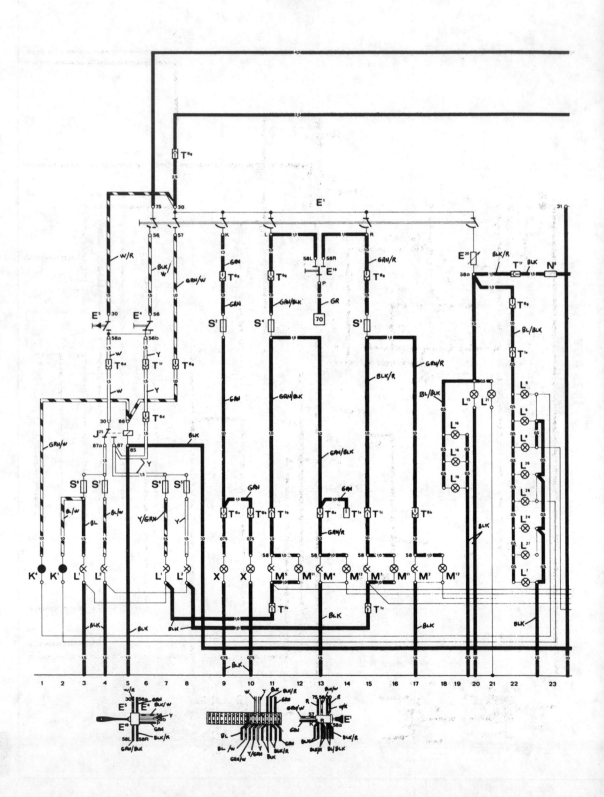

1975
PART II

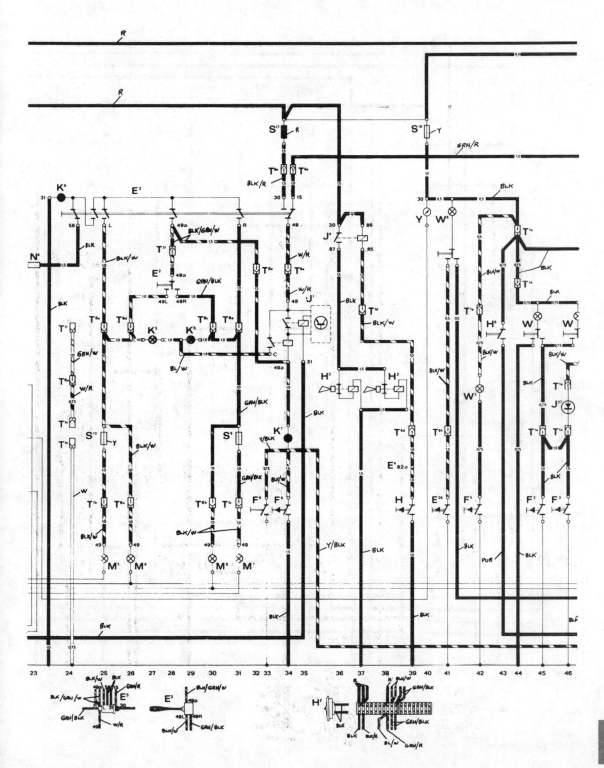

1975
PART III

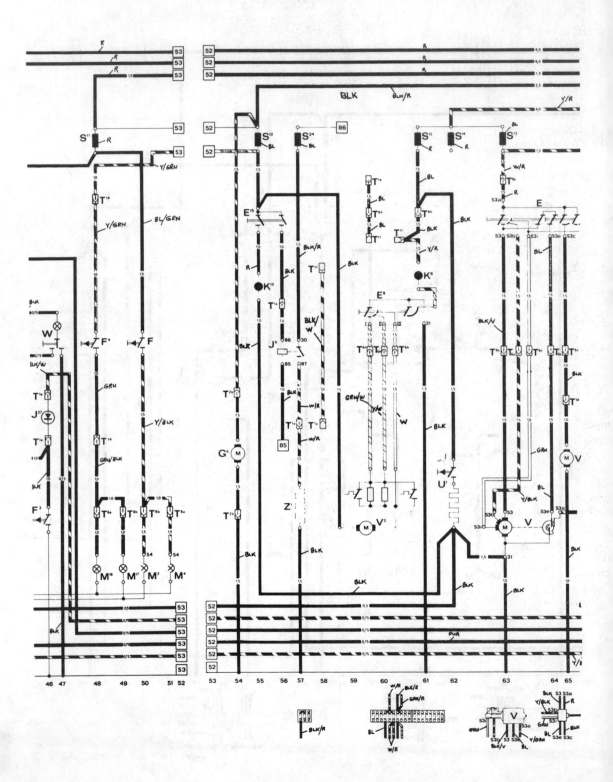

1975
PART IV

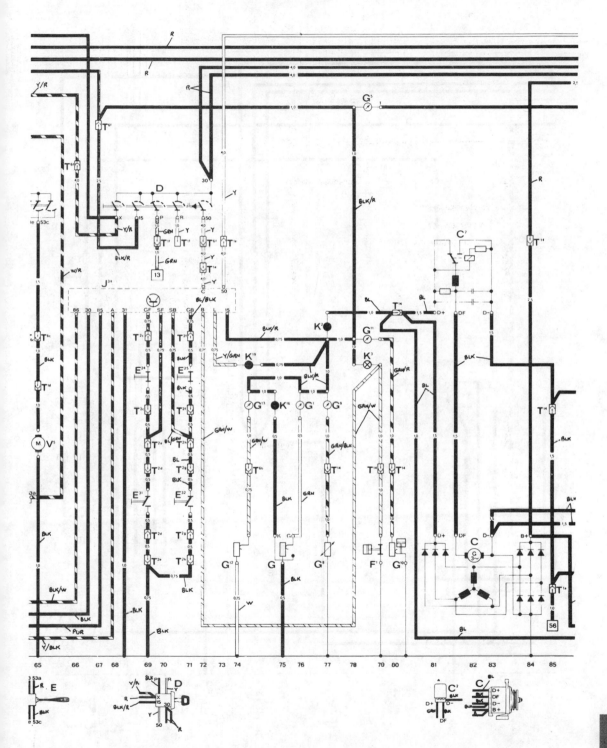

1975
PART V

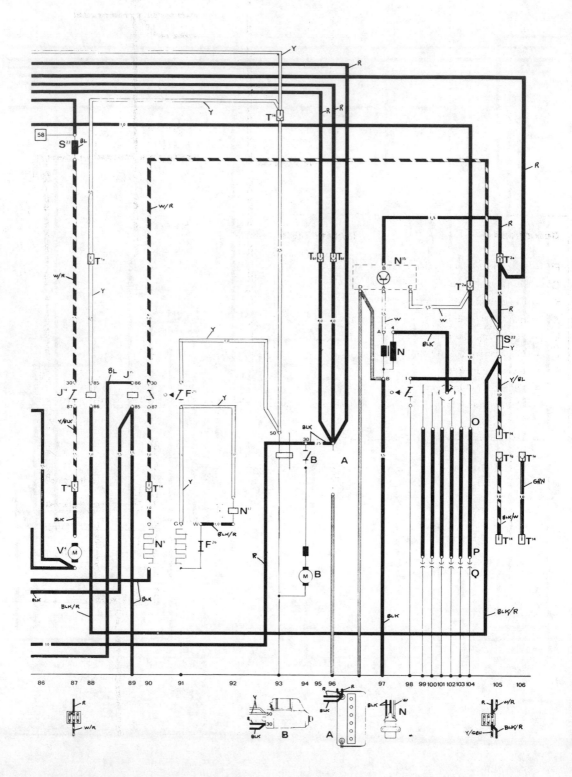

1975 CALIFORNIA (SUPPLEMENT)

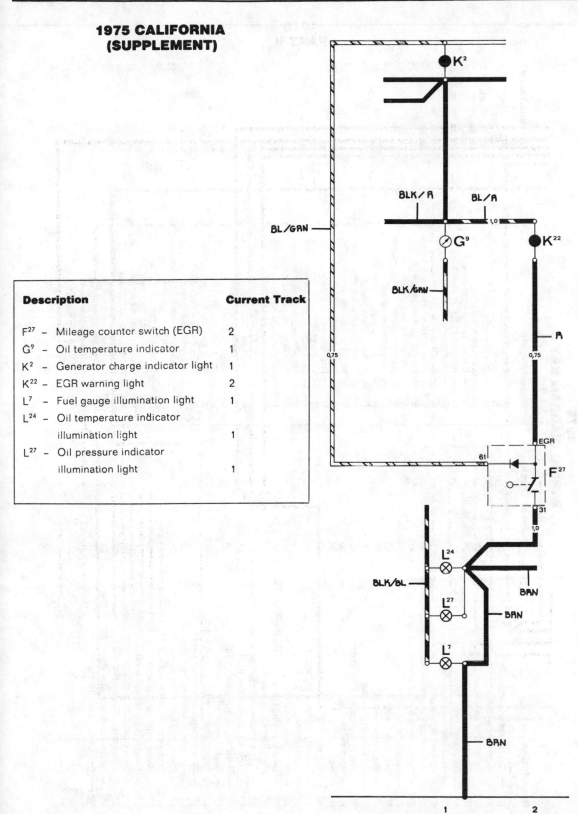

Description	Current Track
F^{27} – Mileage counter switch (EGR)	2
G^9 – Oil temperature indicator	1
K^2 – Generator charge indicator light	1
K^{22} – EGR warning light	2
L^7 – Fuel gauge illumination light	1
L^{24} – Oil temperature indicator illumination light	1
L^{27} – Oil pressure indicator illumination light	1

15

1976
WIRING DIAGRAM KEY

Description	Current Track
E — Windshield wiper switch	39
E¹ — Headlight switch	6, 8, 9, 11, 15, 20
E² — Turn signal switch	28
E³ — Emergency flasher switch	24, 25, 28, 31, 34
E⁴ — Dimmer switch	6, 39
E⁵ — Headlight flasher switch	4
E¹⁹ — Parking light switch	13
E²⁰ — Instrument panel illumination potentiometer	20
E²⁶ — Switch for glove compartment light	41
F — Stop light switch	50
F² — Left door switch	45
F³ — Right door switch	46
F⁴ — Back-up light switch	48
F⁵ — Switch for luggage compartment light	42
H — Horn switch	39
H² — Horns	36, 38
H⁶ — Key warning buzzer contact	43
J¹ — Hazard / turn signal flasher	33, 34, 35
J⁴ — Horn relay	36, 37
J²⁵ — Headlight relay	4, 5
J²⁷ — Diode for seat belt warning system	46
K¹ — High beam indicator light	2
K⁴ — Parking lights indicator light	1
K⁵ — Turn signal indicator light	27, 29
K⁶ — Hazard flasher indicator light	24
L¹ — Sealed beam unit, left headlight	3, 7
L² — Sealed beam unit, right headlight	4, 8
L⁶ — Speedometer illumination light	22
L⁷ — Fuel gauge illumination light	22
L⁸ — Clock illumination light	22
L¹⁵ — Ashtray illumination light	20
L¹⁶ — Heater control assembly illumination light	19
L²¹ — Temperature control lever illumination light	21
L²⁴ — Oil temperature indicator illumination light	22
L²⁶ — Tachometer illumination light	22
L²⁷ — Oil pressure indicator illumination light	22
M² — Right stop / rear light	17, 50

Description	Current Track
A — Battery	105
B — Starter	102, 103
C — Generator	88, 89, 90, 91, 92
C² — Voltage regulator	88, 89, 90
C¹² — Capacitor for ignition unit	116
D — Ignition / starter switch	73, 74, 75, 76, 77
E — Windshield wiper switch	68, 69, 70
E⁹ — Fresh air blower switch	60
E¹⁵ — Rear window defogger switch	55, 56
E¹⁶ — Heater blower switch	99
E²⁴ — Left seat belt switch	74
E⁴³ — Outside mirror control switch	64, 65
F¹ — Oil pressure switch	86
F⁶ — Brake warning switch	78
F⁹ — Parking brake switch	75
F²⁶ — Thermo-switch for cold start valve	100
F²⁷ — Mileage counter switch (EGR)	81, 83, 84
G — Fuel sender unit	82
G¹ — Fuel gauge	83
G⁵ — Tachometer	85
G⁶ — Fuel pump	96
G⁸ — Oil temperature sender unit	84
G⁹ — Oil temperature indicator	84
G¹⁰ — Oil pressure sender unit	87
G¹¹ — Oil pressure indicator	85
G¹² — Oil level sender unit	80
G¹³ — Oil level gauge	80
G¹⁹ — Air meter contact	95
G²¹ — Speedometer	67
G²² — Speedometer sensor	67
J⁹ — Rear window defogger relay	56, 57
J¹⁴ — Relay for heater blower	98, 99
J¹⁶ — Relay for fuel pump	95, 96
J³⁴ — Seat belt warning system relay with integrated buzzer	71, 72, 73, 74, 75, 79
K² — Generator charge indicator light	84
K³ — Oil pressure indicator light	85
K⁷ — Parking brake / brake warning light	75
K⁸ — Blower indicator light	61
K¹⁰ — Rear window defogger indicator light	55
K¹⁶ — Low fuel warning light	81
K¹⁹ — Seat belt warning light	75
K²² — EGR warning light	82
N — Ignition transformer	106

1976 KEY (Continued)

Description	Current Track
M⁴ — Left stop / rear light	13, 51
M⁵ — Left front turn signal / parking light	11, 25
M⁶ — Left rear turn signal	26
M⁷ — Right front turn signal / parking light	15, 31
M⁸ — Right rear turn signal	30
M¹¹ — Front side marker light	12, 16
M¹² — Rear side marker light	14, 18
M¹⁶ — Left back-up light	48
M¹⁷ — Right back-up light	49
N⁶ — Resistor	23
S² — Fuses	9, 15, 11
to — on the	8, 7, 4
S¹¹ — fuse box	3, 31, 25, 48
S¹⁷ —	34
S¹⁸ —	40
T¹ — Cable connector, single	
a — near regulator panel	14
b — behind sealed beam unit, left	11, 25
c — behind sealed beam unit, right	15, 31
d — behind fuse box	37
e — on luggage compartment floor	22, 42, 44, 45, 46
f — behind instrument panel	6, 22, 24, 28
h — near left rear lights	24
T⁶ — Cable connector, sixfold	
a — in the engine compartment, rear left	9, 13, 24, 26, 48, 51
b — in the engine compartment, rear right	10, 17, 30, 49, 50
d — below instrument panel	4, 6, 26, 30, 39
e — below instrument panel	25, 31, 32, 34
g — below instrument panel	8, 9, 11, 15, 22
h — below instrument panel	41
T¹⁴ — Cable connector, fourteenfold on regulator panel	48
W — Interior light	45, 46
W³ — Luggage compartment light	42
W⁶ — Glove compartment light	41
X — License plate light	9, 10
Y — Clock	40

Description	Current Track
N⁹ — Warm-up regulator	93
N¹⁵ — High tension ignition unit	106
N¹⁷ — Cold start valve	101
N²¹ — Supplementary air valve	94
N³⁵ — Magnetic clutch for mirror control	66
O — Distributor	107—113
P — Spark plug connector	108—113
Q — Spark plug	108—113
S¹² — Fuses	55, 68
to — on the	62
S¹⁵ — fuse box	61
S²¹ —	96
S²² — Fuses on the	114
to — rear fuse box (regulator panel)	98
S²⁴ —	57
T¹ — Cable connector, single	56, 57, 58, 95, 99, 116
a — near regulator panel	70, 93
d — behind fuse box	60, 80, 115
e — on luggage compartment floor	58, 60, 61, 75, 76
f — behind instrument panel	114
g — below shift lever housing	114
T² — Cable connector, double	
a — below regulator panel	113, 114
b — in engine compartment, left	91, 98
c — near left seat	74
i — in tunnel, rear	67
k — below regulator panel	95, 96
T⁴ — Cable connector, quadruple, in outside mirror housing	63, 64
T⁶ — Cable connector, sixfold	
b — in engine compartment, right	80
c — below instrument panel	68, 69, 70
f — below instrument panel	71, 72, 77, 104, 105
h — below instrument panel	60, 61
T¹⁴ — Cable connector, fourteenfold on regulator panel	84, 86, 87, 92, 93; 98, 102, 114, 115
U¹ — Cigar lighter	62
V — Windshield wiper motor	68, 69
V² — Blower motor	60
V⁴ — Heater blower	98
V⁵ — Washer pump	70
V¹⁷ — Outside mirror control motor	64
Z¹ — Rear window defogger	57
Z⁴ — Outside mirror defogger	63

15

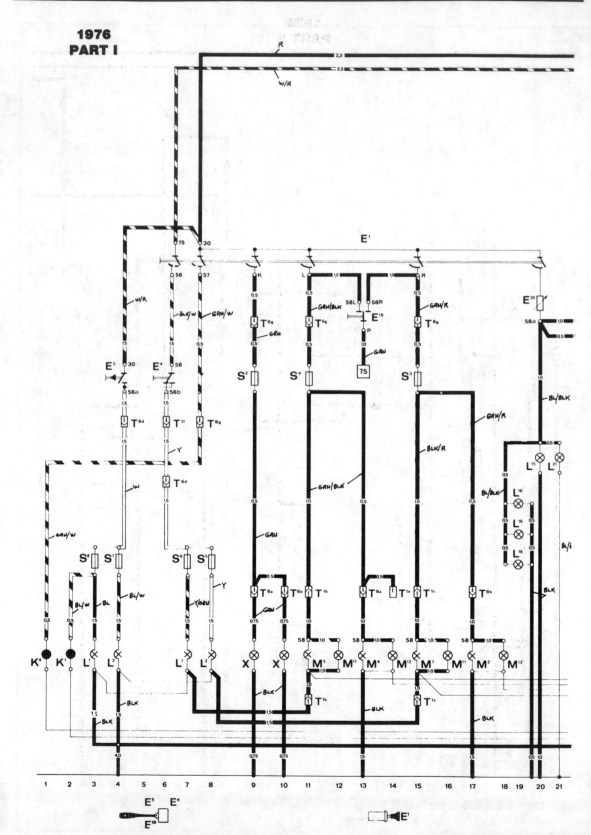

1976
PART I

1976
PART II

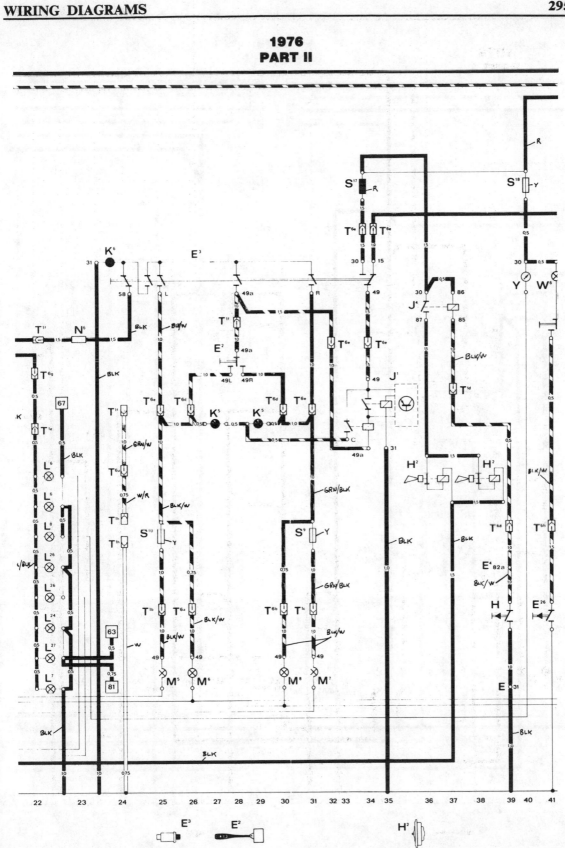

1976
PART III

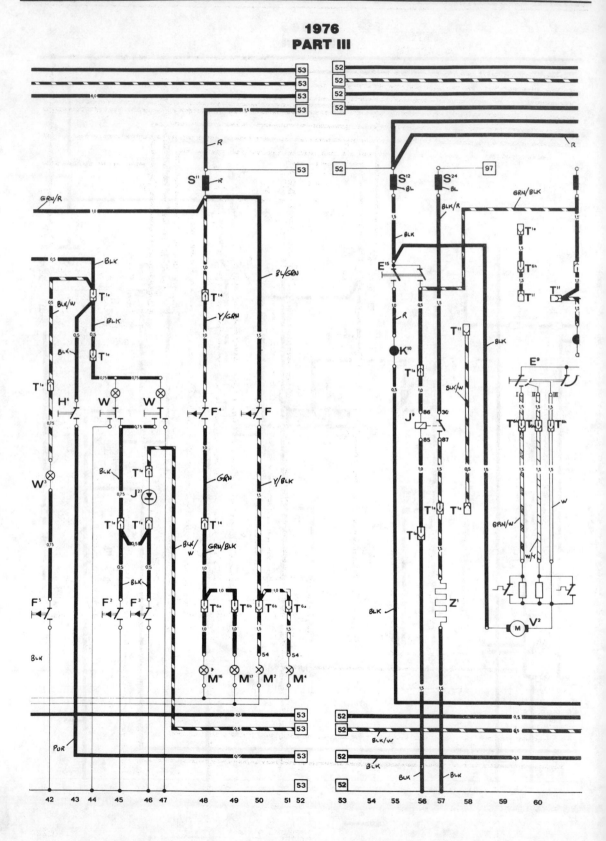

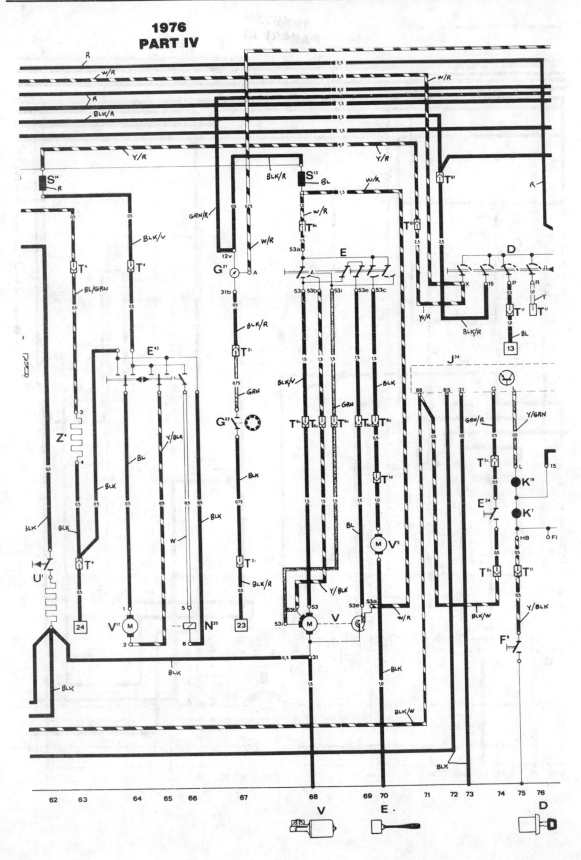

1976
PART IV

1976
PART V

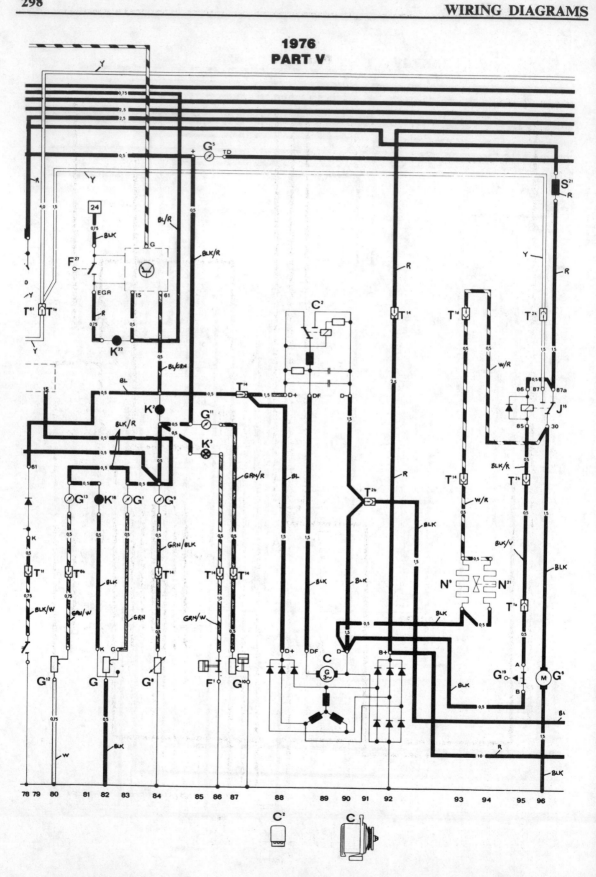

1976
PART VI

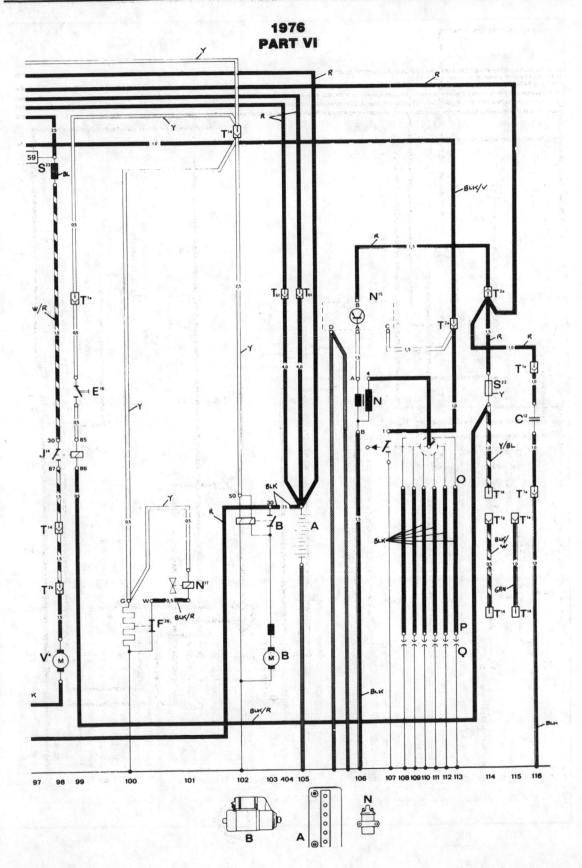

WIRING DIAGRAM KEY

1977

Description		Current Track
E	Windshield wiper switch	39
E 1	Headlight switch	6, 8, 9, 11, 15, 20
E 2	Turn signal switch	28
E 3	Emergency flasher switch	24, 25, 28, 31, 34
E 4	Dimmer switch	6, 39
E 5	Headlight flasher switch	4
E 9	Fresh air blower switch	58, 59, 60
E 15	Rear window defogger switch	53, 54
E 19	Parking light switch	13
E 20	Instrument panel illumination potentiometer	20
E 26	Switch for glove compartment light	41
F 2	Stop light switch	50, 52
F 3	Left door switch	45
F 4	Right door switch	46
F 5	Back-up light switch	48
—	Switch for luggage compartment light	42
H	Horn switch	39
H 2	Horns	36, 38
H 6	Key warning buzzer contact	43
J 1	Hazard / turn signal flasher	33, 34, 35
J 4	Horn relay	36, 37
J 9	Rear window defogger relay	54, 55
J 27	Diode for seat belt warning system	46
K 1	High beam indicator light	2
K 4	Parking lights indicator light	1
K 5	Turn signal indicator light	27, 29
K 6	Hazard flasher indicator light	24
K 8	Blower indicator light	60
K 10	Rear window defogger indicator light	53
L 1	Sealed beam unit, left headlight	3, 7
L 2	Sealed beam unit, right headlight	4, 8
L 6	Speedometer illumination light	22
L 7	Fuel gauge illumination light	22
L 8	Clock illumination light	22
L 15	Ashtray illumination light	20
L 16	Heater control assembly illumination light	19
L 21	Temperature control lever illumination light	21
L 24	Oil temperature indicator illumination light	22
L 26	Tachometer illumination light	22
L 27	Oil pressure indicator illumination light	22
M 2	Right stop / rear light	17, 50
M 4	Left stop / rear light	13, 51

Description		Current Track
A	Battery	116
B	Starter	113, 114
C	Generator	97 – 102
C 2	Voltage regulator	98, 99
C 12	Capacitor for ignition unit	128
D	Ignition / starter switch	83 – 88
E 9	Windshield wiper switch	72 – 80
E 16	Heater blower switch	109
E 24	Left seat belt switch	84
E 38	Potentiometer for intermittent wiper operation	78, 79
E 43	Outside mirror control switch	66, 67, 68
F 1	Oil pressure switch	95
F 9	Parking brake switch	85
F 26	Thermo-switch for cold start valve	110
F 27	Mileage counter switch (EGR)	90 – 93
G	Fuel sender unit	91
G 1	Fuel gauge	92
G 5	Tachometer	94
G 6	Fuel pump	106
G 8	Oil temperature sender unit	93
G 9	Oil temperature indicator	93
G 10	Oil pressure sender unit	96
G 11	Oil pressure indicator	94
G 12	Oil level sender unit	89
G 13	Oil level gauge	89
G 19	Air meter contact	105
G 21	Speedometer	70
G 22	Speedometer sensor	70
J 14	Relay for heater blower	108, 109
J 16	Relay for fuel pump	105, 106
J 31	Relay for intermittent wiper operation	75 – 78
J 34	Seat belt warning system relay with integrated buzzer	81 – 88
K 2	Generator charge indicator light	93
K 3	Oil pressure indicator light	94
K 7	Parking brake / brake warning light	85
K 16	Low fuel warning light	90
K 19	Seat belt warning light	85
K 22	EGR warning light	90
N	Ignition transformer	118

1977 KEY (Continued)

Description	Current Track
M 5 – Left front turn signal / parking light	11, 25
M 6 – Left rear turn signal	26
M 7 – Right front turn signal / parking light	15, 31
M 8 – Right rear turn signal	30
M 11 – Front side marker light	12, 16
M 12 – Rear side marker light	14, 18
M 16 – Left back-up light	48
M 17 – Right back-up light	49
N 6 – Resistor	23
S 2 – Fuses	9, 15, 11
to – on the	8, 7, 4
S 12 – Fuses	3, 31, 25, 48, 53
S 15 – on the	60
S 17 – fuse box	34
S 18 – Fuse on the rear fuse box	40
S 24 – fuse box	55
T 1 – Cable connector, single	14, 54, 55, 56
a – near regulator panel	11, 25
b – behind sealed beam unit, left	15, 31
c – behind sealed beam unit, right	37
d – behind fuse box	22, 42, 44, 45, 46, 51
e – on luggage compartment floor	6, 22, 24, 28, 56
f – behind instrument panel	24
h – near left rear lights	
T 2 d – Cable connector, double, on luggage compartment floor	50
T 6 – Cable connector, sixfold	9, 13, 24, 26, 48, 51
a – in the engine compartment, rear left	10, 17, 30, 49, 50
b – in the engine compartment, rear right	4, 6, 26, 30, 39
d – below instrument panel	25, 31, 32, 34
e – below instrument panel	8, 9, 11, 15, 22
g – below instrument panel	41, 58, 59, 60
h – below instrument panel	
T 14 – Cable connector, fourteenfold on regulator panel	48
U 1 – Cigar lighter	61
V 2 – Blower motor	58, 59
W – Interior light	45, 46
W 3 – Luggage compartment light	42
W 6 – Glove compartment light	41
X – License plate light	9, 10
Y – Clock	40
Z 1 – Rear window defogger	55

Description	Current Track
N 9 – Warm-up regulator	103
N 15 – High tension ignition unit	118
N 17 – Cold start valve	111
N 21 – Supplementary air valve	104
N 35 – Magnetic clutch for mirror control	68
N 43 – Thermovalve	104
O – Distributor	119 – 125
P – Spark plug connector	120 – 125
Q – Spark plug	120 – 125
S 13 – Fuses	72
S 14 – on the	66
S 16 – fuse box	106
S 22 – Fuses on the	126
S 23 – rear fuse box (regulator planel)	108
T 1 – Cable connector, single	105, 109, 128
a – near regulator panel	80, 103
d – behind fuse box	76, 78, 88, 127
e – on luggage compartment floor	85, 86
f – behind instrument panel	126
g – below shift lever housing	
T 2 – Cable connector, double	125, 126
a – below regulator panel	101, 108
b – in engine compartment, left	84
c – near left seat	85
d – on luggage compartment floor	70
i – in tunnel, rear	105, 106
k – below regulator panel	
T 4 – Cable connector, quadruple, on luggage compartment floor	65, 66
T 6 – Cable connector, sixfold	89
b – in engine compartment, right	72, 73, 74, 76, 80
c – below instrument panel	81, 82, 87, 115, 116
f – below instrument panel	93, 95, 96, 102
T 14 – Cable connector, fourteenfold on regulator panel	103, 108, 113, 126, 127
V 4 – Windshield wiper motor	72, 75
V 5 – Heater blower	108
V 17 – Washer pump	80
Z 4 – Outside mirror control motor	66
Z 4 – Outside mirror defogger	65

15

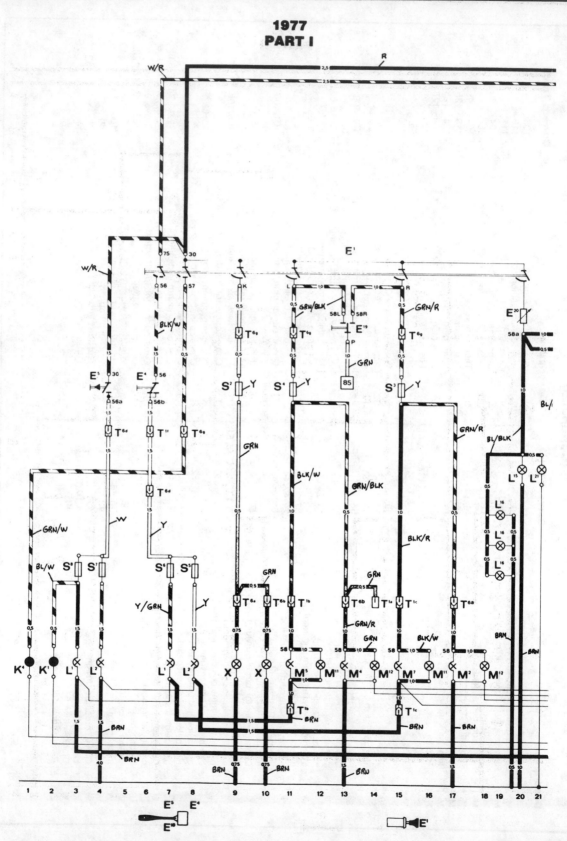

1977
PART II

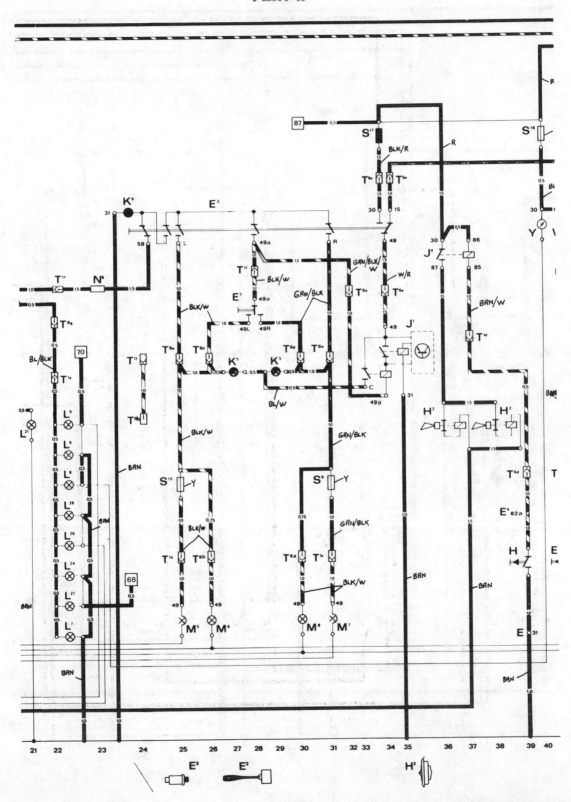

1977
PART III

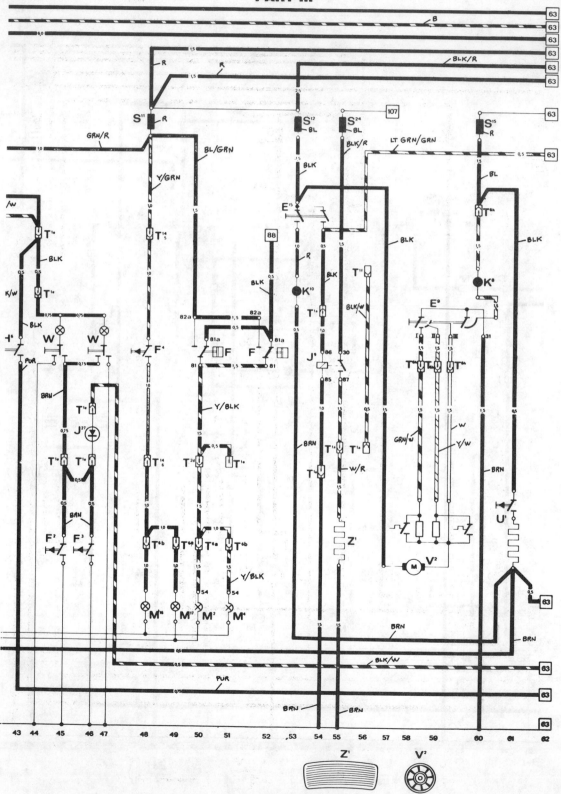

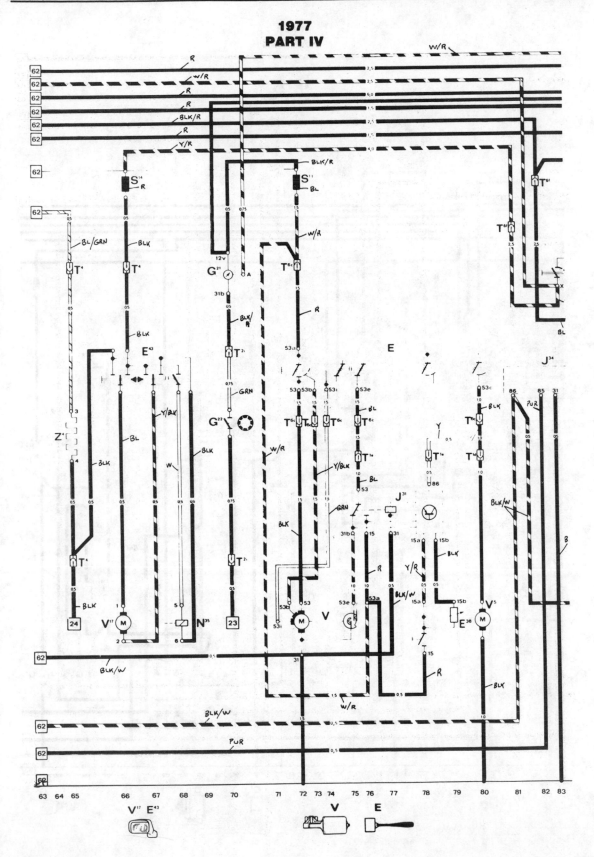

1977
PART V

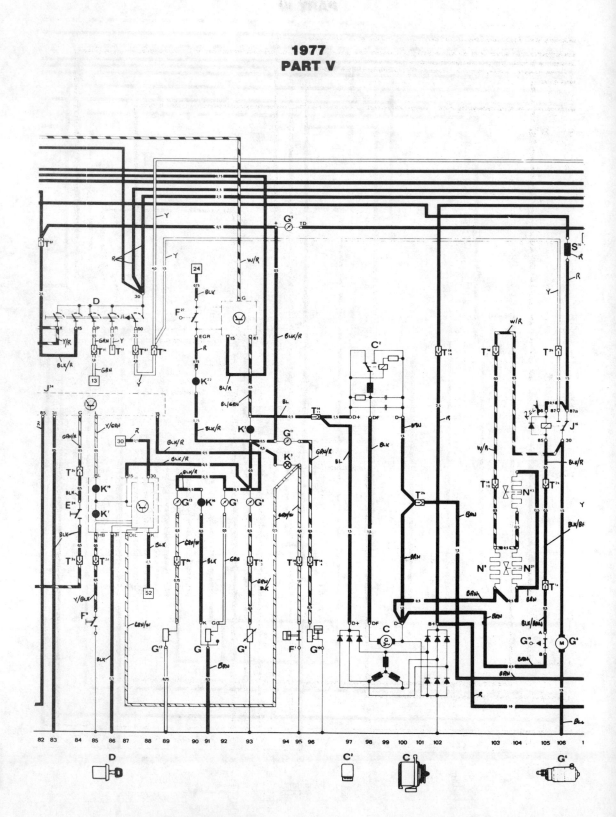

1977
PART VI

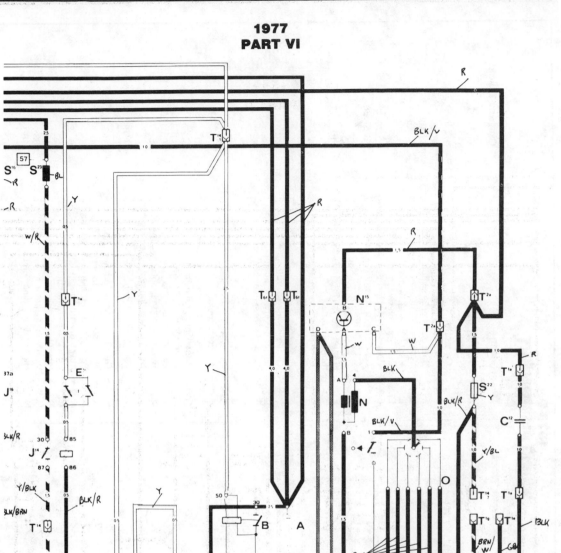

1978-ON WIRING DIAGRAM KEY

Description	Current Track
E — Windshield wiper switch	39
E1 — Headlight switch	6, 8, 9, 11, 15, 20
E2 — Turn signal switch	28
E3 — Emergency flasher switch	24, 25, 28, 31, 34
E4 — Dimmer switch	6, 39
E5 — Headlight flasher switch	4
E9 — Fresh air blower switch	58, 59, 60
E15 — Rear window defogger switch	53, 54
E19 — Parking light switch	13
E20 — Instrument panel illumination potentiometer	20
E26 — Switch for glove compartment light	41
F — Stop light switch	50, 52
F2 — Left door switch	45
F3 — Right door switch	46
F4 — Back-up light switch	48
F5 — Switch for luggage compartment light	42
H — Horn switch	39
H2 — Horns	36, 38
H6 — Key warning buzzer contact	43
J1 — Hazard / turn signal flasher	33, 34, 35
J4 — Horn relay	36, 37
J9 — Rear window defogger relay	54, 55
J27 — Diode for seat belt warning system	46
K1 — High beam indicator light	2
K4 — Parking lights indicator light	1
K5 — Turn signal indicator light	27, 29
K6 — Hazard flasher indicator light	24
K8 — Blower indicator light	60
K10 — Rear window defogger indicator light	53
L1 — Sealed beam unit, left headlight	3, 7
L2 — Sealed beam unit, right headlight	4, 8
L6 — Speedometer illumination light	22
L7 — Fuel gauge illumination light	22
L8 — Clock illumination light	22
L15 — Ashtray illumination light	20
L16 — Heater control assembly illumination light	19
L21 — Temperature control lever illumination light	21
L24 — Oil temperature indicator illumination light	22
L26 — Tachometer illumination light	22
L27 — Oil pressure indicator illumination light	22
M2 — Right stop / rear light	17, 50

Description	Current Track
A — Battery	116
B — Starter	113, 114
C — Generator	97 – 102
C2 — Voltage regulator	98, 99
D — Ignition / starter switch	83 – 88
E16 — Windshield wiper switch	72 – 80
E24 — Heater blower switch	109
E38 — Left seat belt switch	84
E43 — Potentiometer for intermittent wiper operation	78, 79
F1 — Outside mirror control switch	66, 67, 68
F9 — Oil pressure switch	95
F26 — Parking brake switch	85
G — Thermo-switch for cold start valve	110
G1 — Fuel sender unit	91
G5 — Fuel gauge	92
G6 — Tachometer	94
G8 — Fuel pump	106
G9 — Oil temperature sender unit	93
G10 — Oil temperature indicator	93
G11 — Oil pressure sender unit	96
G12 — Oil pressure indicator	94
G13 — Oil level sender unit	89
G19 — Oil level gauge	89
G21 — Air meter contact	105
G22 — Speedometer	70
J14 — Speedometer sensor	70
J16 — Relay for heater blower	108, 109
J31 — Relay for fuel pump	105, 106
J34 — Relay for intermittent wiper operation	75 – 78
— Seat belt warning system relay with integrated buzzer	81 – 88
J35 — Speed switch	103
K2 — Generator charge indicator light	93
K3 — Oil pressure indicator light	94
K7 — Parking brake / brake warning light	85
K16 — Low fuel warning light	90
K19 — Seat belt warning light	85
N — Ignition transformer	118
N9 — Warm-up regulator	103
N15 — High tension ignition unit	118

1978-ON KEY (Continued)

Description	Current Track
M 4 – Left stop / rear light	13, 51
M 5 – Left front turn signal / parking light	11, 25
M 6 – Left rear turn signal	26
M 7 – Right front turn signal / parking light	15, 31
M 8 – Right rear turn signal	30
M 11 – Front side marker light	12, 16
M 12 – Rear side marker light	14, 18
M 16 – Left back-up light	48
M 17 – Right back-up light	49
N 6 – Resistor	23
S 2 – Fuses	9, 15, 11
to – on the	8, 7, 4
S 12 – on the	3, 31, 25, 48, 53
S 15 –	60
S 17 – fuse box	34
S 18 –	40
S 24 – Fuse on the rear fuse box	55
T 1 – Cable connector, single	
a – near regulator panel	14, 54, 55, 56
b – behind sealed beam unit, left	11, 25
c – behind sealed beam unit, right	15, 31
d – behind fuse box	37
e – on luggage compartment floor	22, 42, 44, 45, 46, 51
f – behind instrument panel	6, 22, 24, 28, 56
T 2 d – Cable connector, double, on luggage compartment floor	50
T 6 – Cable connector, sixfold	
a – in the engine compartment, rear left	9, 17, 30, 49, 50
b – in the engine compartment, rear right	10, 24, 26, 48, 51
d – below instrument panel	4, 6, 26, 30, 39
e – below instrument panel	25, 31, 32, 34
g – below instrument panel	8, 9, 11, 15, 22
h – below instrument panel	41, 58, 59, 60
T 14 – Cable connector, fourteenfold on regulator panel	48
U 1 – Cigar lighter	61
V 2 – Blower motor	58, 59
W – Interior light	45, 46
W 3 – Luggage compartment light	42
W 6 – Glove compartment light	41
X – License plate light	9, 10
Y – Clock	40
Z 1 – Rear window defogger	55

Description	Current Track
N 17 – Cold start valve	111
N 21 – Supplementary air valve	104
N 35 – Magnetic clutch for mirror control	68
N 43 – Thermovalve	104
O – Distributor	119 – 125
P – Spark plug connector	120 – 125
Q – Spark plug	120 – 125
S 13 – Fuses	72
S 14 – on the	66
S 16 – fuse box	106
S 22 – Fuses on the	126
S 23 – rear fuse box (regulator planel)	108
T 1 – Cable connector, single	
a – near regulator panel	105, 109,
d – behind fuse box	80, 103
e – on luggage compartment floor	88, 127
f – behind instrument panel	85, 86
g – below shift lever housing	126
h – near battery	84
T 2 – Cable connector, double	
a – below regulator panel	105, 126
b – in engine compartment, left	101, 108
c – near left seat	84
d – on luggage compartment floor	85
e – near distributor	119, 120
i – in tunnel, rear	70
k – below regulator panel	105, 106
T 4 – Cable connector, quadruple, on luggage compartment floor	65, 66, 67
T 6 – Cable connector, sixfold	
a – in engine compartment, right	89
c – below instrument panel	72, 73, 74, 76, 80
f – below instrument panel	81, 82, 87, 115, 116
T 14 – Cable connector, fourteenfold on regulator panel	93, 95, 96, 102, 103, 108, 113, 117, 126,
V – Windshield wiper motor	127
V 4 – Heater blower	72, 75
V 5 – Washer pump	108
V 17 – Outside mirror control motor	80
Z 4 – Outside mirror defogger	66
	65

15

1978-ON
PART I

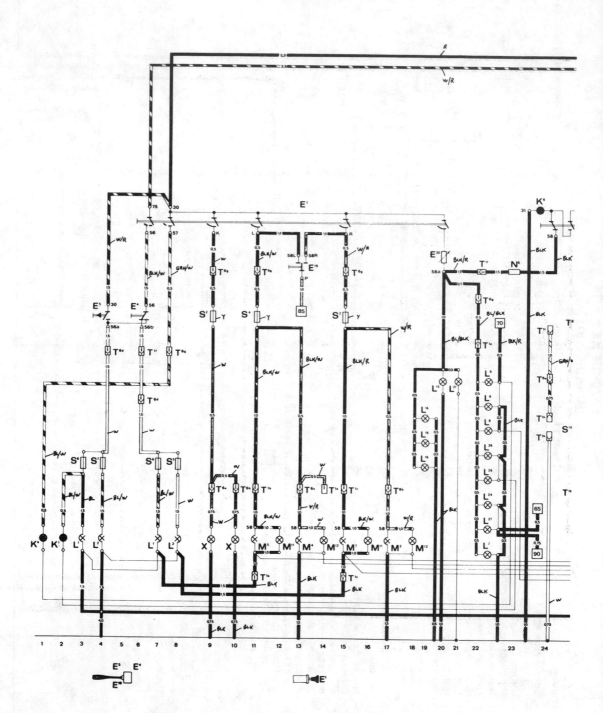

1978-ON
PART II

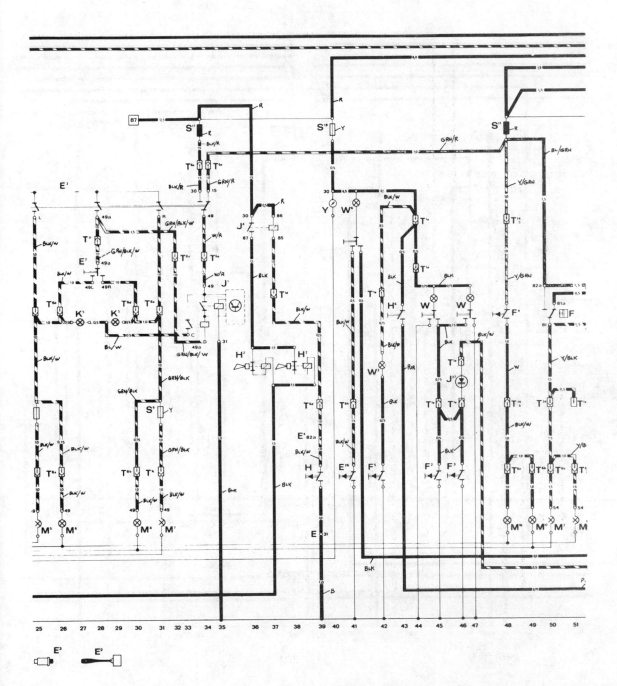

1978-ON
PART III

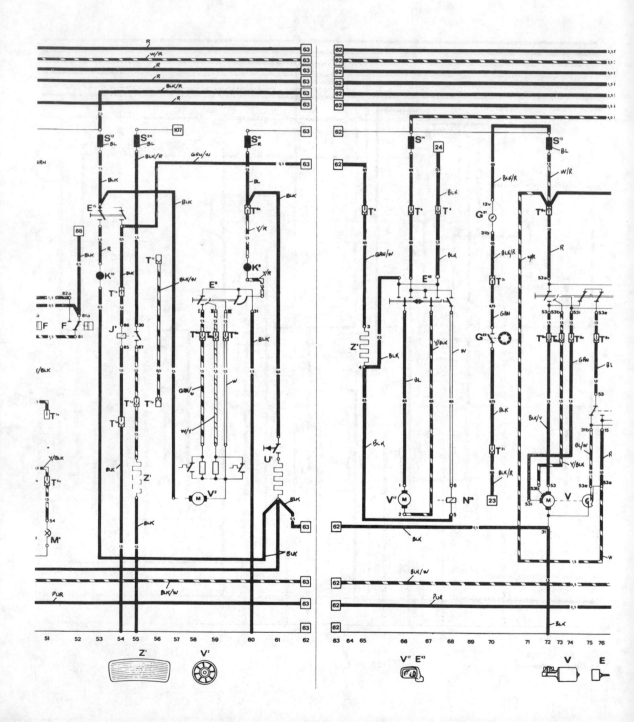

1978-ON
PART IV

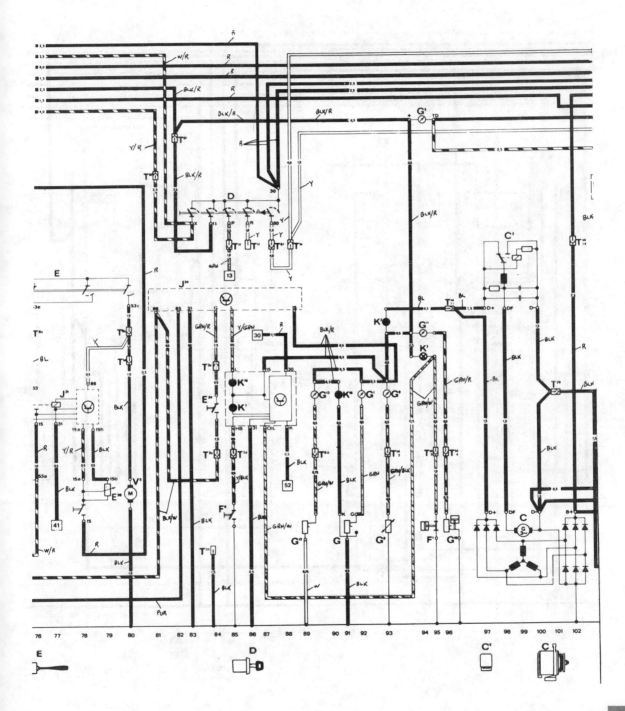

1978-ON
PART V

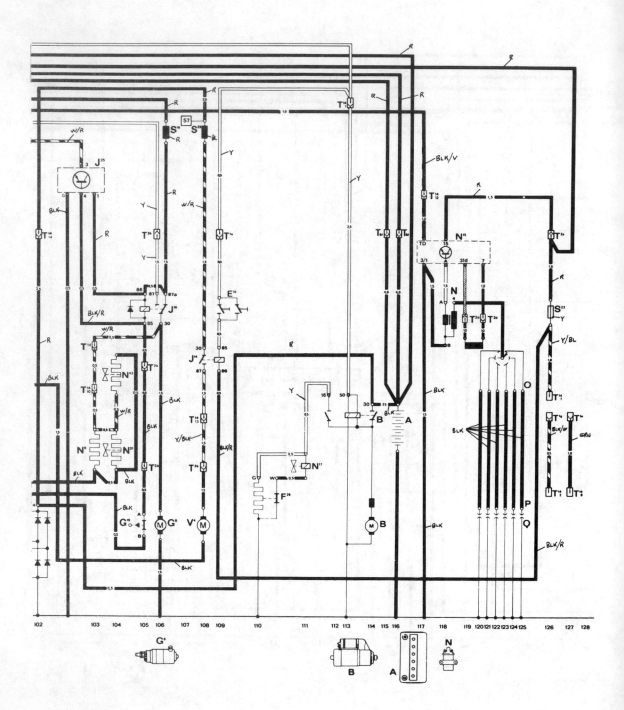

1980-ON U.S. (SUPPLEMENT)

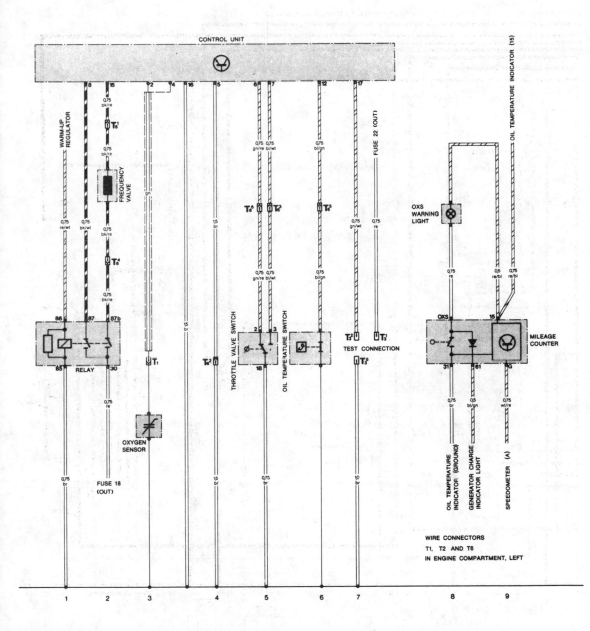

FRONT AND REAR WINDOW DEFOGGER
KEY

Description	Current Track
A – to battery	2
C – to generator	10
C^2 – to voltage regulator	6
D – to ignition/starter switch	7
E^{36} – Windshield and rear window defogger switch	6, 8, 9
J^{45} – Diode for windshield defogger	7
J^{47} – Windshield defogger relay	4, 5
J^{48} – Relay for two-stage rear window defogger	6, 7, 8, 10
K^{23} – Windshield and rear window defogger indicator light	5
S^{12} – Fuses	6
S^{18} – in	1
to – the	2, 3
S^{21} – fuse box	4
S^{23} – Fuses in the	11
S^{24} – rear fuse box	10
T^1 – Cable connector, single	
a – below regulator panel	6, 10
b – behind fuse box	4
T^2 – Cable connector, double, below regulator panel	7, 8
T^{14} – Cable connector, fourteenfold	6
U^1 – to cigar lighter	5
Z^1 – Rear window defogger, stage 1	7
Z^2 – Windshield defogger	4
Z^3 – Rear window defogger, stage 2	8, 9

FRONT AND REAR WINDOW DEFOGGER

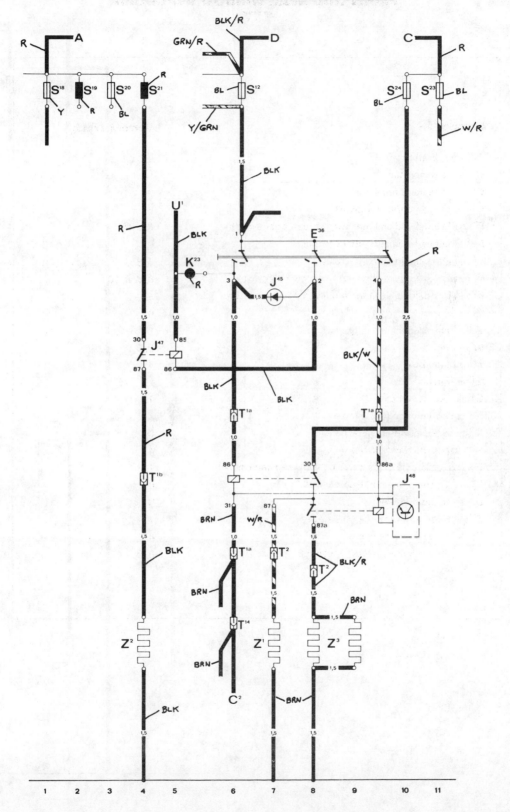

15

AUTOMATIC HEATING SYSTEM

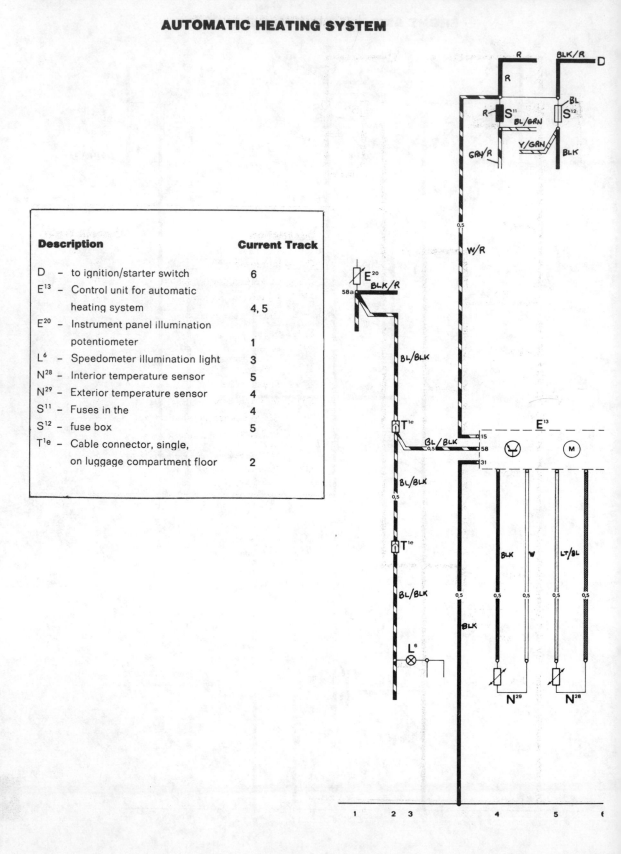

Description	Current Track
D – to ignition/starter switch	6
E[13] – Control unit for automatic heating system	4, 5
E[20] – Instrument panel illumination potentiometer	1
L[6] – Speedometer illumination light	3
N[28] – Interior temperature sensor	5
N[29] – Exterior temperature sensor	4
S[11] – Fuses in the	4
S[12] – fuse box	5
T[1e] – Cable connector, single, on luggage compartment floor	2

REAR WINDOW WIPER

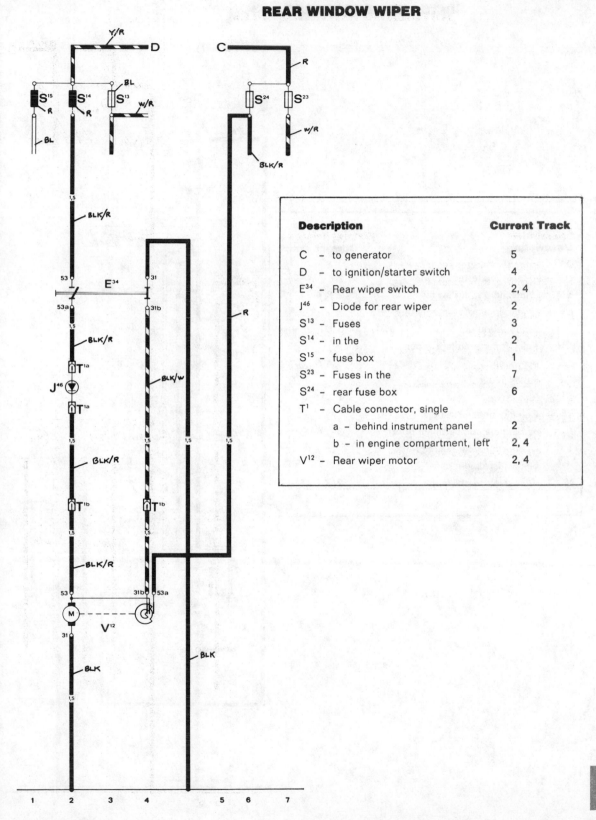

Description		Current Track
C	– to generator	5
D	– to ignition/starter switch	4
E[34]	– Rear wiper switch	2, 4
J[46]	– Diode for rear wiper	2
S[13]	– Fuses	3
S[14]	– in the	2
S[15]	– fuse box	1
S[23]	– Fuses in the	7
S[24]	– rear fuse box	6
T[1]	– Cable connector, single	
	a – behind instrument panel	2
	b – in engine compartment, left	2, 4
V[12]	– Rear wiper motor	2, 4

INTERMITTENT WIPERS

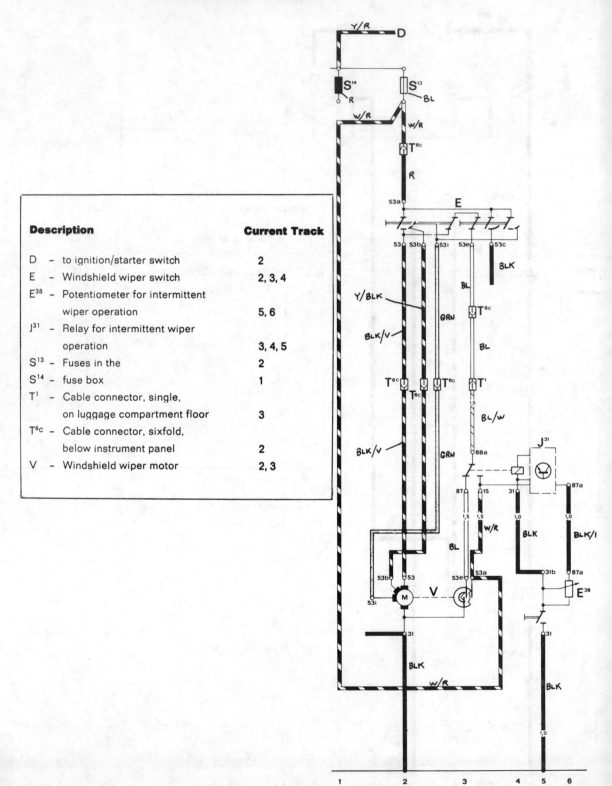

Description		Current Track
D	– to ignition/starter switch	2
E	– Windshield wiper switch	2, 3, 4
E^{38}	– Potentiometer for intermittent wiper operation	5, 6
J^{31}	– Relay for intermittent wiper operation	3, 4, 5
S^{13}	– Fuses in the	2
S^{14}	– fuse box	1
T^1	– Cable connector, single, on luggage compartment floor	3
T^{6c}	– Cable connector, sixfold, below instrument panel	2
V	– Windshield wiper motor	2, 3

1965-1976 ELECTRIC WINDOWS

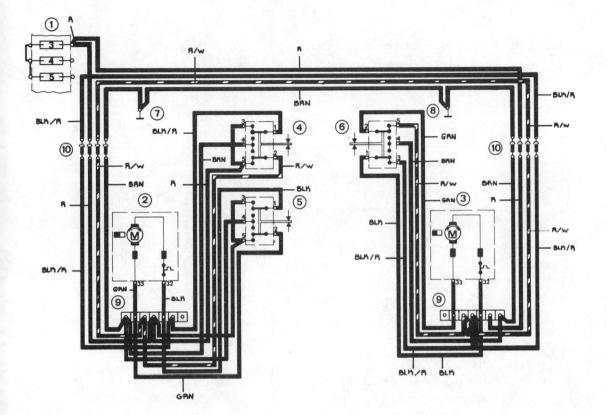

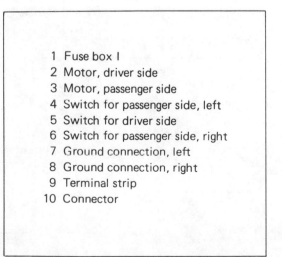

1 Fuse box I
2 Motor, driver side
3 Motor, passenger side
4 Switch for passenger side, left
5 Switch for driver side
6 Switch for passenger side, right
7 Ground connection, left
8 Ground connection, right
9 Terminal strip
10 Connector

15

1977-ON ELECTRIC WINDOWS
KEY

Description	Current Track
A – to battery	9
D – to ignition/starter switch (terminal X)	1
D – to ignition/starter switch (terminal 15)	2
E^{39} – Power window switch, driver side, for passenger side	5, 6
E^{40} – Power window switch, driver side	9, 10
E^{41} – Power window switch, passenger side	5, 6
J^{51} – Power window relay	3, 4
S^{12} – Fuse	2
S^{13} – Fuse	2
S^{14} – Fuse	1
S^{17} – Fuse	8
S^{18} – Fuse	9
S^{21} – Fuse	5
T^{1} – Cable connector, single, behind fuse box	3
T^{6} – Cable connector, sixfold	
) a – in door well, left	5, 6, 8
b – in door well, right	5, 6, 7
V^{14} – Power window motor, left	9, 10
V^{15} – Power window motor, right	5, 6

1977-ON ELECTRIC WINDOWS

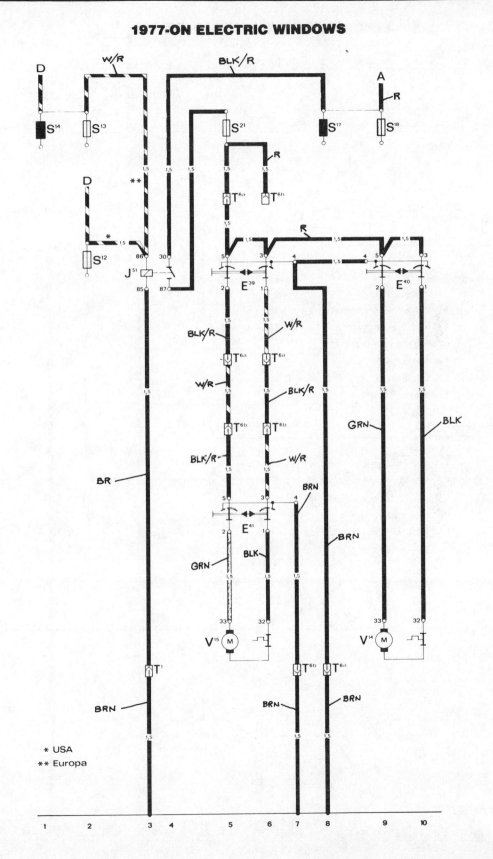

* USA
** Europa

15

ELECTRIC SUNROOF

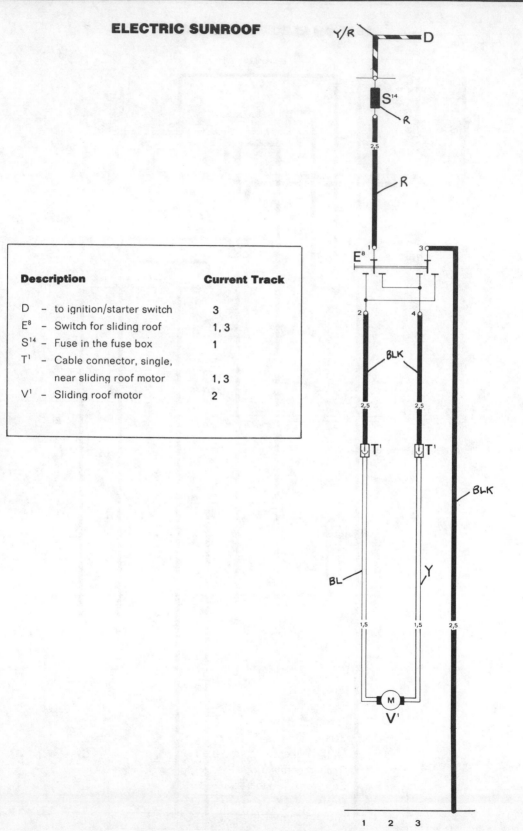

Description		Current Track
D	– to ignition/starter switch	3
E[8]	– Switch for sliding roof	1, 3
S[14]	– Fuse in the fuse box	1
T[1]	– Cable connector, single,	
	near sliding roof motor	1, 3
V[1]	– Sliding roof motor	2

FRONT AND REAR FOG LAMPS

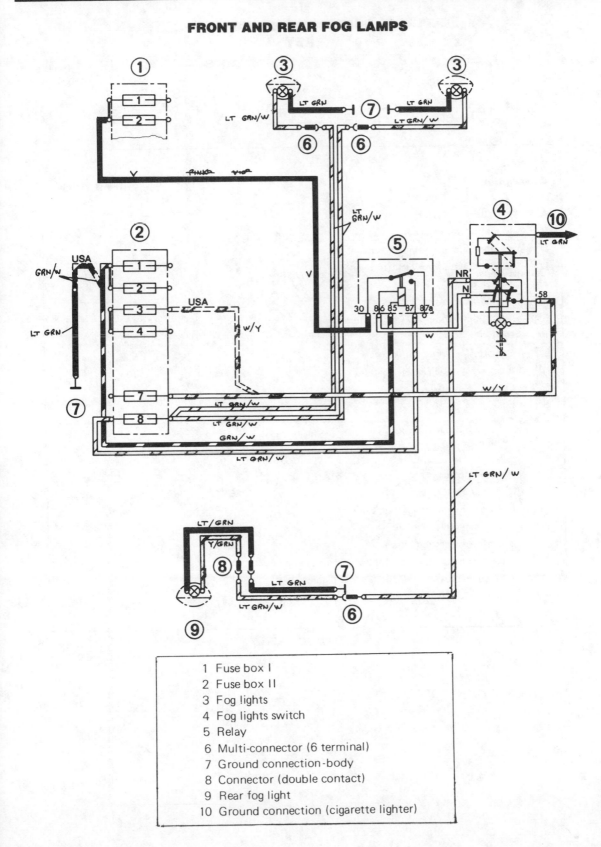

1 Fuse box I
2 Fuse box II
3 Fog lights
4 Fog lights switch
5 Relay
6 Multi-connector (6 terminal)
7 Ground connection-body
8 Connector (double contact)
9 Rear fog light
10 Ground connection (cigarette lighter)

AIR CONDITIONING
KEY

Description	Current Track
A – to battery	9
B – to starter (terminal 50)	2
D – to ignition/starter switch (terminal 15)	1
D – to ignition/starter switch (terminal 50)	4
E^{30} – Switch for AC	5, 6
E^{33} – Temperature switch for AC	10
F^{45} – Thermo-switch for AC (excess temperature)	10
J^{32} – Relay for AC	4, 5
N^{23} – Resistor for evaporator blower	5, 6
N^{25} – Electromagnetic clutch	10
S^{11} – Fuse	3
S^{12} – Fuse	2
S^{18} – Fuse	7
S^{19} – Fuse	6
S^{20} – Fuse	5
T^{1} – Wire connector, single	
a – near compressor	10
e – on luggage compartment floor	2, 4, 10
T^{2} – Wire connector, two-pole	
a – near evaporator blower	8
T^{4} – Wire connector, four-pole, below instrument panel	5, 8, 10
T^{6f} – Wire connector, six-pole, below instrument panel	4
V^{20} – Evaporator blower	8

AIR CONDITIONING

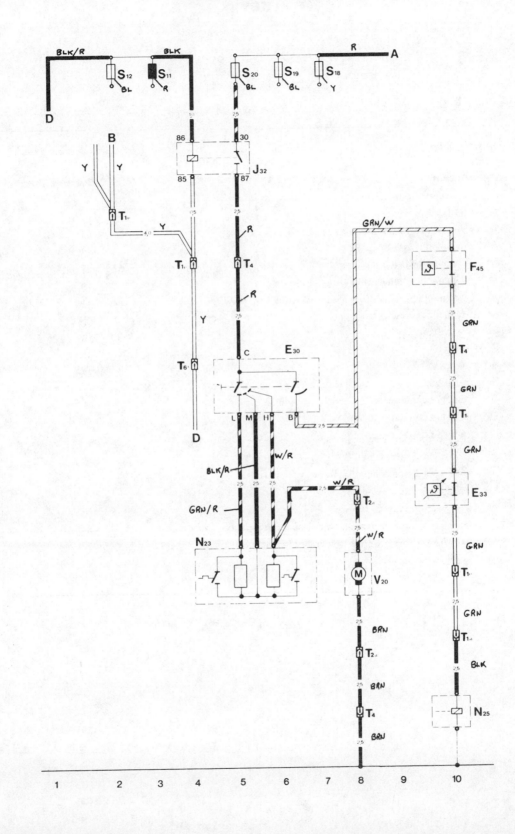

HEADLIGHT WASHERS
KEY

Description	Current Track
A – to battery	7
D – to ignition/starter switch	1
E^1 – Headlight switch	1, 2, 3
E^4 – Dimmer switch	1
E^{37} – Headlight washer switch	4
J^{25} – to headlight relay (from model 76 to fuse S^6)	1
J^{39} – Headlight washer relay	5, 6, 7
S^{17} – to fuse S^{17}	2
S^2 – Fuses	3
S^{18} – in the	6
S^{19} – fuse box	7
T^{1f} – Cable connector, single, behind instrument panel	1
T^2 – Cable connector, double, near battery	7
T^6 – Cable connector, sixfold	
d – below instrument panel	1
g – below instrument panel	3
V^{11} – Headlight washer pump	7

HEADLIGHT WASHERS

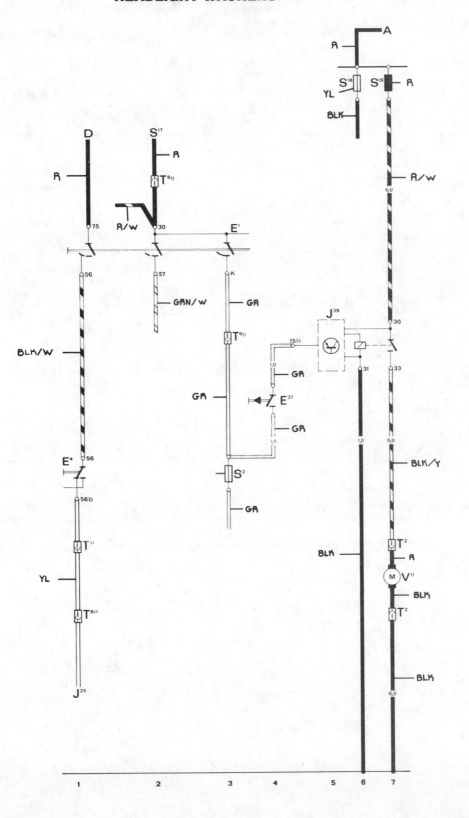

AUTOMATIC SPEED CONTROL
KEY

Description	Current Track
E^{21} – Selector lever contact (Sportomatic)	11
E^{45} – Speed control switch	2, 3, 4
E^{46} – Control unit for speed control	1–9
F – Stop light switch	1
F^{36} – Clutch pedal switch	7
G^{21} – to speedometer (terminal 31 b)	5
G^{21} – to speedometer (ground)	6
J^{54} – Diode for speed control	10
N^{7} – to control valve	12
N^{37} – Solenoid valve for speed control	9
S^{11} – Fuses in the	1
S^{12} – fuse box	2
T^{1} – Cable connector, single, in tunnel	7, 11
T^{3} – Cable connector, triple, in footwell, left	7, 8, 9
T^{4} – Cable connector, quadruple, below instrument panel	2, 3, 4
V^{18} – Control element	9

AUTOMATIC SPEED CONTROL

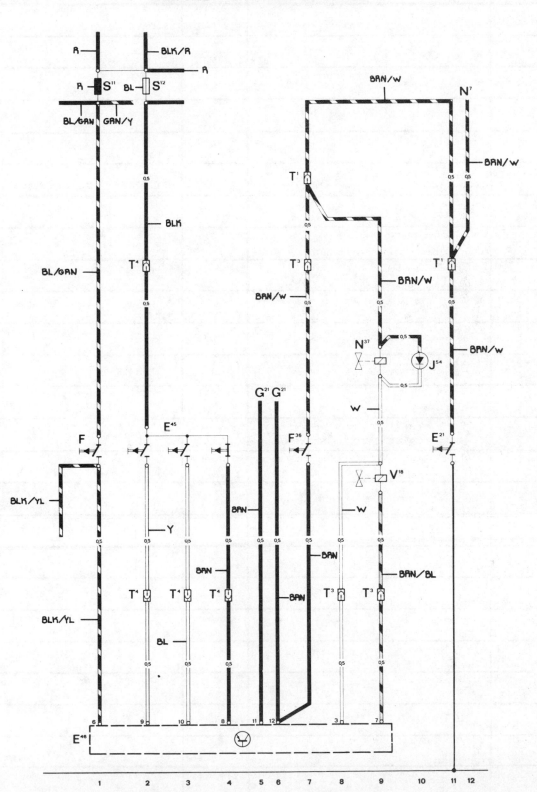

15

MAINTENANCE LOG

DATE	TYPE OF SERVICE	COST	REMARKS

MAINTENANCE LOG

DATE	TYPE OF SERVICE	COST	REMARKS

NOTES

NOTES